Negative, Nonsensical, and Non-Conformist

MICHIGAN MONOGRAPH SERIES IN JAPANESE STUDIES

NUMBER 99

CENTER FOR JAPANESE STUDIES
UNIVERSITY OF MICHIGAN

Negative, Nonsensical, and Non-Conformist

The Films of Suzuki Seijun

PETER A. YACAVONE

University of Michigan Press
Ann Arbor

Copyright © 2023 by Peter A. Yacavone
Some rights reserved

This work is licensed under a Creative Commons Attribution-NonCommercial 4.0 International License. *Note to users:* A Creative Commons license is only valid when it is applied by the person or entity that holds rights to the licensed work. Works may contain components (e.g., photographs, illustrations, or quotations) to which the rightsholder in the work cannot apply the license. It is ultimately your responsibility to independently evaluate the copyright status of any work or component part of a work you use, in light of your intended use. To view a copy of this license, visit http://creativecommons.org/licenses/by-nc/4.0/

For questions or permissions, please contact um.press.perms@umich.edu

Published in the United States of America by the
University of Michigan Press
Manufactured in the United States of America
Printed on acid-free paper
First published April 2023

A CIP catalog record for this book is available from the British Library.

Library of Congress Cataloging-in-Publication data has been applied for.

ISBN 978-0-472-07570-6 (hardcover : alk. paper)
ISBN 978-0-472-05570-8 (paper : alk. paper)
ISBN 978-0-472-90347-4 (open access ebook)

DOI: https://doi.org/10.3998/mpub.11486286

The University of Michigan Press's open access publishing program is made possible thanks to additional funding from the University of Michigan Office of the Provost and the generous support of contributing libraries.

Acknowledgments

I would like to express my gratitude to Associate Professor Alastair Phillips for his painstaking reading of and commentary on the earliest version of this monograph. I thank the editors of the University of Michigan who have brought the book to fruition at various stages of the process: Christopher Dreyer, Anna Pohlod, Kevin Rennells, and the editor of the Center for Japanese Studies series, Professor Markus Nornes. I am grateful to William Carroll for his magnanimity in allowing me to read a pre-publication copy of his book. Lastly, I would like to acknowledge my wife, Olivia Sun, for her ten years of patience with this all-consuming project.

Contents

	List of Illustrations	ix
	INTRODUCTION	1
	A NOTE ON THE TEXT AND TRANSLATIONS THROUGHOUT THIS BOOK	19
1	THE RECUSANT	21
2	THE DOG	42

(*Rajo to kenjū, Ankokugai no bijo, Kagenaki koe, Kaikyō chi ni somete, Kutabare gurentai, Tokyo kishitai, Subete ga kurutteru, Akutarō, Toge wo wataru wakai kaze, Akutarō-den: warui hoshi shita demo*)

3	THE MIRROR	72

(*Yajū no seishun, Tantei Jimusho 2-3: Kutabare akutō-domo, Kemono no nemuri*)

4	THE TATTOO	108

(*Kantō mushuku, Oretachi no chi ga yurusanai, Hana to dotō, Irezumi ichidai*)

5	THE FLESH	142

(*Nikutai no mon, Shunpuden, Kawachi karumen*)

6	THE BREAK	179

(*Tokyo nagaremono, Kenka erejii, Sandanjū no otoko, Mikkō o-rain, 13-go taihisen yori sono gosōsha wo nerae*)

7	THE HINGE	223

(*Koroshi no rakuin, Pisutoru opera*)

8	THE DOUBLE	265

(*Zigeunerweisen, Kagerō-za, Yumeji, Hishū monogatari, Rupan sansei: Babiron no ōgon no densetsu*)

Appendix: A Complete Filmography for Suzuki Seijun, Director   319
Notes   347
Bibliography   379
Filmography   391
Index   397

Digital materials related to this title can be found on the Fulcrum platform via the following citable URL: https://doi.org/10.3998/mpub.11486286

Illustrations

2.1	*Hādo-boirudo* as Transnational Hybridity (*Rajo to kenjū*)	47
2.2	Noguchi Hiroshi's Muted Cityscapes (*Kenjū buraichō: Nukiuchi no Ryūji*, 1960)	48
2.3	Noguchi's Bourgeois Aspirants (*Kenjū buraichō*)	48
2.4	Film as Fashion Shoot, Shot (1): Shiraki Mari "models" for a photographer	49
2.5	Film as Fashion Shoot, Shot (2): an innovative jump cut to Shiraki	49
2.6	That Obscure Object of Desire: the iconic *femme fatale* as cinematic shadow	52
2.7	*Hādo-boirudo* Cinema as Abject Simulacrum	53
2.8	The Birdcage: the spunky teenager (*Ankokugai no bijo*)	55
2.9	Polymorphic Perversity: On the Edge of Taste and Censorship (*Ankokugai no bijo*)	55
2.10	Suzuki's Dog, Shot (1a) (*Kutabare gurentai*)	59
2.11	Suzuki's Dog, Shot (1b)	60
2.12	"Moving Color": Magritte's portrait of the nude (*Black Magic*, 1945)	62
2.13	Post-war Vacancies: *Subete ga kurutteru* (1960)	65
2.14	Atypical Suzuki? Crisp architectural lines (*Akutarō*, 1963)	68
3.1	Out of the Shadows (*Yajū no seishun*)	73
3.2	Authoritarian Containment of Public Information	73
3.3	Out of the Past—hand-painted red camellia links the monochrome and color sequences	74
3.4	Everything Out in the Open (*Yajū no seishun*)	74
3.5	Violence at a Distance	75
3.6	The Third Sequence—narrative as viewed through a one-way mirror	76
3.7	Transforming Film Noir—Kawachi Tamio calmly slashes his opponent's face	81
3.8	The (Mis)Information—Mizuno (Shishido) continually directed to the "wrong number"	82
3.9	A Female Erotic Gaze—Mrs. Nomoto appreciates the wild Mizuno as he enters and beats up her underlings	85
3.10	No Return—the male protagonist does not initiate a returning gaze	86
3.11	Modernity as Fetish	87
3.12	Gendered Violence in a Non-Diegetic Yellow Dust Cloud	89
3.13	The Hooded Eyes of the Vigilante (1)	90
3.14	The Hooded Eyes of the Vigilante (2)	91

3.15	The Face of Dehumanization?	94
3.16	Erotic Spectacle as Hyperbolic Fetishism	95
3.17	Erotic Spectacle as Satire	96
3.18	Mediated—the erotic dancer partitioned by the mirror-screen	97
3.19	Extreme Visual Contrast (1): Shallowness and Depth	97
3.20	Extreme Visual Contrast (2): The Bisected Frame	98
3.21	The Memory Screen (*Kemono no nemuri*)	100
4.1	The Red Thread of Attachment (*Kantō mushuku*)	116
4.2	Color as Emotion or Color as Ambiguity (*Kantō mushuku*)	117
4.3	Haunted Remembrances, Shot (1a)	120
4.4	Haunted Remembrances, Shot (1b)	120
4.5	Lighting and Narrative Meaning, Shot (1c)	121
4.6	Dysfunctional Ellipsis, Shot (2)	122
4.7	Uncanny Passage—the "haunted" blue light shows Katsuta's fear	122
4.8	The Mark of Insecurity—the ghostly apparition of the man who scarred Katsuta's cheek	123
4.9	Dream Lover, Shot (1)	124
4.10	Dream Lover, Shot (2)	124
4.11	Urban Modernity as Spatial Disjuncture (1)	125
4.12	Urban Modernity as Spatial Disjuncture (2)	125
4.13	Attention to Detail—the "stoic" traditionalism of Okaru-Hachi and his "art"	127
4.14	A Cinematic Mirror, Shot (1)	128
4.15	A Cinematic Mirror, Shot (2)	129
4.16	A Cinematic Mirror, Shot (3)	129
4.17	A Cinematic Mirror, Shot (6)—the object of all gazes	130
4.18	Reversals of Gender and Power, Shot (1)	130
4.19	Reversals, Shot (2)	131
4.20	Reversals, Shot (3)	131
4.21	Reversals, Shot (4)—Hanako from the "wrong" side	132
4.22	Suzuki as Kurosawa—fighting men pour into the receding street from beside the camera	134
4.23	History Versus Theatricality (1)—The Dull, Earthen Weight of Labor (*Hana to dotō*)	136
4.24	History Versus Theatricality (2)—the visual textures of Asakusa as a Theatre of Life (*Hana to dotō*)	136
4.25	History *as* Theatre (*Hana to dotō*)	137
4.26	Theatrical (Anti-)Melodrama—the stylized sets of the curt finale	138
5.1	Cinema Palimpsest: superimposition of the protagonist and her imaginary world (*Nikutai no mon*)	143
5.2	Caligari and Frontality	144
5.3	Cinematic "Inter-Subjectivity" (*Nikutai no mon*)	149
5.4	The Hell of Romantic Attachment—Harumi runs toward freedom, only to find she cannot leave the patriotic Mikami behind	153

5.5	The Myth of Domesticity—Sachiko's meager dishes fallen, along with her hopes of "a decent marriage"	154
5.6	Portrait of A Marriage? Harumi "composes herself"	155
5.7	The Stylization of Death	158
5.8	Violence Out-of-Sync, Shot (1)	159
5.9	Violence Out-of-Sync, Shot (2)	159
5.10	Rage Against the System—Harumi reacts to her intolerable entrapment	160
5.11	The Restoration of Order? Prostitutes jeer at Mikami in retaliation for his violence	160
5.12	Sadism and Sexploitation in Suzuki Norifumi's satire *Ero shogun to nijūichi nin no aishō* (1972)	171
5.13	Nakedness as Freedom—Harumi dreams of running free	173
5.14	Nakedness as Art	173
5.15	Masochism and Distance	174
5.16	Masochism and Concealment	174
5.17	Pornography's Threat in a Media Regime	177
6.1	The Frontier as Fashion—Kobayashi Akira as a Japanese film star in Western cowboy dress (*Wataridori*, 1959-62)	182
6.2	The Frontier as Fashion—Montgomery Clift's stylized "Frontier Youth" outfit (*Red River*, 1948)	183
6.3	Discontinuity in Action, Shot (1) (*Tokyo nagaremono*)	186
6.4	Discontinuity in Action, Shot (2)	187
6.5	Discontinuity in Action, Shot (3)	187
6.6	Discontinuity in Action, Shot (5)	188
6.7	Discontinuity in Action, Shot (8)	188
6.8	Discontinuity in Action, Shot (13)	189
6.9	Discontinuity in Action, Shot (15)	189
6.10	Discontinuity in Action, Shot (20)	190
6.11	Discontinuity in Action, Shot (21)	190
6.12	Imposed Style, Shot (1a)	194
6.13	Imposed Style, Shot (1b)	194
6.14	Theatrical Style as Falsity	195
6.15	Heroic Action as Dance	195
6.16	An Icon of the Genre—the gun "triply emphasized" by film style	198
6.17	Iconic Shorthand—the villain Ōtsuka is viewed only by extreme close-ups	200
6.18	The Action Hero as Commodity—Watari Tetsuya as "Third Time Phoenix Tetsu"	200
6.19	The Libidinal Economy—exotic sexual promise of Akasaka's neon signage	201
6.20	Stage Door—the illusive, elusive space of the affluent Club Alulu	203
6.21	Club Manhole: Youth, Sexual Suggestion, and Excess	204
6.22	What Lies Beneath—through "The Manhole" and into the Abject	204
6.23	Women and *yakuza*	205

6.24	Masculinity and Commodity Fetishism	209
6.25	Urban *Flâneur?* (*Tokyo nagaremono*)	210
6.26	Violence and Genre Cinema—Kiroku cajoled into violence (*Kenka erejii*)	212
6.27	"Sex" and the Middle Class—Kiroku masturbates by playing piano	213
6.28	Between a Rock and a Hard Place—Women Under a Militarist Patriarchy	216
6.29	Violence and Sexual Fantasy, Shot (1)	217
6.30	Violence and Sexual Fantasy, (Shot 4a)	218
6.31	Violence, Fantasy, and False Time (Shot 4b)	218
6.32	Natural Imagery and Martial Training—Kiroku receives training from a self-proclaimed "master" in a mountain glade	220
6.33	Symbolic *Méconnaissance*—falling cherry blossoms	221
7.1	Cinematic Negativity, Shot (1) (*Koroshi no rakuin*)	224
7.2	Cinematic Negativity, Shot (3)	224
7.3	Cinematic Negativity, Shot (4)	225
7.4	Surrealism and Abjection	226
7.5	Surrealist Transformation	227
7.6	Butterflies and the Avant-Garde—surrealism and metaphors of femininity (*Tobenai chinmoku*)	228
7.7	The Butterflies of Death (*Koroshi no rakuin*)	228
7.8	Iconicity of *Noir*	229
7.9	The Protagonist as Demon	231
7.10	Sex and Subjugation	232
7.11	In the Tunnel—downward slide of masculine competition	234
7.12	Political Allegory—Who Is Number One?	235
7.13	I am a Bullet (The Fetishization of Violence) (*Performance*, 1968/70)	236
7.14	Reluctant Voyeur—Hanada despairs at the unbridgeable distance (*Koroshi no rakuin*)	237
7.15	The Discreet Charm of the Bourgeoisie	238
7.16	Training for Power—in extreme pursuit of "hardness"	238
7.17	Negativity as Farce	241
7.18	Blocked Up—the frame bisected by a partition while the head of the protagonist is barely glimpsed	243
7.19	Deframing—a composition with Hanada's feet flashing across the bottom of the frame	243
7.20	Empty Space and the Moving Camera	244
7.21	Non-diegetic Style and Satire in the 1960s	245
7.22	Excess Visuality—spotlighting on an area with no narrative function	245
7.23	The Allegory of Excess Visibility	246
7.24	Uncanny Femininity	247
7.25	Disjunction of Sound and Image	247
7.26	Discontinuity Aesthetics, Shot (1)	248

7.27	Discontinuity Aesthetics, Shot (2)	249
7.28	Aesthetics of Death (*Pisutoru opera*)	261
7.29	Aesthetics of Nihilism—the chic Cosmopolitan Killer	264
8.1	The Colors of Hell (Nakagawa's *Jigoku*)	270
8.2	At the Doorway (*Zigeunerweisen*)	271
8.3	The Blue Light of Haunting	272
8.4	Cinema in a False Light	272
8.5	The Return of the Oppressed—Aochi glimpses the three beggars	273
8.6	Interior: Hell	273
8.7	Beguiled by a Fox? Aochi struggles to define the uncanny Sono	274
8.8	Representation Breaks Down (in the face of female sexuality), Shot (1)	275
8.9	Representation Breaks Down, Shot (2)	275
8.10	Representation Breaks Down, Shot (3)	276
8.11	Erotic Grotesque Nonsense	279
8.12	Violence at a Distance, Shot (1)	281
8.13	Violence at a Distance, Shot (2)	281
8.14	Violence at a Distance, Shot (3)	282
8.15	The End	283
8.16	What Price (Male) Freedom? The crimes of Nakasago are laid out for the viewer	284
8.17	Miraculous Transformation	286
8.18	The Phonograph as Technological Uncanny	288
8.19	The Cinema of Painting (*Yumeji*)	291
8.20	Anarchism and Earthiness—a solemn ceremony (*Kagerō-za*)	294
8.21	The Consequence of Power—haunting corpses of birds	205
8.22	Miraculous Transformation (II) (*Kagerō-za*)	296
8.23	Breaking the Wall	297
8.24	"Hysterically Phallic" Capitalism	298
8.25	Cinematic *Keren*, Shot (1)	300
8.26	Cinematic *Keren*, Shot (2)	301
8.27	Cinematic *Keren*, Shot (3)	301
8.28	Backdrop: Shinako willfully brings down the makeshift theatre	302
8.29	In the Realm of the Virtual	307
8.30	Imaginary Signifier—Matsuzaki views different scenes through a spyglass	308
8.31	The (Virtual) Realm of the Dead	309
8.32	The Double as Death—Matsuzaki watches himself watching his double	309
8.33	Whither the Present? Shot (1)	310
8.34	Whither the Present? Shot (2)	311
8.35	Suzuki's Homage to Dreyer—Reiko as Jeanne D'Arc (*Hishū monogatari*)	315

Introduction

In 1958, Suzuki Seitarō was a 35-year-old, lower-ranking, critically unrecognized contract director at Nikkatsu studios, despite the fact that he had already made fifteen feature-length program pictures. When he changed his professional name from "Suzuki Seitarō," his birth name, to the more flamboyant "Suzuki Seijun," no one in the press or film industry seems to have taken notice. They ought to have. Forty-five years later, in 2003, the octogenarian Suzuki was still directing films, long after the economic collapse of the Japanese studio system; he had won every major Japanese film award and significant international awards, including a lifetime achievement award at the 1991 São Paulo International Film Festival. The most prominent directors of the 1990s throughout Japan, East Asia, and the English-speaking world were citing him as an important influence, including Kurosawa Kiyoshi, Miike Takashi, Aoyama Shinji, John Woo, Wong Kar-wai, Quentin Tarantino, Baz Luhrmann, and Jim Jarmusch, who actively sought the master's stamp of approval on his work of hard-boiled homage, *Ghost Dog* (1999). We may add to the list, of late, the director of *La La Land*, Damien Chazelle, who toured Japan and announced his indebtedness to the 93-year old director just one month before Suzuki passed away, in February 2017, from Chronic Obstructive Pulmonary Disease.[1]

I do not relate these facts in order to extol a clichéd narrative of an artist's slow rise from derision to fame and unmitigated triumph. Such judgments are relative. As a filmmaker, Suzuki never attained the same respect nor the degree of centrality to Japanese media discourses as many others (Kurosawa and Ōshima Nagisa, for example). Even in his 70s, he struggled to finance his films. His narrative *is*, however, about the cultural endurance of a notably distinct film practice against remarkable adversity. How did the career of this director, who was fired from his studio and quietly blacklisted by the entire studio system in the late 1960s, outlast by decades the careers of major contemporaries at Nikkatsu and other studios? How did his influence on filmmaking practice arguably come to be more significant and widespread (especially internationally) than that of the younger, more fashionable, and highly publicized directors of the *nuberu bagu* (Japanese New Wave) such as Ōshima and Yoshida Yoshishige? Why did it take Japanese film criticism so long to recognize this powerful strain of influence, and why does it remain so underrepresented in academic film studies today?

The extraordinary circumstances of Suzuki's rise to artistic prominence is self-evidently a worthy subject of historical scholarship, revealing as it does the upheavals of the Japanese film industry since 1960 and the rise of trans-cultural media networks of producers, distributors, critics, and fans through which Japanese studio genre films (and the cult of genre auteurism) took on a virtual life. This book, however, is neither a biography nor an industrial history of a studio or genre, though aspects of all these will come into play. It is an interpretative and cultural study that canvasses the entirety of Suzuki's cinematic *corpus* and asks a range of questions about its significance—questions which rise up from the surface of these extraordinary filmic texts themselves and demand attention. What makes Suzuki's films so different from those of his contemporaries—including his top-ranking Nikkatsu rival Imamura Shōhei, his own mentor Noguchi Hiroshi, and his many successful apprentices such as Hasebe Yasuharu—that they have wielded such an influence and given rise to notorious cultural scandal? And what, in the history of narrative film, is the conceptual significance of a director who gaily asserted that "time and space are nonsense in my films"?[2]

Marking Difference

In a response to the work of the critical theorist Paul de Man, a notable literary critic of the 1970s once posed a question that is applicable to any aesthetic endeavor: "How does meaning get started anyway? Does it arise only in ironic repetition . . . or through excess, usurpation, overflow? . . . Or a cascade of newness . . . metonymic, hyperbolic, metaphorical?"[3] I am inspired by these very rhetorical operations in Suzuki's films—irony, excess, figuration, and the like—to pose a question throughout this study that is parallel to those questions above. How, in narrative film, does *difference* get started? How do we detect difference, and degrees of difference, and how may it be measured? The structuralist legacy of academic media studies has inclined us to analyze mass media productions as instantiations of large, aggregate blocks of dominant structures and ideologies. But an individual film, in all its historical contingency, is better metaphorized as a loose and fragile ball of thread—of countless interwoven formal and ideological strands.

Two decades of puzzled reflection on the distinctly demonstrative film practice of Suzuki Seijun have brought me to the conclusion that it is perilous at best, and foolish at worst, to ignore, misunderstand, or fail to theorize film-textual difference. To take the larger view of Jan Mukařovský: "the history of art, if we examine it from the standpoint of the aesthetic norm, is the history of revolts against reigning norms."[4] My aim throughout this book is to pinpoint the (hitherto unrecognized) contribution of Suzuki's films to such a period of overthrow, to appreciate the semantics and character of an "event in discourse that expands the space of meaning."[5] Film history, perpetually biased and incomplete as it is, has much to gain by isolating what is remarkable about the films of Suzuki even within the well-trodden generic grounds upon which they are built.

How does difference get started? The answer that I derive from my reading of Suzuki's films, and related films, is that it is established primarily through a process of ceaseless *negation* or *negativity*. Of course, to assert that there are such operations of "negation" or, indeed, "irony" within a cinematic text is to presume that there are meaning effects within those texts that are the product of an *intentionality*, a creative agency, at work in and through them, insofar as we can detect it. That creative agency, which is conventionally assigned to the transient collaboration of a set of filmmakers (directors, designers, actors, and the like), is the basis, though a shifting and elusive one, of what the critic or scholar means when he or she speaks of a particular *film practice* whose contours may be traced in the continuities *between* films that, paradoxically, serve to differentiate them from others.

A "negative" film practice operates in a way that is remarkably similar to what Dudley Andrew described as the role of figuration in film discourse: a more or less "calculated introduction of dissonance into any stage of the film process."[6] Difference is also necessarily relational to the constraints of the particular institutional context of its making: in Suzuki's case, the post-war Japanese studio system, with its hierarchies of power, cultures of censorship, and economies and conventions of filmmaking. But it also relates, broadly, to the struggle of any film practice for aesthetic (and, indeed, existential) survival in and amongst those practices associated with one's peers, one's antecedents, one's cultural institutions, and amidst the buffeting tides of cultural and historical change.

Given that Suzuki was a director of modestly budgeted, low priority

"B" pictures, often not in control of the scripts and stars assigned to him, "difference" in his films is often located on the level of editing, narrative structure, cinematic *mise-en-scène*, and stylistic gesture—precisely because these things are not verbalized and therefore do not give up their meanings and ideological subtexts readily, either to the viewer or to the controlling eyes of the studios and other organs of cultural authority. That is, after all, one method of survival.

How do we measure difference and evaluate its meaning in that nexus of formal practice, intentionality, and ideology that constitutes films and groupings of films?[7] This book makes claims for the necessary (and often slighted) work of textual interpretation in establishing sounder methods and evidentiary standards of reading, misreading, and going beyond the meaning effects of individual film texts in order to discover how and what a group of films (like Suzuki's) communicates to its viewers. Therefore, although this study takes as its objects the films of one director (and the films that have a demonstrable relation to them), the guiding methodology throughout is not *auteurism*, as traditionally understood, but close film-textual interpretation.

Nevertheless, to the extent that my use of textual "intentionality" or "agency" may be viewed as a form of "authorship," I must stray very briefly into the contested waters of film theory in order to clarify my operative assumptions about these concepts.

What's in a Name? The Director as Object of Study

In this book, I am designating a composite, yet potentially contradictory, "authorial function" named "Suzuki" that is found within the text and is (re-)constructed in each reception of it—generally with reference to other texts that are associated with "Suzuki."[8] Film scholars, among others, negotiate the continuities between these countless film receptions by bringing to a viewer's attention the evidence of patterns of intentionality that they have gleaned from textual analysis. This level of textual agency, while associated, according to common practice, with the name of the director, nevertheless accommodates a collaborative view of filmmaking that argues for the "significant difference" produced by other creative agents, including actors;[9] it need not oppose itself, like classical auteurism, to the "author function" of these other collaborators,[10] should anyone wish to describe them. Thus, the intentionality and practice that I label as "Suzuki" should be understood as the *directorial endorsement* of a collaborative agency forged by the director and significant creative partners such as cinematographers Nagatsuka Kazue and Shigeyoshi Mine, production designer Kimura Takeo, editor Suzuki Akira, and a host of regular actors and assistant directors.[11] This view is particularly well suited to the *kumi* system of the Japanese studios in which the director would work with the same collaborators from film to film. It leaves open a space for judicious assessment, across the multitude of films associated with the "Suzuki *gumi*" team of collaborators, of what meaning effects of a given film may be more or less representative of their agency and what may have come into being without *necessarily* having been endorsed by them at all (e.g., to take an obvious case, the documented censorship of certain films).

I must acknowledge, nevertheless, that this abstract (in the precise sense of the word), delicate, and fine-tuned definition of "the director" as a textual agency and an object of critical study is not necessarily what most habitual film viewers, film critics, or even academics mean when they discuss the qualities, ideologies, and comparative virtues of a "Suzuki" or a "Kurosawa." Common usage generally conjures up images of an individual creative "talent" on a film set or in an editing suite telling others what to do. Nor, unlike some contemporary media theorists, do I think that this conventional "image" of the director is wholly invalid or irrelevant to the proper object of Film and Cinema Studies. It is both common-sensical and inevitable that we will continue to study film directors of some cultural notoriety and contemplate the potential intersection between directors, the films attributed to them, and the meanings of the films. But if using the name of the director to designate a primary (though not only) source of filmic meaning is to be a coherent, let alone justified, procedure—a problem that Yoshimoto's famous book on Kurosawa could not quite get past—we must distinguish "the author as empirical origin . . . from the author as effect of the text."[12] That is to say, there are always at least two "Suzukis" just as there are at least two "Hitchcocks," two "Kurosawas," and indeed two "Kimura Takeos," since the general principle I am stating holds true for production designers, etc., as well as directors. There is (1) Suzuki the artist and thinker as we know him from his films, which is a construct that both he and his collaborators are responsible for, but not in control of; and (2) Suzuki the man—a career film director making decisions throughout a production process—as we know him from research and reminiscence, memoirs and public appearances. When I use the name "Suzuki" in this text, it will not be difficult for the sensitive reader to estimate, from the context of a given sentence, whether (1) or (2) is being implied. But it is indeed a special and proper object of "director study" to make critical statements and judgements that are true for *both* (1) and (2), that is to say, when I am proposing some kind of an intersection between the two; for example, when I strongly assert that Suzuki's budget limitations and insecure position in the studio system influenced the very meaning of certain film narratives themselves as well as the formal operations by which they appear to have been constructed. At present, I do not see how critics or scholars can justify relating the director as a "real world" creative agent to the intentionality that is manifest in the highly constructed artifact that is a film text without resorting to this "double discourse"; but it is a small price to pay for intellectual pursuits that are enjoyable to a great many and have obvious significance *at least* in reference to the films and filmmaking of the past century. It is worth remembering that throughout the latter, since Griffith if not since Méliès, the "director" (though sometimes confusingly referred to as "producer" in the popular media of the classical Hollywood period) consistently reigned supreme in discourse if not in fact.[13]

Marking Difference

Throughout the following, broadly chronological analysis and interpretation of perhaps forty of the forty-nine feature films attributed to Suzuki as director, I attempt to define the formal and ideological contours of a remarkably consistent filmmaking practice that evolved into the shape of what I have called the "Suzuki Difference," a practice that is defined by the search to differentiate itself from dominant filmmaking practices and ideologies (i.e., the Japanese studio system taken as a whole) and also from received counter-practices, such as the documentarian aesthetics of the *nuberu bagu* as conditioned by the cultural politics of the Japanese New Left of the 1960s.

It would be too easy, perhaps, to interpret the Suzuki Difference aesthetically by reference to a list of formal devices which were unconventional, indeed unacceptable to the studio system at the time when Suzuki and his crew of loyal collaborators first employed them: discontinuous editing and narratively dysfunctional ellipses, non-synchronous sound and visuals, pervasive non-diegetic lighting and coloration, non-diegetic graphics and inserts, flat theatrical backgrounds, etc. Some of these devices were also used in the transformational period of 1959-1961 by younger contemporaries such as Masumura Yasuzō, Ōshima, and (in the West) Jean-Luc Godard. In most cases the "experiments" we find in Suzuki's films significantly pre-dated these, but what is important is not simply a formal/stylistic precedent. Due to the media prominence of the *nuberu bagu* directors and a shrinking audience of mainly young men, the studio system gradually accepted stylistic change to the extent that, by 1969, even formulaic entertainment like *Gojira tai Hedorah/Godzilla vs. the Smog Monster* (Tōhō, 1969) operated according to stylistic parameters that would have been unthinkable in 1966. What is important, then, is the conceptual or critical use to which these formal operations are put. It is the rich semantic complexity of Suzuki's practice that differentiates it from the work of other studio directors, even those of the 1970s who followed Suzuki's lead in applying a much broader palate of filmmaking technique to their work. Ultimately, Suzuki's film practice is perhaps best appreciated not so much in the company of his fellow Nikkatsu directors or those of the *nuberu bagu*, but alongside a broader strand of trans-cultural modernism in the narrative arts encompassing Sōseki Natsume (whose *Botchan* and *Yume Jūya/Ten Nights of Dream* have their analogues amongst Suzuki's output), Luis Buñuel, von Sternberg, Welles, Ichikawa, and Teshigahara. I will argue that Suzuki's films constitute, necessarily within the idiom of popular genre filmmaking, a reflexive cinematic form as an alternative and highly idiosyncratic politics of the image, a critical negation of the workings of patriarchy and social control in popular film—yet without abandoning, and indeed embracing, a cinema of visual pleasure.

A question arises: how do we define unconventional form or elements of style in cinematic practice? Obviously, deviations can only be measured from norms. Another concept of film theory that I have brought to bear on the exploration and elaboration of the "Suzuki Difference" is the "classical narrative style" of the Hollywood and Japanese studio system, by which I mean an unwritten, historically contingent "code" of filmmaking practice, or better, a rigorous "formal economy" of practice that dominated these studios' film productions (and many others) from roughly 1919-1966. Some version of a "classical" cinema predominantly associated with the studio system exists in the diverse and otherwise incongruent theories of Bordwell, Deleuze, Burch, McCabe, and many others. In two articles from the 1990s, Bordwell claimed that the Japanese studios, from the Great Kantō earthquake (1923) to 1945, *more or less* (that is, normatively) obeyed the principles of classic continuity editing, including, for example, shot-reverse shot, axis of action, match on action, POV ("point-of-view") editing, and other facets of the classical narrative cinema.[14] Bordwell's complex argument—based on a sampling of 163 films—includes an "ornamental" function of style that reduced the excessive "redundancy" of Hollywood's stylistic economy without violating it. Moreover, such expressive effects quickly established conventions of their own as "the reigning style reserved a canonized function for them."[15]

What is the "classical narrative" economy to which Bordwell refers? He writes that "in classical filmmaking the overriding principle is to make every instantiation of technique obedient to the ... transmission of *fabula* information. Departures are motivated by longstanding genre conventions (e.g., the musical)."[16] That is to say, the singular priority of this kind of filmmaking is the exposition of narrative, or more precisely, the exposition of what Bordwell calls "an integral *fabula* world"—essentially, the "world" in which the narrative takes place, what I have called "diegesis" throughout this book.[17] The "diegetic" elements of the filmmaking are the elements that exist for the purpose of constructing the "narrative universe" in which the characters (and their thoughts, perceptions, actions) can be said to exist. We could say that the primary (sometimes only) function of these elements is to convey narrative information. On the other hand, the "non-diegetic" elements of filmmaking, which from a certain point of view are much rarer than the diegetic ones, are elements that, logically speaking, do not create or contribute to the "narrative world," but exist for some other purpose. The most obvious example of the latter is the orchestral "underscore" that is ubiquitous in classical Hollywood movies, which "comments" on the story world, so to speak, without being a part of it. Throughout narrative cinema, however, non-diegetic *visual* elements are considerably more unconventional than orchestral soundtracks and the like. I make use of the term "non-diegetic" throughout this book as a way of linking together many disparate formal devices and filmmaking choices that Suzuki employs to various ends. For in addition to their being deliberately non-conformist, they collectively contribute to an experiment in cinematic communication and expression beyond the confines of the story and its basic telling.

According to Bordwell, the structural principle that ensures the efficient transmission of narrative information—the primary engine of classical narration, so to speak—is causality, which "commits classical narration to unambiguous presentation. . . . The viewer concentrates on constructing the *fabula*, not on asking why the narration is representing the *fabula* in this particular way."[18] In other words, "the viewer's interest is entirely suspense oriented."[19] Further, "most explicitly codified into rules is the system of classical continuity editing. The reliance upon an axis of action orients the spectator to the space." Physical space must be represented logically, predictably, and efficiently, but such simplifications come at a cost: the viewer's comprehensive mastery of depicted space imposes far severer restrictions on shot change (i.e., editing): Bordwell judges that " mismatched screen direction and inconsistently angled eye lines are less likely; perceptible jump cuts and unmotivated cutaways are strictly forbidden."[20]

Bordwell's account of "classicism" has been rightfully criticized for its "self-imposed consistency,"[21] but it is not his wealth of textual evidence so much as his qualitative interpretation of "boundary" cases that is legitimately in question.[22] I suggest that we can retool Bordwell's distinction between "problematic" and "unproblematic" violations of classical narrative economy (in regards to the function and intent of a stylistic event) as a useful tool for mapping both the aesthetic and ideological boundaries of the system.[23]

Unfortunately, we do not enjoy a similarly systematic or evidentiary analysis of the Japanese post-war cinema. Eric Crosby provided some textual evidence for the claim that post-war studio practice adhered to "classical" compositional norms. We can moreover supplement the films that Crosby has sampled with the many films of Nikkatsu's higher-ranking directors from 1954-1966 such as Inoue Umetsugu, Saitō Buichi, Noguchi Hiroshi, even the young Masuda Toshio. Even theorists who reject Bordwell's concept of "classicism" would be unable to argue that the practices of these directors differ significantly from the formal economy that Bordwell identified in prewar Japanese film, or indeed in its Hollywood antecedents. In fact, I would argue that most films of the post-war studio system, for myriad historical and economic reasons, were far more conservative in their stylistic economy (continuity, camera movement, reliance on the scene as the principle narrative unit) and more closely oriented towards Hollywood practice than had been the prewar cinema, for instance Itō Daisuke's influential *chanbara*. Noël Burch (in a seminal, though dated, study) viewed a significant number of post-war studio films and came to this same conclusion.[24] The post-war cinema to 1965 simply had no equivalent to the extraordinary stylistic breadth of technique and differential quality of Naruse's astonishing "subjective" montage from 1931's *Koshiben ganbare/Flunky, Work Hard!* It took the films of Suzuki and of a very few contemporaries to violate the normative spatio-temporal economy and narrative functionality described above, in all its tolerance for "ornamental novelty," consistently enough to break it.

Making Difference

As a director, Suzuki was neither born nor bred to be a cinematic iconoclast. He may have come to it via the school of hard knocks. Like hundreds of thousands of others, this undemonstrative, unprepossessing youth of *shitamachi* Tokyo probably felt a sense of pride and duty and few misgivings when he was drafted into the Imperial Navy right out of high school in 1943. Subsequently, his eyes were forced open. Suzuki's post-war experience was, unsurprisingly, marked by severe depression and relative destitution until he joined the assistant director's program at Shōchiku studios. Thereafter, he toiled in obscurity for six years, and spent another two years doing the same after joining the newly reconstituted Nikkatsu Studios. Even after becoming a director in 1956, Suzuki worked near the bottom of the production system in a state of high anxiety, his films repeatedly subject to censorious internal criticism and himself under threat of dismissal, more than once, by Nikkatsu executives. Given Suzuki's war traumas, followed by years of professional insecurity, it is not as surprising as it may seem that between 1958 and 1960, a mind as restless, defensive, and wary as Suzuki's should have gradually hit upon a method—an aesthetic will to power, so to speak—of differentiating his films as far as possible from the conventions accepted and adopted by his studio colleagues; that is to say, of negating received practice.

The process leading up to this strategic awareness that one detects in Suzuki's films was undoubtedly less deliberate, less progressive, and more of a collaborative evolution than the above description implies. But it is a matter of record that Suzuki refused to back down after being told repeatedly by the studio that his filmmaking choices differed sharply from the desired norm. Although it may touch the more problematic borders of auteur criticism to say so, I believe that the studio's criticisms contributed, ironically,[25] to the transformation of an outwardly pensive, anxious, and paranoid novice named Seitarō into the aggressively motivated, satirical, and equally paranoid artistic persona named Seijun. It was the films of "Seijun" that came to reorient popular exploitation filmmaking as a rebellious exercise in reflexivity directed at the very institutions—social, cultural, and commercial—that brought such films into being and which were more or less responsible for turning Suzuki's professional career into an exercise in frustration. (He never described the filmmaking process as anything but nerve-wracking.) If this may seem a trivial motivation for the pursuit of cinematic originality, we should bear in mind, firstly, that something's genesis is not the limit of its outcome. Secondly, we might consider how Christian Metz theorized *all* aesthetic discourse as (in Andrew's words) "the progressive displacement of meaning in relation to a censoring process [that] turns a desire into a pattern of flight and detour that surfaces as discursive figure."[26] Metz's "censor" was the Freudian superego, but the obvious analogy to social-institutional resistance was never lost on his inheritors. Suzuki's relationship to the studio often appears as a masochistic revolt against the symbolic father of institutional authority.

Whatever may have been its genesis and motivation, Suzuki's gamble—or his stubborn impulses—paid off. As the post-war generation came into its own and the cultural ground shifted beneath the feet of Nikkatsu's ageing corporate bosses, Suzuki became an icon of young, urban male cinemagoers and young filmmakers alike (including his own assistants) during the mid-1960s. This only resulted in his being promptly fired (and blacklisted) for stepping out of line. Despite his own personal misgivings about the tide of events, a career of high-risk envelope-pushing and aesthetic self-assertion blossomed, by April 1968, into a culture war waged on the site of cinema. Students, directors, and provocateurs protested Suzuki's dismissal in the streets before Nikkatsu president Hori Kyūsaku's office in a spectacular foretaste of May 1968.

The "Suzuki Problem" of April 1968 being now relegated to the same distant political past as France's "Langlois Affair" of May 1968, the most significant result of Suzuki's struggle for directorial independence is the production of forty-three popular genre films and six independent avant-garde spectacles that continue to demonstrate to viewers an unprecedented degree of ironic self-awareness, narrative and representational ambiguity, expressive inventiveness, and ethical provocation. In their reflexive political modernism, Suzuki's films, as Donald Richie recognized, are recognizably similar to those of his former Shōchiku colleague, the celebrated Ōshima.[27] But whereas Ōshima's films amounted to a Brechtian theatre of gestures directed towards the political and formal debates of his generation, Suzuki's political sense of form compelled him to evade interpretation, even to militate against received processes of cinematic signification in themselves. The European modernists had most notably associated these tendencies with another marginal, alienated, and paranoiac artist, Franz Kafka. Like Kafka, or the writer Uchida Hyakken in his early gothic phase that inspired *Zigeunerweisen* (1980), Suzuki's films never abstain from the descent into an underworld that is essentially "inexpressible." Somewhat closer to the heart of Suzuki's film practice, however, may have been certain Hollywood directors still active in the post-war period, such as the famously defensive John Ford. Contra those Japanese critics who still maintain that Suzuki's films are "uniquely" Japanese and/or unconscious of Hollywood, Suzuki once credited Ford—whose career is cleverly alluded to by a fake movie poster advertising a silent Fox Western in *Kenka erejii/ Fighting Elegy* (1966)—as having directed the finest action sequences in the Occidental cinema. Though formally as much a realist as Suzuki was anti-realist, Ford in his films seemed to delight in highlighting the contradictions within American ethics and values, and between those values and social realities, thus making it virtually impossible to determine his films' ideological position towards the narrative events that they portrayed.

Like Kafka or Ford, then, but unlike Ōshima, Suzuki is not politically constructive or "progressive." He does not set out a program for systemic social or cultural reform; his films do not participate *directly* in the political debates of the time, nor do they propose a direction for revolutionary action. In fact, Suzuki most often dwells on the failure of rebellion by those who are caught in the ideological system against which they struggle. While Ōshima represented (often critically) his own political Left, Suzuki's films examine the long Japanese tradition of rebellion from the right—of reactionary subjectivity. In doing so, they effortlessly attain a sort of universalism in their representation of Japanese culture and its recursive and dominant formations—no small achievement for a director who more or less declined, for forty-nine years, to make "Ozu-like films" that represented the quotidian existence of ordinary post-war Japanese. In comparison to this sense of universality (a notion that is very much out of favor in academic criticism today), the films of Ōshima and Terayama Shūji appear very much more pertinent to *their times* than to ours, if no less sporadically impressive for all that.

On the other hand, because Suzuki's films exist in the idiom of popular genre and involve a culturally familiar subject matter, it has been too easy for critics to dismiss their socio-political analysis as retrograde or non-existent. There were no critics, by contrast, who failed to miss the socio-political intentions of a so-called "classical" director such as Kobayashi Masaki. There is an irony here, for Kobayashi approached the same themes—for example, rebellion from the right—with such sly and understated subversion that the thrust of his political critique was hardly obvious. In *Jōi-uchi: hairyō tsuma shimatsu/Samurai Rebellion* (Tōhō, 1965), Mifune Toshirō plays a mild-mannered, loveable father figure of an exswordsman who cheerfully brings about the death of everyone around him. We too easily forgive him. Whereas the smug, reactionary men of violence of Suzuki's films are distinctly not loveable, even when played by the handsome Kobayashi Akira; nor would Suzuki dream of making excuses for them. Why, then, did the critics miss the critique in Suzuki's case? The fact that a "B-movie" director of the 1960s lacked cultural capital is not quite an adequate explanation; it is more accurate to say that Suzuki addressed this lack, and the restrictions that came with it, by offering a socio-political analysis discoverable only through visual metaphor and other open-ended narrational forms. In contrast, having become a studio director a few years earlier in a time of truly rapid change for the cinema, Kobayashi Masaki retains, for all his truly acerbic social vision, formal energy, and facility in the representation of narrative time, a certain classicism and restraint which Suzuki was indifferent to, but which the critics found accessible. In hindsight, Kobayashi is now widely seen to have self-limited the expression of a radical critique which he himself may have believed, whereas Suzuki's form of critique, indubitably political yet maddeningly refracted and evasive, seems to provoke us even now.

Perhaps we can best appreciate Suzuki's mode of address in light of a politics of the image such as that advanced by Jacques Rivette—among the most militant of the French *nouvelle vague* directors—in 1969:

> I don't believe in a revolutionary cinema ... which is satisfied with taking the revolution as its subject ... The only way to make revolutionary cinema in France is to make sure that it escapes all the bourgeois aesthetic clichés. ... I believe more and more that the role of the cinema is to destroy myths, to be pessimistic. Its role is to take people out of their cocoons and plunge them into horror.[28]

Suzuki's films are pessimistic rather than programmatic; the director viewed the latter orientation as a trap of power. They take negation as an ethical first principle beyond mere aesthetic iconoclasm. Suzuki has variously described his film practice as "destructive" or as a form of nihilism, but it is best described as a *negative* aesthetic, socially, critically, and reflexively:

> When Chuson-ji, the famous Buddhist temple ... was still standing, travelers would simply pass it by. ... They only began to notice it ... after it was in ruins. What is standing now isn't really there. When it is demolished, the consciousness that it ... was there begins to form. Thus, even in terms of ... civilization, the power of destruction is stronger.[29]

What is negation, for Suzuki? On the one hand, it is not at all a Sadean negation, which abhors and violates nature in the name of reason.[30] On the other, it can neither be identified with nor entirely separated from Freudian negation, which is a form of disavowal, a looking away from an intolerable reality. Suzuki's films, considered as a social/aesthetic practice, do not disavow: they actively reject. They deliberately "make false" not reality per se, but the consensual/conventional realities that mask that literally unutterable reality. Like Kurosawa at his boldest, the Suzuki film looks—with a certain masochistic pride in *not* looking away. But if they do not look away from Japanese post-war realities, neither do they instrumentalize cinema as a vehicle to "merely" represent an extra-cinematic actuality—which is in any case impossible. On the contrary, Suzuki's films seem to surpass those of any other Japanese director in actively recognizing the camera's transformation of actuality into image, upon which transformation those images, whatever their political valence, automatically register as a source of fetishistic pleasure for the viewer. If the philosopher Gilles Deleuze is correct to argue that Freudian disavowal, as the basis of fetishism, consists in "radically contesting the validity of that which is" such that it "suspends belief in and neutralizes the given in such a way that new horizons open up...", then there is clearly a relation to Suzuki's sensual, dream-like, artificial mise-en-scène. According to Deleuze, the author von Sacher-Masoch wishes "to put on wings and escape into the world of dreams... He does not believe in negating or destroying the world nor in idealizing it: what he does is disavow it... He questions the validity of existing reality in order to create a pure ideal reality."[31] Suzuki's cinema is correspondingly dreamlike, to be sure, but these are dreams that, like Kafka's, hardly refrain from "negating the world as we know it"; these are dreams, like Hitchcock's, of terror and murder, of intolerable oppression and largely failed rebellion. They are also, often, beautiful.

The Suzuki Difference, then, operates fundamentally on at least two levels: on the first, these images and scenarios constitute a brazen truth—in at least the common usage of the word—on account of their bringing to light an all too real underside of violence inherent in the economic and social systems of modern Japan, and perhaps in the project of modernity itself: a project long held in deep suspicion by Japanese intellectuals and writers, prewar and post-war and across the political spectrum. For to acknowledge—as the idealistic "Phoenix" Tetsu (Watari Tetsuya) in *Tokyo nagaremono/Tokyo Drifter* (1966) is patently unable to do—that Japan cannot and should not wish to retreat into its martial premodern past is not necessarily to validate Japan's (capitalist) present and likely future, which seems in Suzuki's films to be equally coercive, albeit *via* a different route. On another level, perhaps a deeper one, each and every filmic image of social, ideological, and psycho-sexual violence—whether on the part of loyal yakuza foot soldiers, female prostitutes, or plainly psychotic killers—participates in a cinematic and trans-cinematic erotic fantasy: indeed, an erotic *game* akin to those which von Sacher-Masoch plays, and which, for Deleuze and a certain strand of modern philosophy, may constitute a formidable form of cultural resistance. One has a sense of Suzuki's films as part of a game that the popular art of the cinema *must* play out to the bitter end; a game which is plainly dangerous on the level of social representation in the arena of a mass art that is constantly subject to manipulation by corporate, bourgeois, even bureaucratic ideologies. Hence the crucial development of a negative aesthetic of the cinema that can be, as needed, both provocatively reactive and thoughtfully reflexive.

There is an ethical and political risk to this open-endedness of Suzuki's films. Evasive and Janus-faced in tone and representation where Ōshima, by contrast, is more-or-less frank, Suzuki's films nevertheless dwell with equal consistency on motifs and displays of gendered violence. To be sure, these films never came close to employing the "graphic," Sadean representations of the Nikkatsu and Tōei "pinky violence" and similar sub-genres that developed in Suzuki's wake; unlike Wakamatsu Kōji (who is far more celebrated in academic circles), Suzuki's films have little interest in "direct" or "realist" representations of rape or violence. Nevertheless, in navigating these risky waters of the 1960s cinematic scene, in which it was too easy to plunge into sadistic exploitation for a predominantly male audience, these pictures do not always obviously win their "games" against the forces of social and gender cliché; but, as I have found over the course of many years of pondering the meaning of this cinema, they often do.

Perhaps no cliché is so vehemently negated by Suzuki's pictures as the one post-war myth that remains as current and powerful in East Asia today as it was in the 1950s: the myth of historical/economic "progress" and "development." If one could find a single axiom with which to encapsulate the dissentient historical wisdom of Suzuki's films, it would be that "history repeats itself, first as tragedy, second as farce." Their absurdist and baroque presentation of Japanese (sub-)culture from Meiji to Heisei seems always to be neatly poised at the turning of history's wheel from the tragic to the ridiculous. And it is needless to say that despite their sometimes explicit pro-labor orientation, they do not hold out much hope for a Marxian or Utopian teleology.

Suzuki's negativity, then, is a complex operation by which the intolerable truths of Japanese society are represented, but are seen, in the cinema, as within a dream. What are these truths, specifically? As a veteran of the Pacific "theatre" of war whose experience alternated between a soul-destroying tedium and a stunned, panicked fleeing from sites of imminent death, Suzuki as a thinker continually returned to the institutional expression of violence as a fundamental yet intolerable condition of social organization. In his films, the monopoly on the means of violence by governing institutions in Japan (as, for example, during the Tokugawa reformation, the Meiji Restoration, or the U.S. Occupation) evidently did not permit a greater degree of peace or freedom for its "subjects" than other social structures or, indeed, anarchy might have done. Nor did it seem to matter much who exactly had been in power from one generation to the next. Rather, institutional power generally at once suppresses and instrumentalizes the (irrational) violence of the individual in order to wield and justify violence as social control. War, capitalist exploitation, gangsterism, policing, mass media pressures, and prostitution appear in these films as permitting the "institution," one way or another, to unleash an annihilation of its subjects in the name of that control—an annihilation that, at one point in Japan's modern history, had reached the level of the near-total. For Suzuki's films, it seems as if the "hidden" truth of annihilation that underpins "civil" society—including, polemically, that of *post-war* Japan—must be continually invoked. Even the relatively comic milieu of the rural, itinerant performers of *Toge wo wataru wakai kaze / The Wind-of-Youth Crosses the Mountain Pass* (1961) is being forcibly, desperately ground out of existence. If this manner of historical critique, as I describe it, may seem to some to be broad and imprecise, we should remember that highly figural discourses—from the films of Buñuel to the novels of Abe Kōbō—cannot be subject to such a "literal" translation without considerable loss.

Nor does Suzuki's blanket condemnation of post-war military-industrial technocracy, for all its lack of subtlety, lack passionate defenders in fields outside of the aesthetic. In her introduction to Klaus Theweleit's seminal *Male Fantasies* (1987), Barbara Ehrenreich writes:

> Then in our own time—and I write in a time of "peace", meaning that our wars are so far "local" and endured only by peripheral, or third world, people—what do we make of the warrior caste that rules the United States . . . with its counterpart in the Soviet Union . . . ? These men wear civilian clothes . . . [and] go home at night to wives and children. Yet are they not also men who refuse, at all costs, to disarm? Men who have opted

for perpetual war—"the cold war" of nuclear terror? . . . They have succeeded in enlisting the human and mechanical energy of production for the cause of death. . . . Our executive warriors pave over the farm to build a munitions factory. . . . As more and more human and material resources are appropriated by the warrior caste, it becomes harder and harder to draw the line between production, as an innately purposeful human activity, and the production of death.[32]

When we supplement Ehrenreich's picture with the decades of carbon-intensive and otherwise pollutant "production" practices of a profit-driven elite, its menace becomes comprehensive indeed. Theweleit's book famously illustrated a particular (prewar) example of the contribution of lower-middle class and working-class war veterans to the ideological perpetuation of this kind of reactionary (and ironically elitist) military-industrial machine that, materially, was of little benefit to most of them. A veteran himself, Suzuki has more than once taken aboard this very critique in his films; but in general, and in keeping with Japan's unique experiences of the past century, Suzuki blames the generals—and their successors. And as in Theweleit's work on the war veterans of the German *freikorps*, Suzuki's delusional reactionaries are not so much focused on the enemy *outside* as they are bent on the elimination of the gendered and "Othered" enemy *within*, that is to say, within our borders and even, especially, within our skins.

These quasi-anarchical, quasi-Freudian critiques and social representations would not necessarily distinguish Suzuki from younger directors, such as Fukasaku Kinji, if not for their unique cinematic expression. If, as Deleuze controversially argued, a dream-like aesthetic is a form of artistic resistance, then Suzuki uses such a cinema not to construct (elusive) alternative societies, but to "re-present" the truth of violence and oppression in a form that is transmuted by art,[33] a figurative and reflexive form that rejects all notions of realism and distances itself from the signified. Violence as abstract art can be tolerated and indeed can, and perhaps must, become a source of masochistic pleasure. For if not, then where shall those pleasures be found that do not delude us in the service of power?

The specific contours of this negative aesthetic practice—a dynamic and relational negativity, a response to its times—shall be revealed, subsequently, through close textual analysis of Suzuki's films.[34] Although this book treats several of the director's most representative films in chronological order, I have arranged my study so that each chapter invokes a distinct set of theoretical, critical, and cultural frameworks that I find to be most germane to that particular set of films and which can supplement the approaches already advanced. Chapter 1 provides a brief history of Suzuki's life, his film career, and its critical reception. Chapter 2, treating the early films of 1956-1961, focuses on the Japanese adaptation of Western genres and stylistic norms, including the aesthetics of color. Chapter 3 (1962-63) discusses the sexual politics of studio genre films and, above this, how cinematic form and figuration translates to politico-aesthetic meaning, generally. Chapter 4 (1963-65) examines the formal and political context of the vast post-war genre of *yakuza* films to which Suzuki made an early, invaluable contribution. Chapter 5 (1964-66) relates Suzuki's historical representation of the war and the Occupation to the representation of female sexuality, revealing a masochistic aesthetic that determines both. Chapter 6 (1966) examines iconic style, discontinuity, and other formal strategies in relation to a social critique of post-war and prewar masculine and national identities. Chapter 7 (1967) attempts to place Suzuki's use of discontinuity editing and other "negative" formal devices in a transnational context of cinematic evolution in the 1960s, before exploring whether Suzuki's fatalism can be understood as a form of ethical wisdom. Finally, chapter 8 (1980-91) examines the re-appropriation of prewar Japanese art—specifically, gothic literature and classical theatre—in Suzuki's creation of a new mythical and "dream image" within an avant-garde cinema of uncanny and abject pleasures.

A Note on the Text and Translations Throughout This Book

In this book Japanese names are given in the order of surname first and personal name second, as per Japanese custom. In the case of film titles, I have given the Japanese name first, followed initially by an English translation. I have made an exception for the film *Zigeunerweisen* and used the original German title of the musical composition by Pablo de Sarasate after which the film takes its name. The Japanese title, which has been romanized in several sources as *Tsigoineruwaizen*, is simply the Japanese syllabic transliteration of the original German.

At this time of writing there are no recognized standard English titles for Suzuki's films, but instead a large number are variants attached to various theatrical and video releases in different markets. Literature on Suzuki in English has seen a similarly bewildering proliferation of variants. Arrow Films, who are to be celebrated for their heroic efforts in making eleven unreleased Suzuki films available to the public in high definition, have, unfortunately, chosen the worst possible titles for each: with *Akutarō*, for instance, rendered weakly into English as *The Incorrigible*. I have taken the liberty of deciding upon the best translation of the Japanese title, rather than being bound to any one of these variant release titles (which are provided in the Appendix at the end of this book) on some arbitrary basis. Any reader who may find my use of Japanese-language film titles distracting, off-putting, or hard to follow, is strongly recommended to consult the titles and plot summaries in the Appendix whenever encountering an unfamiliar title, before moving on to the rest of the given chapter.

All translations from films and publications in the Japanese language are mine unless otherwise stated in references.

As for the romanization of Japanese words, I have followed the Revised Hepburn System of Romanization which notably represents long vowels by the use of macrons (for example, ō and ū). Exceptions have been made for the extremely commonplace names Tokyo and Osaka, and for multinational corporations, such as Kodansha Ltd., that are officially romanized without a marker of long vowels.

CHAPTER 1

The Recusant

Early Life, 1923-1948

Suzuki Seitarō was born on 24 May 1923, in the heart of central Tokyo, reportedly in Nihonbashi (part of Chūō ward),[1] a neighborhood that in the 19th century had been the commercial and cultural capital of the city and the center from which all geographical distance was measured. It was within walking distance of Marunouchi and Ginza, at that time the respective political and commercial centers of the Japanese Empire. Suzuki was born one hundred days before the Great Kantō Earthquake that would ravage central Tokyo. He was the eldest son of a merchant of dry goods, particularly textiles such as kimonos,[2] who moved his family some years after the quake to nearby Honjō ward (now Sumida). There is little evidence to indicate that the father was consistently prosperous, but his fortunes presumably improved after the move as he allegedly became a manufacturer of bicycle bells.[3] His merchant family did not have the prestige of an aristocratic background (as did the Kurosawa family, for instance); rather, Suzuki has proudly described himself as a lifelong *Edokko*, that is, a descendent of working or middle class residents of the old neighborhoods of Edo. Despite early successes in primary school, Suzuki's academic career was marked by failure, possibly because his parents directed him towards vocational schools. After graduating from a Tokyo trade school in 1941,[4] he twice failed the entrance exam to a Tokyo commercial college, and subsequently took the exam for the colonial "Asian Development Institute" with the intention of going to Indochina.[5] Failing this and several other exams, he finally succeeded in entering the relatively prestigious Hirosaki High School in distant Aomori Prefecture in April 1943.[6]

Suzuki acknowledged being deeply influenced by the urban culture of the Taishō era (officially 1912-1926, but lasting until a climate of cultural nationalism became pervasive in the early 1930s), including the dynamic theatre scene of Asakusa:

> It was Japan's Belle Epoch, different from both the Meiji and Shōwa eras. The Taishō was a period that glorified freedom. Of course, there was con-

trol from above, but within certain bounds the common people were free. There were anarchists, Bolshevists, terrorists. It was an age of ideology. On stage there was opera and new types of theatre.[7]

Suzuki remembers Taishō not only as an age of comparative political freedom, but as an urban culture of transnational hybridity, the result of popularly accessible cultural forms (paperback fiction, popular theatre) and technologies (cinema, gramophone).[8] While there is no question that Suzuki was deeply exposed to kabuki and other forms of theatre in this period, sources agree that throughout the 1930s, Suzuki spent much of his time at the movies. He was affected by the popular *jidai-geki* such as Inagaki Hiroshi's *Edojō saigo no hi/Last Days of Edo Castle* (Tōhō, 1941). Certain European films left a mark as well, including a 1936 film record of Austria's Burgtheater and Erik Charell's *Der Kongress Tanzt/The Congress Dances* (1931),[9] a lightly satirical musical comedy boasting flamboyant tracking shots, opulent costumes and sets. The film was a perfect correlate to what the press depicted as the *ero-guro-nansensu* (Erotic Grotesque Nonsense) culture of the Taishō era.[10]

Only months after his entrance to Hirosaki High School, Suzuki was drafted and sent to Chiba Prefecture for combat training as a Private-Second Class in the 83rd battalion "Imperial Guard" (equivalent to a General Infantry replacement corps). In 1944, the cargo fleet transporting Suzuki to the Philippines was sunk by American submarines, killing nearly half of Suzuki's classmates. In a scenario of military desperation, he and the other survivors in Manila were reassigned to the Air Force but then sent back to Taiwan due to an impending attack.[11] On the way, their freighter was sunk by American planes.[12] Sources differ as to whether Suzuki floated on the open sea for days or hours, but he was eventually rescued.[13] Suzuki's war experience in general seems to have been characterized more by an amazed viewing of the carnage around him than by direct combat: an interesting parallel to his (action film) protagonists who also tend to view situations in uncertainty before (or instead of) acting. In Taiwan, Suzuki spent the rest of the war as a sub-lieutenant at an isolated weather observation outpost. Amidst an atmosphere of sexual deprivation and binge drinking, Suzuki uneasily recalled spending his entire pay on the army prostitutes "assigned" to the unit.[14] He returned to Japan in 1946 utterly destitute, but was able to complete his studies in Aomori. Schilling characterizes Suzuki's war experience as having left a "deep distrust of authority." This is confirmed by Suzuki's bitter observation that during the Occupation "the relatives of Tōjō Hideki and other army staff received generous pensions" while he and other ex-servicemen received a total of ten yen upon demobilization.[15] In 1948, Suzuki graduated with his high school diploma and returned to central Tokyo, briefly working in an office while boarding with his girlfriend and several prostitutes with GI boyfriends.[16] Despite having no ambitions other than financial security, Suzuki took the entrance exam for the nation's top university, Tokyo University. Failing this, Suzuki suffered a period of "severe depression,"[17] but eventually discovered the fledgling Kamakura Film Academy, for which he passed the exam. Suzuki graduated from film school at the end of 1948 and was directed to the exam for the Assistant Director's program at Shōchiku, which he passed. A career seemed to be taking shape.

Assistant Director at Shōchiku and Nikkatsu, 1948–1956

At this time, Shōchiku was the most successful and prestigious studio in Japan. Its 1949 roster of talent included Ozu Yasujirō, Yoshimura Kōzaburō, and Kinoshita Keisuke, then as now acknowledged masters of postwar classical filmmaking.[18] Suzuki's incoming class, including future Nikkatsu director Nakahira Kō, received initial training by Yoshimura, who would soon leave the studio in frustration over artistic interference (a pattern which would become endemic by the end of the decade).[19] As a junior Assistant Director, he was passed from one film set to another for training, beginning with a film by Shibuya Minoru, *Shushin imada kiezu/Red Lips Still Not Gone*, in 1949.

The *kumi* or "crew" system of studio filmmaking was integral to the aesthetic vitality of the Japanese studio system. A director would work with the same creative and technical staff on each film; they would make up his crew, a sort of artistic family whose consistency and loyalty assisted the realization of a "directorial style." Assistant Directors could benefit from having an established director as protégé. As Shōchiku Assistants were able to choose their *kumi*, Suzuki in 1951 joined that of Iwami Tsuruo, a director of melodramas who, at 32, was the youngest director of comparable rank to the studio's masters. Suzuki, now informally married, was receiving a modest living wage and presumably absorbing the techniques of filmmaking. But he described his four years with Iwami as merely "fun," involving hard drinking and womanizing, and did not feel the director had been an influence on him: "after work . . . we were forbidden to talk about movies. The only thing we were allowed to do was drink."[20] Writing in the 1970s, Suzuki was critical of this lack of an intellectual context at Shōchiku: "Seven years passed in which we hadn't read a book, seen a film, or thought about politics and our lives in general."[21] In this climate of stagnation, "I was a melancholy drunk and soon became known as a relatively worthless Assistant Director . . . when we were on location, I stayed in the bus."[22] Despite this self-portrait of indolence, Suzuki in fact wrote some unproduced screenplays.[23]

Clearly, in addition to unsatisfied ambition, Suzuki was experiencing the frustration of being just a cog within a major studio. An important aspect of the *kumi* system was that being Assistant Director was considered as training for becoming Director. "Chief" Assistants were (theoretically) guaranteed a promotion (at least on a trial basis). In actual practice, however, promotion could take as long as a decade.[24] "There were 16 assistant directors ahead of me at Shōchiku. I felt frustrated at ever becoming a director there."[25] Although he seems to have risen to the rank of Chief Assistant,[26] working on war films as well as Iwami's melodramas, he was never promoted, and like many others at Shōchiku, jumped at the offer of a better salary from Nikkatsu when the studio resumed film production in 1954.

Another Chief Assistant who moved to Nikkatsu was Noguchi Hiroshi, an older filmmaker who would have a decisive effect on Suzuki's career. Noguchi had joined Nikkatsu's Tamagawa studios in 1935 and had become a director. But like many underemployed filmmakers after the war, he accepted a demotion to Assistant at Shōchiku. With Nikkatsu's new start as a low budget film producer, Noguchi was quickly promoted and asked Suzuki, his script supervisor on a film called *Karadatachi no hana/Orange Flower*, to join him as Chief Assistant.[27]

Before this partnership, Suzuki worked on a *jidai-geki* (*Kunisada Chūji*) and a melodrama by Yamamura Sō (*Kuroi shio/Black Tide*). In its early days, Nikkatsu, bereft of star actors, made some prestige literary films (Ichikawa's *Kokoro*, 1955) and many cheap *jidai-geki* using the actors from the old-fashioned *shinkokugeki* theatre troupe,[28] which had made its name in the 1920s producing period dramas with more realistic fight scenes. Hasumi Shigehiko described *Kunisada Chūji*, and the other black and white *jidai-geki* made by Nikkatsu at the time, as looking "shoddy" next to the Hollywood films that Nikkatsu itself imported.[29] This had an unfortunate effect on the careers of Noguchi and Suzuki: although the violent, slightly exploitative thrillers they eventually made were seen by millions as the lower half of a Nikkatsu double bill, their déclassé appearance meant that post-war film critics failed to rate them seriously, no matter how original their form.

Noguchi's first post-war film, *Ore no kenjū wa subayai/My Pistol is Quick*, transformed both Nikkatsu and Suzuki. Nikkatsu became the first large-scale producer of *gendai* action pictures, that is, action-oriented melodramas with contemporary rather than historical settings.[30] This tendency developed into the "Nikkatsu *akushon*" brand of the late 1950s, but in a larger context, the three-decade industrial dominance of *yakuza* movies (*yakuza eiga*) would have been impossible without this early development. Noguchi's film seems to have been the first *gendai* action at Nikkatsu, and Suzuki recalled having to borrow a pistol from the police, since the studio did not have one.[31]

Very loosely based on a novel by Mickey Spillane, Noguchi's film showed the hybrid influence of hard-boiled detective literature and the Hollywood crime films that Nikkatsu imported. Suzuki's career would also become inextricably linked to this tendency. *Ore no kenjū wa subayai*, featuring a private detective played by Kawazu Seizaburō, led to a sequel (*Rakujitsu no kettō/Duel at Sunset*, 1955) that was co-written by Suzuki himself. Noguchi, for his part, would work almost exclusively in crime films until his untimely death in 1967.

Suzuki as Director: The Early Films, 1956-1960

By 1956, Nikkatsu's *jidai-geki* were being phased out and replaced by urban thrillers and melodramas featuring teenage protagonists that evolved from the post-war *seishun eiga* (youth films) of other studios (e.g., *Aoi Sanmyaku/Blue Mountains*, Shōchiku, 1949). This was the context of Suzuki's promotion to director of pictures like those of Noguchi. Of Suzuki's first six films (1956-57), four were hard-boiled crime thrillers using Noguchi's stars (Kawazu and Mizushima Michitarō), and staff. His first film, however, *Minato no kanpai: shōri wo wagate ni/Harbour Toast: Victory is in Our Grasp*, was a combination of youth melodrama and light thriller typical of the later *Nikkatsu akushon* style. It focused on two brothers, a sailor and a jockey who, through the romantic wanderings of the latter, get mixed up with a criminal gambler. The thriller trappings and downcast ending of brotherly sacrifice (typical of the time) demonstrate how Nikkatsu's genres tended to bleed into one another, but the film was really designed as a vehicle for its popular theme tune and thus is an early manifestation of one of Nikkatsu's more ephemeral genres, the *kayō eiga* or pop-song film, which reflected the dominance of the youth-oriented record industry. The film would be lost to history amongst many dozens of Nikkatsu "programmers" if it were not for the director's subsequent reputation.

Over the next three years, Suzuki alternated between crime thrillers and teen melodrama. The *topos* of youth romance in Japanese film was changed forever in 1956, when Nikkatsu produced two notorious film adaptations of the abrasive bestselling novels of Ishihara Shintarō,[32] themselves influenced by hard-boiled fiction. These pictures rejected innocent provincial romance with frank teenage sexuality, violence, and the fast, reckless lifestyle of Tokyo's *nouveau riche*. They turned Ishihara's younger brother Yūjirō into Japan's biggest star and started the short-lived but influential *taiyōzoku* or "Sun Tribe" cycle about delinquent youth. Although Suzuki made only two films that recognizably belonged to the trend, his entire career was affected by the revolution in cinema-going tastes, with numerous thrillers and youth melodramas such as *Aoi chibusa/Blue Breasts* (1958) featuring mild exploitation elements and plots involving sexual violence.

As a contract director at the bottom of Nikkatsu's directorial ranking system (where he remained for most of his career), Suzuki had no input or control over scripts or leading actors.[33] While all Nikkatsu directors faced similar constraints, top-ranking directors had access to bigger budgets, longer shooting schedules, top stars like Ishihara (who never worked with Suzuki), and greater involvement in script creation. Like Noguchi, Suzuki was instead assigned low-budget B-pictures to accommodate a theatrical double bill. While he toiled through formulaic scripts and rushed shooting schedules, Nikkatsu promoted two former Shōchiku Assistant Directors, Kurahara Koreyoshi and Imamura Shōhei. Younger and less experienced than Suzuki, Imamura received well-deserved acclaim for his film *Buta to gunkan/Pigs and Battleships* (1961) and became a top-ranking director commanding media prestige, while Suzuki, evidently jealous of his rival, worked in obscurity and fear of dismissal.[34] Suzuki would be given little more than two weeks preparation time for a picture, and often had to devise camera set-ups the night before shooting.[35]

Welded to Nikkatsu's release slate of approximately one new picture per week,[36] B-picture units were largely left alone. As in Hollywood, this somewhat "ghettoized" position allowed the director to get away with creative "negotiated oppositions" to the restrained forms and styles of the prestige pictures.[37] "The studio had no idea what I was doing until I was finished. . . . The set was the director's territory."[38] Suzuki stated frequently that the Nikkatsu scripts he received were formulaic, in fact "almost always [had] the same plot."[39] He was therefore motivated to inject some kind of difference into routine assignments. Apart from reasons of artistic and ideological discomfort with formulae, it was also necessary to stand out from contemporary directors like Kurahara.⁴⁰ Suzuki began to add unscripted visual gestures that might alter the interpretation of the narrative. He later admitted to borrowing techniques that were not part of studio practice from the Hollywood movies of the time,⁴¹ and credited the post-war films of Hitchcock, Huston, and Ford.⁴²

Although one traces a growing assertion of difference, even flamboyance, in the films over time, Suzuki was never free from studio interference. At least two films (*Hachi jikan no kyōfu/8 Hours of Terror*, 1957, and *Suppedaka no nenrei/Naked Age*, 1959) were severely re-edited after Suzuki's cut.⁴³ The case of the former—a suspense drama concerning a stranded bus hounded by two ex-cons—is surprising, since this was the first of Suzuki's films to demonstrate a categorical excellence in every aspect of classical narrative filmmaking, including elaborate camerawork, masterful staging of action in a limited setting, and a brisk, spontaneous delineation of the various social archetypes who collide inside the bus. These archetypes are distributed almost precisely as they were in Ford's *Stagecoach* (released in Japan after the war): the heroic prostitute, the disgraced ex-doctor, etc.⁴⁴ These archetypes, like the *topos* of the isolated group under siege, predate the cinema itself, but appear fresh and contemporary in Suzuki's version; their socially-revealing interactions captured in contrapuntal tones of irony and unforced humor that impart a verisimilitude to what is otherwise formulaic. Nevertheless, it seems to have been these lightly farcical touches that Nikkatsu and its board chairman, Hori Kyūsaku, came to disapprove of. Suzuki's achievements went unrecognized, either by the studio or by *Kinema junpō*'s condescending, Hollywood-obsessed reviewer, who bizarrely wrote that "the interest of the script—because one doesn't see a calculation in its direction to the extent of a John Farrow [!]—comes to nothing, which I find regrettable."⁴⁵

Suzuki was threatened with dismissal, not for the first time, but Nikkatsu managing director Emori Seijurō insisted that Suzuki was talented and emerged as his only executive supporter.⁴⁶ Emori may be the reason for the disjunction between Suzuki's own account of his professional destitution and the evidence of the trailer of *Fumihazushita haru/The Spring That Never Came*, which throws up a text on the screen extolling "the genius direction of Suzuki Seijun." This is all the more ironic considering that this tale of a social worker (Hidari Sachiko) drawn like a moth to the sexual flame of a bullying teen (Kobayashi Akira) is the most conventional of Suzuki's films in every respect excepting its social ideology, which is heavily ironized by the performances: Kobayashi's lower-class sweetheart is entirely mature whereas the older woman's reckless, unprofessional infatuation turns out to be just what the insecure teen needs. A reviewer wrote piously that ". . . in its depiction of violence as Nikkatsu's house style, this [picture] ought to be said to be impossible to have occurred," but conceded that, though exploitation was "the aim of the work, it is clearly saying something that is separate."[47] Given the lack of subsequent publicity attempts, it seems that Nikkatsu quickly abandoned the idea of giving the director some public *cachet*.[48]

Anxious about his career and finances, Suzuki Seitarō adapted the *nom de plume* Suzuki Seijun as a screen credit in 1958. Despite this, the director continued to receive no critical attention whatsoever. Of his 40 Nikkatsu films, only two early pictures were reviewed by the *Asahi shinbun*. In the 1950s, the films were routinely reviewed in *Kinema junpō* only because the magazine's editorial policy at the time was to review nearly every release from the major studios. The reviews considered mostly questions of stars and studio trends and showed no recognition of the director's name; this despite the fact that *Kinema junpō did* endorse some concept of auteurism. The magazine made celebrities out of directors such as Masumura Yasuzō and, most egregiously from Suzuki's point of view, Imamura Shōhei.[49] The simple truth, then, was that most critics of the era could not conceive of a "program picture" as critically significant. One rare directorial evaluation, in the *Kinema junpō* review of *Ankokugai no bijo/Underworld Beauty* (1958), merely proves the point. "One feels that director Suzuki Seijun has gotten used to wide-screen black and white [filmmaking]," the critic wrote, oblivious to the fact that this film was the *first* film credited to the name of Suzuki Seijun.[50] Nevertheless, the positive review of this excellent thriller provides evidence that, with the advent of "Seijun Suzuki," a *potentially* recognizable maturity had emerged in full expressive command of the elements of film style.

Still under the shadow of Noguchi, to whom he was devoted, Suzuki had no consistent *kumi* of his own. This was to change, gradually. On his second film, the obscure romantic melodrama *Umi no junjō/Pure Emotions of the Sea* (1956) he had been assigned Noguchi's cinematographer Nagatsuka Kazue. A director of photography at Nikkatsu since the mid-1920s, Nagatsuka was the first and most important of Suzuki's regular collaborators, a major component of the "signature" style that emerged from his *kumi*. The veteran Nagatsuka remained quietly respectful of the younger man's unconventional visual ideas. Suzuki achieved startling effects with other cinematographers, especially in *Ankokugai no bijo*, the director's first film in NikkatsuScope (the equivalent of CinemaScope) and a fascinating study in expressive framing. But by 1960 Suzuki was working almost exclusively with Nagatsuka and his former apprentice, Shigeyoshi Mine, who photographed Suzuki's films when the older artist worked with Noguchi. By 1959, Suzuki was also collaborating with one of the studio's chief editors, Suzuki Akira, and a "stock company" of Nikkatsu character actors—Kaneko Nobuo, Takashina Kaku, Ashida Shinsuke, Hatsui Kotoe, Kondō Hiroshi, Noro Keisuke, Chō Hiroshi and, later, Kawachi Tamio—some of whom appeared in nearly a dozen of his films.

A Middle Period at Nikkatsu, 1960-1963

Several developments in 1960 influenced the shape of Suzuki's career. Firstly, he was assigned to take over Nikkatsu's *Gurentai* series of films (1960). These were light action melodramas with fanciful stories of pure-hearted street youths starring the teenaged Wada Kōji, an inexperienced "spoiled brat" (in Suzuki's words) who was promoted as one of Nikkatsu's "Diamond Line" of action stars because of his resemblance to Ishihara. This was but a small cycle within the great wheel of Nikkatsu *akushon*, which coalesced around the superstar vehicles of Ishihara, Kobayashi Akira, and Akagi Keihachirō. The term "Nikkatsu *akushon*" remains elusive, as it covered, by design, most of the films that Nikkatsu produced, whether hard-boiled thrillers, action comedies, prewar *yakuza* thrillers, or romantic melodramas, so long as some sort of action set piece was involved.

From 1960-1962, Suzuki was the exclusive director of vehicles for Wada. The first of his eight Wada films, *Kutabare gurentai/Go to Hell Youth Gang!* (1960), was also Suzuki's first color film, and this ephemeral rock 'n' roll action scenario became an extraordinary text of non-diegetic stylization using color and the anamorphic lens. Although Suzuki attempted further experiments in subsequent films, there is evidence that he chafed increasingly at the limitations of the genre and star persona.[51] From the studio perspective, Suzuki and his "contemporary" aesthetic had finally been put to financial good use, and, indeed, Suzuki delivered a few commercial hits, such as the coast guard saga *Kaikyo chi ni somete/Bloody Channel* (1961). Accordingly, Suzuki received a greater amount of control over editing and (crucially) scripting.[52]

Despite this, one reason for Suzuki's discontent may have been professional envy of younger colleagues such as Imamura, who were treated by the media as artists comparable to the much-touted Shōchiku *nuberu bagu* ("New Wave"). Suzuki enjoyed a productive friendship with one *nuberu bagu* director, his former colleague Shinoda Masahiro, often calling the younger director, a superb technician, to ask how to photograph a certain idea.[53] Yet it probably galled Suzuki that he was ignored for even his more politicized films, such as the delinquency picture *Subete ga kurutteru* (1960), which was extremely similar to contemporary films by Ōshima, Shinoda, and Kurahara. Suzuki's fourteen films from 1960 to mid-1963 garnered only a single capsule review in *Kinema junpō*.[54] Such frustrations may have spurred his increasingly bold and differential stylization of visuals and montage beginning in 1963.

The "Mature" Suzuki, 1963-1967

In 1962, Suzuki again allegedly incurred the wrath of the studio president Hori for "extensive use of symbolism within a traditional action picture" and was assigned only two pictures to direct that year, as opposed to the six made the previous year.[55] Fortunately, his film *Akutarō* (1963), adapted from a novel by the early Shōwa author Kon Tōko, caught the youth *zeitgeist* and managed to please audiences, the studio, and Suzuki himself. The story of an intensely combative, pent-up teenager subject to the protofascist oppression of educational bureaucracy, the film garnered a 1965 sequel of sorts and begat an artistic partnership which Nikkatsu had allegedly feared: that of Suzuki and art director Kimura Takeo.[56] Given license by a director like Suzuki, Kimura's work became characterized by a disregard for naturalistic color and design that went beyond the infamous modernist designs of Ken Adam in the James Bond series, who described his work as merely "heightened reality."[57] Kimura thus advanced considerably Suzuki's "differential style," and with this partnership, an essential and dedicated *kumi* had finally coalesced. Over the next three years, joined by future directors Yasuharu Hasebe, Yamatoya Atsushi, Sone Chūsei, and screenwriter Tanaka Yōzō, the *kumi* developed within itself a loose, unauthorized creative clique at Nikkatsu. With the punning pseudonym of *Guryū Hachirō* ("Group of Eight"), the group conceived and wrote several screenplays while discussing the evolution of film language from within the studio system in a more organized fashion than the early *nuberu bagu* had done. Suzuki's 1967 masterpiece *Koroshi no rakuin* (screenplay by "Guryū Hachirō") was the only formal product of this alliance, but its covert influence was tremendous, particularly on the later work of Yamatoya and Hasebe when, in an extension of Suzuki's style, they defined the aesthetics of Nikkatsu's *roman poruno* genre.[58]

By mid-1963, independent exploitation films featuring sex and nudity (including the films of Wakamatsu Kōji) were beginning to steal the crucial young male demographic audience away from major studios, which were already suffering from competition with television. A hard-boiled thriller, *Yajū no seishun/Youth of the Beast* (1963) was assigned to Suzuki by Nikkatsu management as an experiment in a film with an "adults only" certificate. After Suzuki had made the film, Nikkatsu changed its mind about the rating, thus causing problems with *Eirin*, the industry censorship board. Despite this, a unique crime thriller emerged that bordered on the avant-garde, marked by extreme violence filmed at laconic distance and lavish stylization involving the play of sound and silence, primary and pastel colors, and shifts of color and black and white. The film made popular character actor Shishido Jō into a dramatic lead and solidified their versatile eight-film collaboration (despite a testy personal relationship). Although critics reported that the film disappeared with little review and indifferent word of mouth (at least in establishment circles),[59] the largely positive reviews in *Eiga hyōron* and *Kinema junpō* demonstrated a new consciousness of directorial style. Nakahara Yumihiko, of the former, wrote:

> Something with faults such as these . . . is not just a program picture that makes an extravagant impression. . . . Because [Suzuki] is on the poverty-stricken borders of Japanese film, he does not make mistakes, he creates something unique. . . . Suzuki has borrowed the framework of Nikkatsu action, and has molded his own aesthetic universe.[60]

This was evidence of a minor sea-change in popular film criticism: *Eiga hyōron* began to champion Suzuki as a major filmmaker, though very few others followed suit.[61]

Suzuki followed *Yajū no Seishun* with *Kantō mushuku/Kanto Wanderer*, perhaps the director's first *yakuza* film (a genre which came into being virtually simultaneously) but also a haunting trip into memory, dream, and erotic longing. The participation of Kobayashi Akira, who remained loyal to Suzuki from his early career days, undoubtedly helped the director's position at Nikkatsu. Hasumi has noted that, with *Kantō mushuku* as the B-feature to the most critically and financially successful film of the year, Imamura's *Nippon Konchūki/Insect Woman* (1963), Suzuki received more critical exposure than ever before; and yet still *Kinema junpō* awarded *Kantō mushuku* only 29th place on their poll of the year's best films.[62] Although Suzuki was still a minor figure with little "celebrity" amongst viewers or critics, *Kantō mushuku* inspired the first feature article on him, "The Beauty of Suzuki Seijun" by Kajiwara Ryūji, who marveled that "from the space of the [film's] spectators, ridicule flowed. When Japanese encounter anything new (good or bad) it seems they must look at it with a contemptuous eye . . . But if this were not a film by the generally unknown Suzuki Seijun, if it was the work of a great director like Kurosawa or Ichikawa, would they have expressed contempt?"[63] He found Suzuki's colorful theatricality "refreshing" yet paradoxically serious, compared to Nikkatsu's *akushon* formula, in its handling of violence and eroticism: "I haven't seen works which photograph the female body in this way (*Suna no onna* and *Nippon konchūki* came later) . . . Isn't it the case that his growth [as a filmmaker] is the opening of a new phase of Japanese cinema?"[64]

In 1964, Nikkatsu succeeded in producing an "adults only" film with Suzuki's *Nikutai no mon/Gate of Flesh*, an erotic adaptation of Tamura Taijirō's seminal 1948 novella about prostitution amongst the ruins of postwar Tokyo, a novel which extolled the abandonment of tradition and the revolutionary potential of sexuality. Suzuki's oneiric style and Kimura's expressionist sets annoyed Nikkatsu, but the film became Suzuki's greatest commercial success. The conservative media establishment refused to catch on: with his films still ignored by the daily papers, *Nikutai no mon* (and its 1965 "follow-up" of sorts, *Shunpuden/Story of a Prostitute*, a damning portrait of the wartime military based on a Tamura story) was widely excoriated by offended reviewers.[65] Even an ambivalent *Eiga hyōron* critic was confident that "this is a film of unknown nationality . . . it becomes an imitation of Vadim unable to describe [Japanese] post-war morality. If he were a moral author, Suzuki would be below standard. Where is the morality of *Nikutai no mon*. . . ?"[66] Faced with the shock of the new, which, moreover, flouted widespread consensus about the war, the critics floundered with desperate "foreign" comparisons. Nevertheless, Suzuki was now widely recognized amongst the film-critical establishment, as much disliked as praised.

From 1964-1966, Suzuki completed the "Flesh Trilogy" that began with *Nikutai no mon* (and starred his own discovery, the actress Nogawa Yumiko) and produced four *yakuza* pictures ending with *Tokyo nagaremono/ Tokyo Drifter* (1966). A number of articles appeared in *Eiga geijutsu* and *Eiga hyōron*, the latter including an insightful one by Ryōgoku Midori (see chapter 4). Even *Kinema junpō* allowed a feature, in 1966, that compared Suzuki to the popular Tōei director Katō Tai.[67] Critics also mentioned in passing the existence of "Seijun fans."[68] Certainly, we can say that students who had grown up with B-pictures by Nakahira, Katō, Okamoto and others, unburdened by total dependence on the classical cinematic norms of the first post-war decade, accepted Suzuki's differential style with little trouble, especially when it captured their favored stars, like Kobayashi, in iconic postures. They evidently viewed the comic ironies of these films as an entertaining, if not necessarily typical, aspect of Nikkatsu *akushon*.[69] Probably only a tiny minority of enthusiasts would have recognized the director's name. Nevertheless, the Nikkatsu, Tōei, and Tōhō action films that male students adored, some of them made by Suzuki's former associates, began to "catch up" to Suzuki's non-diegetic stylization by 1967, particularly in their use of non-diegetic color and jump cuts.

Suzuki had acquired just enough clout at Nikkatsu to rewrite his scripts from scratch, on occasion.[70] Nikkatsu management however, was far from satisfied. "I got warned about *Gate of Flesh*, too! By that time, I was getting warned every time I made a picture! . . . One producer used to come up to me every time I finished a film and say 'Okay this is it. You can't do anything more. You've gone too far.'"[71] *Tokyo nagaremono*, now considered a prescient work of generic pastiche and urban cultural hybridity, was the last straw for Nikkatsu, who wanted a simple pop-song film to promote their new star, Watari Tetsuya.[72] The film was panned by an uncomprehending *Kinema junpō*,[73] and Suzuki's only supporter, Emori, was fired. However, his next film, *Kenka erejii*, a black comedy of militarization and sexual repression in the 1930s, received strong support from film publications, even *Kinema junpō*, who published the screenplay (originally written by the leftist filmmaker Shindō Kaneto).[74] Yamaguchi Tetsu praised that the war generation could find in *Kenka erejii* an outlet for their experiences: ". . . I laughed to the point of tears, because I was possessed by precious life experiences characterized by a kind of catharsis."[75]

The Suzuki Problem of 1968

In early 1967, Hori Kyūsaku removed a film from his release schedule and directed Suzuki to come up with a replacement in only a few months. Suzuki and Guryū Hachirō capitalized on the situation to make their most extreme film yet, *Koroshi no rakuin*, a spatially disorienting, sexually explicit, temporally circuitous, fatalistic thriller about a brutal killer who challenges the system and is crushed by it. Hori was outraged by this film, which, having no promotional support from Nikkatsu, was a box office failure (albeit an inexpensive one). This gave Hori the excuse he needed, and while Suzuki was working on a television film (*Aisaikun konban wa:*

Aru kettō/Good Evening Dear Husband: A Duel) in April 1968, he learned from a secretary that he had been fired.[76]

The resulting controversy, which galvanized fans and filmmakers, has been called the "Suzuki Seijun Problem" of 1968, and was a surprising component of the nationwide student demonstrations that rocked Japan in May and June of that year.[77] When approached on Suzuki's behalf, Hori said, insultingly, that "Suzuki's films do not make money...therefore they are not good. Suzuki is no good as a director.... he should open up a noodle shop or something instead."[78] As it turned out, Kawakita Kazuko—director of the Ciné Club, the most prominent film society in Tokyo with connections to the avant-garde scene and the Art Theatre Guild (ATG), a new producer and distributor for *nuberu bagu* directors—had requested prints of Suzuki's film for a retrospective of his career. Hori refused, responding to Kawakita that it reflected badly on Nikkatsu to show such "incomprehensible" films aimed at an "exclusive audience," and that the prints were "prohibited" from further screenings.[79] Hori's public behavior, based on his personal irritation with Suzuki's films, demonstrated that the studio's prewar management was out of touch with the times, comprehending neither the tastes nor the culture of its urban, largely male, audience. What had started as an internal contract dispute had now become a question of the censorship and perhaps destruction of a filmmaker's work.[80] The Association of Japanese Film Directors tried and failed to negotiate with Hori about Suzuki's contract, then publicly condemned his behavior as a violation of constitutional rights to creative freedom.[81] On June 7, Suzuki sued Nikkatsu for approximately 7,000,000 yen for breach of contract and personal damages and demanded a public apology. The Ciné Club, ATG, the Actor's and Scriptwriter's Guilds, and various student political organizations helped Suzuki organize a press conference on that day. This was followed by a demonstration of hundreds of protestors in front of Nikkatsu's offices in Hibiya on June 12,[82] including prominent industry figures as well as radical and Marxist student groups wearing red helmets.[83] A "Joint Committee for the Problem of Suzuki Seijun" was formed and the Suzuki Problem ballooned as the student Left seized upon it as an opportunity to attack the authoritarian corporate and government combine that had ruled Japan since the end of the Occupation.[84] Suzuki received public support at various stages from prominent artists such as Ōshima, Shinoda, Terayama Shūji, and Director's Association president Gosho Heinosuke. He received tacit support from Kurosawa and Mishima Yukio.[85]

In July, Hori revealed that Nikkatsu studios was in enormous debt and that a sizable percentage of staff were to be laid off. Based on the evidence considered by Ueno Kōshi in his book *Suzuki Seijun zen eiga*, it seems clear that Suzuki was both an economic scapegoat for the troubled Nikkatsu and the vessel for an ideological, generational clash between mutually exclusive views of the cinema: a classical narrative cinema based on the Hollywood model aimed at an imaginary *general* audience that was long lost to television, and a "modernist" cinema that excited a younger audience tending towards cinephilia.

Suzuki's court case dragged on until December 1971 and involved nineteen witnesses. Up to that time, *Kinema junpō* and, especially, *Eiga hyōron* published several updates on the developing Suzuki Problem;[86] most of these articles were not substantive so much as ardent declarations of activist commitment. The circumstances of *Koroshi no rakuin*, whose production Hori had personally approved, were damning, but not as much as Hori's shocking financial mismanagement of the studio.[87] Suzuki was forced to accept an underwhelming settlement of 1,000,000 yen out of fear that Nikkatsu would become insolvent.[88] Suzuki's challenge to the studio system had already met with reprisals. In 1969, the five major film studios implemented an informal blacklist on Suzuki. Unable to direct, Suzuki turned to commercials and to writing. His many books, beginning with *Kenka erejii* (1970), combined impressionistic essays, cultural observation, biographical sketches, and interviews. Suzuki continued to write until the late 1990s, though with few discussions of his actual film work.

Late Suzuki, 1977-2005

Ironically, despite blacklisting and financial desperation, Suzuki had become the most famous of Japanese directors. The period 1969-1981 was a "golden age" of Suzuki criticism, with feature articles in major and minor film magazines and,[89] eventually, more prestigious general arts publications such as *Bijutsu techō*, *Asahi Journal*, *Bungei*, and *Kokubungaku*.[90] In the latter, Tayama Rikiya's appreciation of Suzuki's "sensuous beauty of imagery" set the tone for much future criticism in Japan by overstating, indeed, imposing on Suzuki's films a cultural/aesthetic binary characterized by a "decidedly Japanese" nostalgic lyricism as against a "European modernism" of style. *Kinema junpō*, by now fashionably committed to supporting the director, published a multi-part anecdotal memoir by Kimura, entitled "To Shoot a Film For Suzuki Seijun This Year!"[91] Satō Tadao, the *Eiga hyōron* founder, included a chapter on Suzuki in his seminal book *Nihon eiga shisōshi*,[92] forever establishing the major themes of Suzuki criticism: a cinema of aesthetic "destructiveness" characterized by abrupt formal transitions, the multi-faceted filmic traces of Suzuki's war experiences, and a consequent sense of the ironic quality of violent spectacle.[93] We must pause on this insight for a moment, for Satō remains, after a half-century, the most important critic of Suzuki, and not only because his was the first piece of writing on the director to appear in English (in 1983). Satō's greatest contribution was to situate Suzuki, despite his work in studio entertainment, as a consistently political director who represented the anxieties and violence of post-war society as a reflection of his own wartime experience: an at once personal and collective working through of an ex-serviceman's all-too-real sensory-motor experiences of bodily disintegration, annihilation, and authoritarian coercion *via* what has proven to be, in the right hands, the perfect vehicle for such a process: the violent spectacle of action cinema. In *Shinema '69* Suzuki was asked why violence is depicted humorously in his films. "It is inexcusable to say so but . . . when you go to war . . . it *is* humorous." As an example, Suzuki gives an account of naval burial at sea: the ridiculous sound of dead bodies plunking into the ocean, one after another, followed by the rat-tat-tat of the trumpet.[94] Satō gives a superb gloss to this notion: "for Suzuki, who had lived amid annihilation, it was necessary to view oneself objectively, even to the point where mutability appeared pathetic and humorous at the same time."[95] Satō thereby equates humor (irony) with objectivity. This in turn may help us to understand the tone of Suzuki's address to the spectator. Wherever, in the subsequent chapters of this book, I emphasize the modes and affects of irony, detachment, alienation, and masochism in conjunction with the spectacle of violence, the reader must, as Satō demands, bear Suzuki's wartime experience in mind, as palpable as the ever-present backbeat in the rock compositions of Suzuki's contemporary, Chuck Berry.

Satō's championship of Suzuki was one of several factors that inspired a younger generation of film critics, including Hasumi, Ueno, Yamane Sadao, and Nishikawa Hideo, to emerge as a sort of core group of interpreters of Suzuki's work. They, in turn, inspired both critics and viewers: by 1975, a contrarian critic would write exasperatedly about "fully occupied" screenings and events and about "how many film magazines, how many roundtable discussions surrounding Suzuki" would "make the mistake" of treating the director as a film auteur.[96] At least in Tokyo, this was clearly the high-water mark of public exposure to Suzuki's films. However, it was not his burgeoning critical reputation but his Guryū Hachirō assistants who kept Suzuki in business. The last generation of Nikkatsu studio filmmakers before the collapse of the industry, they connected Suzuki to directing jobs on anthology television, notably for the CM network.[97] His most famous collaboration was as director of two episodes of the second *Rupan sansei/Lupin III* TV anime series (1977-1980), based on the manga series by Monkey Punch. This led, in turn, to Suzuki supervising the big screen adventure *Rupan sansei: Babiron no ōgon no densetsu/Lupin III: Golden Legend of Babylon* (1986). Richie has inferred that the conceptual association of Suzuki's aesthetic with manga and *anime* (Miyazaki Hayao was another collaborator on the series) gave Suzuki a *cachet* and staying power with younger spectators who had not seen his Nikkatsu films.[98]

During frequent dry periods, Suzuki would meet at his house with his former subordinates to discuss the creation of a "new kind of film."[99] Yamatoya Atsushi adapted a script from the manga artist Kajiwara Ikki about the media creation of a golf pro, and convinced Shōchiku to allow Suzuki to direct the film. In 1977, after a decade, Suzuki returned to cinema with *Hishū monogatari/A Tale of Sorrow*. The magazines, especially *Eiga geijutsu*, heralded the return of a "master" with on-set visits, interviews, retrospective essays and screenplay publications.[100] However, *Hishū monogatari* demonstrated a filmmaker no longer willing or able to operate within the aesthetic or ideological confines of established media. Revisiting the avant-garde style of *Koroshi no rakuin*, Suzuki bit the hand that fed him and produced a devastating, bitter satire of television and its colonization of subjectivity. The remarkable male lead, Harada Yoshio, would collaborate with Suzuki on four subsequent projects, but despite the enthusiasm prior to release, the film's reviews were close to disastrous, as was the box office.

With the "failure" of *Hishū*, it was something of a miracle that Yamatoya's former producer Arato Genjirō, who had made his career in avant-garde political theatre, suddenly offered Suzuki and his friends *carte blanche* to produce a low budget film. Suzuki and Tanaka Yōzō chose to adapt the oneiric novella *Sarasate no ban/The Sarasate Record* (1952) by the Taishō/Shōwa writer Uchida Hyakken. For the resulting film, *Zigeunerweisen*, Suzuki and former Nikkatsu collaborators Kimura, Nagatsuka, and Suzuki Akira capitalized on the Japanese obsession with ghost stories to create a project concerned with irrational erotic obsession, the haunting presence of Japan's pre-modern past, and the cinematic representation of time. Articles in art journals as well as film periodicals followed upon word of mouth,[101] and Suzuki's film ended up winning every major award that year including the number one spot of *Kinema junpō*'s Best Ten. In another first, Suzuki's film entered and won the Jury Prize at the Berlin Film Festival. Overnight, Suzuki had become the inheritor of several now defunct legacies: the independent cinema, the *nuberu bagu*, and the avant-garde theatre world of the late 1960s. There were, as always, condescending voices.[102] Nevertheless, Suzuki felt more free than ever to express his connection with prewar history through a cinema of painterly images influenced by Taishō theatre and surrealism and unencumbered by narrative causality. With Aratō's company, Cinema Placet, he made two avant-garde epics of the Taishō era, *Kagerō-za* (1981) (from the story *Shunchū* by the great Meiji writer Izumi Kyōka), and *Yumeji* (1991), a fantasia on the career of the painter Yumeji Takehisa (1884-1934).

In between, Suzuki directed a radical deconstruction of the American crime film, *Kapone ōi ni naku/Capone Cries a Lot* (1985), but this film, like *Yumeji*, did not repeat the critical impact of *Zigeunerweisen*. Suzuki's currency in Japan as an "auteurist touchstone" for the media had long since faded before *Yumeji*'s release.[103] It did not matter, for Suzuki's films were for the first time beginning to be shown around the world, with retrospectives at the Pesaro Film Festival in 1984 and the Edinburgh Festival in 1988, followed by Vancouver, London, Rotterdam, San Francisco, San Paolo, New York, Melbourne, and Bologna throughout the 1990s. Suzuki's currency on the festival circuit inspired the respected DVD-video distributor, The Criterion Collection, to introduce two Suzuki films to the American public (in 1999). It also influenced a generation of international filmmakers, as well as emerging Japanese directors.[104] In a reversal of fortune, Suzuki's films, along with those of his contemporary Fukasaku Kinji, came to be seen as a greater influence on contemporary East Asian cinema than the films of the *nuberu bagu*.[105]

In this climate, Suzuki (at 77) produced a sort of synthesis of *Koroshi no rakuin* and the aesthetics of the Taishō trilogy. A modest *succes d'estime* in Japan, *Pisutoru opera* (2001) was the first Suzuki film to be reviewed upon release by major American periodicals such as the *New York Times* and *Chicago Reader* (in which Jonathan Rosenbaum enthusiastically praised the film).[106] Over the next three years Suzuki gathered the finances for his final film, the musical *Opereta tanuki goten/Princess Raccoon* (2005). A remake of Suzuki's favorite Japanese film, the 1939 *Operetta Tanuki goten* by Kimura Keigo, the film was truly international, featuring Chinese superstar Ziyi Zhang and audaciously using international pop songs and CGI effects to present a fantasia on Japanese mythology. It saw multiple releases throughout Asia and Europe, including at the Cannes Film Festival. This international presence of Suzuki as auteur and the availability of his films on DVD, Blu-ray and (latterly) on streaming have stimulated a slow, often halting, but ongoing wave of critical and scholarly re-evaluation. Film criticism in Japan, marked by nostalgia for the heyday of Nikkatsu and Yūjirō, has tended to view Suzuki as a (somewhat distinctive) representative of the studio flavor.[107] His critical treatment has been hampered more than most by tendencies towards anecdotal history and roundtable conversations. Even Suzuki's most powerful critics (e.g., Hasumi) were content, in Ueno Kōshi's 1986 book, with a genial roundtable discussion that contained very little analysis, extended interpretation, or theoretically informed argument, and a familiar unwillingness to pursue disagreement.[108]

Nevertheless, the theoretical views of Hasumi, Ueno, and Yamane, as established in other writings but surfacing in their occasional essays on Suzuki, form much of the subject matter and approach of the first monograph on Suzuki to be published in English, by William Carroll. Carroll's book, which was published while this present volume was going to press, to some extent typifies the main concerns of Japanese film studies as an academic sub-discipline: the Japanese New Left of the 1960s and 1970s and the films (particularly the politicized exploitation films) and film-theoretical discourses that were associated with it. But Carroll's book also quite usefully devotes space to what he defines as the "cinephilic" criticism of Ueno, Yamane, and Hasumi, and how it set the terms by which certain prominent critics, cineastes, and film directors would understand Suzuki in the three decades following the Suzuki Problem of 1968. Carroll's thorough analysis of this corpus, as well as his extended translations of Japanese critics of a number of different stripes and orientations, is certainly a welcome addition to the relatively small amount of English-language scholarship on the director. Nevertheless, the focus on the critical heritage differentiates Carroll's study from my own, despite some similarities and some overlap in argument and analysis (e.g., concerning Suzuki's achievement of "multiple points of interest within the same [Cinemascopic] frame";[109] and Carroll's anticipation, as it were, of the social critique of yakuza films that I elucidate in chapter 4).[110] Whereas Carroll's book emphasizes what are essentially modes and cultures of *reception*, such as cinephilia, this present volume consistently emphasizes reflexivity and negation as textual features and as progenitors of meaning, including socio-political meaning, that condition a structured encounter between text and viewer. Carroll entertains a view of Suzuki's films as being either *non-pori* (a frequent term of the New Left which is translated by Carroll as only "potentially political") or "pre-political" (defined by Hobsbawm as those "who have not found, or only begun to find, a specific language" of political expression).[111] I prefer to consider narrative cinema generally as deploying semiotic systems alternative to language with necessarily alternate, usually figurative, rhetorics of political consciousness (e.g., Fassbinder's "lighting and camera angles are a director's philosophy"). These are not easily translated into an activist language of immediate responsiveness to a shifting political landscape—a problem about which the early films of the *nuberu bagu,* made in an era of student protest, seemed to be acutely self-conscious. This formal disjunction was exacerbated by a historical one, i.e., that Suzuki's political consciousness was that of a member of the war generation. Carroll offers many astute and original observations on the formal dimensions of Suzuki's films throughout (particularly in his survey of color usage across Suzuki's entire career, and in his attentiveness to the presence of various kinds of "subimages," including filmswithin-films).[112] However, his textual analysis—for example, on *Yajū no seishun*'s mirror scene, which I treat extensively in chapter 3—frequently takes place in reference to and *within* the theoretical frameworks and distinctions established by the critics of an earlier period[113]—for example, within the framework of Hasumi's notorious obsession with cinema as being destined to constantly reflect the materiality and concreteness of the film frame and thus to acknowledge its own limitations, or else to try to disavow them. In certain sections, this has the effect of decentering Suzuki's films, in all their heterogeneity and potential meanings, as examples rather than as works and objects of analysis on their own terms. This present book, in contrast, favors close readings of individual films, bringing them into (at least a fleeting) contact with a great variety of theoretical frameworks emanating from transnational developments in film theory, and brought together, so I hope, by analytic concepts of diegesis, difference, and negation, which cut across the bewildering heterogeneity of Suzuki's array of formal and stylistic gestures throughout 49 features.

Carroll's translation and presentation of the Japanese critical episteme for the benefit of English readers and cineastes is a (very recent) anomaly and a corrective since, as Carroll recognizes, most criticism in English, lacking adequate contextual information, has come from a sector that treats Suzuki, with his recognizable visual style, as a quintessential "Asian cult cinema" director—the discourse of "cult" being, ironically, a kind of circumscribed auteur discourse within a popular idiom. Neither this tendency, nor the narrowly Nikkatsu-centered approach of the Japanese critical establishment, is adequate. In 1984, an unnamed French critic identified the broader picture upon which I want to concentrate when he challenged Suzuki, "how did the language and spaces of your movies change course in a big way in the mid-sixties?" The perpetually paranoiac and evasive surrealist responded with the slyly ambiguous, "I don't think at all about language and space...."[114] Suzuki may well have realized that the radical naiveté or unconsciousness that he pretended to might itself pose a formidable challenge to the system. Whatever the director may have meant, his films speak their own singular discourse, to which this book will now attend. They reveal a "director" within them who can be pigeonholed neither as a "genre auteur" nor a journeyman of the Nikkatsu house style and ideology, but one whose prescient and idiosyncratic transformation of narrative film "language" anticipated and instigated transnational developments, carrying a historical and philosophical weight comparable to the work of Kurosawa and Antonioni before him, Godard and Ōshima after him.

CHAPTER 2

The Dog

(Rajo to kenjū, Ankokugai no bijo, Kagenaki koe, Kaikyō chi ni somete, Kutabare gurentai, Tokyo kishitai, Subete ga kurutteru, Akutarō, Toge wo wataru wakai kaze, Akutarō-den: warui hoshi shita demo)

Between 1959 and 1960, three Assistant Directors at Shōchiku studios—Ōshima Nagisa, Shinoda Masahiro, and Yoshida Yoshishige—made their respective directorial debuts. Although Suzuki Seitarō had been an A.D. at Shōchiku far senior to these three, no one in 1960 within Japan's filmmaking or critical establishment would have considered that he belonged to the same aesthetic universe as the *nuberu bagu*. Few critics were aware that Suzuki existed, except perhaps as a screen credit on Nikkatsu's B-pictures.[1] By comparison, Ōshima was already a prominent film critic who received widespread acclaim for his second film (*Seishun zankoku monogatari/Cruel Story of Youth*, 1960); the early films of Yoshida and Shinoda received lavish attention in film magazines such as *Kinema junpō* as Japan's answer to the already legendary directors of the French *nouvelle vague*, Jean-Luc Godard and François Truffaut. Following the tremendous success of Nikkatsu's *taiyōzoku* "Sun Tribe" films, which signified to the industry that many Japanese cinemagoers were ready to embrace "the new," Shōchiku's publicity machine assured that the *nuberu bagu* directors would be empowered as "instant auteurs" with public and cultural cachet;[2] although, as Ōshima was soon to discover, this empowerment, and the backing of the studios, had its limits.

At the same time, Suzuki toiled through low-budget crime films and pop song films (*kayō eiga*) with second-rate Nikkatsu stars, each film serving as the lower half of a double feature at Nikkatsu theatres. Suzuki's career was being outpaced, even by younger Nikkatsu directors such as Imamura Shōhei, who commanded media prestige and high budgets, much to Suzuki's eventual resentment. Imamura's films were viewed, then and now, as a kind of Nikkatsu cohort of the *nuberu bagu*; a consideration never yet granted to Suzuki's films. The Nihon University-educated Kurahara Koreyoshi was another example. Another former Shōchiku A.D., Kurahara became a top-ranking director after only his first film, the impressive Ishihara vehicle *Ore wa matteiru ze/I am Waiting* (1957).[3] For more than 30 years, Suzuki and the self-consciously Godardian Kurahara shared the same editor, Suzuki Akira, with the two directors reacting competitively to each other's work through this essential intermediary. "Maybe Kurahara uses too much film," judged Suzuki.[4]

It took until 1963, seven years after he started as director, for a tiny subset of critics to recognize the director of *Yajū no seishun* as a figure of aesthetic interest. In 1970, Satō Tadao established the orthodox view that Suzuki had made only "routine job assignments" in the 1950s.[5] At that time, Satō had little means of reviewing those early films. I would argue, in contrast, that Suzuki's "hard-boiled" B movies of the 1950s are among the studio's most significant and transformative genre films. At first imitative of American thrillers, their transnational stylistic and cultural hybridity enabled the young director to take occasional risks with film narration and form that were unheard of in the studio cinema of the 1950s; they pioneered a distinctive use of jump cuts, problematized the cinematic gaze through visual allegories of the mediation of the camera, and utilized eccentric widescreen framing as a sort of hyper-textual commentary on filmmaking practice. I will argue, further, that experiments with color, even in Suzuki's innocuous pop song films, represent a break with classical filmmaking of an equally profound conceptual significance as the early films of the *nuberu bagu*. In the conclusion of this chapter, I will also discuss how in 1960 Suzuki made at least one film related to the *taiyōzoku* cycle. *Subete ga kurutteru/Everything Goes Crazy* explored the youth-oriented social realism that was associated with Kurahara and Imamura's films, to which it is a kind of riposte, being as audacious in form and as dissenting in its view of Japanese society (c. 1960) as the contemporary *nuberu bagu* films on the subject.

Yet despite this essentially realist and discursive "social problem" film, the films of Suzuki as a whole had long since demonstrated an alternative mode of self-reflexive filmmaking practice, evidencing a deep inquiry into the phenomenology and image-politics of the erotic and violent representations that had made these genre films so indispensable to the public.

This reflexivity pulled Suzuki away from the (stylized) social realism of *Subete ga kurutteru* towards a "generic-ironic" practice; that is, one which reinvests in the discursive potential of cinematic spectacle in genre films by bending it, haltingly, towards a critique of the same mass culture and media establishment that produced these very films: that very establishment within which the director, by his own account, had found himself unappreciated, isolated, and trapped.

Hard-Boiled Wonderland

Between 1957 and 1958, a distinct formal practice emerged from Suzuki's imitation of the hard-boiled crime films of his mentor at Nikkatsu, Noguchi Hiroshi.[6] It is possible to illustrate the emergence of Suzuki's "differential" style through a comparison of two early but notable hard-boiled thrillers that Suzuki made with the stars Mizushima Michitarō and Shiraki Mari: *Rajo to kenjū/Nude Girl and a Gun* (1957) and *Ankokugai no bijo* (1958).

I want to justify my use of the term "hard-boiled" to mark some dozens of unsentimental, black-and-white Japanese crime films from the 1950s, chiefly, but not exclusively, from Nikkatsu. Even though Suzuki frequently used the equivalent Japanese term (*hādo-boirudo*) to describe his own crime films,[7] my use of the term to describe this cycle of films from the mid-to late 1950s is not necessarily warranted by the critical vocabulary of the time. Rather, I am classifying a cycle of films that has *never* been properly recognized by Japanese film historians. Certainly, film magazines were using the term *hādo-boirudo* by 1960 to describe the generic affiliation of not only Suzuki's films, but those of contemporaries such as Okamoto Kihachi,[8] while *Eiga hyōron* compared Suzuki to the "hard-boiled" writer James Hadley Chase.[9] The Nikkatsu historian Watanabe Takenobu classified the studio crime thrillers starring Shishido Jō from 1963-1967 as a *hādo-boirudo* cycle, but did not give a name to the earlier 1950s crime films dominated by Noguchi. Critics often referred to the early crime films of a number of different studios as *gangu mono* (gangster subjects), but the term is too general and somewhat misleading.[10] Crime thrillers of the 1950s conspicuously did *not* attempt to represent the culture of the *yakuza* gangs (no doubt for fear of causing offence). Thus I prefer, throughout this book, to use *hādo-boirudo* as the best historical term available to describe this cycle of films. Despite terminological confusion, this is a significant body of at least thirty studio films, produced under the influence of a wave of American popular literature and media exported to Japan throughout the decade, and producing an initially imitative, then dynamic and evolving cycle.

The hard-boiled literary movement in America has a well-defined time and place of origin. Despite its long roots in "sensationalized American pulp fiction addressed chiefly to working-class men,"[11] hard-boiled fiction came into the world in 1923 through the writings of Dashiell Hammett and *Black Mask Magazine* under the editorship of Jack "Captain" Shaw. One of the major qualities which differentiated Hammett from the gentlemanly detective fiction which came before him was the terse, vernacular, quasi-objective diction that Hammett adapted from the quasi-modernist style of H.L. Mencken. Originally, the term "hard-boiled" focused exclusively on the tough character of the urban private detective. The twin emphasis of this literature, then, was on the detective himself and on the journey of investigation into society's hidden corners. As the decades progressed, "hard-boiled" came into a broader usage and denoted a larger variety of crime thriller scenarios.[12] In the 1940s, Raymond Chandler could speak in a very general sense about Hollywood crime melodramas when he wrote that "people can take the hard-boiled stuff nowadays."[13] It was this more encompassing use of the term that some Japanese critics would adapt, as *hādo-boirudo*, to describe the vigorous crime literature (and the occasional film) coming out of post-war Tokyo.[14]

From 1950 to 1955, an influx of translations of American crime stories descended on the Japanese reading public, alongside the films of Humphrey Bogart and other stars of iconic status in Japan. With thirty years of American literary developments introduced in one wave, the prewar writings of Hammett, Chandler, and Cain appeared at the same time as, and sometimes later than, the pulp fictions of younger authors like Ross MacDonald and Mickey Spillane. This had several consequences. Since simultaneity of exposure emphasized similarities more than distinctions, hard-boiled fiction appeared to Japanese readers as a more compressed and consistent movement or genre.[15] The term "hard-boiled" thus denoted for Japanese readers a characteristically American and contemporary literary mode and a wide collection of narrative *topoi* concerning urban crime and violence.

The effect on Japanese crime and detection literature was tremendous. Younger writers in the mid-1950s such as Ōyabu Haruhiko and Kōjō Kō met with instant commercial success adapting hard-boiled American prose (and its violent criminal brutality) to a Japanese idiom in novels like Ōyabu's *Yajū shisu beshi/The Beast Must Die* (1958).[16] It was inevitable that Japanese studios would cash in on this trend. It was arguably Kurosawa who produced the first examples of "hard-boiled" films in Japan, *Yoidore tenshi/Drunken Angel* (Tōhō, 1948) and *Nora inu/Stray Dog* (1949).[17] The great backlog of 1940s American crime films released throughout Japan's post-war period, the very same films which French critics had called *films noir Americain*,[18] had clearly established a taste for a recognizably similar Japanese product. And the rise of the double feature in Japan, which made Suzuki's career as a B-movie auteur possible, had established a viable market for this kind of film.[19]

Thus, directors of the mid-1950s, like Noguchi at Nikkatsu and Okamoto Kihachi and Makino Masahiro at Tōei, were soon followed by younger cohorts such as Sugawa Eizō at Tōho and Ishii Teruo at Shin-Tōhō, who assembled films that showed this hybrid influence of American hard-boiled literature, *film noir*, the Japanese *hādo-boirudo* fiction discussed above, and established, indigenous thriller writers such as Matsumoto Seichō. This transnational hybridity is not a theoretical construct; it is overt and self-conscious in the films themselves: Suzuki's *Rajo to kenjū* begins with a cabaret act in which the *femme fatale*, a dancer, wears an American cowboy hat and boots (Fig. 2.1) while shooting six guns from a holster.

Most of the iconography of the American *films noir* of the 1940s and 50s are consciously represented in these Japanese "translations" of the genre: scenes of low-key lighting, expressive uses of shadows, tawdry night club acts with alluring singers, guns, trench coats, brutal psychotics, torture, and professional criminals in hidden, tangled networks.

It is not surprising that this trend took root particularly at Nikkatsu, which produced the majority of these thrillers. The studio had acted as a successful importer of American crime films, among others, for nearly ten years before venturing back into film production in 1954. Noguchi's *Ore no kenjū wa subayai*, Nikkatsu's earliest thriller, began the trend, and over the next two years crime thrillers replaced low-budget *chanbara* as the studio's characteristic product. *Chitei no uta/Song of the Underworld* (1956) was one of Noguchi's best films, and Suzuki joined the trend with his third effort *Akuma no machi/Demon Town* (1956)—a film so obscure, despite the presence of actor Kawazu Seizaburō, that it appears to never have been re-released in any form (unless it were at the private "Ciné-clubs" of the late 1960s). At its height of popularity, the cycle included even vehicles for Ishihara Yūjirō such as Masuda Toshio's *Sabita naifu/Rusty Knife* (1958).

It is Noguchi's iteration of the formula that most concerns us here. Suzuki's hard-boiled films were no doubt influenced by his own reading and viewing of the American hard-boiled mode,[20] and it is worth noting the American hard-boiled influence on many other renowned Japanese

Fig. 2.1. *Hādo-boirudo* as Transnational Hybridity: Shiraki Mari as a cabaret dancer fetishistically dressed as a cowboy (*Rajo to kenjū* / *Nude Girl With a Gun*)

artists, including Abe Kōbō and (later) Murakami Haruki. Nevertheless, a number of local and culturally specific features of Suzuki's early films can be traced back directly to his mentor, Noguchi. The latter was a reliable studio filmmaker who rarely departed from the stylistic norms of classical filmmaking. As a crime film innovator, nevertheless, Noguchi effortlessly adapted the seedy milieu of American urban thrillers to Tokyo in the midst of a long post-war reconstruction that often served the demands of industry over population. Noguchi depicts, in muted tones, a post-industrial cityscape of empty, somewhat alienated modern structures. He used spare yet modern interiors that made the milieu, rather than the film, look cheap.

In some ways a comic filmmaker, Noguchi takes a tongue-in-cheek notice of 1950s consumerism, and would often cut away from a scene prematurely, though not disruptively, in order to make a character or situation look absurd.

For the most part, however, his style is as muted as the low-key cabaret acts in his underworld nightclubs. This is a legitimate aesthetic choice, a hard-boiled universe in fact, and Noguchi deserves to be better known for it. But Suzuki, who used cabaret scenes for gaudy and outrageous spectacle, took the opposite course, pushing the boundaries of taste and narrative credulity.

This is evident in Suzuki's baroque fourth film, *Rajo to kenjū* (1957), which strikingly anticipates Hitchcock's *Vertigo* (1958) as the story of an innocent man manipulated by two women (played by the same actress, Mari Shiraki) who may or may not be the same. It is also a stylistic manifesto that makes a significant use of jump cuts two years before Godard was credited with revolutionizing the cinema for doing the same in *À Bout de souffle*/*Breathless* (1960). Suzuki's film is an unpredictable mix of rather generic *policier* conventions and erotic titillation, as reviewers were quick to point out.[21] But it also exhibits dynamic stylistic deformations that

Fig. 2.2. Noguchi Hiroshi's Muted Cityscapes (*Kenjū buraichō: Nukiuchi no Ryūji / Ryūji the Gunslinger*, 1960)

Fig.2.3. Noguchi's Bourgeois Aspirants: bored *yakuza* attend a (rather conservative) fashion show (*Kenjū buraichō: Nukiuchi no Ryūji*)

anticipate the revision of hard-boiled material in the much later films of the *nouvelle vague* such as *Tirez sur la Pianiste* (1962).

The inventiveness of the opening sequence is palpable, a tour-de-force of confusion, artifice, and eroticism. It begins with the meta-textual "cowboy cabaret" number mentioned above. As the strip artist fires off her imitation six-guns, a glass breaks on a table, suggesting that a real shot has been fired. In the ensuing montage of countenances, confused movement, and running feet, the film refuses to establish who shot who, but an innocent photographer (Mizushima Michitarō, Nikkatsu's answer to Bogart) soon finds himself on the street, being lured into the dancer's apartment.

Fig. 2.4. Film as Fashion Shoot (shot 1): Shiraki Mari 'models' for a photographer, but the only camera shooting her is cinematographer Nagatsuka Kazue's (*Rajo to kenjū*)

Fig. 2.5. Film as Fashion Shoot (shot 2): an innovative jump cut to Shiraki in a different pose (*Rajo to kenjū*; reminiscent of Rita Hayworth in *Gilda*, 1946)

As the girl strips to her underwear, Mizushima whips out his camera and starts to photograph her. Soon, the girl is "play-modeling" for Mizushima, posing erotically up against the brick wall of her apartment. A medium shot captures Shiraki, gazing erotically into the camera, which is angled sharply to the left.

Suddenly, a jump cut frames Shiraki in close-up, from a frontal angle, as she is creating a different pose, whipping her head and long hair from the bottom to the top of the frame.

Regardless of whether anyone in the Suzuki-*gumi* had seen and remembered a similarly voyeuristic jump cut on Rita Hayworth in Orson Welles' pathbreaking, baroque, critically reviled *Lady from Shanghai* (1947),[22] the inevitably self-reflexive context in which it is used here allows *Rajo to kenjū*'s jump cut to depart entirely from the diegesis of this narrative film, momentarily, to become a photomontage, a moving magazine. It artfully depicts a social milieu of commercialized eroticism and subjectivity: the model who lives for the camera. To throw a further cog into the diegesis, this "photomontage" occurs while the protagonist is *not*, so far as the viewer can tell, using his camera, but gazing directly at Shiraki. The temporal and diegetic status of the image becomes completely indeterminate, appearing as a pure bravura imposition of directorial style. It is a sign of things to come.

The jump cut appears only twice in this film, however, and the style of *Rajo to kenjū* from this point on is both confident and largely conventional. Apart from a certain tendency to avoid shot-reverse shot patterns,[23] the framing, editing, stock music, and even the location views of the stereotypically "bustling" city are unremarkable and perfectly typical of the genre. There are exceptions: on one occasion the *femme fatale* looks into the black slate cover of her posh record player and sees there a superimposed view of the protagonist as he drives his car. This view of the character has not occurred in the narrative prior: it is not precisely a flashback, but a sort of "re-created" vision.[24] Although these flamboyant touches, upon consideration, seem to challenge any reductive understanding of narrative time in the cinema, at this stage of Suzuki's career they are infrequent and not terribly disruptive of the hegemony of classical film form.

On the narrative level, a number of clichés are executed with seeming earnestness. Instead of focusing on the anxieties of a man who has been framed for murder, the film represents a police force bending over backwards to help him prove his innocence. This typically white-washed celebration of the Tokyo Metropolitan police is utterly reactionary for a director who would later (as early as *Kagenaki koe*, 1958) depict the manipulative police, and all other aggregates of institutional power, as dreadful.

Other genre elements, however, are fresh and surprising: in a fight scene between the gangsters and the hero, the latter improbably passes off the flash pan of his camera as a gun. This is another emphasis, like the "cowboy cabaret," on the fanciful "make-believe" that characterizes the whole of this scenario. Other such touches include a villain (Sugai Ichirō) absurdly made to resemble V.I. Lenin, a fight scene executed as pure farce, with both sides scurrying around without the slightest agility or courage, and a hero deftly portrayed by Mizushima as the ultimate everyman, devoid of any special heroic or romantic qualities until the disappointingly conventional finale.

Despite a formidable performance from Shiraki Mari, the characterization of the *femme fatale* (or non-characterization, as her identity remains unfixed) tends towards the Hollywood idiom by which, as Janey Place writes, "we observe both the social [agency] of myth which damns the sexual woman and all who become enmeshed by her, and a particularly potent stylistic presentation of the sexual strength of woman which man fears."[25] Constantly undressed, Shiraki is a pure male projection of seductive availability. Correspondingly, the film comes across at times as an extended advert for a new style of ladies' underwear and bra; after *Kinema junpō* fumed that the film's "transparent commercialism is disgusting," the director seems to have responded, in some sense, in *Ankokugai no bijo* by featuring young *men* in ladies' underwear at a frivolous dance party. In the typical fashion of both Japanese melodrama and American *film noir*, the *femme fatale* must die, though not before bombing her villainous ex-lover. In doing so, one could say that Shiraki's "gusto" all-too-briefly allows the Japanese *femme fatale* to inhabit the mythic territory of the ancient female shaman and her uncanny superiority over men. It is a territory much-explored in Suzuki's later films, yet here it is effectively reined in by narrative economy, by genre, by thematic focus, by modern patriarchy in itself.

Given her seductive wiles and the exploitative nature of the picture, it is remarkable that the protagonist passes up every chance of making love to Shiraki. Here is the film's satirical sting: given a script that largely reproduces the sexual politics of American and Japanese hard-boiled thrillers, the resulting film places a baroque over-emphasis on voyeurism. On two occasions, the hero gazes at the silhouette of Shiraki as she strips behind an opaque window (a window, moreover, that opens onto a public landing).

Later, on the justification of "collecting evidence" for the police, the hero sets his camera on an adjacent rooftop and takes pictures of the heroine as she showers nude. As in *Rear Window* (1954), voyeurism has replaced any and all desire for sexual contact. Perhaps this should be taken as symptomatic of a post-war crisis of masculinity, or perhaps the voyeurism of the middle-aged hero, in full cooperation with the police, connotes a prewar patriarchal order in its surveillance and control of femininity. The scene features a number of extreme close-ups on Mizushima's camera that emphasize what normative Hollywood cinema, through techniques such as eyeline matching, aims to conceal: that the notorious male gaze of the cinema, the gaze of mastery, is conditional upon its filmic mediation. Mizushima's camera stands for the film camera and makes a critical point to which Suzuki's films will obsessively return: the gaze should not function in the vacuum of a diegesis. That is to say, the film rejects what would be considered a normative use of the male gaze in the narrative cin-

Fig. 2.6. That Obscure Object of Desire: the iconic *femme fatale* as cinematic shadow (*Rajo to kenjū*)

ema, an example of which might be a male and female character gazing at one another, their respective POVs captured by over-the-shoulder reverse shots which allow the actors to avoid looking directly into the camera (a potential disruption). Suzuki's films evidently object to this attempt to conceal the mediation of the camera, and resort to often non-diegetic means to reinstate it. The viewers must be made aware of mediation, which creates (and effectively replaces) the male gaze just as surely as its object—like the silhouette of the nude *femme fatale* in the window—is a fantasy on a screen, a cinematic shadow.

Appearing six months later, *Ankokugai no bijo/Underworld Beauty* (1958) inhabits the same narrative and stylistic idiom as its predecessor. It demonstrates a fuller command of classical studio narration, and yet is determined to manifest its own textual difference. The largely conventional visual schema of *Rajo to kenjū* is replaced here by the spectacular use of what Hasumi has called the "previously neglected [visual] details" of genre.[26] In one instance, a gunfight is portrayed by means of an empty, darkened, opulent stairway, punctuated by enchanting bursts of gunpowder. In another, the audience views a mannequin made up to look like the heroine and containing a diamond in its breast. But now the mannequin is twisted apart, with the limbs and clumps of the breast torn off, and half sunk in the slime of a dank and abject sewer where the protagonist has dumped it. The shot is magnificently eerie and full of foreboding, expressive of desires so abject that they can only be expressed by simulacra, and only in passing.

For Hasumi, this hypostatization of the generic and the conventional *is* the authorial signature of a Suzuki film. But already in *Ankokugai no*

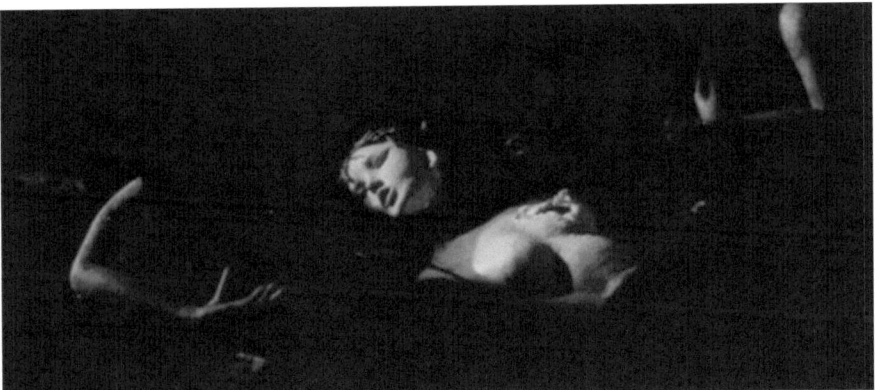

Fig. 2.7. *Hādo-boirudo* Cinema as Abject Simulacrum: the terrifying inexpressible, by proxy (*Ankokugai no bijo / Underworld Beauty*)

bijo, as Eric Crosby has shown, we see evidence of a more radical bifurcation between textual intentionality (the agency at work "behind" the film text) and the dominant stylistic norms of studio cinema. Grappling creatively with its designation as one of the first "NikkatsuScope" films and with the problems of CinemaScope composition, it managed to introduce a highly differential style of framing.

After demonstrating that Japanese studios necessarily adapted their widescreen compositional strategies from Hollywood, who created and exported the technology, Crosby analyzes the director's penchant for "unbalanced" compositions utilizing extreme edge-framing, extreme foreground and multi-planar staging, and the "obtrusive" use of tracking shots to introduce new characters and information.[27] Crosby recognizes these as departures from demonstrable stylistic norms:

> Surely, Suzuki could have avoided such compositional awkwardness, but the crucial point here is that he understands the convention, employs it, and.... frequently ... takes this one step further by creating an expectation for compositional payoff ... then ultimately subvert[ing] it.[28]

Crosby seems uncertain as to whether Suzuki's "flamboyant devices" serve a function related to "the articulation of narrative information and character psychology," or whether a fine line has been crossed between "articulation" and disruption: "in other instances, such compositional imbalances will seem to have no function other than the purely decorative.... We hope for some ... significant narrative information but we are thwarted as often as . . . satisfied."²⁹ Yet I cannot improve upon Crosby's concluding description of the director's early aesthetics: "Suzuki's early widescreen cinema seems to abide selectively by American norms while *also highlighting the arbitrariness of their functions*."³⁰ Alongside a mastery of accepted convention, these films develop a reflexive critique of the same. Their differential compositions suggest alternative cinematic potentialities but also carry a negative critical force in pointing to the "arbitrary" studio reliance on one set of norms. This is not only in relation to framing. *Ankokugai no bijo* includes a similar deformation of narrative time involving a montage of gazes of gangsters reacting to the arrival of a hero who does not in fact enter the door until a later shot.

The sexual politics of the film, rather than problematizing male voyeurism as before, depict the hard-boiled urban milieu as a quasi-surrealist fantasia of polymorphic perversity. The figure of the store mannequin is the iconic, narrative, and ideological center of the film.³¹ The plot involves a hero (Mizushima) who contends not only with the cold, repressed sadism of the *yakuza*, but also the heroine's boyfriend, a perverted sculptor of mannequins who is obsessed with human anatomy. Only this sculptor can retrieve stolen diamonds by dissecting the stomach of a corpse of a man who swallowed them, and he does so—accompanied by the eerie sound of twinkling bells on the soundtrack—with an expression resembling surprised ecstasy. In this hard-boiled myth of Pygmalion, both hero and perverse sculptor want to "mold" the rebellious heroine (a defiant performance by Shiraki that escapes all containment), but while the sculptor is an isolated predator resembling Peter Lorre's *M* (1931), the patriarchal hero carries the full weight of institutionalized masculine prerogative. Small wonder that the film ends with a shot of a birdcage, suggesting the heroine's entrapment in stifling domesticity with the injured hero.

Along the way, the viewer sees nude mannequins displayed at every stage of their production, from eerie shelves of detached heads with lewd expressions to fully formed figures with what appears to be artificial pubic hair (Fig. 2.9). At one point the workers on the factory floor begin to fondle their mannequins sexually.

The store mannequin is a double allegory, not only for male fetish, but for the post-war consumerism that renders everything as fetish. With Nikkatsu B-pictures at this time flirting along the edge of exploitation (with partial female nudity, for instance),³² Suzuki takes the plastic fetishism of the crime thriller to an outrageous, and yet cleverly uncensorable, degree, producing a sophisticated reflection on the genre.

Released later in the year (1958), *Kagenaki koe* continued to showcase

Fig. 2.8. The Birdcage: the spunky teenager in domestic partnership with the bullying elder she had previously repulsed (*Ankokugai no bijo*)

Fig. 2.9. Polymorphic Perversity: On the Edge of Taste and Censorship. Note the shadows that barely conceal the 'artificial pubic hair,' a bodily feature that for years was an obsession of the Japanese film censors (*Ankokugai no bijo*)

a technical proficiency of expressive technique, but, at the same time, seemed to "step outside" of the hard-boiled continuities and developments that we have noted across the prior two films. The hard-boiled tendency continues in *Ankoku no ryoken* and *Kemono no nemuri*, two films from 1960 that, despite sporadic formal highlights, suggest that Suzuki's career was repeating itself. Although *Kagenaki koe* is, in my evaluation, a near masterpiece, it is also one of the few films by Suzuki whose formal and stylistic economy, impressive as it is, seems dominated by its textual antecedents. By this I mean to say that it is based on a story by the revered Matsumoto Seichō and also betrays the powerful influence of German expressionism. Never before had the youthful Suzuki-*gumi* been confronted with such preeminent source material as Matsumoto's, and this undoubtedly accounts for the overreliance on conventions such as a murder mystery plot (instead of a byzantine *gangu mono* scenario), a gallant reporter (Nitani Hideaki), informational charts and voiceovers, and a setting not in the shady bars of Roppongi and Shibuya but within Tokyo's *yamanote* "commuter rail" suburbs.

Kagenaki koe is thus the exception that proves the rule; but its handling of its material is striking and distinctive in all departments—from Nagatsuka's low-key stylization to an unforgettably thuggish supporting performance by Shishido Jō. Indeed, *Kagenaki koe* has some profound connection to later films such as *Koroshi no rakuin*, which turned to surrealism, rather than expressionism, for inspiration. Most notable is a roughly tripartite structure that is not at all the cumulative three-act structure of mainstream screenwriting, then and now, but rather, three parts characterized by radical shifts of setting, stylistic economy, character perspective, identification, and mysteriously weak transitions and narrative links between the parts. The first section presents the travails of a telephone operator (Shimizu Mayumi) in the workaday world of Tokyo's lower-middle class commuter labor force, portrayed with something akin to the social realism of Kurosawa's *Nora inu* (1947) as variously corruptible types who gamble their money away while awaiting decent employment. So economical is this section that one might well miss the horizontal compositions (suburban apartment blocks, fences, ubiquitous rail lines) gradually overtaken by a sense of the heroine's entrapment in interior shots favoring right angles, verticals, and, paradoxically, extreme depth. Once the heroine's supersensitive hearing—and her increasing distress—is established by an extreme, frontal close-up of her ear, followed by a frequent repetition of the grotesquely loud sound of mahjong tiles being shuffled in the next room, we become aware that we are in the grip of a self-consciously expressionist approach.

The second section unfolds in a series of semi-rural outskirts visited by Nitani's reporter, whose winding investigation rediscovers the now sidelined, relocated heroine and several other witnesses from the night of the murder, incorporating several of what we may, for brevity's sake, call "flashbacks." This includes a harrowing montage sequence in which every shot is a canted angle, a gesture which may or may not relate to the drunkenness of one of the characters involved. While enthralled by its stylistic excess, viewers will not, as a rule, question the diegetic status of these visual distortions, because they function as markers of the "flashback" and are also fairly clearly the objective correlative of the characters' emotions or heightened perceptions. This suits the conceit of Matsumoto's story, which hinges on the heroine's hearing. In short, *Kagenaki koe* is a notable classic of expressionist crime films in the wake of Fritz Lang's *M*; but its contemporary and relatively undistorted social representations are more congenial to Nikkatsu's commercialism than the early expressionism of a Shōwa period film like *Kurutta ippēji* (Kinugasa, 1926), for instance, would have been. While Kurosawa, for his part, was also deeply influenced by Lang and Joe May, Suzuki's film is more recognizably expressionist: yet it thereby lacks the singular self-identity of a film like *Nora inu* (or *Ankokugai no bijo*, for that matter). Instead, it is a sophisticated and formally agile representative of a 1950s crime cinema that was practiced, across the globe, by a number of expert craftsmen, now mostly forgotten. In *Kagenaki koe*, in essence, we know what the filmmakers are doing and why. When Suzuki's career was deliberately directed away from "B" thrillers towards teenage "pop song" films, however, the "what" of this unmistakable filmmaking practice became obvious, while the "whys" became permanently, tantalizingly out of reach.

Suzuki's Dog: Color, Comedy, and Modernity

From 1960-1962, the heyday of the "Nikkatsu *akushon*" mega-genre, Suzuki's career was dominated, against his will, by a series of star vehicles for Wada Kōji, the youngest member of Nikkatsu's much-touted "Diamond Line" of action stars. The association was a blessing and a curse: while Suzuki gained some success and security as a contract director, his 1950s narratives of disorientation and unconventional subjectivity were made impossible by the fixed, dimensionless persona of Wada, a teen-aged studio creation. These types of films, branded "youngster action" (*kozō akushon*) by critics, were generally a mix of mild action, light melodrama, and comedy, with rock 'n' roll thrown in. Some of these efforts, despite incidental pleasures of humor and setting, are so conventional as to be utterly dated. Suzuki's most remunerative film of the period, *Kaikyō chi ni somete/Bloody Channel* (1960), was a hoary melodramatic scenario of brother against brother, enlivened only by expansive color vistas of a Japanese coastal town and finely choreographed action. Nothing about the picture—save for a single jump cut that is shocking within the straightforward economy of the whole—is out of the ordinary for, or beyond the capabilities of, such competent studio professionals as Noguchi or Masuda.

But a few films in the Wada cycle served as an experimental ground for the advancement of the "language" of popular film. *Kutabare gurentai*, Suzuki's first film with Wada and his first in color, was highly unusual in suffusing a blatantly commercial teen pop song vehicle with what can only be considered an avant-garde spirit and visual surface. Here, along with extremely differential framing, appears the non-diegetic color stylization that would characterize Suzuki's directorial practice in films such as *Nikutai no mon* (1964). The improbable story concerns a lower-class teen whose adoptive father is killed by a greedy developer in a hit-and-run incident, but who suddenly inherits the leadership of the Matsudaira clan of Awaji Island. If *Kutabare gurentai* was, by studio design, a pop culture confection, its deployment of color and movement creates a cinematic equivalent of the *matsuri* (street festivals) that are woven into the picture.

The scenario—by, of all people, the liberal democratic politician Hara Kenzaburō, a future Speaker of the Diet—is a bizarre displacement of teen romance (the credited female lead is all-but-invisible) in favor of an "Oedipal romance" in which the teen hero pursues his estranged mother (Higashi Emiko), demanding that she renounce her "sordid" sexual life with a despicable industrialist. There is a certain resonance with post-war social psychology. It is played out seemingly earnestly, but the film may be a reflexive criticism of itself, and Nikkatsu's *kozō akushon* cycle of films, as symptoms of a cultural arrested development.

Hara's scenario also advances a suspect, or perhaps simply naïve, ideology proposing a facile reconciliation of the major class and cultural divisions of the era: new American-style consumer aspirations, symbolized by rock 'n' roll and leisure sports, and *Nihonjinron* discourses of Japanese uniqueness represented by the "feudal" traditionalism of the Matsudaira clan. To be fair, the film itself undercuts the out of touch gentry at every turn, whether by a retainer who loses his shoe while making his ceremonial approach to the dais, or by the street urchin hero, who dismantles the clan coat of arms while telling the matriarch to "quit the *jidai-geki*," thus emphasizing the constructed (or fabricated) nature of "tradition." Moreover, the conflict between the Matsudaira clan and the development cartel from Tokyo seems to put the lie to the very synthesis proposed.

At one point, when the teenagers have successfully resisted the cartel's plots, they link arm-and-arm and sing a song from the war era that was well known to veterans like Suzuki, but most likely obscure to the younger generation. The intention may be a far-fetched display of transgenerational solidarity, against precisely what we do not know. But any such display, in the fall of 1960, could not help but recall the massive student protests against the ANPO treaty.[33] Bizarrely, the scene is filmed with a deliberate distortion of the anamorphic lens that creates an effect of "waving" parallel lines over the entire frame. What is the relation, here, of content to form? It is a question that viewers were rarely compelled to ask of a post-war Nikkatsu picture, however stylish. Yet it is an inevitable reaction to the kind of recurring, unconventional gestures in Suzuki's films, which tantalize us to seek what is probably impossible to find: namely, the ability to determine whether gestures such as this bear an *ironic* or an instantiating relation to the picture's narrative and ideological positioning.

Kutabare gurentai opens with a jolt of color, style, and speed. The third shot following the titles finds a car heading down a Tokyo street to the accompaniment of upbeat New Orleans jazz. The next shot is a close-up view, from inside the car, of a stuffed animal—a white dog—placed on top of the back seat.

As the shot and the music continues, the color of the white dog shifts to a gaudy purple, as if sprayed by an invisible hand.

The following two shots reveal the driver, a greedy businessman (Kondō Hiroshi), in a rapid match on action as he is kissing his mistress (the boy hero's mother). The film then cuts back to the stuffed dog, which now shifts from purple to aqua blue, then falls forward as the car hits and kills the adoptive father of the hero.

Nothing in post-war Japanese cinema—not even the overtly theatrical stylization of kabuki-esque films like Kinoshita's *Narayama bushikō/Bal-*

Fig. 2.10. Suzuki's Dog: Color, Modernity, and Meaning (shot 1a) (*Kutabare gurentai / Go to Hell Youth Gang*)

Fig. 2.11. Suzuki's Dog: Color, Modernity, and Meaning (shot 1b), the white dog turns purple (*Kutabare gurentai*)

lad of Narayama (Shōchiku 1958)—prepares one for this flourish of non-diegetic coloration. It transforms a trivial object whose relation to the narrative is either totally arbitrary, or open to a thousand interpretations. It is a pure, non-diegetic imposition of the filmmakers' intentionality, but to what purpose? It is a visual metaphor, but for what?

I have written elsewhere about this gesture in reference to an aesthetic of "colorism," a term used by the film theorist Gilles Deleuze in order to synthesize disparate, pathbreaking experiments in cinematic color by Minnelli, Antonioni, and Godard, the latter of whom made the definitive pronouncement, "it's not blood, it's red."[34] Similarly, when asked by a critic why the heroine's fingernails suddenly turn to a yellow color in *Hishū monogatari* (1977), Suzuki replied that it was because the room was yellow.[35] But *Kutabare gurentai* goes even further than the examples that Deleuze considered in its use of a "moving color" effect that asks its viewers to make meaning out of the "virtual conjunction" of a series of non-diegetic colors and the trivial, innocuous object (the toy dog) to which they become transiently attached. Although a conventionalized rhetoric of moving color in Japanese theatre, particularly *kabuki*, is relevant here, I am tempted to read the moving color of *Kutabare gurentai* metaphorically, as a form of "unsettlement" that relates it to a visual sense of the instability of demolished and rebuilt,[36] rapidly changing, and electrified post-war cityscapes (consider, for example, post-war Tokyo's iconic neon signage, which appeared prominently in *Kagenaki koe*, among others). When, in

Aoi chibusa/*Blue Breasts* (1958), an abandoned, bombed out shack is the site of a real or possibly imagined rape, it becomes a similarly allegorical site of amorphous cultural anxiety.[37] *Kutabare gurentai* bends color itself, rather than any particular or significant colored *object*, to this purpose (albeit within a semi-comical idiom). The "wild" detachment of the colors combines with the out-of-control automobile as symptoms of an anxious post-war era, characterized by speed and visual excitement but heading (like the hit-and-run driver) in a risky direction.

The "colorism" of *Kutabare gurentai*, through its diegetic "falseness," opens for the viewer a window on a larger film world in which meaning effects are not dictated by or restricted to a narrative world, and in which cinema represents the "form and pressure of the time" through (often abstract) visual associations. Such a gesture, at the time, was inevitably disruptive. It violated every dictate of the predictable spatial relations and closed narrative realism of classical studio norms. It violated the balanced, earthy color scheme of classical Japanese painting,[38] instead recalling the "virtual" movements of color in Taishō and European modernism, particularly surrealism (see Figure 2.12). It soon landed Suzuki in trouble with Nikkatsu, when Hori Kyūsaku reprimanded him for "extensive use of symbolism within a traditional action picture" in the final Wada vehicle, *Ore ni kaketa yatsura*/*Those Who Bet on Me* (1962).[39] (In this pressurized atmosphere, it is no surprise that *Kutabare gurentai* was followed by the "scaling-back" of *Tokyo kishitai* [1960], a film which evinces no formal ambitions whatsoever, but to some extent compensates for this by the charmingly goofy comic business of its first half, including the only example, in Suzuki's notably anti-American oeuvre, of a positively represented American character: the amusing George Ruika as an irascible music teacher.)

The "false" conjunction between colors and objects in *Kutabare gurentai*,[40] quite apart from the metaphoric associations we might wish to glean from it or impose upon it, witnesses an early birth of the consequential non-diegetic stylization of the cinema of the 1960s. It uses color as a modernist "shorthand" to create non-diegetic observers of the spectacle—a reflexive, essentially non-fictional intimacy between viewer and screen: a moment somehow suited to particular historical conditions, yet also simply there "to be looked at" in way that, perhaps, operates beyond and above *any* schema of meaning effects. *Kutabare gurentai*'s abstract colorism seems to do for all colors what Kandinsky attributed to whiteness: "White . . . works upon us negatively, like . . . pauses in music that break temporarily the melody. . . . not a dead silence, but one pregnant with pos-

Fig. 2.12. "Moving Color": Magritte's portrait of the nude bisected by color contrast. *Black Magic*, 1945. (Photograph by Alan Hall, reprinted by permission of Musée Magritte/RMFAB.)

sibilities."[41] The film, and Suzuki's dog in particular, is similarly an example of loud, brash "silence" signifying nothing, and everything.

From Realism to Reflexivity

The color stylization of Suzuki's B-pictures, beginning with *Kutabare gurentai*, was more conceptually radical and arguably more philosophically consequential than the early stylistics of the Shōchiku *nuberu bagu*, which included such techniques by Ōshima as the limited use of non-diegetic sound (in *Seishun zankoku monogatari*, 1960), complex flashback structures, and a rhetoric of political figuration (people or emblems set against a non-diegetic black background in *Nihon no yoru to kiri*/Night and Fog in Japan), which actually had a number of cinematic antecedents.[42]

Like the *nuberu bagu*, moreover, though not so inclined towards the topical, these Suzuki pictures are a site of ideological contestation, political as much as aesthetic: just as we have seen in regards to the gender representations and catalogued perversities of his hard-boiled films. One might argue that, before 1963, a fully developed connection between visual abstraction, stylistic impertinence, and ideological reversal—the negation of dominant assumptions—had yet to emerge in Suzuki's films or in the studio system generally.

This search for a politics of the image, a synthetic grounding of the pleasures of spectacle in a space of social representation very consciously marked by ideological contradiction and critique, may help to explain how Suzuki's career could embrace the realist social problem film of the early 1960s, only to quickly abandon it. *Subete ga kurutteru* is an urban teen delinquency film, a cycle that had begun with Nikkatsu's own *taiyōzoku* melodramas. By 1961, it had embraced the more political films of Ōshima and Hani (*Furyō shōnen/Bad Boys*). Suzuki's film—which unquestionably reflects the filmmaking practices of the French *nouvelle vague*, with over two-thirds of the film shot on exterior location in Shinjuku and other areas—has an equal claim to membership in the early phase of the *nuberu bagu* as two more famous Nikkatsu films, Imamura's *Buta to gunkan* (1961) and Kurahara's *Kyonetsu no kisetsu/Season of Heat* (which debuted only a week before the Suzuki picture). Only Suzuki's "low" status as a "cult" or "*yakuza*" director has prevented this obvious association.

Moreover, I would argue that *Subete ga kurutteru* advances, on certain political readings, beyond the early *nuberu bagu*, and certainly beyond Kurahara's rather exploitative film. *Kyonetsu no kisetsu* seems to encourage a materialist or naturalist reading of teen delinquency: it as if the summer heat itself, and the teenage libido that it stokes, drives the protagonist to rape a female passerby. The morality of contemporary culture is secondary until the thorny issue of pregnancy comes up. But there is nothing "naturalist" about *Subete ga kurutteru*. Rather than proposing the positive or negative political significance of the masculine, teen-aged, sexualized body engaged in all manner of crime and sexual violence[43] (which was after all the basis of the *taiyōzoku* films that had made Nikkatsu so wealthy), Suzuki's film represents an arrested and pathologically anxious post-war masculinity, marked, in particular, by a profound fear of female sexuality. It relates this fear of the feminine to the prewar culture of a patriarchal order that, as is openly declared in the film, was responsible for the war, and now looks on in horror at the generation it has created.

The title, *Subete ga kurutteru* or *Everything Goes Wrong*, applies not only to the characters, but to post-war Japan: every aspect is misdirected, out-of-kilter. It is the most direct and sweeping indictment of post-war society to come out of Nikkatsu's first decade of production—its *"Burial of the Sun"* (1960), so to speak. Society is a blighted urban holocaust of emotional despair, sexual predation, and enslavement to the dollar. Where Suzuki's later films are, broadly speaking, allegorical and open-ended, tending towards the critique of institutional structures rather than the epiphenomenal constraints of ordinary lives, *Subete ga kurutteru* addresses these concerns through dialogue and a rather contrived plot set against the backdrop of the great student protests of 1960 against the ANPO treaty.[44] It concerns a high school student, Jirō (Kawachi Tamio), who cannot get over the fact that his mother is the long-time mistress of a prominent businessman, the arms manufacturer Nanbara (Ashida Shinsuke). The mild, all-too-human Nanbara metonymically serves as a figure of responsibility for the war (Jirō's father was run over in a "friendly fire" incident by the tanks that Nanbara manufactured) and as an agent of post-war reconstruction, of which the Cold War arms trade was a principal part.

Jirō's problem with his mother has led to a pathological correlation between female sexuality and money. There is an alarming innocence to the moment when he throws coins at the free-spirited girl, Tani (Nezu Yoshiko), who has ended his virginity; he really does assume that women have sex for money. His delusion is no one's fault, but it drives Jirō mad, like Orestes or Hamlet, until he destroys himself and all around him. When he confronts Nanbara at the climax, Jirō veers between acute perception of the failings of the war generation and an animalistic rage in which he murders the only father-figure he has ever known.

It seems as if Jirō cannot escape the war he never saw—the desperate entanglements that survival necessitated. But this is surely an incomplete reading. For each of the characters, it is not the war, but the "money-or-nothing" pattern of life under capitalism that bedevils their every step. Jirō's desperate search for money (through increasingly criminal behavior) is ironically accompanied by an idealist's disgust for its tainting of all relationships. The idealism only feeds his abominable treatment of Tani, herself a troubled victim/participant of a gang which pays for its thrills by prostituting female members.

Tani's friend Etsuko (Nakagawa Shinako) is trying to raise money for an abortion. Etsuko is treated with casual misogyny by her boyfriend, an otherwise estimable leader of a protest group whose attitude towards her illustrates the limitations of the student movement. This is a prescient critique in an era in which younger directors (one might say a whole generation of Japanese filmmakers) were tending in the opposite direction when

Fig. 2.13. Post-war Vacancies: *Subete ga kurutteru* (1960) and the emptiness of youth

it came to the relations between New Left political discourse and gender difference—wherein rape constantly appears as a symbolic, often sacral, act of political dissent or, at the very least, dissident rage.

The desperate Etsuko waylays Nanbara into sleeping with her for money. We should and have been sympathetic to Etsuko's plight, but as she veers wildly between seduction, extortion, and beggary, Nanbara can only look upon her pityingly. A close-up of Etsuko shows not simply desperation, but total vacancy—a vacuum devoid of values, dreams, or sense of self. Not even personal desire lives there, only moment-to-moment need.

One can imagine such faces were common in the starving post-war Tokyo of late 1945. In this film, the new prosperity and the much-vaunted doubling of average incomes have seemingly made little difference for the children of the working class. Why not? Throughout the narrative, their desperation is economic, but the finale of the film seems interested in tracing its roots to a cultural scene that is, in turn, driven by market forces heading in no clear direction. If the question is, "what do these teenagers want?", then clearly they do not know what they want beyond a daily cycle of sexualized stimulation and response. Their desperate and circuitous behavior continually orbits around the question, neither answering it nor escaping from it. And the consequences of that behavior, when it comes up against an entrenched socio-economic structure seemingly at odds with the leisure economy and commodity culture that floats on the surface, leads to a vicious circle of entrapment.

Beyond this, the film offers no answers or solutions—it is a characteristically negative analysis. Everyone is responsible and yet no one is to blame. Nostalgia, or return to the world of Nanbara, is no answer. Jirō's mother admits at one point that she has become calculating, valuing her lover's money rather than their relationship. In response, Nanbara answers enigmatically: "We didn't have the freedom of young people today, unfortunately." Energy, at least, and a rebellious determination not to be told what to do still belongs to the young, and though this is hardly a fulfilling ethic or a *raison d'être*, one can imagine that the filmmakers share Nanbara's envy, despite the seeming inferno they make out of the youths' cultural environment.

The final scene of the film follows a hack journalist and a hostess who are mystified by the haplessness and misfortunes of these teenagers. The camera then tracks with seeming aimlessness around the hostess's bar, revealing an almost endless supply of useless, alienated and alienating American-style consumer paraphernalia. Has the institutionalized commercialism of desire, in partnership with a sensationalist popular media,[45] created the teen degeneracy that it profitably feeds on?

In a similar film of the same year, *Taiyō no hakaba*, Ōshima enables a social critique through his film's "look" and visual style, but approaches this in quite a different manner from *Subete ga kurutteru*'s enigmatic nominalism. *Taiyō no hakaba* uses a gory red and brown color palette to sink its viewers into the mud of a burning junkyard on Tokyo's swampy outskirts: the waste environment allegorizes the lives of its truly lower-class denizens. In contrast, Suzuki's film about spoiled teens features a rather slick black-and-white surface—Tokyo's media-image of itself and its burgeoning "economic miracle," through which Nagatsuka's camera work, as an interrogatory narrator, must penetrate. The same procedure is more strikingly operative in the color cityscapes of *Tokyo nagaremono* (1966). If Ōshima's film creates an existentialist or naturalist (what Deleuze would call an "originary") image of (ex-)urban Japan, Suzuki's film lies squarely within the Society of the Spectacle—a surprisingly Godardian vision of the sub-bourgeois junkyard (I am thinking in particular of Godard's diatribe in *Prénom: Carmen* [1978], perhaps the best thing about that film, on the subject of superfluous plastic coffee mugs). From the vantage point of 2022, which of the two visions, Suzuki's or Ōshima's, is the more prescient in its manner of critique? The answer seems obvious. But if Ōshima's film is something of a period piece today, neither is *Subete ga kurutteru* above critique. Does its surface orientation and quasi-realist choice of form limit its critique to the superficial as well? Unlike some of the other films discussed in this chapter, in the creation of which we can well imagine the filmmakers strategizing how to push beyond what Suzuki had seen in *À Bout de Souffle*, the stylistic audacity (e.g., use of jump cuts) in *Subete ga *kurutteru* is not nearly as provocative as Godard's. And if the film lacks a strong flavor of experimentation, so too does it seem to lack a certain quality of *expansiveness* common to Suzuki's films. Even in hard-boiled efforts that managed to differentiate themselves from Noguchi, there is a sense of a unique, irreplaceable world created and embodied by each film and between films: not simply a larger narrative world, though this is certainly an achievement, but a critical and ideological world. This is what Wayne C. Booth called an *ethos* that connects narrative moments and gestures of a formal nature to the creative agency that produces them (as in, i.e., the popular adjectives "Capraesque" or "Hitchcockian").

It would have been interesting to see the development of a craftsman of the empirical, in some ways Ozu-like social melodrama that is evident in *Subete ga kurutteru*. Not one to repeat himself, however, Suzuki somehow managed to use his unpredictable assignment roster at Nikkatsu in order to forge ahead in the new direction that would become associated with his name. But how to characterize that direction? Hasumi considered teen melodramas such as *Akutarō* (1963) the most important pictures of Suzuki's earlier years because they achieved the "perfection" of the Shōchiku Ōfuna melodramas that Suzuki had encountered as an Assistant Director. This was a genre of "simplistic sentiment" about the "everyday joys and sorrows of the countryside" that lacked, to its detriment, a "crucial sense of loss."[46] In regards to *Akutarō*, about the schooling of a Taishō teenager, it would be hubris to attempt to improve on Hasumi's description:

> The dialogue, in flawless dialect . . . is superior to the so-called realism of someone like Shindō. Suzuki sticks to the story and the vague nostalgia for the Twenties it embodies, like a hermit in a world of abstract beauty. . . . Suzuki suddenly rises above Ōfuna melodrama and, remarkably, seems to harken back to the days of Ozu and Naruse. The way in which the fatal attraction of the young adolescent is portrayed against the background of the period is unmistakably lyrical and in no way sentimental. . . . The merely workmanlike *Akutarō* is neither more nor less than a juvenile melodrama in its purest form. Perhaps the film was the last melodrama, [giving] the declining Ōfuna melodrama a worthy funeral.

Despite Suzuki's attraction to the Taishō imaginary, Hasumi nevertheless subtly corroborates my own sense that pictures such as *Akutarō* are hardly more representative of Suzuki's career than a film like *Subete ga kurutteru*. He writes, "Suzuki made a film of a kind he was not familiar with himself."[47] This is particularly evident when we consider that a "flash-

Fig. 2.14. Atypical Suzuki? The crisp architectural lines of *Akutarō* (1963)

back" sequence in *Akutarō* is not less interesting or impressive than the rest of the picture, even though it is shot on a small studio set in a somewhat stylized way that is closer to Suzuki's earlier films than to *Akutarō*'s restrained "lyrical realism," which is defined by location shooting that captures a quiet, airy country town in crisp compositional and architectural lines.

The same is true of a humbler exercise in "lyricism" such as the Wada vehicle *Toge wo wataru wakai kaze/The Wind of Youth Crosses the Mountain Pass* (1961), which is even more atypical of Suzuki's pictures before and after it. This film, a tribute to the endurance of a penny-ante magic show that travels from town to town, is steeped in semi-nostalgic rural vistas, repressed youthful attractions, and a spirit of camaraderie (even amongst *yakuza*) that is ideologically unchallenging but enlivened by brisk pacing and sly, deprecating humor. If we ignore the self-consciousness of Suzuki's later films and attend to specific aspects of diegetic style—such as the static, single-shot compositions that shift, without any disjunction, from breezy hillsides to interiors pouring over with incidental plastic detail (the paraphernalia of the troupe)—than this film is aesthetically without peer amongst Nikkatsu's output. Beloved in certain quarters (like *Akutarō*, which boasts a far more streamlined and precise formal economy), the picture seems at times to grasp at being a definitive representation of the lower end of show business. Why it does not do so is a matter of some critical puzzlement, since the filmmakers make the best of a scenario that has sufficient, if unremarkable, narrative interest. Perhaps the film is too concise; perhaps it is too "handsome" in representing the humiliations and anxieties of performing life, from the players' mildly sordid lives to the deathly encroach of big business upon them. Perhaps the troupe's performances are filmed in a too muted and frontal manner (though in any case they are supposed to be, at best, humble); or perhaps the film is so comfortable in the vein of Shōchiku nostalgia that it never reaches, at any point, a critical mass of energy. The troupe's amusing final performance is perhaps too faithful to the script to fully represent the sense of what is possible when performers are given the sudden freedom and motivation to improvise. The fully cinematic energy and immediacy of the great cinematic evocations of stage work (including the *noh* play in Ozu's *Banshun/ Late Spring* and Suzuki's own *Kagero-za*) is absent here.

It is nevertheless true that Suzuki's earlier efforts in the more *contemporary* sub-genres of romantic melodrama (whether the adult-oriented *Raburetaa* or the semi-exploitative *Aoi chibusa*) had been less successful than these nostalgia pieces, and even betrayed a feeling of disengagement between filmmaker and material. Yamane Sadao opined, "if we try to look again at something like *Raburetaa*, it's completely not what became the so-called Suzuki Aesthetic. . . . That said, it is beyond doubt a Suzuki film."[48] The comparative obscurity of these films is probably not accidental. Nevertheless, the critics who associate Suzuki's filmmaking practice (and its formal-thematic continuities across forty Nikkatsu features) with a particularly "Japanese" and prewar lyrical nostalgia, in the vein of *Akutarō*,[49] should not forget that the very essence of the Taishō and early Shōwa imaginary was its characteristically *modan* impurity: the fluidity of "code-switching" between cultural rhetorics, the earnest engagement with European thought,[50] the "negative capability" of simultaneous adaptation of and irony towards Western leisure culture. All of these qualities are on display, for instance, in the theatre troupe's offerings in *Toge wo wataru wakai kaze*.

In final analysis, I believe that the most formative and underappreciated aspects of Suzuki's early films, in terms of their continuity with the later ones, are the modernist experiments with color and the mastery of the hard-boiled idiom. The latter demonstrated (on a modest scale) a cultural dynamic that was analogous to that of Taishō in its hybrid, intertextual, transnational characteristics. Hasumi notably downplays this hard-boiled influence, just as he downplays the awareness of Hollywood forms and conventions in Suzuki's films. (Suzuki reflected on Hollywood deeply enough to be moved, later on, to pen a tribute to the actress Susan Hayward.) Few would argue that in the 1960s, Suzuki's films achieved a consistency that concentrated on action spectacle as well as a certain kind of reflexivity. Both of these things were congenial to the hard-boiled cinema, with its expressionist and surrealist undertones; neither of them, by the most inclusive measure, were hallmarks of Shōchiku Ōfuna melodrama. I argue that Suzuki's name today—as a marker of the textual intentionalities that are conventionally attributed to a film's director—is most typically and justifiably associated with a modernist, self-authenticating cinema practice that declared itself antithetical to realism. Made in 1965, the film *Akutarō-den: warui hoshi no shita demo/Bastards: Born Under a Bad Star*, plays like a parody of this transition from a rhetoric of realism to a rhetoric of reflexivity, just as it is a parody of the original *Akutarō* and of *seishun eiga* generally. It tells in its outlines the same story as *Akutarō*, but this time in an idiom of broad, often grotesque sex comedy at a rapid pace catalyzed by incessant wipe cuts, three-or-four second flashbacks, mysterious ellipses, subjective camera movements, verbal *double entendres*, extended comic digressions, and cartoonish performances that border on expressionistic—particularly the magnificent Nogawa Yumiko as a pixie-like temptress who goes to great lengths to uncover the protagonist's member. There is even an unmotivated repetition of a shot of the hero moving from Right to Left with the screen direction reversed. Most memorable are the metaphorical sight gags, one of which (replacing a baby with a monkey) is completely non-diegetic whilst the other—which compares *kendo* students, in a cutaway, to quarrelsome, rapacious roosters—turns out, eventually, to be a diegetic intercut of the gambling activities of the hero's father. As Bordwell wrote of Godard, "the more or less arbitrary juxtaposition of lighting options . . . camera angles, decoupage options, musical styles, and so forth . . . tends to be not systematically oppositional but purely 'differential' . . . [and] makes a whole film out of the discrete narrational flourishes. . . ."[51] Whereas the political context of the setting of the original *Akutarō* emerges gradually through the youthful protagonist's own, limited, point of view, the sequel is a familiar of the freewheeling, satirical comedies of the 1960s condemning provincial repressiveness through the use of historical allegory (Tony Richardson's *Tom Jones*, from 1963, was a notable example).

What was the problem with "realism" such that Suzuki's films of the mid-1960s had to go to such lengths to distance themselves from it? The problem with (at least) the version that emerges in *Subete ga kurutteru*, and which Suzuki must have observed in his rivals Kurahara and Imamura, seems to have been that it relegated politics and philosophy too much to the realm of the diegesis, rather than to the role of the camera, which had established the potential to be *openly discursive* (in a sense) in the films of Godard. Realism also tended (certainly with Kurahara) to naturalize exploitation through the sway of narrative and identification with the male protagonist. Suzuki as a director was either unable or unwilling to achieve the kind of pared-down realism that could become truly differential and philosophically expressive—although some may read *Akutarō* as a step in that direction. The influence, moreover, of the silent era on Suzuki—expressionism, French surrealism, and Carl Theodor Dreyer—likely inclined him in the opposite direction.[52] From what we know of his artistic persona, Suzuki was of no temperament to take up the position of follower of either the *nouvelle vague* or the *nuberu bagu*. Partly for this reason, and partly out of necessity as a Nikkatsu director, he would henceforth explore his formal and political concerns through genre, particularly in the allegory of crime and in the landscape of the dream-image, the collective desiring unconscious of a nation.

CHAPTER 3

The Mirror

*(Yajū no seishun,
Tantei Jimusho 2-3: Kutabare akutō-domo,
Kemono no nemuri)*

The first five minutes of Suzuki's early masterpiece, *Yajū no seishun/Youth of the Beast* (1963), consists of three short sequences, each jarringly distinct in editing, pacing, and mise-en-scène. Together they function as "master keys" to the interpretation of the film as a whole.

In black and white, the first post-titles sequence depicts a crime scene at one of Tokyo's "love hotels": an apparent double suicide between a young singer and an older policeman. The sequence is full of partially obscured views. It begins with the white coat of an unidentified technician blocking the camera's view, then quickly moving off-screen to reveal the strewn corpse of the policeman. The camera than pans upward to reveal the previously unseen corpse of the young woman. The white coat passes through the frame again and the camera travels off-screen right to follow it, only to reframe on a diamond-shaped window-pane, with the bisected countenance of a detective peering out (Fig. 3.1).

A reverse-angle medium shot reveals in full two middle-aged detectives who are peering out the window where a small crowd of onlookers has gathered. The camera tracks to follow one detective as he methodically covers the window with curtains, as if to reassert control over the visibility that the harmless onlookers are seeking.

The same detective turns, looks down at the corpse, and says wistfully, "At least there's some benefit in having been loved by a woman that much." The other detective agrees; it is, after all, a perfectly typical sentiment in Japanese melodrama whether pre-war or post-war, action or romance.

As it turns out, the none-too-bright detectives are looking at a double murder framed to *look* like a suicide. Their sentimentality merely perpetuates the lie. This sequence depicts an old world of romantic and moral

Fig. 3.1. Out of the Shadows: the obscured world of the 1950s crime thriller (*Yajū no seishun* / *Youth of the Beast*)

Fig. 3.2. Authoritarian Containment of Public Information (*Yajū no seishun*)

absolutes reflecting the post-war Japanese fascination with American hard-boiled detective fiction,[1] in which Sam Spade and Philip Marlowe were the tarnished knights protector of a culture of "values" as against the fast, loose leisure class cultures of the city. At the same time, it connotes a prewar Japanese landscape in which "things were as they seem" and in which double suicide (*shinjū*) could still be regarded as an aesthetic, erotic, even moral apotheosis. But Suzuki's film will soon undercut this belief system. The opaque and blocked compositions complement the predictable attempt by the police to conceal, control, and interpret information ostensibly on behalf of the public. As the authorities entertain their romantic thoughts, there is a cut to a drawing table on which a single camellia

Fig. 3.3. Out of the Past: the hand-painted red camellia links the contrary monochrome and color sequences

Fig. 3.4. Everything Out in the Open: the second sequence of *Yajū no seishun*

reaches out from a table full of sordid evidence: drugs, beer, and playing cards. The camellia is saturated with hand-painted color in an otherwise completely monochrome composition.

With an abrupt cut, the second sequence erupts upon us in full color. A group of schoolgirls at a local train station are doubled over and laughing hysterically, as if making light of the deathly melodrama of the previous sequence. We are no longer in the same social or aesthetic universe, as if the older state of things has exploded from an excess of youthful desire out of sync with the social order.

In a series of eight shots, the new sequence quickly goes about its main business: apparently random acts of violence and brutality (*bōryoku*). A shot lasting merely two seconds shows a young man emerging from the

Fig. 3.5. Violence at a Distance: a brutal, unidentified protagonist

station to meet the girls. Rather than developing this narrative any further, the film cuts to an extreme long shot of a busy street corner where some roistering youths, probably those from the station, are milling around. A stranger in a black trench coat appears and knocks down three of the teenagers with his fists.

He kicks one repeatedly in the head and we cut to a harshly angled shot of the bloodied, prostrate youth as the stranger wipes the blood from his shoe on the young man's shirt. For 1963, this is excessive cinematic brutality, all the more so because rapid cutting and obscure compositions make it arbitrary: the viewer is unable to identify the characters or even the situation. The stranger is only ever seen from behind. Another abrupt cut then brings us to a pachinko parlor. The stranger in black, shot only from below the knee, steps on the hand of a customer who has attempted to retrieve a pachinko ball from under the stranger's feet. The next shot is the exterior of a cabaret club. Inside, the stranger is revealed to be Shishido Jō—a familiar face to moviegoers—as he intimidates an unfortunate waiter. Later, this inebriated stranger stuffs a wad of bills into the bra of a demure and self-possessed hostess. She is visibly unimpressed, so the stranger pours a bucket of ice down her dress.

As Shishido bullies this woman, there is a startling transition to a third sequence. We are now viewing the stranger in the cabaret from an entirely different place. The giant mirror forming the wall of the cabaret is in fact a one-way mirror, and on the other side of it an elegant woman and some well-dressed gangsters are observing the stranger through this vast, partitioned observation window.

Fig. 3.6. The Third Sequence: the narrative as viewed through a one-way mirror

In place of the short cuts of the previous sequence, the new location is revealed in a complex travelling shot lasting 40 seconds. The room is soundproof, so that the criminals (and the viewer) observe Shishido's offensive behavior in dead silence, through the mediation of the partitioned screen. Two minutes later, the gangsters operate state-of-the-art recording equipment in order to restore the music and sounds of the cabaret. The criminals, like the police, are in the business of capturing information.

Each sequence announces a certain motif which carries through the rest of the film. The first "detective" scene is a kind of generic quotation and initiates a discourse on film genres and their potential transformation. The second sequence problematizes the representation of (gendered) violence in cinema. The third, in teasing relations of power, spectacle, and sound, "transparently" allegorizes a cinematic practice that reflects on itself by means of, and in relation to, the preceding, provocative narrative representations. The three sections of this chapter correspond to these three sequences, the cinematic ideas that they embody, and how they make *Yajū no seishun* a transformational film, not only in a director's *oeuvre* and in the studio's history, but in the evolution of a transnational genre.

The Japanese are Making Noirs, *Too*

As a reflection on the legacy of hard-boiled crime fiction, the opening detective sequence introduces its major motifs of the controlling hand of the authorities and the problem of (mis)information (Fig. 3.2). It initiates a dialectic of old and new, black and white and color, stasis and movement, cultural permanence and chaotic upheaval. The red camellia (Fig. 3.3) "sticks out" of the monochrome hard-boiled milieu and acts as a thread leading into the color sequences that follow, finally returning in the film's final, and once again monochrome, shot. Similarly, the hard-boiled stranger in the black trench coat "sticks out" like a sore thumb amongst the hip denizens of a colorful modern Tokyo (Fig. 3.5), encased on all sides by advertisements and centers of consumer diversion including pachinko, cabaret, strip shows, and, in another self-reflexive gesture, a Nikkatsu cinema in Asakusa advertising movie stars, including Shishido himself. With this sequence in mind, it is important to begin with the way in which Suzuki's film negotiates the influence of cinematic genre and deploys its aesthetics in the service of social allegory.

Hard-Boiled, *Noir*, and Not-So-*Noir*

Suzuki recently acknowledged the direct influence of the American crime writer Dashiell Hammett.[2] Hammett also looms large over the 1962 novella *Hitokari/Manhunt*, by Ōyabu Haruhiko, on which *Yajū no seishun* was based.[3] Throughout the post-war decade, translations of Hammett, Chandler, Spillane, and others exploded on the Japanese literary scene, and with his 1958 novella *Yajū no shisu beshi/The Beast Must Die*, Ōyabu was one of the first Japanese writers to make a career by adapting the "Western" hard-boiled style to the liminal, criminal spaces of Tokyo. This almost immediately led to competing series of films based on the author's work at Tōhō and at Nikkatsu under the direction of Noguchi Hiroshi. We must therefore view *Yajū no seishun* (1963) as marking both the beginning and the end of a *hādo-boirudo* cycle in Japanese film. Although it straggled on as a sub-genre until at least 1961, the initial cycle of films in the mid-fifties waned in popularity in favor of the more variegated (but equally formulaic) "Nikkatsu *akushon*" brand, which began as early as 1957. With the development of its "Diamond Line" of the most popular movie stars in Japan (Ishihara, Kobayashi, Akagi Keihachirō), Nikkatsu was more interested in promoting likeable personalities than fatalistic melodrama, and as early as 1959 Noguchi's *Kenjū buraichō/Tales of a Gunman* series began to tone down the hard-boiled context of these films in order to present a more "audience-friendly" gunman.[4] This style was more-or-less adapted by Suzuki himself in another Ōyabu adaptation, *Tantei jimusho 2-3: Kutabare akutō-domo/Detective bureau 2-3: Go to Hell Bastards!* (1963), which amply demonstrated that hard-boiled source material, even from a best-selling author, was far less important than Nikkatsu's "house style" in determining the form and tone of the resulting adaptation. I do not know whether Nikkatsu originally envisioned this property as a genuine crime and suspense thriller with a light touch, or as a violent comedy reminiscent of Nakahira's *Yabai ni nara zeni ni naru/Danger Pays* (1962), which also made use of Shishido Jō's ability to add dimensions of comic awkwardness and sometimes outright absurdity to moments of actions and suspense. But the studio was probably surprised at the extent to which Suzuki—evidently bored with three years of Wada Kōji vehicles—decided to take the comedy route to new extremes. Essentially telling the same story as *Yajū no seishun*, that of a tough, devious protagonist (in this case a private detective) infiltrating a gang for the purpose of bringing it down, *Tantei jimusho 2-3* is light thriller material, occasionally hilariously so, as when Shishido's character bends the film audience's suspension of disbelief by inserting himself, rather too smoothly and suddenly, into a nightclub cabaret act in order to communicate surreptitiously with his (ex-girlfriend) singing partner. Packed with absurd social portraiture and narrative situations, gunfights that mow down *yakuza* foot soldiers like so many ants, and punctured by an occasional, shocking sobriety (as when the heroine reflects on the state of her soul following a terrible history of sexual exploitation), *Tantei jimusho 2-3* seems just as willing to construct a highly efficient, elaborate suspense sequence as it is to cut away from the narrative tension in favor of amusing bits of business. The picture has an understandably mixed critical reputation, with some finding it fresh and spontaneous and others dismissing it as neither fish nor fowl on account of its humor being the driest of the dry, relying (for the most part) on neither jokes nor action pratfalls; as when Shishido's office manager calls up the *yakuza* headquarters and tries to "call off" a mob hit on account of the target "not showing up," only to be told by a janitor of sorts that "it's too late . . . they've already left." It surely says something about Suzuki's unique handling of this genre material that the heart of the film is not Ōyabu's intricate cat-and-mouse machinations, however amusingly deployed, but the comic shenanigans of Shishido's two practically useless employees, including the priceless Hatsui Kotoe (Suzuki's most distinctive actress, next to Nogawa Yumiko) as a sexually ambiguous magazine editor whom we would nowadays call a "true crime *ōtaku*," that is, a crime-obsessed nerd. Tony Rayns finds the character irritating, evidence of the film's failure as a comedy,[5] but her weird and grating personality is precisely the point, being of a type that would never appear in a Nikkatsu thriller before or after *Tantei jimusho 2-3*, and would be more germane to a sharply observed social (and sexual) comedy of manners.[6] The gauche Hatsui, refreshingly liberated from all then-current gender stereotypes while at the same time extremely unreliable, reflects an "urban contemporary" culture that parallels the setting of the film amidst Tokyo's semi-suburban outskirts, with signs everywhere of construction and rapid commercial development, a cultural megalopolis in the making.

It is illuminating to compare the tone of *Tantei jimusho 2-3* with the brutal and frequently terrifying *Yajū no seishun*, which declares its difference by establishing a new relationship between itself and its cinematic predecessors of the 1950s. This difference also illuminates how Nikkatsu *akushon*, by 1964, was struggling to reinvent itself for a shrinking audience. Contemporary offerings by other Nikkatsu directors went off in various directions, including variations on the Bond films, a trend mocked in *Yajū no seishun* through its cat-stroking supervillain Nomoto (Kobayashi Akiji). But Shishido's stunning and abrasive performance, combined with the "contemporary" feel of Suzuki's film as a colorful variation on the long out-of-fashion 1950s *hādo-boirudo*, made an impact by working counter to other trends.[7] Having recently graduated from the role of the villain or second lead into a light leading man, Shishido now became the leading dramatic actor of a cycle of "new" *hādo-boirudo* films of the 1960s,[8] some of them directed by Suzuki's former assistants. Although reportedly not commercially successful on its initial release,[9] *Yajū no seishun* was nevertheless on the critical radar. *Eiga hyōron*'s Nakahara Yumihiko called it an "action film aimed at art theatre."[10] It was the second Suzuki film of the decade that *Kinema junpō* deigned to review, with the director himself given only a passing mention.

As a hybrid, transnational revision of the already hybrid, transnational mode of "hard-boiled," the picture also has claims to international significance, not least because its aesthetic "newness" would serve as a point of departure for what I have called the Suzuki Difference, a set of bold stylistic reformulations of narration that would appear with increasing consistency from this point forwards. But while the director's subsequent films took the road of genre pastiche and conceptual provocation (rather like his young contemporary Jean-Luc Godard in *Alphaville* and *Pierrot le Fou*, both 1965), *Yajū no seishun* is a contradictory text that attempts in part a serious and purposeful reformulation of genre. Both American and Japanese hard-boiled fiction is radically retooled, in form and ideology, for a new era. In addition, Suzuki has said that when he started at Shōchiku in 1948 he was ignorant of even such important American filmmakers as Huston.¹¹ This is a sly acknowledgment that by the time Suzuki had become a "mature" director, he had seen and learned from such films as Huston's *Maltese Falcon* (1941) and Dassin's *Night and the City*, which, initially for the French, had become key representatives of the critical discourse of *film noir*.¹² Although unaware of these discourses or even the term *film noir*, Suzuki's film is a direct engagement with these American predecessors. Even as it follows many other thrillers in lifting the "servant of two masters" narrative pattern that was made instantly canonical by Kurosawa's *Yōjinbo*, *Yajū no seishun* (1963) is also recognizable as a revisionist variation on *The Maltese Falcon*.

Is it too late to insert Suzuki and the Japanese hard-boiled film into the contested, but ever-expansive, category of *film noir* (as Roberto Cueto has attempted to do)?¹³ Certainly, many critics would question the usefulness of doing so. On the other hand, there is a certain inadequacy to the Hollywood and Eurocentric focus of *film noir* criticism, then as now, which ought to be addressed. Noguchi had been making urban crime thrillers such as *Ore no kenjū wa subayai* (1954) during the heyday of American *noir*, while Suzuki was making variations on these thrillers, with a psychological emphasis and a low-key aesthetic, even before such critical touchstones of *noir* as *Odds Against Tomorrow* (Robert Wise, 1957) and *Murder By Contract* (Irving Lerner, 1958). The 1950s *hādo-boirudo* was historically coextensive with late American *noir*: it is not simply a *post-facto* revisionism. *Yajū no seishun*, a later and more self-conscious reflection on crime films, hypostasizes those qualities which the surrealist-influenced French critics praised in American *film noir*. As James Naremore sums up, *film noir* "was a kind of modernism in the popular cinema: it used unorthodox narration; it resisted sentiment and censorship; it reveled in the 'social fantastic' . . . [and] the ambiguity of human motives; it made commodity culture seem like a wasteland."¹⁴

Given the contested usage and delimitation of the term *film noir*, it may be preferable to categorize *Yajū no seishun* and other Nikkatsu films according to a term from contemporary Japanese discourses such as *hādo-boirudo*. But it is no less true that the greatly under-theorized hard-boiled film in Japan (which stretches from *Yoidore tenchi* in 1947) can help us extend and perhaps retool our understanding of *film noir*, as much as *noir* can help us to understand the cinematic *hādo-boirudo*. Indeed, by extending the aesthetics of American crime thrillers into new areas of color and reflexive allegory, the prescient *Yajū no seishun* compels us to revise our critical histories of *noir*. Naremore has written the following of Hollywood's *neo-noir* cycle:

Fig. 3.7. Transforming Film Noir . . . "into a kind of neo-expressionism . . . ideally suited to color and widescreens": Kawachi Tamio calmly slashes his opponent's face

> *Taxi Driver* belongs in company with several . . . productions of the decade—including the *Long Goodbye* and *Chinatown*—which were made with the nostalgic idea of film noir in mind. However, despite its allusiveness and almost scholarly self-awareness, it is neither a period movie nor a pastiche. Instead . . . it transforms . . . *film noir* into a kind of neo-expressionism that is ideally suited to color and widescreens.[15]

Has not Suzuki's brutal yet "self-aware" film, composed in NikkatsuScope with bold primary colors and "neither a period recreation nor pastiche," anticipated by more than a decade the revisionism for which Scorsese, Schrader, and Polanski have been so widely celebrated? Rather like Altman's belated *Long Goodbye* (1973), one may consider *Yajū no seishun* a sort of "nostalgic rejection" of American *noir* (and its Japanese contemporaries), a conclusion that the *noir* aesthetic is inadequate to "post-postwar" social representation and must be replaced by a newer, freer mode of cinematic presentation. But what form would this take?

Information Networks and the "Big Lie"

The motif of (mis)information that dominates the first three sequences of *Yajū no seishun* provides a concrete example of its revision and adaptation of American *noir* to the contemporary cityscapes of Tokyo. Like late *noir* films such as *Kiss Me Deadly* (1955) and Suzuki's own *Kagenaki koe* (1958), *Yajū no seishun* raises questions about the social effects of infor-

Fig. 3.8. The (Mis)Information Society: Mizuno (Shishido) continually directed to the "wrong number"

mation technologies. Both gangsters and police operate hidden telephone networks, tape recorders, microphones, and one-way mirrors (the latter an obvious precursor to video surveillance). None of this applied technology seems able to clear up the misrecognition that bedevils a deceitful urban milieu which seems to be going wildly off track. Several cop killers are never found out by the law, while the ex-detective Mizuno Jō (Shishido) is able to hide his identity from the two *yakuza* factions, in a bewildering game of feint and double-feint, just long enough to destroy them both. Jō seeks the hidden secrets of the Nomoto operation which lie at the end of a mysterious telephone number. But the telephone keeps *misdirecting* him, along with the viewer, even to the point where the investigation structure of the plot itself gets lost in a bewildering accumulation of sub-plots and incidents.

The gangsters themselves are unable to *recognize* Jō as being any different from themselves. This leads to their downfall, for when it comes to the extraction and misdirection of information, Jō outclasses them all. He seduces (more accurately, counter-seduces) Nomoto's wife for information, coerces secrets out of his friends, and finally catches the murderer by means of a tape recorder which dominates the mise-en-scène of the film's final sequence. These activities seem to relate him to the criminals, not simply on account of his callous brutality but in his complicit exploitation of networks and technologies of power. This is highly reminiscent of Aldrich's evolution of *film noir*, *Kiss Me Deadly*, in which detective Mike Hammer is not so much a lone wolf as a key strategist in a great electronic network that grants anonymity to the clever. J.P. Telotte observes that this flawed protagonist is a failure at personal communication because, for Hammer, communication has been reduced to "information. . . . a thing or commodity to be extracted" from unwilling subjects, rather than a natural, collaborative process.[16] Conventional speech acts involve mutuality, a sequenced exchange of the roles of speaker and listener, whereas recording technologies either distance and disembody the poles of communication, or render speech unidirectional (e.g., the tape recorder). Mizuno similarly arrests and reifies the communication process as he approaches it through deception or, worse, interrogation. As a cop, Mizuno once "questioned" a suspect and "knocked him badly, so badly he couldn't talk." Utilizing "righteous" violence in the search for the killer of his partner and surrogate father, Jō would like to view himself as an upholder of masculine virtues in contradistinction to postwar mores embodied by a ruthless gang of women, sadomasochists, and homosexuals who exploit desire. But Jō, like the cops and *yakuza*, deals in the business of domination, imposing repression so fanatically that it becomes *annihilation*, and therefore self-defeating: the subject can no longer speak, and Mizuno learns, and gains, nothing.

Mizuno is not just a liar; he is complicit in "the big lie" that, for Suzuki establishes a continuity between prewar authoritarian censorship and post-war capitalism's regime of the commodity. Unknowingly, Jō participates in a consumer society's fragmentation and consequent domination of subjectivity. This may be inevitable, for how can one escape the literal "mechanisms" by which society now operates? But by linking Jō's romantic defense of older values (so often a posture of Japan's pro-corporate Liberal Democratic Party) to domination, deception, and technocracy, the film threatens to overturn what the independent "lone-wolf" detective of hard-boiled fiction is presumed to stand for.

Electronic technologies had an urgent resonance in 1960s Japan. For thoughtful observers, they could function as dystopian metaphors for a society that was "misdirected," increasingly reliant on information networks and surveillance for the maintenance of power. Marilyn Ivy writes that the 1960s "witnessed the first coherent policy studies of the 'information society' (*jōhō shakai*) in which government . . . and think tanks outlined their plans for the coming shift towards information industries—computers, robotics, new media networks, automated production systems."[17] How much of this shift Suzuki could have understood is questionable, but he would have been sensitive to the fact that Tokyo Tower (as prominently seen in *Tokyo nagaremono*) was initially planned as an electronic transmitter even as it announced the economic ascendency of Japan within the international marketplace, in part due to the success of companies like Sony. Suzuki's films consistently magnify the suspicion that excess amongst the consumer generation (the hysterical teenagers of the film's second sequence) benefits Japan's patriarchal institutions, which, through organized collusion between bureaucracy, monopoly corporations, and *yakuza*, are thus able to mass produce both the objects and, to a great extent, the subjects of desire. Nikkatsu's mostly escapist entertainments, which gave rise to and advertised pop records, gossip magazines, and the nation's biggest celebrities, were hardly irrelevant to this transformation; while Tōei's *ninkyō* pictures, financially backed by the *yakuza* themselves, were downright suspect.[18] Thus *Yajū no seishun*, by adapting the American *noir* motif of misdirected communication, advances a contemporary critique while demonstrating the answer to the question proposed above: the need to replace the aesthetics of hard-boiled thrillers with a form that was both more direct and more reflexive; which could represent and even criticize a media society by considering the cinematic process itself.

Masculinity in Crisis

In the second sequence of the film, we glimpse a young and frivolous *chinpira* (punk), a representative of aggressive masculinity at a specific post-war moment: the early 1960s. This *taiyōzoku* character gets kicked in the head by Mizuno, whose unsympathetic (if humorously outrageous) character is a fragile avatar of the reactionary imagination, an unstable middle-aged fantasy of stoic masculinity able to contain the *imagined* causes of post-war social anxiety and urban malaise: sexually liberated women, open homosexuality, wild teenagers. *Yajū no seishun*, however, holds the fantasy at a critical distance.

More than forty minutes of the running time elapses before we learn that he is an ex-cop who has joined the *yakuza* to discover the murderer of his ex-partner. This narrational strategy inhibits the all-too-easy process of empathetic identification as it refuses to contextualize the motives of a protagonist who bullies women and wipes a bloody shoe on a teenager's chest. With Mizuno's past as an ex-detective withheld from us, the cinema's conventional "hero morality" cannot bridge this empathetic gap. Shishido's beating of the teenager is filmed in a detached, extreme long shot followed by "grotesque" camera angles that obscure our view of the situation while heightening the brutality of his actions.[19] This mise-en-scène, which contains not a single POV shot, hinders the triple identification of viewer = camera = male pro-

Fig. 3.9. A Female Erotic Gaze: Mrs. Nomoto appreciates the wild Mizuno as he enters and beats up her underlings

tagonist,[20] denying the viewer the impression of mastery over the visual and narrative content of the film which, for many film theorists of the 1970s, was the precondition for identification and ideological alignment with characters. Even if we turn to an alternate, cognitive theory of identification, such as that of Murray D. Smith,[21] the inability to identify with Mizuno's context, thoughts, and often his feelings, is crucial to understanding the film's disposition toward a masculinity that erupts into gendered violence.

Consider the central example of the cabaret/mirror scene in which Mizuno meets Mrs. Nomoto. Cabaret seems essential to the world of *film noir*: in *Gilda* (1946), *Du Rififi chez les hommes* (Dassin, 1955) and *Rajo to kenjū*, the nightclub scenes depend, in more or less the way that Mulvey has proposed, on identification with the hero and his POV in order to establish the erotic gaze at the female performer, initiating a play of gazes and aligning his erotic desire with the pleasure of the viewer. In Mulvey's view, this familiar ploy normalizes not only voyeurism, but a hierarchy of social relations. But in this cabaret scene presented by Suzuki, Mizuno is seen only in long shot as he carouses with various women, with again no usage of POV. When the camera cuts from the cabaret set to the gangster headquarters behind the one-way mirror, it is a woman, the powerful Mrs. Nomoto (Kazuki Minako), who is the voyeur behind the mirror, gazing at Mizuno and at the entire cabaret spectacle as if controlling it. The scene takes place in silence, but silence is not, here, equated with submissiveness, but with authority and mastery of vision. The scene in fact contains several instances of Mrs. Nomoto's frankly erotic gaze (Fig. 3.9), but Mizuno, for his part, makes eye contact with no one; the male gaze is never initiated.

Fig. 3.10. No Return: the male protagonist does not have a close-up, or initiate a returning gaze

Mizuno compliments Mrs. Nomoto's beauty without looking at her. When their eyes do meet, moments later, it is an angle at which Mizuno's countenance faces away from the viewer. We must rely on Mrs. Nomoto's visible gaze as an acknowledgment of whatever has passed between them. The camera refuses to establish this sexual attraction *via* the male POV. Although there are notable exceptions to this pattern as the film progresses (a scene of strategic seduction, for example), the film as a whole does not *authorize* the male gaze as a matter of course, but rather, selectively deploys it. The POV of Mizuno as *an investigator* is frequently a surrogate for the audience's own (futile) quest to *make sense* of this bizarre narrative.

When Mizuno is revealed to be an ex-cop, one might argue that authority and empathetic appeal is being restored to the male protagonist. Only minutes later, however, Mizuno reacts with a very naked and hysterical agony when Boss Nomoto perforates his fingernail. In *ninkyō yakuza* films, the protagonist endures torture with stoic endurance. Not so here. The fantasy of Mizuno's heroic omnipotence is quickly at an end: from this point, the narrative and character unwind into a violent chaos as Mizuno tries and fails to control the fictive scenario of the gang war that he has created, even to the point of fatally shooting his only friend, Minami (the versatile Esumi Eimei), in the instant after Minami has loyally saved Mizuno's life. A supreme irony caps all of this chaos when Mizuno, a seducer and deceiver, finds that he himself has been manipulated, all along, by a woman. Suzuki presents not the fantasy of male control, but its breakdown and implosion in an excess of wild brutality. Unlike Chan-

Fig. 3.11. Modernity as Fetish: the Nomoto operation characterized by gaudy colors, ostentatious or eroticized objects of modern art, surfaces as smooth and polished as Nomoto's fancy throwing knives

dler's Philip Marlowe, or Noguchi's hard-boiled heroes, the pent-up, anxious Mizuno is too deeply divided to represent any unified construct of values. Since he has put his former partner and his wife on a pedestal as idealized parents, the film's emphasis is not on man's social or psychological maturity, but on the titular "youth" (*seishun*) of someone (Mizuno?) or something (society?) that has degraded what it means to be human to the level of the bestial. Mizuno's own unprofessional sadism, moreover, is mirrored by that of the Nomoto brothers, who seem to act out his impulses towards violence against women. Shishido, who has physical power but little mental discipline, is a definitively "post-war" hero of uncertainty, a mirror of the very identity crisis that moved Japanese audiences of all persuasions to take refuge in the stoic heroism of Tsuruta Kōji or Takakura Ken, the emerging star of Tōei's *ninkyō eiga*.[22] This cultural uprooting, which even at the time was labelled in the popular press as "The Age of Neurosis" (*noirōse jidai*),[23] was the result of a transition, in fifteen short years, from the transcendental patriarchal values of the imperial *kokutai* to foreign occupation, disillusionment, and the material values of a market-driven culture. If Takakura's rock-hard persona is an escape from that reality, surely Shishido represents the failure of escape.

Too young to have experienced the war, Mizuno lacks perspective in confronting the post-war crisis of values. Belonging to the famous "generation without fathers," Mizuno's condition is haunted by the post-war vacuum of values and identity, a "troubled character of self-denial" clinging desperately to mythic values of male professionalism.[24] Like Mizuno, the Nomoto brothers are haunted by their deceased mother, who was a *yōpan* (a prostitute working amongst American soldiers), and as a result are pathologically anxious about their own masculinity. They operate a sleek, modernized gangster operation, devoid of traditional *yakuza* iconography and portrayed in highly fetishistic visual terms. This is contrasted with the *yakuza* faction of Onodera (Shin Kinzō),[25] whose Asakusa-based gang sports tattoos and traditional robes. Onodera's death, in what is essentially a *kamikaze* attack with a bomb-laden car, is a parodic symbol of the war experience and the death of Old Japan. The film represents both the pre- and post-war generations as symbolically "impotent," with Jō anxiously stranded in between.

Violence and the Containment of the Feminine

Mizuno's strongest adversaries prove to be two women on the wrong side of the law: Mrs. Nomoto and Mrs. Takeshita (Watanabe Misako), wife of the slain policeman and Nomoto's mysterious "7th Mistress," who is secretly in charge of the entire operation. As the second half of the narrative descends into frenetic chaos, itself resembling masculinity in crisis, the male characters struggle to contain this feminine power. This results in two unforgettable scenes of gendered violence. In the first, Boss Nomoto whips his scheming wife on a velvet red carpet, then throws her into a tuft of reeds in the backyard; they have sex. The violence has a ludic aspect: when his subordinates try to leave the room the excited Nomoto tells them to "stand there and shut up." One gangster indicates that he has seen this kind of exhibition before. While they make love on the reeds, a cloud of dust with an unnatural yellow color wafts over them in one of Suzuki's most interesting non-diegetic effects up to that time.

The masculine anxiety underlying the violence is not at all covert, while the detective hero is problematically implicated in the scene not as a "phallic agent" but as fascinated voyeur. If the sequence distresses us with the sadism of a powerful exploiter, it is also attuned to the subversive political provocations of extreme and "deviant" sexuality—just like the surrealists and like Suzuki's younger contemporary Wakamatsu Koji, who began making outrageous, politicized sex films in 1963.[26] As with these auteurs and those of later Nikkatsu *roman poruno*, it is certainly possible to construct a reading of *Yajū no seishun* that is thoroughly misogynist.[27] Whether one subscribes to such an interpretation may depend on whether one views the scene as a form of rape or as the sadomasochistic game of a bored, entitled couple in violation of sexual propriety. A comparison with

Fig. 3.12. Gendered Violence in a Non-Diegetic Yellow Dust Cloud

a very similar sequence in *Tantei jimusho 2-3* lends credence to the latter. But Suzuki is certainly working within a set of broadly exploitative hard-boiled conventions. As Chandler's Marlowe states, economically, "women make me sick."[28] Suzuki's film questions hard-boiled ethics, in particular the detective himself as a defender of a pragmatic and communal morality. But, equally, it does not negate them unambiguously. Of all directorial bodies of work, that of Suzuki seems to me to most consistently refuse the possibility of any constructive (or comforting) "message" to his films.[29] What Suzuki said, in 1972, about sentimentalism applies, also, to ideological manipulation: ". . . a thing that pulls you along like that is no good. . . . Because you mustn't 'drag' [the viewer]."[30] Because any attempt to discover the film's intentions and dispositions must take into account not only the studio-mandated script but visual interpolations like the unexplained yellow dust cloud, viewers are free to interpret such metaphors in different ways according to their perspective, or simply to see reflected those values (including radical values) that they have brought with them to the cinema. *Yajū no seishun* and descendants take the "democratic" neutrality of popular studio cinema to a new extreme in which inherent narrative structures of moral and political judgement, left or right, seem no longer to have any place.

The visual subtext of the film and its unsympathetic protagonist counter what might in other hands be a justification of gendered violence through an appeal to law and order (e.g., the hard-boiled tradition in some manifestations) or a deeper appeal to mythic structures of the sacrifice of women-as-symbol.[31] When Jō discovers that Mrs. Takeshita is the power behind the throne, manipulating Nomoto and murdering her husband

Fig. 3.13. The Hooded Eyes of the Vigilante (1)

and a young dancer, his response to the discovery is unexpectedly horrific. With his signature deceit, he coerces Mrs. Takeshita into denouncing Nomoto while the younger Nomoto brother, Hideo (Kawachi Tamio), is listening. She calls Nomoto's mother "a whore who specialized in black men," enraging the unbalanced Hideo. Jō locks the two of them together in Mrs. Takeshita's parlor room, while Hideo, acting out his childhood horror of female sexuality, slashes Mrs. Takeshita's face with a razor blade. This act of violence occurs off-screen while Jō stands outside the door with a look of disbelief on his face, marveling at his own capacity for cruelty. Finally, he reveals that he has recorded everything on a tape recorder, which he plays over the phone for the police.

The interior lighting (like the yellow dust) gives the sequence a dreamlike quality. Mrs. Takeshita's apartment is excessively dark, with large areas of deep shadow, seemingly from a non-diegetic source, cast on the walls. Violence in Suzuki is almost never treated as realism, but is marked out by the mise-en-scène as a kind of ideological fantasy. While Jō listens to the violence behind the door, Nagatsuka and Onishi Mitsu's exquisite lighting creates a harsh, jagged shadow over his eyes.

This may be a gesture towards Ford's *The Searchers*, which Suzuki considered to be the greatest American "action film."[32] At one point in that film, John Wayne's Ethan Edwards gazes at a white woman who has been driven mad by culture shock. After becoming fully integrated into Comanche society, she has been unwillingly recaptured by white soldiers. As Ethan looks at her, his hat creates a sinister band of shadow that appears across his violent eyes.

Fig. 3.14. The Hooded Eyes of the Vigilante (2): note the similarity of composition, including the bisected background

The gesture betrays Ethan's obsession with "miscegenation," an obsession so strong that he is willing to kill his own niece because she has become the wife of a Comanche. Ethan will do anything to maintain a "code" or a set of borders (racial, familial, and concerning legitimate/illegitimate violence) that he feels is threatened, perhaps because it is these very borders that allows a vigilante like Ethan to regard his actions as justified vis-à-vis his "Othered" enemies.[33]

It seems to be this general point at play in *Yajū no seishun*—an "adults-only" film by design—with a director who reflexively contemplates borders and transgressions in cinematic representation.[34] In the Japanese post-war context, the borders in question pertain, mainly, to the patriarchal regulation of sexual roles. Jō has turned down the chance to kill Nomoto and his actions will allow Hideo to escape scot-free; Mrs. Takeshita is the sole object of "punishment." Why not simply turn her into the police? Siding, instead, with Hideo the pimp, Jō acts desperately to contain the emasculating social and sexual power of The Woman. Mrs. Takeshita had represented Jō's last contact with any social/moral "legitimacy." When she crosses from "mother" figure, the supposed embodiment of civilization, to "whore," his violent reaction betrays a desperation to retain his own faltering identity as a "decent" member of the middle class in opposition to the underclass of gangsters and "deviants" that surrounds him. Part of this reactionary fantasy is the legacy of the "loyal wife, wise mother" (*ryōsai kenbo*) social code established by the Meiji patriarchal order and in force until the end of the war. Although *ryōsai kenbo* was technically outlawed by the post-war government as an unwelcome phrase from the past, nevertheless, as Kathleen Uno describes, state education policies of the paternalistic Liberal Democratic Party encouraged the first two post-war generations of women to think of themselves primarily as "homebound wives and mothers."[35] In context, the concept of middle class decency that Jō inflicts on his "mother" connotes not obedience to the law as such, which is the legitimate function of the police, but to the patriarchal Law of the Father. Though he may be avenging the murder of a good man and an innocent girl, Jō's excessive, gendered solution defends patriarchy against the effrontery of a woman who is simultaneously a housewife, a mistress, and a powerful criminal.[36]

There is perhaps a satirical point being made here about women in the "planned society" of post-war Japan. Market capitalism had a hand in proposing new forms of gender regulation, for in addition to being subject to new social mores concerning role prescription and household domestication, women were *also* the principal target of advertising. Mrs. Takeshita's *noirish* and lonely house contains, incongruously, all the fashionable household goods of the late 1950s: electric oven and range, electric rice cooker, and kettle. As Marilyn Ivy describes:

> Electrical appliances fueled the consumer revolution. . . . they became the objects of desire, the signs of middle class inclusion, the unparalleled commodity fetishes. . . . Electric appliance manufacturers were the leading advertisers. . . . Appliances standardized the image of the average household and what the housewife should possess. . . . Some view this process as one of homogenization, an elimination of differences as nuclear familial units constructed themselves as micro-utopias sealed off from external conflict.[37]

The fact that these metaphors of socio-economic change have been grafted to a hard-boiled scenario of vigilante detectives and *femmes fatales* is part of the revisionist genius of *Yajū no seishun*, but is also a cause of its fundamental ideological ambiguity. The threat to the social order presented by the *femme fatale* could sometimes overwhelm the intentions of her male creators, who often crudely deployed the woman-as-symbol in a "gendered opposition to establishment culture."[38] As Janey Place writes, "the primary crime that the 'liberated' woman is guilty of is refusing to be defined in such a way, and this refusal can be perversely seen (in art, or in life) as an attack on man's very existence."[39] Mrs. Takeshita has literally mounted an attack by murdering her husband. Moreover, whereas Sylvia Harvey asserts that figures such as the prostitute in American *film noir* actually "reconfirm the primacy of monogamy,"[40] Mrs. Takeshita is far more subversive since, as Nomoto's "7th Mistress," she dominates a perverse crime family in which adultery supersedes monogamy as the structuring foundation. She represents a kind of grotesque inversion of the post-war Japanese state's "valorization of the conjugal couple and the nuclear household."[41] Since she has arranged, in service of a criminal plot, a childless marriage to the police detective, first as a front for adultery, then in order to murder him and live comfortably alone in an appliance-filled house, her plan is akin to a staged satire of post-war domestic womanhood, a collection of conformist signifiers (husband, appliances) re-purposed in the service of her own eroticized exercise of power. Once discovered, her manipulation of domestic iconography presents, like adultery itself, a blatant challenge to patriarchy.

If nothing else, the film resembles the work of Suzuki's contemporary Harold Pinter in demonstrating that social control *is* violence, and Mizuno, as the avenger of the middle class, reasserts that control with an excessive force far beyond that which he had applied as a police detective. But there is a crucial difference: rather than wielding the knife himself, the ever-manipulative Mizuno acts as an orchestrator of events through the use of technology (the hand-held tape recorder), thus potentially redeeming his vigilante status through alignment with the oligarchic planners of the "Information Society." Utilizing the mastery of information that Nomoto's operation aspired to, will Mizuno remain a vigilante, or has he nailed himself to the cross of power? Mizuno's own ambivalent expression seems to recognize that the price of success in this milieu is high: dehumanization.

Because it dwells on the excessive violence of patriarchy when that regime is threatened, the film may be seen as a provocation of gender norms. On the other hand, it may be that Suzuki's images of misogynistic violence communicate the same antipathy towards a supposedly "feminine" mass culture that high modernism and hard-boiled fiction (its disreputable cousin) had shown. Is Mrs. Takeshita being punished by the film itself through the agency of Mizuno—the director of this climactic scenario—or is she, a powerful challenger, simply the final victim of "the beast"?

Fig. 3.15. The Face of Dehumanization? Mizuno's own revulsion toward the vigilante "justice" he inflicts on a mother figure

Aesthetic Departures; or, the Polysemy of Eros

The Lady in the Mirror/Window/Screen

The third sequence of *Yajū no seishun*—the mirror sequence—problematizes the violence of its predecessor through a variety of effects that seem designed to put a distance between the spectator and their involvement or investment in the narrative, the spectacle, or both. We might therefore call them "distantiation effects" and in this sequence they appear in the form of partitioned windows and the manipulation of sound. The erotic spectacle of a semi-nude dancer in this sequence is mediated and rendered abstract when viewed through a vast one-way mirror. This seems to be a key sequence not just for the film itself, but for the entirety of Suzuki's self-reflexive cinema practice, especially in this fertile "middle period" of his career, from 1963-1967. We need to grapple with three facets of this practice that are brought to light, so to speak, by the allegorical presence of this mirror/screen: the representation of voyeurism and the body, the use of metaphor, and the polysemic nature of cinematic spectacle. The mirror/screen, especially in its function of linking similar gestures from previous Suzuki films that relate voyeurism to the proliferation of screens, announces to us that Suzuki is continuously pursuing a quintessentially self-reflexive kind of cinema. But it also informs us that reflexivity in his films appears in the form of a question, not an assertion. The question finds its center in the nature of cinematic spectacle, its relation to viewers, and its definitively erotic aspects. Though a primarily negative thinker,

Fig. 3.16. Erotic Spectacle as Hyperbolic Fetishism: the Cabaret Feather-Dancer as Budding Flower (*Yajū no seishun*)

Suzuki manages here to problematize cinematic spectacle and its commercial exploitation without endorsing some sort of purely negative or anti-erotic form of "unpleasurable" anti-cinema.

The erotic objectification of the body is a constant throughout the sequence, which begins with Mizuno pouring a bucket of ice down a hostess's dress. But this outrageous act is viewed in extreme long shot, with the camera stationed behind the one-way mirror where Mrs. Nomoto watches with voyeuristic intensity. As Mizuno is shuffled off-screen by the bouncers, the camera pans to follow him and then abruptly stops, in order to frame an empty area of the cabaret illuminated by only a small lamp. A semi-nude dancer holding gigantic purple feathers then rises up from the floor beneath the screen and unfolds the feathers like the blossoming of a flower.

As viewed from behind the soundproof HQ, this action occurs in complete silence. Although the image is highly fetishistic, there is a hyperbole to the gaudy staging which is reminiscent of the just-plain-silly "Christmas cabaret" in *Tantei jimusho 2-3*, which satirizes the libidinal consumerism of the 1960s by dressing a dozen semi-nude dancing girls as Santa's elves.

Furthermore, as the dancer turns to begin her routine, the camera does an intrusive flash-pan back to the HQ. Except for one brief (and strangely out of place) cutaway to the feather dancer from *within* the cabaret, the dancer remains in the extreme background, behind the one way mirror, for the rest of this lengthy scene in the HQ. She makes a jarring contrast to the violence taking place nearby, while the luxurious purple of the cabaret is offset by the sterile off-white décor of the HQ. Moreover, the filmmak-

Fig. 3.17. Erotic Spectacle as Satire: Christmas and Libidinal Consumerism (*Tantei jimusho 2-3: Kutabare akutō-domo / Detective Bureau 2-3: Go to Hell Bastards!*)

ers have chosen to partition the one-way mirror with black-lined window panes that divide it into smaller panels, thus appearing to divide the dancer's body among the panels. (Among other things, this suggests that the one-way mirror is in production terms simply a rear-screen projection, meaning that it is merely a narrative construct, an illusion of the film's diegesis.) In one long shot, the black band of the window frame exactly covers the dancer's breasts.

This strategy of representation is certainly conducive of a far different kind of erotic sensibility than that which would be conjured by multiple close shots and partial views of the strip artist's body from *inside* the cabaret.[42] While we are not entitled to say that the eccentric staging (deep background, partitioning, primary colors) *negates* the eroticism of the dancer's image, it certainly does transform the specular relations between the viewer and the eroticized body. Perhaps the key to the seminude dancer is her inaccessibility: her alluring performance is triply distantiated from us—first by the separation of the screen, secondly by the fact that she recedes into the far background, and thirdly by the interposed sections of the mirror that partition her. Instead, Suzuki's film emphasizes the kind of fetishism associated with distance, denial, and the spectacular, theatrical deployment of light, color, costume. It positions the eroticized body as a portion of a larger composition, moreover a composition which emphasizes not one unified effect, but constantly subdivides the frame to create prominent visual contrasts.

Thus emphasis is on the heterogeneous composition, the variegated

The Mirror / 97

Fig. 3.18. Mediated: the erotic dancer partitioned by the mirror-screen (*Yajū no seishun*)

Fig. 3.19. Extreme Visual Contrast (1): Shallowness and Depth (the small HQ is represented in multiplanar depth while the large, deep cabaret space appears flattened and two-dimensional)

spectacle of multiple attractions taken as a whole,[43] rather than inviting the viewer to extract the erotic female body from out of it. Since the mediation of the mirror-screen is a virtual double for what the movie camera is doing, *Yajū no seishun* refuses to short-circuit the viewer's awareness of the camera's mediation of the image and, in doing so, reminds the spectator that *all* cinematic eroticism is so mediated and lacks a third dimension.[44] In this sense the mirror corresponds to the mediated sounds and voices of information technology, but there is a larger cinematic reflection at work, suggesting that the eroticism of the cinematic body is different in kind and quality from eroticism-in-the-world, and not simply a sec-

Fig. 3.20. Extreme Visual Contrast (2): The Bisected Frame: contrast the "decadent" mise-en-scène of the cabaret with the sterile office

ondhand or illegitimate reflection. This is a key point, because the latter, basically platonic idea of the image as a degraded reflection of "the real" tends to be the default assumption of both cinema spectators and a great many theorists.

The mirror scene therefore allegorizes but does not quite clarify the director's practice as regards the sexual politics of the image. Certainly it clarifies that his practice *and* politics are inseparable from and perhaps determined by Suzuki's reflexive exploration of what cinema *is*.

From Allegory to Metaphor: Suzuki's Reflexive Practice

In art criticism generally, reflexive aesthetics have often been polemically opposed to realism. That is to say, they have been opposed to conventional aesthetic practices that have presented themselves as "realist" at certain periods in art history.[45] This simple opposition may be hard to sustain throughout the broad canvas of film history, especially if one takes the position, as did Christian Metz in his later work, that *all* narrative films must be regarded as being, by their nature, self-reflexive to a greater or lesser degree.[46] But if all cinematic address is reflexive, how do we critically estimate the formal differences (and the ideological differences they enable) between ordinary Nikkatsu or Hollywood program pictures and the neo-modernist self-consciousness of Antonioni, Godard, and Ōshima? Or, for that matter, Shinoda's formally complex, hard-boiled masterpiece *Kawaita hana* (1964)? It is undeniable that something like an opposition between realism and reflexivity, or perhaps a high degree of tension between the two, is evident in the case of films like *Yajū no seishun* and its relation to the conventional, "consensual" realism of the studio cinema.

It is easy to see why this tension, however one interprets the critical intention behind it, may be regarded as a definitive feature of Suzuki's practice (as well as the source of the inevitable, unbridgeable impasse between himself and Nikkatsu's management with their unproblematic "house style"). The mirror scene witnesses an opening out, perhaps a bold declaration, of a tendency which had its roots in his earlier hard-boiled films.

Kemono no nemuri/Sleep of the Beast (1960), in particular, is the most conventional of Suzuki's darker, more sober thrillers; it is chiefly memorable for its all too brief, but universally relatable "bourgeois tragedy" of a middle-aged, laid off *sarariman* (Ashida Shinsuke) who turns to crime only to find that he cannot "catch a break" either in the underworld or in the workaday world. Unlike *Yajū no seishun*, the film's investigation structure, which only gradually reveals Ashida's guilt, is a distraction to its essential strength. However, the film contains one extended sequence involving a "screen" of sorts that raises it, as an original exercise in narration, above virtually anything the director had done to that point. Tom Vick, in his handsome art-style book on Suzuki, justifiably highlights this scene. In a standard medium shot, the film's two protagonists ask the bar girl Akemi (Chishiro Yūko) to recount her memories of the mysteriously disappeared *sarariman*. As she responds at length, the camera moves in to isolate her, then quickly moves to reframe her at the extreme right-of-screen while the background behind her goes completely black. The background—taking up the entire frame—is then replaced with a superimposed image of the *sarariman*'s recent past and his encounter with Akemi. These background images transpire in complete silence, with Akemi now seen in the background "story" as well as in the right foreground, where the latter, "present" version of herself has become lightly translucent (Fig 3.21). Akemi recounts her memories, frequently turning her head over shoulder to "look" at the image as if narrating the silent footage.

None of the film's viewers had ever seen such a boldly artificial narrational device before in the post-war cinema, but anyone over 30 would have associated Akemi's narration with the famous *benshi*, the onstage performers who, for decades, explained and narrated Japanese silent films in front of, and to the side of, the cinema screen. So the association between Akemi's "memory-screen" and the cinema screen is inevitable, and has (as we shall see) similar metaphoric and reflexive connotations to the cabaret mirror/screen in *Yajū no seishun*. Arguably, Suzuki innovated an even bolder *benshi*-like narrative device in *Tantei jimusho 2-3* by getting

Fig. 3.21. The Memory Screen: viewing herself and others onscreen, Akemi narrates, *benshi*-like, her own life (*Kemono no nemuri* / *Sleep of the Beast*)

rid of the presence of screens altogether. Instead, the picture uses a cabaret performer to sing a song about a contest between a rabbit and an old fox that encapsulates, allegorically, exactly what is going on in the elaborate suspense plot of the film at that point: a series of complex, life-and-death double-crosses between Shishido's protagonist and his devious *yakuza* bosses. But let us put this aside in order to pursue the present topic of the allegorical links between cinema screens and the "secondary" screens within Suzuki's films.

In *Yajū no seishun* and *Kemono no nemuri*, the unexpected gestures involving screens appear as the sort of disharmonious and (briefly) alienating spectacle that Robert Stam, citing Benjamin, compares to the "sudden freezing of a domestic quarrel when a stranger enters the room.... The interruption has made the condition strange." Mizuno's obnoxious behavior and the dancer's routine are similarly estranged on the other side of the mirror-screen. Such self-conscious deployments of disruptive spectacle are linked by Stam to the long history of parodic, subversive lower-class entertainments that Bakhtin famously categorized as the *carnivalesque*. But Stam adds that "with the advent of modernism, discontinuity becomes programmatic and rather aggressive. Interruption pre-empts spectacle; in fact it *becomes* the spectacle." In *Yajū no seishun*, the effect may not be quite so aggressive as that, but it is true that the "interrupted" compositions of the mirror-screen do indeed "become" the spectacle. The mirror-screen's mediation of the "proximity" of the (erotic) objects of view places the viewer in a unique position to appreciate the indirectness of all cinematic representation. If the realist image of the classical studio cinema is essentially an attempt to disavow that fact, as I believe it is, then Suzuki's film, by its calculated difference, negates both the myth and the political valence of the so-called "direct" photographic representation of the cinematic image.

By 1963, a challenge to the conventions of realist melodrama was already well under way through the Brechtian cinema of Ōshima. Part of Suzuki's enduring value as a Japanese filmmaker is that his films deployed such a challenge in the form of a playful, ironic spectacle reminiscent of the theatrical modernism of a Beckett or a Pinter: all three of them were influenced by their respective national traditions of popular music hall or "vaudeville" entertainment. A humorous spirit of subversion was notably lacking in the dead serious, anti-ludic modernism of the early 1960s as represented by Ōshima, Yoshida, Wakamatsu, and epitomized by Hijikata Tatsumi's lugubrious theatrical *butoh*.

But Suzuki's allegory of the mirror offers more than simply a playful disruption of realism: it amounts to a meditation on cinematic signification, or symbolic presentation, itself. Speaking to Isoda and Todoroki, Suzuki vehemently denied attempting to attach a certain fixed meaning or message to the device of the mirror-screen:

> SUZUKI: But what about a generally boring storyline? It's boring, so one tries to revise it—because Nikkatsu films were easy to understand. So, with an ordinary cabaret, I'm thinking 'What should we do here?' . . . and [because of my] crossing through the mirror, everyone thinks, 'Wasn't there some meaning in doing this?', *and that isn't right.* . . . If one says . . . 'How about this?', *it's not a matter of trying to say something.*
>
> ISODA/TODOROKI: Now, on the contrary, in that portion [of the film] everyone is uncertain.
>
> SUZUKI: Yes . . .
>
> ISODA/TODOROKI: [It] is richly fruitful . . . fit for appreciation any number of times.[47]

One notes the questioning, exploratory rhetoric with which Suzuki approaches *his own* filmmaking choices, even though those choices required a firm, precise hand to capture them on film. Suzuki claims that he decides on his camera set-ups (and therefore many of his expressive effects) on the morning of the shoot, then immediately puts them into practice.[48] He claims not to make fixed decisions beforehand about color and mise-enscène. We need not take everything that Suzuki says at face value, but certainly the time constraints and urgency of B-movie filmmaking give credence to his methods, since whatever exploratory images his team creates cannot fundamentally be altered after the fact, even in editing.

Suzuki's denial of message-making may be a more revealing approach to the allegory of the mirror than any other. In a loosely surrealist approach,[49] he seems to use the limitations of filmmaking in order to *prevent* himself from creating a self-consciously "interpreted" image; that is, an image which provides its viewer with the means to make a conclusive interpretation of it. Could it be that such images, in addition to being deliberately evasive, embody a certain fear or horror of interpretation? Could they be an attack on meaning itself, that is, an attack on cinema as a vehicle of meaning, or at least, semantic meaning?

Therefore, while I have frequently described Suzuki's reflexive image practice as "allegorical," the term should be used with some reservations. It is allegorical insofar as the director invites us to consider the *significance* of what he has filmed, rather than simply to accept its existence as a matter of narration and visual phenomenology. Here I differ with Hasumi Shigehiko's treatment of Suzuki: as a constituent of a larger narrative film, the Suzuki image (*contra* Hasumi) confronts us with its own formal tensions and demands to be investigated; it is a cinema not of observation, but of intellectual relations.[50]

In its standard denotation, allegory is an *explicit* "conventional and rational"[51] correlation between something textual (or filmic) and something extra-textual that is determinate and clearly recognizable "within a particular culture,"[52] Does this sense of "allegory" apply to Suzuki's mirror/screen?

Firstly, and most obviously, the one-way mirror is closer to a cinema screen than to a standard mirror: an audience is on one side and the object of spectacle is on the other, unconscious of the voyeur but acting *as-if-to-be-seen* nonetheless.

Unlike standard allegory, the "Suzuki image" attracts associations which do not have a clear pre-existent source or ground in the culture at large. Although the images created by his team naturally stem from their cultural experiences, beliefs, and ideas, Suzuki presents this cultural baggage as an undiscrete and undifferentiated tissue, which can be rolled out indefinitely, revealing new threads as it goes. These images do not lead us to one set of pro-filmic sources or only in one direction. The mirror-screen is one of Suzuki's grand symbols, or, to propose a more specific nomenclature, a grand *open metaphor*, a richer and more precise term than "allegory" or "symbol" to describe what Suzuki is doing with his reflexive screens.

What do we mean by "metaphor" when we are speaking about the cinema? Christian Metz recognized a category of "metaphoric juxtaposition" within his *"grande syntagmatique"* of the cinema and noted that it could take both diegetic and non-diegetic forms. But he dismissed such juxtapositions as "fairly limited" and "fairly crude."[53] Trevor Whittock's *Metaphor in Film* hews closer to contemporary metaphor theory in making a strong case for the notion that *tropes*, and especially visual metaphors, are a fundamental aspect of the hermeneutic process by which we comprehend all narrative film, since the process is always a matter of being *seen as* rather than simply being *seen*.[54] Whittock draws on some neglected corners of 1960s film theory, such as Yves Laurot's provocative distinction between ordinary visual symbolism and "properly cinematic metaphor."[55] For Laurot, a symbol is something like a bank that looks like a church or somehow exhibits the properties of both a bank and a church in one place. (Noel Carroll privileged this kind of device, under the term *homospatiality*, as the crux of his clear but highly restrictive definition of cinematic metaphor.)[56] For Laurot, a metaphor is better understood by figures that *begin* with perceptual and/or formal resemblance but *proceed* through comparing what is present to what is evoked only virtually or in thought.

In the cabaret sequence, for example, we may contrast what I call the "open metaphor" of the mirror/screen with a clear, direct, or "closed" visual figure like the dancer resembling a flower (see Fig. 3.16). If cinematic metaphors exist, the latter is surely one of them, albeit of the simplest kind, in which the relationship between the dancer and the flower is based on physical resemblance and formal symmetry and is immediately comprehensible to the viewer. Effective as it is, such a device is neither disharmonious nor particularly reflexive in character. Suzuki utilizes such direct metaphors as the dancer-flower (necessarily) but does not rest with them: he shifts the focus to the contiguity of the dancer-flower with the mirror-screen, the décor, the foreground action, etc., all within the same frame. A compound metaphor such as this does not give us the means to comprehend, fully and immediately, the *grounds* of the relationship between the two or three things that are commonly called, in metaphor theory, the *source* and *target domains* of the metaphor. To put it in layman's terms, the picture does not make manifest the *reason* why it is so insistent on juxtaposing two or three things together in the viewer's mind in a relationship or interaction that is characterized by a tension between their shared resemblance and their immediately recognizable, categorical differences. In some cases, we may even be invited, or tempted, to look for a metaphorical meaning without being able to identify one of the two things (i.e., the source domain) that are being compared. This was the case with Suzuki's bizarrely colored dog in *Kutabare gurentai* (see chapter 2). Hence the necessity of an expansive term such as "open metaphor" to designate such interpretative viewing experiences. Akemi's memory of events as compared to a *benshi*-like screen presentation in *Kemono no nemuri* is a more abstract, though still comprehensible, juxtaposition of the *target* and *source* domains of a metaphor. And while the one-way mirror in *Yajū no seishun* is a part of the narrative rather than an obviously eccentric and non-diegetic device like Akemi's "memory-screen," when we consider the mirror *as a metaphor*, it is far more complex. In the compound figure of the dancer viewed through the mirror/screen, the viewer is forced to reckon all at once with a series of symbolic associations or relationships all interacting with one another: to name a few, (1) the mirror as window and the window as mirror, (2) the window as cinema frame, (3) the mirror as cinema frame, (4) the world seen directly compared to the world seen through cinema, (5) the body seen up close and from a distance, (6) the body seen in-the-world and the body in cinema, and, finally (as discussed below), (7) the female body as erotic object and the (mediated) female body as "something else." Not all of these associations are metaphoric in character, but together, they give rise to a number of different kinds of metaphor. If we consider just (2) and (3) above, the one-way mirror and the cinema-screen are brought into metaphoric juxtaposition, but only one of the two objects (the mirror) is clearly visually present in the film, whereas the other (e.g., the cinema screen) exists either in the mind of the viewer (as Laurot emphasized) or, as the case may be, outside of the film's diegesis in the movie theater in which the film is being watched. This gives just a hint of its complexity. In contrast to explicit metaphors of comparison (like Suzuki's dancer/flower), Whittock's privileging of the category of *diaphoric* metaphor to describe "the synthesis arriving from the juxtaposition of disparate elements"[57] is particularly relevant here. Just as the variegated spectacle absorbs the dancer into multiple centers of visual interest, the mirror-screen itself enables endless chains of connotation or association for the viewer, as gauged and chosen by his or her own cognitive process. Amongst and because of this polysemy of interpretation, it also functions both literally and metaphorically as the site of the erotic spectacle of the cinema.

Ethics and Erotic Spectacle: The Meaning of Non-Meaning

If Suzuki's mirror is an open metaphor, it is also a reflexive one. Like many of Suzuki's visual gestures, it leads back to the cinema or, at least, Suzuki's understanding of it. In this sense, Suzuki emerges as a quintessential self-reflexive artist. As Ricoeur defines it, "reflexion is the act of turning back upon itself by which a subject grasps in a moment of intellectual clarity and moral responsibility, the unifying principle of the operations among which it is dispersed and forgets itself as a subject."[58] To relate this definition, then, to cinematic practice—especially Ricouer's evocation of fundamental principles that compel and clarify the "moral responsibility" of the filmmaker—Suzuki turns the cinema back upon itself (the mirror-screen) to reveal, indirectly, its forgotten operations (for example, the role of the camera's mediation of events). Not only that, but Suzuki uses those revelations to define and defend a particular authorial practice at the very same moment at which that practice is constituted.

But how do we "read" a reflexive discourse about the cinema within an evasive image practice dedicated (as Suzuki assures us in his quote above) to a pervasive skepticism that includes the negation of objective meaning relations? One must remember that the mirror-screen is polysemic precisely because it does *not*, like the dancer-flower, call up a readily recognizable connection of ideas. New conceptual associations must be forged. We might consider the particularly reflexive cinematic associations that arise from the mirror-screen as just some of the many ripples caused by the splash of this image creation, yet upon which we see a distorted reflection of that creation. Suzuki negates certain kind of meanings found in representational art in order that metaphorical associations and potentialities may proliferate in all directions. We may reconsider the "allegory" of the mirror-screen, then, by asking not only what associations does it bring to mind (i.e., through metaphor), but what associations does it not; that is, what may it be thought to negate?

On the viewing side of the one-way mirror, the gangsters watch Mizuno and the cabaret in silence. Since the purpose of the mirror is to provide information, why not include dialogue and reaction? The silence recalls that of the cinematic audience, but further, it is also a refusal of communication, hence, of interpretation. The image is viewed but problematized as a text: nothing is articulated discursively. The image is an open question. This is doubly emphasized by the silence of the cabaret beyond the mirror: it will not speak for itself. What we were once privy to—the synchronized image and sound of the classical cinema—now becomes inaccessible, like the erotic dancer through the mirror; and in fact the image acquires new qualities and relations on account of its "muteness." If Suzuki is evasive of interpretation, his very gestures of evasion, like so many other aspects of his practice, depend on the negation of the conventional—the Nikkatsu cinema which Suzuki found too easy to understand. In this sense, too, the denial of "the message" and the allegory of a "differential" cinema practice are related. All of it has aesthetic and political implications (Ricoeur's "moral responsibilities"), which become more clearly defined in the mature films that follow *Yajū no seishun*.

One obvious implication is the question of who controls the voyeuristic image on one side of the one-way mirror. The dancer appears in the dark, from below the screen, like the cinema itself, in which the image of desire appears mysteriously out of nothing, at the turn of the switch, in the hands of the manipulators of mass media. It may appear that the gangsters, the unseen observers, are the controllers of this image, but like the audience, they struggle to decipher its meaning. Who is this unknown man who has appeared on the screen? They make out the cause and effect of his behavior, but cannot discern his motive or purpose, nor place his action in an explanatory (narrative) context. The gangsters are in thrall to the image despite their attempts to actively interpret it. These are images of desire both for men (the dancer) and women (Mizuno himself, the object of Mrs. Nomoto's gaze). But Suzuki's images are neither ascetic nor prurient: they do not deny cinematic pleasure, in fact channel it in certain directions; but they also recognize the potential for manipulation by the powerful. What Suzuki seems to negate is the unidirectionality of the pleasure-image, the way in which a mise-en-scène manipulates pleasure rather than allowing it to operate freely, to rove over a broad canvas of varied attractions, as we do when viewing the splendid, two-dimensional "scattered attribute" spaces of many East Asian, Buddhist, and pre-Columbian paintings before the introduction of perspective.

At this point the modernist dichotomy "that rejects naturalism in favor of reflexive, hyper-fabulatory or carnivalesque strategies" reappears.[59] Suzuki upholds the pleasures of spectatorship but subverts its directional manipulation, either opening it out onto a collage-like and carnivalesque mise-en-scène (captured in heterodox widescreen rather than close-up) or simply asserting, through his female characters, the reversibility of the gaze.

It is telling that, in *Yajū no seishun*, Suzuki's grand metaphor of the cinema (the one-way mirror) remains a diegetic metaphor: which is to say, to expand on a remark by Whittock, that the object depicted is "given a metaphoric function without in any way detracting from the probability of its appearance there."[60] The symbol of the mirror-screen appears more or less unproblematically as existing within the film's diegesis (though even in this regard, as we have seen, Suzuki cheats!). The "classical" nature of this kind of symbolism, therefore, contrasts with the non-diegetic effects that appear in the earlier program pictures (e.g., *Kutabare gurentai*), and reappear with a vengeance in the subsequent films that would mark out, for viewers, a consistent and characteristic directorial approach. Apart from its play of color and monochrome, *Yajū no seishun* remains by and large a classical film experience, perfectly aligned with Metz's theoretical preference for cinematic metaphors and reflexive "figures of thought" that arise "naturally" within the visual world that makes up and conveys the narrative content of the film.

This is not to say that audiences in April 1963 were not confronted with three sequences—the initial ten minutes of the film's narrative—that constituted the most startling, abrasive, and formally provocative opening they had seen in a commercial cinema since the early 1930s—easily surpassing stylish contemporaries like Ichikawa's *Yuki nojō henge* and Ōshima's films of the period. *Yajū no seishun* struggles magnificently, through eccentric color and figuration and narrative indirection, to break free from the limiting confines of genre and from the very paradigm—the cinema-as-mirror/screen—that it so elegantly expresses and deploys. It reminds us that Suzuki's cinema is not a straight line of stylistic progression towards a unified worldview, but a chronicle of exploration, one that pauses, regroups, asks questions, goes off on tangents. *Yajū no seishun* is not as formally disruptive as other, subsequent efforts, and its potentially radical ideological thrust may be said to conditioned, even limited, by the priority that Suzuki gives to his emerging, exploratory doctrine of the inherent ambiguity and the eroticism of spectacle. But that doctrine would become increasingly consequential, in itself, as its own radical politics of the image. Gilles Deleuze would have called *Yajū no seishun* a cinema of *mental* or *intellectual* relations, perched at the boundaries of classical form and best exemplified by Hitchcock. Situations and actions are no longer clearly or causally linked (e.g., why do Hitchcock's *Birds* attack?). The breakdown in linkages implies a surplus meaning that must be related and interpreted through a "third term,"[61] whether it be, in this film, the mirror-screen or the voice-capturing telephones and tape recorders. It is a cinema of at once surplus and castrated, dysfunctional significations. This stage in the development of a self-reflexive cinematic signification may only momentarily shatter the limits of classical form; but it amounts to a differential cinematic practice put forward, with increasing sophistication, as a political imperative, a response to the times.

CHAPTER 4

The Tattoo

(Kantō mushuku, Oretachi no chi ga yurusanai, Hana to dotō, Irezumi ichidai)

What I have called the "Yakuza Sequence," comprising *Kantō mushuku* (1963), *Hana to dotō*/*Flowers and Angry Waves*, *Oretachi no chi ga yurusanai*/*Our Blood Will Not Forgive* (1964) and *Irezumi ichidai*/*A Generation of Tattoos* (1965), was not made consecutively, but regularly alternated with Suzuki's "*Nikutai* Trilogy." All four films involve a *yakuza* or ex-*yakuza* protagonist as played by Kobayashi Akira, with Takahashi Hideki taking the role for the final film. *Hana to dotō* and *Irezumi ichidai* are period dramas of the early Taishō and Shōwa eras, respectively. *Kantō mushuku*, though a contemporary fiction set in 1963, reaches back into Japan's historical imaginary and initiates a discourse on the continuities of (anti-) social ideology that runs through the subsequent films. These films also established a pattern of self-conscious invention and *intervention* in the conventional structures of genre, and, more broadly, the parameters of cinematic narration.

To view these genre films as therefore significantly constitutive of the "mature" Suzuki Style—which is best encapsulated by the films he made in 1966 and 1967 from *Karumen no kawachi* to *Koroshi no rakuin*—may seem at first to be a perverse interpretation in light of Suzuki's own retrospective comments:

> "*Kantō Wanderer* is a straight *yakuza* film and nothing more. . . . The fact that I made it is a little strange. Because there are plenty of good yakuza films. . . . Why is *Kanto Wanderer* being shown tonight, rather than [Sawashima Tadashi's] *Three Wandering Yakuza*?"[1]

When Suzuki said this, he was at his most strategically deprecating. But we can take him at face value to a certain extent. His four *yakuza* films are, in certain ways, the most conventional of Suzuki's pictures to come after the Wada vehicles that came to an end in 1962. They generally operate according to the traditional strengths of classical narrative film under the studio system: engaging, suspenseful plots; romantic melodramas of love and loss; identification with and (at least partial) empathy for the protagonists. Particularly in regards to the male hero, the films resemble Tōei studios' so-called *ninkyō eiga* (chivalrous film), the most popular form of the *yakuza* picture from the mid-1960s. This far more "nativist" genre would come to dominate the film industry with over 300 films made before the decade was out.[2] It was no accident that Suzuki's rise to prominence as a "genre *auteur*" coincided with the beginnings of a *yakuza* mega-genre still in the process of assimilating various influences. Film critics at the time went so far as to compare Suzuki to a definitive talent at Tōei, Katō Tai.[3]

Nevertheless, it is actually *Kantō mushuku*, the first entry in his *Yakuza* Sequence, that most strongly establishes Suzuki's difference from, and even impertinence towards the *ninkyō eiga* as an (emergent) genre space for ideological fantasy; and also, crucially, towards the post-war studio genre picture as a narrative and stylistic economy of practice. Suzuki's take on the contemporary *yakuza* narrative confronts these conventions with what could be described as a liberating and dynamic nihilism (often coded as feminine in these films) that opposes itself to the rigid, deadening ideological self-imprisonment of the classic *ninkyō* protagonist who appears in *Kantō mushuku*, albeit in a far less glorified form. It may be that in Suzuki's version, the repressed *ninkyō* hero can be interpreted as an allegory of the self-imposed conventions and limitations of studio genre practice. The shape of this nihilistic "opposition" to ideology is also due in no small part to a new aesthetic confidence, an assertiveness fostered by the emergence, in late 1963, of a loyal and near exclusive team of collaborators surrounding Suzuki—most prominently the designer and occasional co-writer Kimura Takeo—willing to challenge the perceived status quo on multiple fronts.

Progress, paradoxically, is rarely linear. With the Suzuki *gumi* firing on all cylinders for perhaps the first time, it should not surprise us that *Kantō mushuku* is, in fact, a more confident provocation, on every level, than some of Suzuki's later films in this vein were allowed to be. *Oretachi no chi ga yurusanai* features Kobayashi and Takahashi—Nikkatsu's *yakuza* stars of choice—together as brothers who become enmeshed in gang life. But its narrative topology and stylistic economy bears a more trenchant relation to the Nikkatsu *akushon* of the late 1950s than it does to the later fashion for *yakuza/ninkyō eiga*. Its ultimate critical significance may be as a mark of transition between these two genre cycles, for Suzuki as for Nikkatsu. The relation of the film to Suzuki's early career assignments is obvious, as the plot of the film, in its bare outlines, pits an innocent brother against a shady brother and then both against a criminal organization. This is a standard formula that both Nikkatsu and Suzuki had used all too frequently in the past (e.g., *Kaikyō chi ni somete*). At the same time, the film seems in retrospect to be an interesting precedent to *Kenka erejii* (1966), which is by far Suzuki's most respected film amongst Japanese critics. Both pictures feature Takahashi as a high-spirited youth who manages, almost like an addict, to get into brawls on all manner of occasion. In this initial, less ambitious incarnation, Takahashi is unable to settle down into the middle class bubble of an office job as an advertiser. This occasions some rather droll, if hardly abrasive, satire on the corporate workplace.

Despite this foreshadowing of later developments, *Oretachi no chi ga yurusanai* remains something of a "throwback" entry in Suzuki's filmography, sandwiched as it is between the two *nikutai* films discussed in the following chapter, both of them abrasive confrontations with Japan's recent past as seen through the eyes of marginalized women, and both potent, disruptive formal documents of a (political) late modernism in Japanese cinema. In contrast, *Oretachi no chi ga yurusanai* seems the most conservative Suzuki film of the period in terms of script and style, if not ideologically. Its most famous sequence is its opening, a mostly continuous and extremely long-lasting lateral tracking shot representing the POV of an assassin watching the interactions of a bourgeois household from the outside as he prepares to enter the house and kill the father of the film's young protagonists. The elaborate choreography and technical achievement of this sequence is indubitable, but it seems not to aim for, nor achieve, the kind of provocative tour de force of Godard's (much later) lateral tracking sequence in *Tout va bien* (1972). This seeming failure is rather strange considering that this slow-paced, anti-climactic sequence is, as the opening of a studio picture, inevitably self-reflexive in terms of the "distantiation" effect that it has on any ordinary cinemagoer expecting a typical crime melodrama on a double bill. But whether it has really added something, in terms of conceptual dynamism, to the Suzuki *gumi*'s well-established *modus operandi* is uncertain. Following that sequence, the mise-en-scène and montage of the film settle down into a series of comparatively measured, stately compositions that capture a very familiar Nikkatsu world of handsome, semi-criminal bars and night clubs west of central Tokyo. A slightly more presentational variation on a 1950s Noguchi thriller rather than the impressionistic, often non-diegetic portrait of that same milieu that Suzuki would create in *Tokyo nagaremono* (1966), the film is perhaps most notable as a highly polished "last word," in handsome color, on Suzuki's early career. Perhaps the filmmakers wished to record their preference for this sort of genre material as opposed to recent trends? The revisionism here is neither radical nor provocative, despite select moments of stunning filmmaking, including a fiery climax that possesses the dynamism that the film's opening so lacks; and a conversation within a car pelted by a driving rain that is effortlessly more expressive (and expressionistic) than Kurosawa had managed with his infamous cascades of "black rain" in *Rashōmon* (1950). But even this scene, much admired by Aaron Gerow among others, is a recreation of a similar scene in *Kagenaki koe* (1958).

By 1964, Nikkatsu had moved on from the old *akushon* formula and was striving to imitate the glorified portrait of *yakuza* gang membership—as seen from within the ranks—characteristic of Tōei's *ninkyō eiga*. I have no doubt that the three remaining *yakuza eiga* discussed in this chapter represent the Suzuki *gumi*'s conscious reaction to the trend; in contrast, the ideological structure of *ninkyō eiga* is rather tangential to *Oretachi no chi*, with Takahashi's protagonist not being a *yakuza* at all. Where the adult *yakuza* characters in *Kantō mushuku* wear formal and traditional dress, obsess over their tattoos, and contemplate the established rituals and symbols of "clan" life, the gangsters of *Oretachi no chi* are sleek businessmen with contemporary offices and operations. Yet it is, ironically, the former that best embodies the principal "argument" of this sequence of films: the *yakuza* as an ideological mirror image of a "legitimate" but alarmingly regulative post-war social order.

Kantō mushuku: *Dreams and Reversals*

Yakuza, ninkyō, and nagaremono

The term "*ninkyō eiga*" may, arguably, be a fine way to categorize Nikkatsu's slavish, inferior imitations of Tōei's original *ninkyō* films of 1963 to (roughly) 1969; but it should not necessarily embrace the more expansive and challenging *yakuza eiga* of Suzuki at Nikkatsu, Shinoda at Shōchiku, and Gosha Hideo at Tōhō, despite their "family resemblance" to the Tōei genre and to each other—a resemblance determined by common cultural and industrial contexts and by the ebb and flow of cinemagoers' tastes. We cannot assume or impose *a priori* the bulk of the *ninkyō eiga*'s rather uniform and well-defined narrative formulae and ideological structures.

Nevertheless, since the *ninkyō eiga* of the 1960s remains at the center of film-critical discourse on post-war Japanese studio pictures featuring *yakuza* protagonists, I will offer a brief summary of its relevance to Suzuki's *yakuza* efforts.

McDonald and Isolde Standish have offered notable commentaries on the structure and ideology of Tōei's *ninkyō* films.[4] For McDonald these films emphasize the pre-modern ideological structure of *giri* and *ninjō* (the conflict and/or balance between "duty" and "personal feeling"). The *ninkyō* protagonist is a sympathetic *yakuza* who commands the empathy and, arguably, the ideological consensus of the audience through the charisma and sexual glamour of stars such as Takakura Ken. Paul Schrader comments that even in his youth, Takakura represented "everything that is old, strong, and virtuous in Japan, and stands as a symbol against Westernization and compromise. As such he is revered by student radicals, the far right, and the . . . guilt-ridden sections of the middle class."[5] Takakura at Tōei constructed a highly successful ego ideal and fantasy of self-reliance for a male audience. As McDonald has shown, when the principled hero breaks into a killing spree at the end of each film, a combination of narrative manipulation (usually involving revenge), the vicarious thrill of cinematic violence, and the likeability of the protagonist serve to justify the use of "righteous" or honorific violence that defines the *ninkyō* genre.[6] Japanese studios (including Nikkatsu) came to whitewash and aggrandize this criminal subset of Japanese society despite the *yakuza*'s highly suspect ties to the "legitimate" power structures of business and politics, including the then highly unpopular Prime Minister Kishi Nobusuke, who resigned in 1960.[7] In these films, often financially backed by the *yakuza* themselves, gangsters appear as the inheritors of the samurai tradition and as the exemplar of an idealized Japanese masculinity. This ideal was predicated, as Standish has explained, on the *topoi* of physical superiority, homosocial bonding, and self-sacrificing stoicism.[8]

In some ways this ideal was continuous with prewar film culture, for example *chanbara* films like *Chūji no tabi nikki/Chūji's Travel Diary* (Itō, 1927), and therefore not terribly original. It is no accident that most of Tōei's *ninkyō eiga* were period dramas while speaking, allegorically, to the culture of the 1960s. Like prewar *chanbara*, the *ninkyō eiga* often posits the gambler hero as a *nagaremono*, a wanderer or drifter,[9] despite the binding paternalistic ties of the *yakuza* gang structure evident in such formulaic sequences as the gang meeting in formal dress and the ritual breaking of the *sake* cup. As Suzuki once pointed out satirically, the rule-bound *yakuza* "drifter" is even less of an "outlaw" than the heroine of melodrama, who in her forbidden emotions is often *truly* forced outside of society.[10] Indeed, if the *nagaremono* ideal was a distant, mythic posture for Tōei's period pictures, in *yakuza* films with contemporary settings it was a total anachronism, an ideological convenience allowing the hero to operate according to a strict, binding "code" emanating from society while taking on the appearance of a rebel outside society. This explains the immense popularity of *ninkyō eiga* even amongst leftist students of the 1960s, as Satō noted.[11] Like oppressed *sarariman*, activists were able to indulge in fantasies of rebellion through these stylized films, even while facing down the real *yakuza* across the picket lines of the Miike coal strike (1959) and other sites of political struggle. With hindsight, though, we can see that it is the righteous, empathetic cinematic hero who sustains the fantasy of the "chivalrous" gangster and reifies the *yakuza*'s very existence even when the narrative opposes him to degenerate, corrupt, or capitalist bosses who expose the reality of the system. Similarly, as Standish has shown in reference to the popular *Abashiri bangaichi/Abashiri Prison* (1965-1967) series at Tōei, even when Takakura's *nagaremono* is placed at the furthest possible removal from "polite" society—the notorious Abashiri Prison—he still occupies a place in an idealized but rigid patriarchal gang structure within the prison.[12] Again, with hindsight, there is very little reason to equate the yakuza hero with social subversion.

In the Suzuki *yakuza* sequence, as a few critics noticed, it is the very failure of rebellion and independence that is the object of fascination, whereas in *ninkyō eiga*, as Standish argues, it is conversely the *nagaremono*'s failure to sustain a homosocial "connectedness" that generates pathos.[13] Yamaguchi Tetsu in *Eiga hyōron* cleverly uses the motif of the *yakuza* tattoo when he writes of Suzuki's films that "this is the fate of the rebel, to wipe and wipe and be unable to wipe it off." Further, he argues that "the essence of Suzuki is *wandering* and *treachery*."[14] Since the *nagaremono* was a popular fictional icon across studios, and since the hero of *Kantō mushuku*, as Suzuki insisted, was not much of an outcast, we must take this with a grain of salt. Nevertheless, Yamaguchi makes a compelling point: one only has to recall the ambivalence and hypocrisy of Mizuno's status in *Yajū no seishun* as a vigilante/policeman in order to understand Suzuki's interest in the *nagaremono* motif and the *yakuza* genre at this stage of development. Suzuki's films are fascinated by the boundary case.

Still, we must be cautious of retro-actively reading the ideology of Suzuki's "Yakuza Sequence" in the light of the later *ninkyō eiga* formula. Although that genre had a long line of precedents, it was not yet established by 1963, with one of the earliest recognizable iterations of the formula, *Hishakaku: Jinsei gekijō/Hishakaku: Theater of Life* (1963) appearing contemporaneously with *Kantō mushuku*. Suzuki's films, once again in the vanguard of popular genre, had no set form either to follow or negate. Their own sense of the potential of *yakuza eiga*, with its characteristic discourses of masculinity and post-war identity, may amount to a road not taken.

Therefore, if the masculine ideal of the *nagaremono* appears to permeate *Kantō mushuku* as it permeates the *ninkyō eiga*, I do not use the word "appears" lightly. On the one hand, it is important to understand the ideological and other limitations imposed on a Nikkatsu contract director. Suzuki testified later that he had a problem with *ninkyō* ideology,[15] but that he was constrained by Nikkatsu scripts which were handed down by an executive committee.[16] *Kantō mushuku*'s script is in fact distantly based on an episode of what ought to have been, for Suzuki, an unimpeachable source: the serialized novel *Chitei no Uta/Song of the Underworld* (1953) by Hirabayashi Taiko.[17] The immediate source, however, was the popular 1956 adaptation of *Chitei no uta* by his mentor Noguchi (with Suzuki as assistant director). But the limitations on a contract director extended beyond the choice of source material to Nikkatsu's enforcement of conventional structures of plot, melodrama, and secondary identification, all of which had been studiously obeyed by Noguchi's classical, realist version. Despite all this, there are significant formal and narrative elements in Suzuki's *yakuza* sequence which depart from and even contradict what would become the dominant ideology of the *ninkyō eiga*. In this sense, Suzuki's earlier statement about *Kantō mushuku* is utterly misleading.

Wandering Narrative, Wandering Heroism

There is a meandering quality to the narrative of *Kantō mushuku* that results in a meandering of the film's ideological thrust. By the end of the film, things are not so simple as in the *ninkyō eiga*, which depends on the honorific predictability of the main character. Where the Tōei films avoid reference to the post-war election fraud, prostitution, and strike-breaking activities of the *yakuza*, *Kantō mushuku* gleefully insists upon them. If, however, it is the hero rather than his corrupt environment who reifies the ideals that the *yakuza* are supposed to uphold, then it is only through the hero, and/or the ideal itself, that the dominant ideology can be questioned. This is precisely the achievement of *Kantō mushuku*.

It is crucial to note that such ideological reversals are achieved, as if *covertly*, through formal strategies of distantiation that subject heroic melodrama to an ironic, often purely visual, authorial commentary. Suzuki's mature stylistic preoccupations are consistently in evidence here, suggesting aberrant readings even while in tension with a linear melodrama that offers conventional ones. At this stage, the "Suzuki Difference" is only a partial "threat" to the coherence of the studio film; it forces cracks in the armor of classical film style, and this in turn outlines the cracks in the armor of ideology that the genre system, as many film theorists believe, was meant to shore up.

Stylistically, *Kantō mushuku* was like no other film made up to that time by the post-war studios. Its closest formal relative is perhaps Ōshima's *Nihon no yoru to kiri* (1960), which had created an experimental political iconography through non-diegetic color and moving camera sequence shots. But Suzuki and Suzuki Akira's ambitious editing practices operated within a far less restricted set of stylistic parameters, as did the stylized use of location shooting to capture Tokyo's urban environment as an allegory of the times. The aesthetic newness of *Kantō mushuku* may also be found in its narrative emphasis on dream and vision, presented through non-diegetic formal effects and signifying the collective, largely masculine social fantasy of empowerment through seduction and violence. Equally important is the startling use of non-diegetic color and lighting and discontinuity editing. These qualities—oneiric narrative, color/lighting, and discontinuity, are the foci of the analytical sections below.

If the narrative of *Kantō mushuku* is largely linear in a strictly temporal sense, it does not develop in a straightforward manner. Refusing to follow its protagonist throughout the first third of the film, the narrative literally wanders through multiple plots and protagonists towards an anti-climax. The film begins with schoolgirl Tokiko (Matsubara Chieko) and her crush on the strait-laced *yakuza* hero, Katsuta (Kobayashi). This romantic situation is soon sidelined and disappears entirely (along with Tokiko) in the second half of the film. After one scene which introduces, as per the *yakuza* formula, the internecine gang conflict that causes problems for Katsuta, the film turns to a seemingly unrelated subplot involving the exploitation of Tokiko's school friend, Hanako, by a *yakuza* punk. In the second third of the film, a further subplot intervenes as Katsuta meets an old love interest, the female card sharp Mrs. Iwata (Itō Hiroko). Conflict develops between Katsuta and Mrs. Iwata's gambler husband, with Mrs. Iwata increasingly prominent as the melodramatic protagonist. In the final thirty minutes, this in turn is replaced by a new conflict involving Katsuta's new job and his intransigent boss. There are aspects of the plot that remain incomprehensible (what is the off-screen relationship between Oyama the businessman, Yoshida the *oyabun*, and Okaru-Hachi the con artist?). Most

Fig. 4.1. The Red Thread of Attachment: a non-diegetic red line, like a brush stroke, moves across the wide screen (and Katsuta's countenance) (*Kantō mushuku*)

importantly, the climactic violence that dominates the ending of the film proves not to be a "climax" at all, for it does not resolve any of the conflicts that the narrative has presented to us: it is only a climax of Katsuta's physical and psychological energy. This is an essential point. The violence that provides a resolution in the *ninkyō* film can, in this case, only call into question a formulaic structure, and, most importantly, the formulaic masculine hero. In this scene, Katsuta has taken a second job as a dealer to support his worthless, cash-strapped Boss Izu (Tonoyama Taiji). Seething from these tensions, Katsuta slaughters two low level, drunken gamblers who disrupt the game in order to borrow money. This is clearly a murderous release of pent-up erotic and Oedipal frustration: the real targets of Katsuta's rage should have been the arrogant husband of Mrs. Iwata and his own corrupt father-figure Izu. As an analogue to Katsuta's turbulence, the scene features perhaps the most iconic visual gesture throughout Suzuki's body of work. In an extreme long shot, the *shōji* (sliding paper doors) of the studio set representing the gambling den collapse and fall backward to reveal nothing but a non-diegetic red glow on all three sides. During a previous conversation with Boss Izu, Suzuki inserts a parallel gesture, a non-diegetic red line which moves randomly over Katsuta's countenance, possibly as an indicator of suppressed rage.

This sort of visualization is our only access to Katsuta's thoughts; more so than in *Yajū no seishun*, potentially symbolic effects "tell us" what the script does not; but such visuality renders all events as matters of interpretation rather than causality. This is true of much of the film's

Fig. 4.2. Color as Emotion or Color as Ambiguity: non-diegetic yellow flairs on the window behind the suffering Mrs. Iwata. Is it the misfortune of romantic attachment, or its loss, or neither? (*Kantō mushuku*)

memorable color stylization: it may express a psychological transition in the characters, but its nature and significance is unclear. Suzuki has often expressed that certain colors have a particular emotional resonance (e.g., purple = anxiety).[18] But contrary to Satō's tentative, seemingly unverifiable suggestion that these color effects were related to character empathy,[19] Suzuki had already rejected the subordination of style to empathetic identification. "In my way of seeing . . . I've gone for empathy completely or not at all."[20] The relational uncertainty between character and non-diegetic color replaces the manipulated emotions of the *ninkyō* genre's "structure of judgment."

What a contrast this makes between this particular *yakuza* tale and a canonical entry in the Tōei genre such as Takakura Ken's first movie in the *Shōwa zankyō-den/Brutal Tales of Chivalry* (1965) series. What strikes me upon viewing the latter is its utter conservatism of color, composition, montage, and plot construction. A less judgmental critic might prefer to call this "economy," and the term would be accurate, since the focus of the film is laid solely and squarely on *jingi* (the *yakuza* code of morality) and whatever constructs of plot and identification that help put *jingi* into action. Director Saeki Kiyoshi's climactic action sequence is not, for all that, poorly handled, but for a picture that aims toward thrilling an audience with a relatively "new" genre of action, this 1965 studio production , as a formal and stylistic construct, offers no difference from a 1955 studio production; despite being made nearly two years after the provocative *Kantō mushuku*.

In comparison to such staidness, the palpable tension of ambiguity in Suzuki's film is not only a product of ironic stylization and wandering plot, but is instilled directly into (what passes for) the film's ideological discourse. Alexander Jacoby writes that "*Kanto Wanderer* was a subtly subversive commentary on the obsolescence of the *yakuza* code: here, the protagonist's efforts to act honourably fail to avert bloodshed and, indeed, trigger the death of his own patron."[21] Katsuta bullies the rival boss Yoshida (Tōru Abe) into respecting the authority of Boss Izu. But in the next scene, once Katsuta is safely in jail, Yoshida does the exact opposite and assassinates Izu. Katsuta's code of violence resolves nothing, including the narrative of the film. Is it the case that the ideal itself cannot stand, or is the post-war hero merely incapable of embodying it? Suzuki said of his main character, "Kobayashi plays an *oyabun* [gang boss] to be, radiating self-confidence, smugly striding along the broad path of crime. . . . An increasingly proud criminal: one who could only flourish within the Japanese system. In other words: as an outlaw, he's a bit too much."[22] This suggests a satirical attitude towards Katsuta's old-fashioned and smug ideological certainty. Out of step with society, Katsuta's "honorific" behavior spells disaster not simply for himself—for this alone would reinforce the "tragic hero" motif, the positive sense of self-sacrifice that permeates the *ninkyō eiga*—but for everyone around him, and particularly the innocent. When Katsuta's brutish gang brother (Noro Keisuke, playing a purely bestial character) has sold the schoolgirl Hanako into sexual slavery, Katsuta resolves to buy her freedom. In a fit of egoism and jealousy, however, Katsuta blows the money away in a gambling contest with Mrs. Iwata's husband. So much for Hanako. For a while, everything (including the *yakuza* "code") is sacrificed to Kobayashi's sexual obsession; but in the violent anti-climax, he reverses course in what he calls a "last chance for the Izu clan's honor."

Because Kobayashi is an attractive protagonist whom the viewers, no doubt, will readily forgive for all his sins, the film does not unambiguously demystify the *yakuza* and its ideal masculinity. Katsuta is a half-formed prototype for the simply delusional characters who dominate the second half of Suzuki's career. The only "resolution" that *Kantō mushuku* offers is the entrapment that each character has brought upon his or her self. The filmmakers emphasize a dialectic of the role of chance (various meetings and coincidences) and that of economic determination (the decline and capitalization of the old *yakuza* gangs) over the strength of will, stoic perseverance, and force of tradition that underpins the cinematic myth of *jingi*.

Wandering through and between all these threads of narrative is the character of Hanako, a precocious, flirtatious high school girl fascinated with *yakuza* (read: power). She serves as the picture's counterpoint to Katsuta's masculinity. Initially bartered and sexually exploited by a *chinpira* (punk) and a businessman in a harrowing scene in the country, she ends up as a geisha to the *yakuza* bosses and, indeed, as a kind of power broker. Hanako's natural talent for manipulating men through sex (or rather, the promise of sex) gives the lie to the prewar myth of idealized masculinity that is enshrined in the *yakuza* subculture and predicated on the subjugation of the feminine. The other female characters, such as Mrs. Iwata who is trapped in this culture because of family attachment, are harshly treated by a patriarchal structure. Hanako becomes its master. *Kantō mushuku* lavishes attention on this character: she is the first in a line of "masterful" women in Suzuki's films, like Misako in *Koroshi no rakuin*, whose extremity brooks no concession to men. At the same time, she is a "dangerously" free and frivolous woman, like the clownish O-Roku of *Nikutai no mon*. She is one of Suzuki's first nihilistic heroes. The *yakuza* are sensual or sadistic thugs, but the perpetually smiling Hanako, like Shakespeare's Edmund or Odysseus, "says nothing that [s]he believes, and believes nothing that [s]he says."[23] Like Iago, Hanako is self-delighted by her growing talent for controlling the slower-witted.[24] At the end, she casually dumps her boyfriend Fuyu after he has killed her new lover, Boss Izu. The culture of the *yakuza* has created its own scourge. In this manner, Suzuki both respects and updates what was differential about his source material, namely, Hirabayashi's focus on trapped (and not-so-trapped) women within the yakuza subculture. No Suzuki film is more conscious of the collision between reactionary cultural nostalgia and the awakening of what we might broadly call "female self-discovery" in the 1960s.

Dream and Reverie

Kantō mushuku is Suzuki's first major exploration of dream and mental vision in the cinema. Long before Kurosawa did, *Kantō mushuku* used bold, non-diegetic colors and "color expressionist" lighting effects to create a cinematic "dreamscape" in the midst of a semi-classical narrative. These techniques were so unconventional in 1963 that the disoriented viewer enjoys no clear demarcation, in the manner of "the Hollywood flashback," between the diegetic space of the narrative and the space of dream.

When Katsuta enters the home of his bewitching love interest, Mrs. Iwata, an important flashback occurs that tells how the characters first met in a dark, wintry *ryōkan* (a symbolic locus of violence between the sexes). Later, we find the characters sitting together in the tatami room,

Fig. 4.3. Haunted Remembrances (shot 1a): artificial pale blue light outlines the characters as they reminisce

Fig. 4.4. Haunted Remembrances (shot 1b): The blue light fades but the actors are re-illuminated from the right before the lights fade again and Katsuta violently "seduces" Mrs. Iwata and pulls her under the camera

silently recalling their acquaintance. This long held shot is a tour de-force of expressive non-diegetic lighting. The key light fades out completely, leaving an artificial pale blue light, which supposedly comes from a window on the upper screen right. It shines on the entrance to Mrs. Iwata's garden in the background of the shot, and a pale reflection of this blue light is cast on the profiles of the two actors (Fig. 4.3).

The blue light then fades, leaving the background in darkness, but a new, more delicate lighting scheme re-illuminates the actors in the foreground.

Fig. 4.5. Lighting and Narrative Meaning (shot 1c): after a moment of darkness, as Katsuta and Mrs. Iwata have intercourse off-screen, a fade-in on the flowers in the background center. Does it have narrative significance?

Katsuta suddenly grabs hold of Mrs. Iwata and pulls her to the floor, below the frame; the lights fade again as they have sex off-screen. All of this takes place in a single, elaborately choreographed take. At the end of the shot, following several seconds of darkness, a spotlight slowly rises on a vase of flowers which is placed behind the lovers in the exact center of the frame.

This fade in on the flowers is a key and characteristic effect: it either has no narrational motivation at all, or else it accomplishes an unconventional, some might say dysfunctional, form of ellipsis. If we assume the latter to be the case, then even though only a few seconds of real time has passed, the viewer is being cued by the lighting to believe that time has passed in the narrative, the time in which the characters made love. There has been no cutting to mark the ellipsis, as would be necessitated by classical and conventional practice. When the shot finally ends, there is a cut to an overhead shot of Mrs. Iwata, awkwardly prostrate on the floor, while Katsuta is shamefacedly turned away from her.

This transition confirms what has occurred, but did it occur before or between the cut? No definitive interpretation is possible, but since these shots introduce a sequence of the film that passes outside of the normal flow of space and time, interpretation based on causality becomes irrelevant.

Following another elliptical cut, Katsuta steps outside of Mrs. Iwata's house with a satisfied, rather cruel expression on his face. Katsuta is walking away from the house when he suddenly starts up in a panic and

Fig. 4.6. Dysfunctional Ellipsis (shot 2): after the cut, the intercourse is long since ended. Is the ellipsis of time indicated by the change of lighting (shots 1a and 1b), or by the cut?

throws his back against a bamboo fence, falling into an area of the fence bathed in the haunting blue light of the previous scene. We soon see that Katsuta's absurdly fearful reaction has been caused by Mrs. Iwata's black cat running across his path! Clearly, the film has entered a space in which memory intersects with either the hallucinatory or the uncanny.

As the camera follows Katsuta's gaze, it pans dreamily away from the front door and along the fence to the right, and suddenly a superimposition of a mysterious man, looking into the camera, appears in front of the fence.

Fig. 4.7. Uncanny Passage: the "haunted" blue light shows Katsuta's fear—of Mrs. Iwata's black cat? Masculinity runs afoul of uncanny femininity.

Fig. 4.8. The Mark of Insecurity: the ghostly apparition of the man who scarred Katsuta's cheek

This character was Mrs. Iwata's con artist partner in the flashback, and his fight with Katsuta left a permanent scar on the hero's face: an allegorical mark of sexual jealousy.

After an abrupt simple cut, we find that Katsuta is in his own bed at home. He wakes up startled, as if from a dream. This may be a simple ellipsis, but what follows forces the viewer to ask how much of the foregoing scene was, indeed, the product of a dream? As Katsuta goes back to sleep, he hears the voice of Mrs. Iwata and the lighting fades to black. Mrs. Iwata then enters Katsuta's room in the next, dimly lit shot, and slowly, lovingly insinuates herself into Katsuta's arms (Fig. 4.9). Katsuta moves to kiss her.

Another abrupt cut follows in which the camera captures Katsuta and the woman in his arms from an angle exactly opposite to the previous.

This new shot is a close-up of the two lovers in which the lighting scheme has suddenly returned to the normative, three-point lighting scheme of typical studio practice. The viewer now finds that it is the schoolgirl Tokiko, and not Mrs. Iwata, who is in Katsuta's arms. The shot, which highlights Katsuta's POV, is a violation of the classical axis of action. Yet what is chiefly of interest is not its disruptive effect but its thematic relation to the periphery lying between dream and truth as visualized on the boundaries of classical form. How much of what passed onscreen actually happened between Katsuta and Mrs. Iwata, and how much has passed off-screen between Katsuta and Tokiko? These moments of "haunting" are connected to traumatic memory but also to Japanese tradition (the timeless, iconic space of the *ryōkan*), and characterize Katsuta's unstable, borderless personal/national past.

Fig. 4.9. Dream Lover (shot 1): Mrs. Iwata in Katsuta's arms

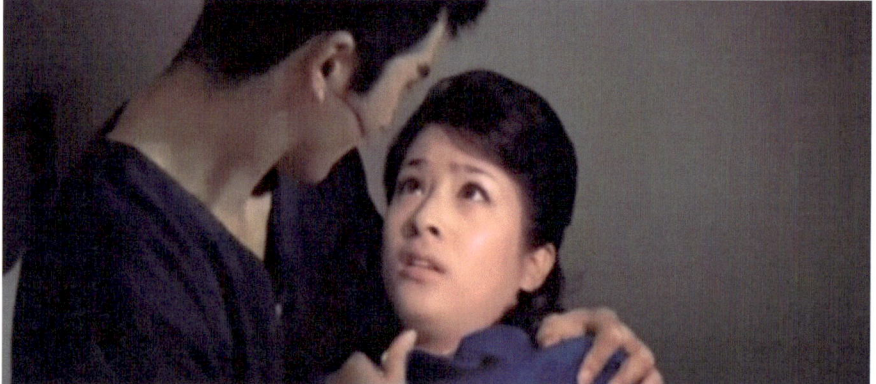

Fig. 4.10. Dream Lover (shot 2): an abrupt cut from the reverse angle. Now Tokiko is in Katsuta's arms—what really transpired?

The Old and the New

A dialectic of past and present, traditional and contemporary, runs through *Kantō mushuku*, centered around the Tokyo *shitamachi* Tokyo locations and the cultures that inhabit it. The first shots of the film depict the encroachment of an abrasive urban modernity: first, a close-up of Hanako with a crowd of commuters behind her; then a shot of Tokiko with a bright red train rushing behind. Finally, a third schoolgirl in front of a busy line of cars is seen.

The girls are clustered in a circle at the train station and the backgrounds are all typical sights of the rapidly expanding mass transport sys-

Fig. 4.11. Urban Modernity as Spatial Disjuncture (1)

Fig. 4.12. Urban Modernity as Spatial Disjuncture (2)

tem of the early 1960s. However, there is no graphic continuity between the backgrounds depicted in these shots; such large public spaces (train tracks, a commuter road) cannot be as spatially contiguous as the film suggests. The opening thus allegorizes "the contemporary" as spatial disjuncture: an unbridgeable gap between the cultural environment of modern youth and the prewar fixation of *yakuza* like Katsuta.

Moments later, an on-location street scene reveals a group of musicians dressed in the archaic costumes used for *matsuri*. These musicians are *chinchin donya*, or performers advertising a sale at a department store. Such unscripted observations of then-contemporary culture reveal the link between capitalism and prewar nostalgia. On this basis it is possible to see the film, or the filmmaker's code within it, as a debunking, an exposure of Japan's vaunted traditional culture as deceptive and hypocritical as the *yakuza* themselves, whose bosses are nothing but corrupt capitalists and pimps. This latter observation often appears in the conservative *ninkyō* films, however, and their success at defining the ideological terrain of the *yakuza eiga*, through a disavowal of post-war contradictions, has perhaps permanently blunted what satirical force *Kantō mushuku* may have had upon its original release.

Kantō mushuku emphasizes its own location shooting in Asakusa and nearby *shitamachi* neighborhoods. However, as Tony Rayns noted, "realism evaporates as the film enters the character's memories and obsessions."[25] Dreaming and waking, Katsuta belongs to a different world, consisting of traditional *ryōkan* and Asakusa gambling dens. The film accordingly retreats from location footage into the stylized, abstract studio sets that represent these environments. They are often drenched in falling snow, which, as Hasumi recognized, is not a representation of the actual weather,[26] being, instead, a complex displacement of cultural metaphors that seems to visualize the primacy of Katsuta's worldview: Japan's historical imaginary in the mind of one inflexible, idealistic character at one remove from reality.

As in Ozu's post-war films, the everyday coexistence of contemporary and traditional culture is unnoticed by the characters, but Suzuki's camera imparts a heightened awareness of incongruity. When the innocent Tokiko meets Katsuta at the boss's house, she asks about the inscriptions on some old-fashioned oil paper umbrellas (*wagasa*) which read "red kimono, white kimono." Katsuta replies, "Before the war, prisoners wore red kimonos. . . . [White ones] are for the honorable departed. . . . That's the *yakuza* way." Tokiko is shocked; her idol, Katsuta, lives in a world of associations totally alien even to the boss's daughter.

Surely the most interesting of the film's social insights is that, having denied any legitimacy to the *yakuza* as representatives of traditional (prewar) values, these same values are located in the professional con artists, Mrs. Iwata and her husband, Okaru-Hachi (the great character actor Itō Yūnosuke). This is perhaps not surprising, for whenever Suzuki's films represent the surviving aspects of pre-restoration culture in a non-pejorative way, it is invariably in the form of art and craft: Edo painting, Edo theatre in its copious manifestations, vintage popular music, and, above all, the emphasis on dreams, ghosts, and erotic obsession handed down from Heian literature to *kabuki*. In contrast to the house of Boss Izu, in which record players, TVs, and empty beer bottles are prominent

Fig. 4.13. Attention to Detail: the "stoic" traditionalism of Okaru-Hachi and his "art," contrasted to the "wild" body posturing of the *yakuza*

features, the immaculate house of Mrs. Iwata and Okaru-Hachi is replete with signifiers of tradition such as *shōji* and wooden porches on a water garden.[27] The contrast is clear. The con man, with his dedication to an old-fashioned (if criminal) craft, demonstrates a rigorousness of purpose that represents traditional artisanship lost in the age of mass production; he also represents an austere, stoic attention to duty that the samurai of the Edo period applied to the tea ceremony as fervently as they did to the sword. One scene in particular contrasts Diamond Fuyu, the rock 'n' roll loving punk with no understanding of *yakuza* culture, with Okaru-Hachi as he is seated on a tatami performing a meticulous task, the marking of cards, with the utmost precision and stillness. The drunken Fuyu callously hints that his sister is in love with Katsuta. But Okaru-Hachi continues his task, outwardly undistracted by this revelation of infidelity and demonstrating the kind of stoic indifference of body posture that characterizes the heroic Takakura in his *ninkyō eiga*.[28]

In this way, *Kantō mushuku* turns the tables on the ideology of the masculine genre cinema that it outwardly embodies. At the end of this scene, Mrs. Iwata expects remonstrance from Okaru-Hachi, but he will not pause from his work; it is at this point that she realizes, with desolation, that she can expect nothing from her marriage other than professional likemindedness. This is metonymic for the exclusion of women from "traditional" culture, and it is far from certain whether *Kantō mushuku* has more sympathy for a dedicated artist (Okaru-Hachi) or for a confused teenager like Fuyu who has no tradition to guide him.

Crossing the Line

Okaru-Hachi's favorite trick is to use mirrors and shiny objects to see the facedown cards that he is dealing. In this new variation on the "mirror" motif, a set of virtual mirrors propose metaphorical relations of "virtual" identity through spatial opposition. In taking this visual motif to logical extremes, *Kantō mushuku* uses mirroring to prepare us for the breaking of the standard "180 Degree Rule" of studio editing practice. This rule ensures constant screen direction, efficient and predictable camera position, and complete spatial clarity. But here, the audience is forced to reckon with problematic, and sometimes inexplicable, visual disjuncture as a form of expression that grows more pronounced as the film progresses. Consider a shot breakdown of this scene in which Katsuta enters the gambling den in order to watch the famous Okaru-Hachi at work.

Before Shot (3), Katsuta is looking towards Okaru-Hachi (off-screen left). The viewer expects to follow Katsuta's glance when he turns his head to see what is off-screen to the right. Instead, we find Okaru-Hachi gazing back at us (Fig. 4.16). Suzuki and Mine are capitalizing on our assumption that Shot (3) should represent Katsuta's POV in a typical shot-reverse shot pattern. They seem, at first, to have broken the 180 Degree Rule: how can Katsuta see Okaru-Hachi on both the right and the left? In order for this to be "true," Shots (1), (2), or (3) would have to be reflections in a mirror. No such mirror is present, but since Okaru-Hachi uses a "mirror trick" a few minutes later, this strange continuity is entirely appropriate.

Fig. 4.14. A Cinematic Mirror (shot 1): Katsuta's head appears above the painted screen of a geisha (*right background*), looking to screen left at Okaru-Hachi gambling. Okaru-Hachi casts a fleeting glance at something off-screen (*toward right foreground*)

The Tattoo / 129

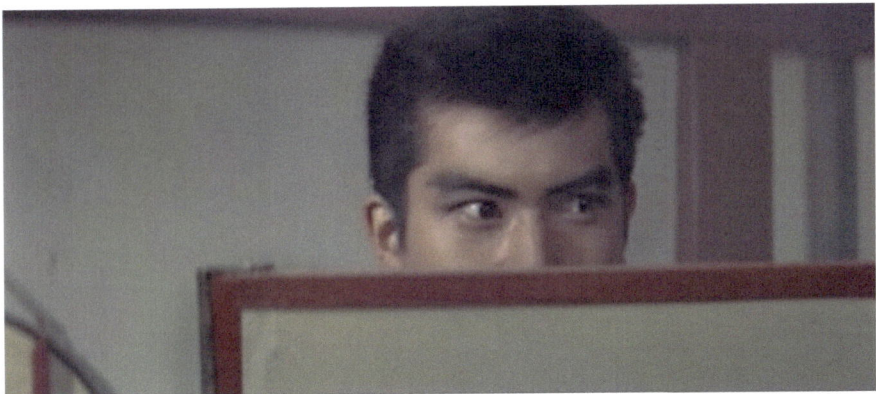

Fig. 4.15. A Cinematic Mirror (shot 2): Close-up on Katsuta suddenly turning his head and looking to extreme right of screen, apparently to follow Okaru-Hachi's glance. Katsuta draws back in surprise.

Fig. 4.16. A Cinematic Mirror (shot 3): Okaru-Hachi raises his eyes and looks directly into the camera, <u>not</u> directly at the woman's head (*left-of-center foreground, out-of-focus*)

In Shot (6), the viewer discovers that Shot (3) was not a POV shot after all. This occurs only after Shot (5), a longish pan, has delayed the solution to the "spatial mystery." Shot (6) is a medium shot of Katsuta's lover, Mrs. Iwata; she is the woman whom both Katsuta and Okaru-Hachi were looking at in Shot (3).

Mrs. Iwata's position, in a part of the room previously unrevealed, makes her the mirror opposite of the Edo-period beauty on the screen painting. Moreover, she is placed by a large red chest that "mirrors" a red chest in

Fig. 4.17. A Cinematic Mirror (shot 6): the object of all gazes

the opposite corner. Thus, the previous shots did not actually break with classical continuity; they simply *appear* to have done so for a considerable length of time: an at once metaphorical and brilliantly cinematic evocation of illusionism, reversal, and mirrored identities.

The end of the film makes a more unequivocal break with the 180 Degree Rule. Hanako tosses aside the jail-bound Fuyu, who is hopelessly begging her to wait for him for "seven or eight years." Shot (1) shows Fuyu on screen right, with Hanako concealed by a screen on the left (perhaps underscoring the character's inscrutability).

Shot (2) shows Hanako from Fuyu's POV, just left of center frame.

Shot (3) repeats the pattern of Shot (1).

Fig. 4.18. Reversals of Gender and Power (shot 1): Fuyu (*right*), and Hanako (*left, concealed*)

Fig. 4.19. Reversals (shot 2): Close-up on Hanako from Fuyu's POV

Fig. 4.20. Reversals (shot 3): repeat of the Shot (1) composition, as in standard Shot-Reverse Shot patterning

But Shot (4), instead of repeating Shot (2), abruptly cuts to a profile shot of Hanako right of center frame, showing a side of her body which cannot represent the POV of any character. Her eyeline does not match that of Fuyu in Shot (3).

This is a "textbook" violation of the 180° axis of action. The breaking of continuity coincides with Hanako's challenge to a coercive, traditionalist subculture: she brandishes infidelity as a weapon against the patriarchal exploitation that has failed to subdue her. *Kantō mushuku* challenges social and formal/cinematic "constructionism" at the same time. The three continuity "violations" I have discussed above (one unproblematic in Katsuta's dream, one temporarily problematic, one thoroughly so) pro-

Fig. 4.21. Reversals (shot 4): Hanako from the "wrong" side of the classical axis of action (*Kantō mushuku*)

gressively reverse the gendered social relations of hierarchy and control implied by the male gaze. Dissentient technique is aligned with dissentient ideology along gendered lines. Hanako, more successfully than Mrs. Iwata, is still operating in an irredeemably oppressive patriarchy, but she is turning her objectification into power.

If Hanako enables the film's most radical departure from accepted technique, nevertheless the cinematic "mirror" of the gambling sequence is an interpretive key to *Kantō mushuku*. It allows the mirror—ironically the mythological symbol of Japanese sincerity and another icon of wartime nationalism—to return to its concrete function of reversing the image. Far from embodying the outcast, the *yakuza*, in their intractable power relations, are simply the mirror image of "legitimate" society. Reversal is not negation, and does not yet permit the wholly "negative" view of The Violence Trilogy. Nevertheless, reversal is the order of the day: martial heroism guarantees defeat (another wartime reflection); con artists are more traditional than *yakuza*; tradition itself is simply a hollow vessel through which its antithesis, capitalism, moves freely. Rather than "treachery" or "wandering," the great motif on display here—that which melds style and subject—is relativism or skepticism, both moderate forms of negativity with respect to convention. In important scenes such as the encounters with Mrs. Iwata, the narration will not tell us what is happening when; the visual style will not specify its significance, nor restrict itself to the culture's signifying conventions. The hero is as inscrutable as the colors that envelop him, yet in the end is ideologically determined; he is never a free individual making a legitimate choice. In such a deliberately uncertain universe, with patriarchal codes eroded everywhere by femininity and by reality, and where impermanence (*mujō*) is the only universal, how can the masculine ideal assert its claim to truth? Is it not just another "fever dream"? *Kantō mushuku* separates nostalgia from the possibility of truth.

The mirror is also a sort of "window" onto a new world of filmmaking, a world now definitively marked by the directorial "signature" of Suzuki that, within a prescriptive mass media, must be inscribed as oppositional. In this "looking glass" cinema, causality, continuity, and the ideological/emotional coherence permitted by secondary identification are still structurally present; but they can now be selectively reversed or de-emphasized in reverse proportion to visual spectacle, artifice, and semantic ambiguity. A new balance is achieved within stylistic parameters much larger than the old "closed narrative realism." Rather than manipulated sympathy, ideological judgment, and the satisfaction of closure, the audience (as Satō noted) now reacts multi-directionally: at one time, with the pleasure of irony; at another, with spontaneous enjoyment of the play of color, movement, form. In *Kantō mushuku* we are given a glimpse of this new world.

The Period Melodramas: History, Theatricality, and Colonial Dreams

Hana to dotō and *Irezumi ichidai* follow *Kantō mushuku* chronologically, but they add little to its portrait of idealized masculinity. What they do contribute is a gorgeously realized historical setting that enables Suzuki to reflect directly on the prewar past. Ironically, these two of Suzuki's most conventional melodramas are also the most overtly political: they constitute his only direct representation of marginalized laborers, exploitative managers, and colonial expansion in the Japan of his youth. In a straightforwardly leftist critique, these tales of the uphill battle against a corporate/political machine recall the great urban protests of the 1910s in which it seemed that the dominance of the Meiji oligarchs and *zaibatsu* industrial barons might finally be challenged by the masses; but the nationalist episteme that compromised those very protests comes to the fore as the outcast male heroes attempt to flee from domestic attachment towards the "Utopian" dream of imperialism. Unsurprisingly, both films were castigated by Nikkatsu bosses: like the early *nuberu bagu*, they exposed the limits of direct political discourse in the studio system.

Two intersecting narrative threads run through these films: a drama of labor politics and a melodrama of failed heterosexual coupling. They are intersected by the hero (Kobayashi and then Takahashi Hideki), an outcast ex-*yakuza* who wants to go straight and joins the lowest of the lowest construction laborers.

Hana to dotō involves a choice between two women. A young wife (the "starlet" Matsubara Chieko) in need of protection for whom the hero, Kikuji, feels nothing but pity, is gleefully sidelined to make way for the bold heroine of the filmmakers' choosing: the tattooed "super geisha" Manryū (played splendidly by Kubō Naoko), an "untamable" ex-prostitute of occupied Manchuria. Kikuji's wife Ōshige is a responsibility rather than a partner, while Manryū is an allegory of instinct and passion, the freedom that was associated, in the Taisho working class imagination, with the vast wilderness of Manchuria.[29] Kikuji and Manryū represent a rare partnership of sexual desire founded on equality and respect. But it is not to be: Manryū risks her own life a record four times to save Kikuji, and is paid for her passion by being stabbed in a ditch by the *yakuza*. The hero barely notices her sacrifice, for by this time he has learned that Ōshige is pregnant. Patriarchy and pride trump intersubjectivity and the freedom of choice.

Irezumi ichidai is even more invested in melodrama and its mechanisms of identification. Suzuki's hand over this largely conventional material is so assured that at times it seems like he is making a Kurosawa film rather than a Suzuki film; indeed, several shots are in homage to *Yōjinbo* (Tōhō, 1961).

Suzuki defined his approach as a deliberate "feminization" of a masculine action narrative: "All the violent actions were transformed into senti-

Fig. 4.22. Suzuki as Kurosawa: fighting men pour into the receding street from directly behind or beside the camera, recalling the deep-focus framing of the destruction of the brewery in *Yōjinbo* (Tōhō 1961). The superfluous combatant on the top of the set memorializes Mifune Toshirō perching on the water tower in the earlier film.

mental and romantic actions. It was a very feminine film."[30] This extends, at least according to Suzuki's way of thinking, to an unusual emphasis on landscape and nature, with earthen, autumnal colors supplanting Suzuki's preference for the bold and the non-representational. The image of running water is a constant throughout, and frequently serves as a graphic match cut between shots and scenes. The boss's sister, Midori (Izumi Masako), is another strong female character, ebullient and heedless of the strict gender proprieties of the day, and not, this time, a prostitute. And in a scene which inverts the usual gendered hierarchy of specular relations in popular cinema, the middle-aged wife of the company boss silently observes the young, sensitive art student Kenji as he removes his shirt and bathes. Nor does the film, from this point, find it necessary to attempt to reassert the male gaze. Kenji is mother-obsessed, while the sexuality of his brother Tetsu, the conventional hero, has a similarly childish aspect: he is too ashamed to face the bar hostess he is sleeping with, and red-faced when Midori pursues him with affection. In the final scene, Tetsu's back is turned to Midori as he looks out to sea towards Manchuria. Another *yakuza* through and through, Tetsu goes off to prison and stoically suppresses his desire to look back as Midori calls to him; when he finally does, it is already too late. *Irezumi ichidai* infers that the martial masculinity of the *yakuza* is not so much defined by the gaze of mastery; rather, it necessitates a kind of arrested naiveté, a total disavowal of feminine attachment. This anticipates the extreme gender dynamics of The Violence Trilogy (1966-67).

In both period films, our interpretation of the politics of melodrama is qualified by a turn towards the aesthetics of theatre for inspiration. In *Irezumi ichidai*, the final ten minutes of the film sees an aesthetic reverse course, likely because the narrative has removed all familial and relational ties from Tetsu and allowed him to be what he is: a killer. Natural locations give way to a studio action set piece reminiscent of 1920s *chanbara* in an expressionist, mythic space of unicolored rooms, endless doors, and non-diegetic lighting. In *Hana to dotō*, Suzuki's theatricality is accomplished through color and the contrast of surface and depth. Extreme long shots of landscapes and recessed architectural interiors (some of them shot in deep focus) characterize the naturalist world of the laborers, as do the muted, earthy colors. Nagatsuka's widescreen compositions devote half of the horizontal frame to mud and straw, the dull irremediable world of labor.

In this location footage, Suzuki uses the NikkatsuScope frame to concentrate on landscape for first time since 1960: the hero wading through wide reedy marshes, the laborers hauling a gravel train across the seem-

Fig. 4.23. History versus Theatricality (1): The Dull, Earthen Weight of Labor. Note the compositional depth applied to the worker's world (*Hana to dotō / The Flowers and the Angry Waves*)

Fig. 4.24. History versus Theatricality (2): the visual textures of Asakusa as a Theatre of Life. Note the seemingly shallow depth between the camera and urban surfaces created by an emphasis on foreground objects (*Hana to dotō*)

ingly endless wide screen. The location sequences, however, are sharply contrasted by urban scenes of an exaggerated and theatrical frontality.

Kimura Takeo stages Asakusa crowd scenes on highly theatrical sets that have the atmosphere of a Taishō stage revue, full of social types and vintage iconography such as a stylized backdrop of the famous Ryōunkaku (Twelve Story Tower).[31] This is a historical fantasia representing Taishō life through its popular arts, depicting Asakusa as one great show.

The Tattoo / 137

Fig. 4.25. History *as* Theatre: the improbably costumed, *grand guignol* villain (Kawachi Tamio) beneath Kimura's stylized recreation of Taishō's Ryōunkaku tower (note the dispropionate scaling) (*Hana to dotō*)

Theatrical technique comes to a head in the film's absurdist climax. Kikuji is heading for a port town from which he wants to ship to Manchuria. An elaborate pan shot moves from window to window of a northeast-bound train establishing that all the major characters are (coincidentally) on board. The snowy port of his destination is represented by one stylized set of ten giant, blatantly artificial snowdrifts improbably packed together like the columns of a temple, with a matted tower at the top of the frame.

As soon as the film imposes this theatricality, its melodrama becomes feverish. After Manryū is abruptly slaughtered and forgotten, the policeman decides to let Kikuji escape to Manchuria. He does so by pretending to talk loudly to the assassin, despite the fact that the latter is quite dead, so that Kikuji, who is concealed only a few feet away, will overhear his message. This bizarre resolution underscores the film's playful alternation of reality, illusion, and artifice. Speaking to the dead man, the policeman promises that Ōshige will be able to join Kikuji in Manchuria at a later time, but as Ōshige leaves, Kikuji comes out of concealment in great distress. The narrative thus ends in total uncertainty. Is the policeman's "happy ending scenario" just another illusion? Will Kikuji once again be torn between responsibility (wife and child) and freedom (Manchuria)?

Hana to dotō brings theatrical artifice into direct confrontation with the viewer's expectation of a narrative and emotional resolution, and to some extent with the patriarchal structures of closure in the popular cinema. It may also be a way of impressing a directorial "stamp" on a narrative full of liberal but less-than-radical content, by suggesting that the historical sit-

Fig. 4.26. Theatrical (Anti-)Melodrama: the stylized sets of the curt finale (*Hana to dotō*)

uation of the workers is too serious, too much a "reality," to belong in the false, aestheticized framework of the heroic *yakuza* melodrama. Hence the division of color and technique between the two principal milieux in both films: the world of cops and gangsters is blatantly, gleefully artificial, the other semi-realistic and burdened with the pessimistic weight of history (the failure of unionism).

Yet the director clearly felt more empowered in the realm of the former; in any event, he made it his signature. It is a mistake to view this stylized, self-consciously cinematic world of action melodrama as having a fixed (i.e., retrograde) ideological weight on account of its past. The cinema is reinvented far easier than reality. If stylization often represents a space of male ideological fantasy, it also demarcates it *as fantasy*, refusing a naturalistic depiction of the world of *giri* and *ninjō* (which I propose to define as the irreversible ideological relation between "honorific" male violence and heterosexual relationships) that would render it as an interpretation of reality. The pleasure we take in Kimura's fantastic and artisanal spaces only encourages the establishment of a critical distance. This is exemplified by the death of Manryū; Suzuki's curt, rapid, anti-melodramatic climax forces the question that a sentimental finale would blunt: why doesn't Kikuji really care about his lover? *Irezumi ichidai*, by contrast, makes an abortive attempt to present a (differential) romantic melodrama within the economy of naturalism: although this treatment permits many fascinating reversals, it comes up against the limits of classical narrative, that is, against the ideological limits that had encrusted around it. Even the independent character of Midori is ultimately measured by her degree of loyalty to the male hero; indeed, this limitation makes the familiar romantic promises at the end of the film—for example, "I'll wait for you until you get out of jail"—as thoroughly unbelievable as a Hollywood happy ending, and unworthy of this intriguing film.

Perhaps Suzuki's finest achievement, in terms of social and historical representation, is to underscore the colonial subtext of even the most marginal Japanese lives of unskilled laborers, bar girls, and small-time crooks. The working class characters speak with almost mythical fervor about the freedom and golden economic opportunities that lie awaiting in the colonies. In *Hana to dotō*, Kikuji will stop at nothing to escape to Manchuria, where he expects to find freedom from the law. In *Irezumi ichidai*, Kenji's last words, as he dies under *yakuza* swords, underscore the terrible delusion of it all: "Brother, let's go to Manchuria!"

The emergent Japanese colonial empire is vilified, mocked, and personified in the character of the pathetic swindler, Yamano (Komatsu Hōsei). Suzuki's most despicable character, he combines the stereotype of the ageing colonial blowhard with the political informer and the crass exploiter. Yamano is a man who can only come to prominence in an era of colonial expansion: a perpetually hard up liar and braggart who was, at one time, an agent of the "Manchurian Land Development Program," Yamano now acts as a liaison between grafted politicians, *yakuza* bosses, industrial spies. When not serving his betters, he makes money by scamming the poor and desperate, including the two protagonists, who are searching for a cheap passage to Manchuria by sea. The dream of working class opportunity through expansion is strangled, symbolically, from the start. Yamano wins their confidence by telling wildly improbable stories to bar girls about his adventures as a government spy with the Kwantung Army, whose reputation was itself based upon a notorious lie.[32] The fact that Yamano is both a con artist *and* some sort of genuine corporate agent, a representative of power on a small scale, is a political gesture on Suzuki's part, an undisguised attack on the broadest possible swathe of prewar imperial culture. Colonialism, which was almost universally viewed, in early Shōwa Japan, as a nationalist and spiritual crusade, a quasi-benevolent Pan-Asian scheme of unification, a bulwark against communism, and a necessary component of national defense, is treated here as the swindle of the century. The studios, on the other hand, continued to churn out "war-retro" pictures throughout the early 1960s,[33] in which the nationalist, racial, and quasi-sacred concept of the *kokutai* remained entrenched, while the history of the Manchurian occupation was largely avoided.

What Is the Nagaremono Ideal?

It is illuminating to compare the three protagonists whom we encounter in the films of the "Yakuza Sequence." In some ways, Kikuji and the more sympathetic Tetsu are both "stunted growths" of prewar militarism. They are not only afraid of femininity, but incapable of intersubjective relations except for those male ties which lead, inevitably, to gang ties. Their behavior relates not simply to Oedipal overdetermination but to a prescriptive, pathological culture of martial masculinity. Standish notices this in the Japanese cinema as "the rejection and denial of the feminine aspects of male nature. Symbolically, this is built into the narrative through the negation of women completely as in . . . wartime productions *or* . . . in the post-war cinema, the rejection of lovers."[34] We have seen many examples of the latter in the *yakuza* sequence, but one can also infer that Suzuki sympathizes with these men as part of his afflicted generation, arrested in its maturation by the war. For such men, gang life and wandering are the only options, but these paths are neither separable nor sustainable: both lead to death.

Ryōgoku Midori, in a fascinating, rambling 1966 article on the fear of domesticity in Suzuki's films, sees an attempt to construct a different type of *nagaremono* protagonist (although she does not, in fact, use the term "*nagaremono*"). She relates this subtler version of the male loner to the "guilty conscience of stability" that she traces back to the great writer Sakaguchi Ango.[35] This entails a post-war socio-political guilt at investing in domestic arrangements which had become writ large, in the wartime era, as private property and the coercive family-state (*kazoku kokka*). For Ryōgoku, Suzuki's protagonists follow a romantic ideal of nomadism as "opting out" of society: an anti-social ethical choice.[36] Certainly the fate of Katsuta represents a masochistic renunciation of a romantic longing so intense that, as he says in voice-over, "I threw away my ambitions and the chivalrous (*ninkyō*) path . . . I had the impulse to follow this swindling woman . . ." His later renunciation of romance is not necessarily based on the fear of femininity, yet rejects any possibility of domestic arrangements.

Standish seems to read the *nagaremono* ideal, like other masculine idealities, as pure psycho-social flight from the feminine, both internally and externally, towards a (mythical) masculine grouping that permits "true intimacy."[37] Ryōgoku, on the other hand, seems to see the *nagaremono*'s search for independence as an intervening state between successful heterosexual relationships and homosocial bonding. One might infer that in order to accomplish the true outcast ideal, the drifter must not only renounce the romantic relations he yearns for, he must also renounce the "primacy of the male group," just as Tetsu is ready to flee from the homosocial solidarity of the laborers in order to "go it alone" as a colonial drifter.[38] In such a situation, as Standish noted, the homosocial relations between individual men (other drifters) become the only, necessarily fleeting, forms of social existence.[39]

Ryōgoku identifies a conflicted, perhaps self-imploding masculine project rather than the more triumphant and linear patriarchal construct that Standish explores in relation to the Tōei films. There is an important theoretical distinction to be made between the ethical renunciation of domesticity and a pure psycho-social reflex of misogyny—or between attachment to a brother and attachment to a whole patriarchal ethos. But in practice and reality, such distinctions often collapse. This is the strength of Standish's critique. According to Ryōgoku, Suzuki remains invested in the *nagaremono* ideal;[40] yet he emphasizes, more than most, its failure. For many of the viewers of *yakuza* films in the 1960s, political dissent from the right—in the form of the martial outcast—may have seemed preferable to no dissent at all. But in Suzuki's version, as Ryōgoku noted, the hero's independence is always bound by the contract of *ninkyō*, an internalized and inescapable social commitment. It is in Suzuki's version, above all others, that masculine essentialism and the erotics of violence render the idea of rebellion from the right as delusional. For Suzuki, then, the only ideal that remains is a negative and unattainable one: a desire to discover how the outsider lives at the price of *all* emotional bonds.

There is an irony here that Ryōgoku does not address. Katsuta, the romantic, goes to jail full of self-righteous pride. But White Fox Tetsu, a preternatural killing animal, is jealous of the fact that his brother died for love. For Standish, the tragic hero trope is built on the notion that a "pure" masculine ideal must be opposed by the forces of social control. But in regretting his incapacity for romance (in contrast to sublimated, libidinal violence), it is Tetsu who recognizes the ultimate futility of his own persona; the sense of failure becomes more important than the ideal. Again, for Standish, the structuring conflict of the Tōei *ninkyō/nagaremono* films is that between *jingi* (honorific masculinity) and the law (social control).[41] For Suzuki—who recognizes and yet departs from this structure through dream and vision—the supervening struggle is simply that between *jingi* and sexuality, or better, between sexuality and *all* social codes.

CHAPTER 5

The Flesh

(Nikutai no mon, Shunpuden, Kawachi karumen)

Discomfiting Continuities: The Flesh Trilogy and the Social Order

Of all Suzuki's films, *Nikutai no mon/Gate of Flesh*, *Shunpuden/Story of a Prostitute*, and *Kawachi karumen/Carmen from Kawachi* are most clearly connected thematically, and they have been referred to, retrospectively, as the *Nikutai* (Flesh) Trilogy.[1] The three films allegorically address the state of Japan during the war years, the immediate post-war period, and the 1960s, respectively. The first two were adapted from stories by Tamura Taijirō, founder and exponent of the *Nikutai bungaku* (Literature of the Flesh) that emerged in the late 1940s.[2] *Kawachi karumen* is a *gendai-geki* adapted from Suzuki's favored contemporary author, Tōkō Kon (the original author of *Akutarō*), and is tailored to expand upon questions raised by the earlier films concerning sex and society, the culture of capitalism, and the post-war continuity of the Japanese social order.

Each film stars the remarkable actress Nogawa Yumiko, playing essentially the same role of a country girl compelled into prostitution by hard times. Nogawa was the only star to be entirely discovered by Suzuki. Her screen presence demonstrates an earthy, vital physicality, a frank sexuality, and a capacious inner life through which she perceives and negotiates the (obstructed) path of her own desires. These qualities, the director claims, could not have been achieved by the composed, prestigious contract stars at Nikkatsu in the 1960s.[3] Nogawa was intended by both director and studio to push the boundaries of sexual representation; a star personality would have been inappropriate. Nogawa's character represents a lower-class "everywoman,"[4] much as Imamura's *Nippon konchūki/Insect Woman* (Nikkatsu, 1963) is a panorama of recent Japanese history seen through its heroine's eyes. One might view the *Nikutai* Trilogy as competition with and an aesthetic response to Suzuki's rival, Imamura.[5]

Fig. 5.1. Cinema Palimpsest: superimposition of the protagonist and her imaginary world in the same frame (*Nikutai no mon / Gate of Flesh*)

The Flesh Trilogy is of vital importance to the development of a "differential" style and textuality in Suzuki's films. Notwithstanding the blatantly commercial derivation of the project, *Nikutai no mon* was the Suzuki *gumi*'s most audacious visual tapestry up to that time. I use the word "tapestry" because the film's most notable visual features include the superimposition of two different POV images onto the same frame at the same time, utilizing both sides of the long NikkatsuScope frame to literally realize the "polysemic" image that was only nascent in *Yajū no seishun*'s mirror sequence. The picture goes even further, incorporating narrative events and the mental images of the protagonist into the same frame.

Because such combinatory images deny perspective, they emphasize by their very nature the flatness of the cinema screen, and may represent an homage to the seemingly two dimensional artistry of German expressionist films such as Wiene's *Das Cabinet des Caligari* (1919).

Suzuki's film creates the effect of an early pre-modern Japanese narrative screen (*emaki*). It also approaches the "scattered attribute space" of Western non-perspectival painting, including the modernist works of Magritte and Matisse, in which various images are placed on the canvas in no particular spatial or thematic order. In addition, *Nikutai no mon* made famous the experiments with primary and non-diegetic colors discussed in the previous chapter. A meticulous recreation of the streets of Tokyo in 1946 becomes, simultaneously, an abstract canvas of often non-diegetic primary colors and stylized, disproportionate set designs. Suzuki and Kimura Takeo choose to "re-present" recent Japanese history *via* an anti-realist mise-en-scène that projects a sort of garish beauty in spite

Fig. 5.2. *Caligari* and Frontality: expressionism's shallow proximity, shading, and flat theatrical backdrops conceal the actual depth of the filmed space

of sordid narrative events, including the actual, on-screen slaughter of a cow, which is intercut with expressions of lust/hunger from the prostitutes who watch this "spectacle." This scene brings home the savagery of everyday street life in 1946 in a way that the cinema's dramatic scenarios never could.[6] Suzuki's stylized representation of this violent milieu turns historical recreation into a subject not for melodrama, but for political and social psychological reflection.

Shunpuden also contains such remarkable non-diegetic, two-dimensional effects such as a man turning into a cardboard cut-out as a representation of his internal disintegration. Not willing to repeat themselves, Suzuki and Nagatsuka opted to visualize the narrative not through superimpositions, but multi-planar compositions of recessed spaces and a more intensive use of discontinuity editing. The result is a more experimental work which owes less to expressionism than to the avant-garde.

Relating the Alice-like encounters of a wide-eyed rural girl with the ersatz spectacle of contemporary, commercial Osaka, *Kawachi karumen* ends the trilogy in a cavalcade of discontinuity, quasi-Brechtian gesture, and occasional surrealist transformation that is suited to its disorienting urban milieu. Yet, above all, it enables a critical reflection on the place of women in it, as Tsuyuko (the picture's "Carmen") manages to surmount the unbearable disappointments of her relationships with variously corrupted men.

Nikutai no mon and Shunpuden are milestones in Japanese cinema history for reasons that are clearer in retrospect than they were at the time. The former, a story about a gang of female prostitutes who band together only to fall apart over sexual jealousy, was specifically commissioned by Nikkatsu as an erotic entertainment showcasing (limited) female nudity and sadomasochistic scenarios.[7] It is the first recognizable model for Nikkatsu roman poruno, a variation on the pinku eiga (soft-core sex films called "pink cinema") that would dominate studio production in the 1970s.[8] Nikutai no mon was Suzuki's biggest commercial success, giving rise to four remakes.[9] It thus had a great, if indirect, influence on Nikkatsu's decision to develop and, from 1971, to concentrate exclusively on erotic productions (erodokushon). Tōei and Daiei studios quickly followed this trend. Suzuki in fact disliked the roman poruno genre,[10] and his films are not responsible for Nikkatsu's subsequent decisions. But their historical impact on the cinema was immense and remains unappreciated; it may even include being the first films to use maebari, a hygienic covering for genitalia.[11]

Shunpuden, marketed as an erotic romance, turned out to be the commercial cinema's most abrasive confrontation with its imperialist past, and hence was reviled by establishment critics. It did not help that both Nikutai no mon and Shunpuden had been successfully adapted to film before by well-reputed directors, the former in 1948 by Makino Masahiro, the latter in 1950 by Taniguchi Senkichi, with a cautious script by Kurosawa.[12] Both films, particularly the latter, were celebrated by establishment critics. However, Occupation film policy, the threat of censorship, and the representational mores of the period ensured that these films entirely avoided the sexual frankness of Tamura's stories, and in the case of Taniguchi's film, avoided the subject of wartime prostitution altogether. In light of this, Nikkatsu management was astute in judging that the time was ripe for a revisitation of Tamura's work, even if their interests were squarely commercial. While the critical reception of Suzuki's Nikutai trilogy was hampered by negative comparison to the original films, in retrospect it clearly differentiates its own politicized aesthetic from, and in many cases actively negates, those originals. In doing so, it furthered Suzuki's reputation for having a distinct stylistic signature and a politics of representation in resistance to the limitations of classical studio realism and the so-called post-war "liberal humanism" of Taniguchi, Kurosawa, and Tamura himself.[13]

It is impossible to fully understand the Suzuki version of *Nikutai no mon* without reference to the rest of the trilogy. Because of its damning of the American Occupation, in part through the common *topos* of rape by American Military Police, *Nikutai no mon* has seemed to some critics (despite its equally hostile portrayal of the *yakuza*) like an all-too-familiar scenario of Japanese "victim consciousness,"[14] that is to say, a facile opposition between the evils of Americanism and nostalgia for an unblemished prewar Japan. This ideological binary had been apparent in many "war-retro" studio films of the 1950s.[15] Although this characterization is inaccurate, it is only with *Shunpuden*, one of the most uncompromising portraits of Japanese colonialism, that the full breadth of the filmmakers' critique emerges. The American occupation is merely one side of a bad equation. At the other side is the solidification of prewar corruption in the form of a militaristic patriarchy followed by a regimented, bourgeois, commoditized one. Taken together, the purpose of Suzuki's trilogy is to demonstrate analogous, coercive dynamics and hierarchies of power across the bridge of war, including the continuity of an entrenched patriarchal elite.

It is necessary to revisit, at least superficially, the post-war ideological landscape in order to appreciate just how counter-hegemonic the representation of history in the *Nikutai* trilogy actually was. For Carol Gluck, Japanese post-war reconstruction depended on widespread belief in a "fundamental break" from the (wartime) past and a new beginning:

> The time of the surrender broadcast was inscribed in Japanese memory as the fictive moment when the past ended and the present began. Willing time to be broken and history severed, Japan turned towards the future. . . . The New Japan, as so many called it. . . . [but] the prewar past, to be obliterated, had first to be retold.[16]

This retelling required a "heroic narrative . . . of an unjust war with clearly identified villains. . . . [The Pacific War] could have been avoided only if its armed forces had kept away from politics."[17] Yoshikuni Igarashi's *Bodies of Memory* reconstructs in detail this "official narrative" of the war that saw defeat as a "sacrifice needed for Japan's future betterment" and the survival of its *kokutai*, its national (and imperial) body politic. This narrative of its "rescue and conversion" paralleled that which the mass media and the cinema had applied to Japan's colonial acquisitions of the 1930s. Just as Japan had "rescued" China and Manchuria for its betterment, so "the United States rescued Japan from the menace of its militarists, and Japan was converted into a peaceful, democratic country under its tutelage."[18] Igarashi believes that this narrative, upon which MacArthur's SCAP collaborated with the Imperial office, remains ingrained in the Japanese consciousness, albeit co-extensive with resentment over American interference.

The *Nikutai* Trilogy appears as an almost point-by-point negation of the official narrative from the hindsight of the mid-1960s. In this vision, Japan—the "lower" Japan, the *shitamachi* world of working or striving people—was never rescued from its patriarchal class of military, bureaucratic, and business elites. The U.S., far from being the rescuer, acted as the guarantor of this elitism, re-establishing a regime of capital under a government/corporate conglomerate. Of course, *Nikutai no mon* is not alone in this view. Even ignoring this collusion with former imperial elites, leftist and libertarian thinkers in post-war Japan had little reason to support the cold war politics and ham-fisted censoriousness of the U.S. Occupation.[19] From the *Nikutai* Trilogy's vantage point, the post-war future was not bright; they suggest that Suzuki and his collaborators doubted that the individual sacrifices of the war were worth making for the survival of any body politic. What they most profoundly negate, however, is the notion of a fundamental "break" for post-war Japanese culture. They represent a Japan only nominally converted to democracy: it remains an authoritarian state organized at the lower levels by deep and inherited social coding through which ordinary social groups—working girls, salarymen, *yakuza*—re-enacted varieties of fascistic behavior that "the official narrative" attributed to military leaders. In *Nikutai no mon* the ex-soldiers cannot escape their indoctrination, while the clique of post-war prostitutes will only sleep with Japanese men as a point of racial pride; they govern each other's behavior through invasive rules and punishments; their leader dons *yakuza* tattoos and declares that her only interest is in power; and even the "innocent" heroine (Nogawa) spitefully seduces and destroys an African-American priest (Chico Roland).

This is a point at which the film diverges from Tamura, its source author, in what is otherwise a faithful adaptation. Tamura viewed female sexuality as a force of nature that could counter and overcome a repressive Japanese tradition of thought.[20] Suzuki's version is characteristically more negative, and in my view a stronger, more complex misreading. The female body may be a site of political resistance precisely because the history of Japanese patriarchal thought had attempted to control it with only partial success (as dramatized in Mizoguchi's 1936 masterwork *Naniwa erejii/Osaka Elegy*). In *Nikutai no mon*, the radical possibilities of the body are contingent and ephemeral. Having endured the bodily conditioning of the war regime, Suzuki could appreciate the power of ideology. The history of the young woman, played in each film by Nogawa, is the history of the *loss* of "natural sexuality" (however we conceive that term), whether to the war, the struggle to survive, or to post-war market forces, even including pornography. She recovers only a desperate and limited freedom through personal rebellion and through a kind of masochism that, ironically, reverses the sadistic presumption of Tamura's story, in which only (masculine) violence can release a truly dynamic female sexuality.[21] Where Tamura used the female body as a permanent laboratory of democracy, a site for escaping the historical past and forging a (brighter?) future, *Nikutai no mon*, looking back from that anxious future, demonstrates a bifurcation between (bodily) resistance and survival. Igarashi theorizes that popular post-war melodrama overwhelmingly associated the reconstruction ideal with the resubmission of female bodies to the control of law and order.[22] But in the film, Borneo Maya's decision to die as a lover, rather than live as a fascist, is a rebellion against a society in which survival means the regimentation of sexuality to new market forces and old authoritarianisms. It is an extraordinary personal act for a heroine as exotic and non-conformist as her name, but politically it changes nothing: history is implacable. However, in the sex scene between Maya and the war veteran (played by Shishido Jō) leading up to her rebellion, Suzuki and Mine produce a non-diegetic shimmering effect around each body which renders bodily boundaries amorphous and permeable. This proposes a new standard for inter-subjectivity and gender fluidity, if only visually and if only through intercourse.

The scene affirms the non-conformist "here and now-ness" of the body: but without affirming the political efficacy of post-war sexual "liberation" in the new order of things. The opportunistic, survivalist heroine in Ōshima's *Taiyō no hakaba*—which contrives to relate fascism and the war experience to the degradations of contemporary slum life—similarly discovers that "vitality is not enough."[23] This pessimistic hindsight connotes not only a regard for the limitations of post-war (democratic/sexual) "liberation," but for the limitations of the post-war artistic discourses of "liberal humanism," personal melodrama, and narrative realism.[24]

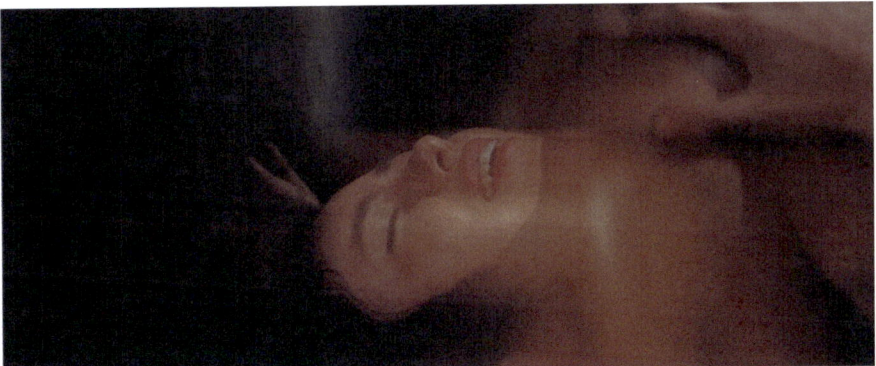

Fig. 5.3. Cinematic "Inter-Subjectivity": a non-diegetic shimmering effect around bodies wrapped in intercourse (*Nikutai no mon*)

Mythologies of Group Dynamics: Domesticity and Yamato Damashii

Post-War "Groupies"

In the *Nikutai* Trilogy, the negative aesthetic I ascribe to Suzuki's films comes into force as a nexus of formal practice and social critique. The following section treats the latter, for the trilogy amounts to a broad indictment of Japanese social organization as satirized through the allegorical figure of the prostitute. The films propose a damning structural critique by representing the group dynamics of Japanese society as inherently unstable and undemocratic. The director has said, "When you watch a Western ... its foundation is the spirit of sacrifice. The Japanese don't have that element. A code is the foundation for us, for each group. As an army has its own code, the prostitutes have *their* own code."[25] Since Suzuki is fully aware of the elitist male tradition of martial heroism and self-sacrifice, he evidently would view that tradition as a hysterical overreaction to broader, deeper Japanese social structures. So did Ikku Jippensha, whose 19th-century *Hizakurige* was the foundation of modern Japanese social comedy; whilst the mature Suzuki, for his part, usually appears to maintain an Ikku-like comic irony even in tackling these most serious and lamentable subjects. Only the key moments, as it were, of each film, depart from that mode and stun us with a sudden sobriety of tone and an evocation of the terror of social coercion.

The characters of the trilogy are organized into gendered groups whose ethics and behaviors are analogous. The male group, represented by the military or the *yakuza*, demonstrates a continuity of power through gendered oppression. As the adjutant general (Tamagawa Isao) in *Shunpuden* batters a "comfort woman" who has been forced to serve the soldiers at the front, he rages at her for letting "the name of His Majesty pass the mouth of an impure bitch like you!" Here is one of the great, succinct expressions of the grand hypocrisy of Japanese patriarchy. The female group—the prostitutes—are symptomatic of the commodification of Japanese life and its regulation of personal desire, whether sexual or material.

It quickly emerges that prostitution, not flesh, is the grand metaphor of the trilogy: prostitution as an institutionalized (gendered) dependency imposed by force. In *Shunpuden*, Harumi's romantic enslavement to the dislikeable lieutenant (Kawachi Tamio) is likewise a prostitution of the soul, reinforced by the sexual paradigms of wartime culture and constantly at war with Harumi's instincts towards self-preservation and sexual fulfillment. Throughout the film, her enslavement is likened to the abuse of the minds and bodies of the male soldiers by the military hierarchy.

Prostitution in *Nikutai no mon* allegorizes the failure of Japan to achieve a "new start" in the post-war era. The disastrous implosion of a potentially benign "union" of female prostitutes is itself allegorical of two interrelated forces. The first is the "Americanized" post-war regime of capital. As the brutish Roku (Ishii Tomiko) puts it, imitating the signs of the fish vendors, the girls sell their bodies "straight from producer to consumer." This libidinal economy is expressed in the narrative by the ironclad, yet totally absurd first principle of the gang: never have sexual relations for free. The second, more subtle, factor is the destabilization of a horizontal union of equals by power relations of domination and submission that substitute for the body's lack of free pleasure and find their outlet in unstable violence. The leader, Sen (Kasai Satoko), who is unable to have an orgasm, punishes "insubordination" based on her own compensatory needs. This mutual dependency of ruler and subjugated looks backward, historically, to the military state, and forward to Japan's submission to the economic and Cold War directives of the United States.

In both cases—the enslavement of women and soldiers to military hierarchy and the enslavement of post-war survivors to a ruthless black market culture—the state of patriarchal subjugation is challenged by a potential for revolutionary change within each subject. In *Shunpuden*, that potential is represented by Harumi, a woman capable of biting the tongue off of a male lover who has lied to her. Her deliberate sexual betrayal of the adjutant general attempts to undermine patriarchy with the only force—female infidelity—that it can never fully accommodate. *Nikutai no mon*, similarly, recognizes the promise of a commune of prostitutes who pool their resources for survival in a time of starvation and protect themselves from pimps and predators. Unfortunately, this revolutionary potential, even in the "Tokyo Year Zero" environment in which survival was popularly thought to supervene over Japanese mores, goes unrealized. In the film's reductive analysis, it is neither the environment nor direct patriarchal intervention that undermines the possibility of change. It is the entropic nature of group dynamics in and of themselves—their susceptibility to corruption in the form of hierarchies of domination and submission—that subverts that potential and ensures the continuity of social inequities across the "break" of the war.

Suzuki's "case studies"—soldiers, *yakuza*, and prostitutes—maintain themselves by codes of conduct informed by social ideologies of such longstanding importance to the Japanese social structure as to deserve to be called "mythologies." In the case of the male groups, the mythology is largely that of *"yamato damashii,"* the oldest and most resonant slogan of Japanese nationalism.[26] The examination of female groups is more surprising. Rather than presenting them simply in relation to wartime ideology, the trilogy confronts the more trenchant "bourgeois" myth of domesticity as the natural outcome of heterosexual romance.

Nikutai no mon begins with the charismatic figure of a young *yakuza* (Wada Kōji) who acts as a pimp for American soldiers. Despite this unpatriotic line of work, the *yakuza* exclaims that *"yamato damashii* still lives!" when he learns that a GI has been knifed by a Japanese veteran. It is remarkable that the *yakuza*, seemingly too young to have fought in the war himself, perpetuates a metaphysical slogan of empire despite military defeat, occupation, and the renunciation of imperial divinity only months before the story takes place. Has the wartime ethos of "national mobilization" proven unassailable by fact, or is the young man simply mouthing a slogan of the *yakuza*? The post-war decade was a watershed era of conservative political activity (mostly in the form of union busting) on the part of *yakuza* and ultranationalist ex-military activists, with extensive (and wealthy) networks of association running between the two groups.[27] *Nikutai no mon* represents this conservative nationalism as a psychosocial reaction to fears of diminished masculinity and condemns its hypocrisy, not only because the *yakuza* were only too happy to participate in American capitalism for gain, but because their prominence and political connections represented business as usual for the ruling elites. Fukasaku, in a famous interview, claimed the desire to memorialize the rough (*arashii*) lower-class male characters of the post-war black market, to whom he felt a kinship.[28] The Suzuki version of black market culture displays an indifference to the *yakuza* bordering on contempt. It recognizes only exploitation and a bogus illusionism derived from social coding.

Corporal Mikami, the male protagonist of *Shunpuden*, is one in a long line of young, delusional fanatics in Suzuki's films. He remains steadfast to the ideal of dying for the emperor even after experiencing first-hand the utter hypocrisy of the military hierarchy and the crimes committed in the imperial name: that is, an adjutant who wants to have him executed out of sexual jealousy, a general who lies about deserters and incompetents to protect the (undeserved) reputation of the battalion, and a bureaucracy that court-martials Mikami himself for cowardice and desertion merely because the other soldiers abandoned him, unconscious, in a trench. Fully aware of the worthlessness of the hierarchy, Mikami's patriotism is so deep that, given the choice of being executed by the Japanese or fleeing with the PLA in the company of other Japanese deserters, Mikami chooses the former without hesitation, and at Harumi's expense. When Harumi sings a sentimental Chinese ballad with the PLA soldiers, achieving a rare moment of inter-cultural subjectivity, Mikami begins to bleed, a physiognomic symptom of his deep xenophobic distress.

The widespread duplicity inherent in a supposedly transcendental hierarchy seems to be the film's way of suggesting that the military elite, in reality, was more self-interested than fanatical: elitism and group dynamics superseded ultranationalism. In contrast, the "purely" fanatical Mikami is one of those faithful, rather than thoughtful, souls who would serve a code of conduct at all costs rather than exploit it for his own gain. But the film is equally unsparing in its critical representation toward this character who, awaiting an unjust execution in his cell, continues to recite over and over again the military Field Service Code (itself derived by Yamamoto Tsunetomo's Edo-period treatise on suicide for the samurai): "Never let wine or women distract from thoughts of death." In keeping with these (common) misogynistic sentiments, Mikami's execrable treatment of his lover, Harumi, is the ultimate condemnation of patriotism, accomplishing a remarkably proto-feminist critique on the part of the filmmakers. As Mikami prepares to commit a useless suicide, Harumi berates him for an ideology that she has long since discarded. But at the last moment, she is unable to resist her romantic attachment and joins him in a double suicide. What are the roots of this perhaps equally fanatical attachment?

Fig. 5.4. The Hell of Romantic Attachment: Harumi runs across the vast plain toward the departing PLA troops (and freedom), only to finally collapse in the mud. She cannot bring herself to leave the patriotic Mikami behind (*Shunpuden / Story of a Prostitute*)

The Home: That Elusive Object of Desire

In *Shunpuden*, Harumi goes from one bad relationship—the sexual pleasure of domination by the hideous, abusive adjutant—to another, when she falls in love with the quietly fanatical Mikami. Misguided loyalty being a constant of Suzuki's films since at least *Ankokugai no bijō*, the central question of *Shunpuden* is why Harumi stays with Mikami literally to the bitter end. At one crucial point, Harumi abandons the invalid Mikami as the PLA are leaving the battlefield and the couple are threatened with starvation or worse. In a slow, extreme long shot, Harumi makes it halfway across a vast, muddy plain, only to collapse in despair. An abrupt ellipsis sees her returned to Mikami's bedside, unable to leave him behind.

Harumi's eventual double suicide is shocking, not because of its historical context, nor its routineness as a narrative resolution from Chikamatsu to Mizoguchi, but because Harumi is a rebellious and uncompromising heroine who rejects the pull of patriarchal values. The suicide is tantamount to a surrender of her individuality to a discredited cultural norm, a terrible sacrifice made for the unappreciative Mikami. But Harumi's fate is prefigured in an earlier scene where another prostitute, Sachiko (Imai Kazuko), returns to the base after the failure of an arranged marriage with a man who turned out to be dangerously disturbed. Speaking of her hopes for the marriage earlier, Sachiko had said that their pimp "can't understand how much people like us feel about marriage. . . ." As she returns in bitter

Fig. 5.5. The Myth of Domesticity: Sachiko's meager dishes fallen in the mud along with her hopes of "a decent marriage" (*Shunpuden*)

disillusionment, her suitcase falls open, revealing the dishes and cutlery that she had lovingly cared for across half a continent. The dishes fall into the mud, an example of visual poetry at its most adroit, and unusual in the context of Suzuki's other films for its sincere and devastating emotive potential. The feminist power of images such as this lead me to resist the facile assumption of Suzuki as yet another modernist practitioner of politicized misogyny.

It is Harumi alone who stoops to pick up the dishes, and in doing so the perspicacious viewer may predict that she is similarly doomed. Harumi is in thrall to a group ideology, which, in this version of the story, is a kind of sentimental romanticism about marriage. In a touching moment of absurd romantic fantasy, Harumi finds the wounded Mikami in the trench and carefully lies down beside him, posing as if to create the mise-en-scène for a standard portrait photo of a young married couple. This romanticism is of a kind nourished by mass circulation women's magazines and textbooks alike during the Taishō and early Shōwa periods.[29]

As the case of Sachiko reveals, these diasporic prostitutes cling to a factually unlikely hope of marriage and economic security with a Japanese man in China. The fact that they do not consider the Chinese farmers for marriage acknowledges the limited world-view of these otherwise sympathetic characters. Sacrifice—of a woman for her lover—was as much a part of Taishō sentimental melodrama as it was a part of the wartime patriotic ethos for men, and *Shunpuden* thus finds the romanticism of the prostitutes to be, tragically, just as destructive. Harumi is turned from the path of rebellion out of her desperate love for Mikami, who in 96 minutes of

Fig. 5.6. Portrait of A Marriage? Harumi "composes herself" beside Mikami's unconscious body in the trenches (*Shunpuden*)

the film neither says nor does a single decent thing for her, and on several occasions reveals the shallowness of his own affections. But her romanticism is as ingrained as Mikami's chauvinistic patriotism. However, there remains at least some hope for the prostitutes that survive Harumi. Led by a Korean elder (Hatsui Kotoe),[30] they decide, in the final scene of the film, that survival is the most important thing, after all. Ironically, they come to the opposite conclusion of Borneo Maya in *Nikutai no mon*, who prepares for death when survival means complicity. The trilogy holds out both as legitimate—and subversive—within the respective circumstances of war and peace. There is an acute historical situation to its ethical analysis. There are no transcendent solutions to the universal reality of social corruption, subjugation, and death.

The group ethics of the female gang of *Nikutai no mon* are tested by the highly ambiguous character of Machiko, a kimono-clad, traditionalist prostitute who is savagely beaten by the other girls for sleeping with a married commuter businessman who reminds her of her late husband. Machiko is creatively invested in the myth of domestic romance. "Somehow women are most happy when married," she sighs, and idealizes the marriage of her parents in a rural Japanese town. Accompanied by *shamisen* strings on the soundtrack, Machiko (who is under the impression that she is a geisha) intrudes on the mise-en-scène like a ghost from the prewar past, but also seems to satirize the 1960s "nostalgia boom" that William Kelly identifies: ". . . throughout the 1960s . . . Japanese culture was . . . frequently expressed as an exultation of . . . rural nostalgia. A feverish *furusato būmu* (home village boom) idealized country folk as true exemplars of . . . Japanese values."³¹ Machiko espouses a sort of erotics of monogamy with metaphysical overtones. She believes that the relation between men and woman is principally physical, but finds its highest attainment in marriage. "You're jealous! You've never had a man's love . . . only I know secrets of the body!" she cries as she is beaten, in reference to her previous marriage. Machiko incarnates a nostalgic myth definitively at odds with the real conditions of post-war culture. She enjoys the fantasy role play of a submissive "domestic woman" but even she cannot sustain this charade until the end of the film. In Suzuki's version, her bizarre mixage of *furusato*, geisha, and domestic sexuality appears as a retrograde prop of the patriarchal status quo, or post-war consumerism, or both.

The Aesthetics of Masochism

Violence and Difference

Satō Tadao, an admirer of *Shunpuden*, remembers that "the majority of film critics were puzzled. . . . Why was this outrageous film made when we already have [the 1948 version]? . . . Critics saw it as exploiting the erotic to sell tickets . . . they viewed it as a dirty film."³² The reviewer for *Kinema junpō* sneered, "as the work of Suzuki Seijun and [screenwriter] Takaiwa Hajime, this cannot be a matter for boasting. . . . For those who know *Akatsuki no dassō*, this [*Shunpuden*] offers disappointment and has only accomplished making us perceive the degradation of Japanese cinema."³³ Such reviewers did not care that the Taniguchi film, because of Occupation censorship and prevailing middle class taste, was so bowdlerized that it denied the existence of "comfort women" (prostitutes) on the war front, thus gutting Tamura's original. Whatever the anti-war sympathies of Taniguchi and Kurosawa, the 1948 film is a victim of history and today represents the whitewashing of a national disgrace on the part of the media establishment. Although Suzuki's film, under studio pressures of its own, sidesteps the question of the forced prostitution of *Chinese* women on the front, its representation of sexual violence under fascism, as well as its unapologetic female sexuality generally, discomfited critics who did not expect political satire from Nikkatsu "B" pictures. Their disavowing sleight of hand thus dismissed the *Nikutai* Trilogy as exploitative, unworthy of consideration. The *Kinema junpō* reviewer of *Nikutai no mon* took offense at any attempt to "re-present" the post-war sex trade, and opined that the film "hangs on nudity and cruelty so simplemindedly it even becomes rather pitiable"[34]; while Kazuki Ryōsuke wrote that "the auteur (i.e., Suzuki) is enjoying himself leisurely, capriciously, as if he may be a sadist as well."[35]

Is the Suzuki film sadistic? Instead of reviving debates about the value of popular exploitation films as political critique, I want to conduct a narrower investigation into the extent to which the representation of gendered violence in these films is representative of, or distinct from, a broader range of its contemporaries (for instance, the studio-produced or widely-seen independent *erodokushon*). This can be assessed in myriad ways—for instance, from the prism of a particular genre, as in chapter 3—and thus I wish to concentrate here, as seems *apropos* to the *Nikutai Trilogy*, on the question of whether it is legitimate to describe some representational, thematic, and formal continuities across Suzuki's many films as "sadistic." Or are they something other?

Certainly, on-screen gendered violence had been commonplace in hard-boiled, horror, and other "B" genres since the mid-1950s. Suzuki's films often invest such moments of violence with enormous visual significance, such as the frequent motif of a woman shot, offscreen, through the breast, her resultant corpse often captured in a lingering, still composition accompanied by non-diegetic stylization (Fig. 5.7). Yet there are telling variations on this motif over time. In *13-go taihisen yori sono gosōsha wo nerae* (1960), the immediate aftermath of a prostitute's lethal penetration by an arrow is the focus of a quasi-sadistic spectacle that, indeed, is ghoulishly repeated throughout the film. The composition is highly plastic, with a medium shot that captures the victim standing upright, still, and composed in death, like a statue of St. Matthews' passion. While violence against the maternal (here, the breast) is at the center of de Sade's aesthetics, it is interesting that the victim in Suzuki's films is always a relatively innocent ingénue, and not the maternal figures within a given narrative. More notable, still, is a slow, emotionally charged travelling shot that imparts a paradoxical sense of "hiatus through motion" as it moves 360 degrees around the room before finally revealing the original site of the arrow's penetration (in front of a window), all the while taking in the fascinated, palpably erotic stares of the not-so-innocent bystanders. This gesture mobilizes a powerful affect of the horror of violence and a self-reflexive layer of spectatorial guilt at the inevitable male eroticization of that violence. This kind of gesture appears masochistic in character and notably absent in Nikkatsu's graphic *roman poruno* films of the 1970s. This complicates the film's emphasis on the graphic description of a violent penetration. The lethal gunshot wound of a young secretary in *Tokyo*

158 / NEGATIVE, NONSENSICAL, AND NON-CONFORMIST

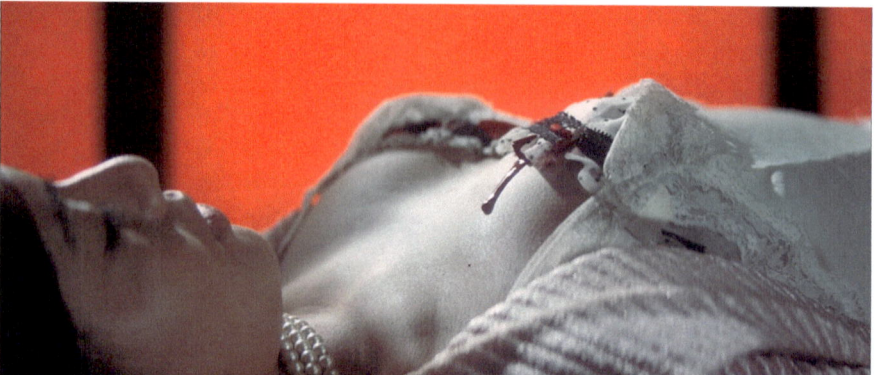

Fig. 5.7. The Stylization of Death: shot in the breast behind a non-diegetic red screen in place of a wall (*Shunpuden*)

nagaremono (1966) goes further in this direction, since the bullet's impact is not only completely unseen, but is multiply displaced by an eccentric, delayed arrangement of narrative information through cutting: we do not know that the secretary has been wounded until several shots after it has occurred, and when we do, the resulting composition can only be described as oneiric rather than graphic. It also immediately alters our perception of the character, who goes from an irritant to a young life cut short by patriarchal caprice.

If Suzuki's films, like other B-pictures, sometimes appear like a catalogue of gendered sadistic acts, does it follow that they present a sadistic mise-en-scène? Satō asserted, to the contrary, that "Suzuki's best films have the appearance of a masochistic cartoon."[36] Perhaps the most revealing moment of *Shunpuden* comes when Harumi demands physical and emotional love from Mikami. Mikami rebuffs her embraces and throws her off; when she persists, Mikami strikes her hard enough to catapult her out of the doorway. But the strike itself is not shown in a linear fashion: first, there is a long shot of the cold outer courtyard, where Harumi has fallen.

This is followed by Harumi on the ground, turning to look at Mikami, and then what *seems* to be the equally stunned reaction shot of Mikami (Fig. 5.9) inside the barn. As it turns out, the latter shot of Mikami is not a reaction shot at all, but a return to the "past," the moment of the slap several seconds before.

The next shot is also of the pitiless Mikami as he hits Harumi. We then return to a close-up of Harumi on the ground as she evidently recalls the moment of violence. She begins to scream in rage and emotional pain,

Fig. 5.8. Violence Out-of-Sync (shot 1): Harumi falls out of the door after Mikami has slapped her (*Shunpuden*)

Fig. 5.9. Violence Out-of-Sync (shot 2): what seems to be Mikami's reaction shot to his own violence is actually the moment before he slaps Harumi (*Shunpuden*)

a scream so fierce (Fig. 5.10) that it is captured in slow motion, causing the scream on the soundtrack to go out of sync with the image.

She continues her seemingly endless howl in two long shots as the other prostitutes crowd the doorway to jeer at Mikami for mistreating a woman. Yet another close-up of Harumi's scream follows, again out of sync; but this time her fury is tinged with concern for the humiliated Mikami.

In this remarkable sequence, Harumi expresses unconquerable rage when faced with the *"Catch-22"* situation of a woman on the war front: either prostitution or monogamy-as-submission to an increasingly intolerable state of things. Standish (briefly) interprets Harumi's scream as

Fig. 5.10. Rage Against the System (shot 5): Harumi reacts to her intolerable entrapment (prostitution or romantic attachment to the contemptuous Mikami)—a continuous scream for five shots, with sound and visuals out-of-sync (*Shunpuden*)

Fig. 5.11. The Restoration of Order? (shot 10): The prostitutes jeer at Mikami in retaliation for his violence. When they mock that Harumi prefers the monstrous adjutant, Harumi is forced to defend her romantic feelings for Mikami. But the formal discontinuity (like Harumi's entrapment) does not cease (*Shunpuden*)

that of the archetypal "hysterical female" whose sexuality must be recontained,[37] but this does not account for the enormous formal and gestural significance of the scene. The scream is so powerful that it shatters the norms of classical cinema. Continuity editing is broken down more severely than in any previous Suzuki film, and the ideological efficacy of linear narrative is powerfully, if temporarily, rejected. Classical realism becomes inadequate as a representational system, either to the representation of female subjectivity generally, or to the intolerable situation of marginalized women at this point in history. Discontinuity and nondiegetic mise-en-scène, corresponding here to subjectivity, must take the place of realism, in order to allow for minor perspectives and admit the possibility of critique. This enables the Suzuki version to subtly declare its superiority to Taniguchi's 1948 classical version, then a critical milestone of realism and "humanism."

In this scene, there is no reason at all to equate Suzuki's avant-garde representation of violence with cinematic sadism, which tends by definition to take on an aesthetic of linear description, control, and mastery. By contrast, here is a form that, while spinning out of control, becomes highly empathetic to the female protagonist and indeed represents her memory. As Standish points out,[38] this form is related to a masochistic context. The camerawork and Suzuki Akira's editing defies the progress of time in order to *suspend* the suffering cry of Harumi through duration, over cranking (slow motion), and repetition. Harumi has escaped from prostitution to the Adjutant only to find herself in another chauvinist "double bind" (romantic commitment = disappointment and abuse) from which she cannot escape. In the final close-up, showing Harumi's sympathy for her tormentor, her positive rage against entrapment (the truly rebellious aspect of *Shunpuden*'s aesthetic) is curtailed by a negative realization. The moment of the "break" has passed. Like all unrequited or masochistic attractions, this is a hell from which Harumi does not entirely want to escape. The film's aesthetic negates the intolerable status quo, but does not indulge in the fantasy of an easy escape from an all-encompassing psycho-social dynamic of sadism/masochism—which can be understood, in Japanese prewar narrative traditions, as a patriarchy that is only bolstered by gestures of female self-sacrifice.

The Whipping Scene: Masochism as Social Allegory

One particular scene in *Nikutai no mon*, in which Borneo Maya is stripped and beaten by the other prostitutes, excited critical charges of sadism and "masturbatory" exploitation.[39] I shall argue, however, that the scene expresses the essence of what Gaylyn Studlar and Gilles Deleuze have identified as a masochistic aesthetic—that is to say, a structural and representational economy—in film and literature.[40] This encompasses, first, masochism as a social allegory expressed largely through narrative arrangements and character interaction. Here, a masochistic dynamic assumed to be present within the family is projected as a relation towards the social order. Secondly, masochism is considered as a quality of mise-en-scène, a visual economy or rhetoric marked by such qualities as ironic distance, suspension, and multi-sensory excess.

To unpack these claims, we must briefly comprehend masochism as a symptomology. While the dominant Freudian view of sadomasochism as a complex anchored in castration anxiety and a female sense of "lack" is still very much in evidence, a number of feminist film theorists have drawn on Deleuze's theory of masochism as a process fundamentally independent, *contra* Freud, from sadism.[41] While Studlar's account of masochistic development in her book, *In the Realm of Pleasure: Von Sternberg, Dietrich, and the Masochistic Aesthetic* is flawed in some of its particulars,[42] it productively expands on Deleuze's central conceit that masochism and sadism are not just clinical conditions but entrenched *cultural* and *representational* tropes with a variable relation to the clinical.[43] It applies Deleuze's analysis of masochism as a *literary language* to cinematic mise-en-scène, and in doing so helps to identify an ambivalently differentiated male and female masochistic dynamic at work in Suzuki's films.

Studlar develops the argument that fetishistic masochism derives from pre-Oedipal sexuality and the infant child's separation from the mother, who is "simultaneously a love object and controlling agent."[44] An impossible search for reunion with an ambivalently idealized mother and for "wholeness" carries on in adult life in the form of masochism and the fetishes associated with it. The psychologist Theodor Reik argued that when the child enters the Oedipal stage, there is a "price" that must be paid "for the mature genital sexuality that is at odds with infant desire" and the pleasure principle. The "price" is that pleasure must be achieved by "another road," through pain. Because of the punishing condemnation of the superego, the masochist "submits voluntarily to punishment, suffering and humiliation, and thus has defiantly purchased the right to enjoy gratification denied before."[45]

Studlar asserts that masochism is, on the level of social interaction and representations, unavoidable as the individual's relation to an oppressive society that he or she has internalized. This renders the boundaries between the self, the familial, and the political all too porous for comfort. Indeed, even the most subtle Freudian-Lacanian orientations of academic film theory have generally underestimated the inevitability of masochism in socialization—first as a reflection on our parents' sexual past, and then as a creator of our mature self and persona. The latter functions as a negotiation of our public standing in the social world and our desire for eminence.

If we can assent to Studlar's point, it is reasonable to hypothesize that all forms of political resistance must negotiate and work through a kind of masochism. Certainly in post-war political cinema across cultures, it is relatively easy to identify a political analogue to the scenario of suffering as a route or a way of working through the guilt incurred in the revolt against the father (Theodor Reik) or, alternately, the desire to expiate the presence of the dreaded father within us (Deleuze).[46]

The sympathetic protagonists of the *Nikutai* Trilogy and the *Akutarō* films (as well as the less sympathetic ones of the *yakuza* films) submit voluntarily to society's (or a subculture's) inescapable punishment, not in capitulation to fear, but in order to purchase *the right of rebellion*. In political terms, of course, the significance of that (largely personal) rebellion differs according to genders and social positions.

Why, then, is rebellion in Suzuki's films so rarely successful? One could argue that in these films, unlike the later films of the *nuberu bagu* and the *pinku eiga* that are deeply entrenched in the political fervor of the New Left, the grand object of desire is, *pace* Lacan, permanently out of reach and unobtainable—whether that object be a fulfilling intersubjective relationship or a sexual-political revolution. Nevertheless, it is still important to distinguish between variant modes of resistance, that is (on this reading), variant modes of masochism as a social motivator. The suicide of Mikami, engaged in a "passive" rebellion against his abusive "father" (the adjutant), is, like samurai *seppuku*, a useless symbolic protest: the rebel gains nothing and the oppressor is strengthened. This failure broadly characterizes the masculine wartime *ethos* of so-called *bushidō* and the "beautiful death," which, with its erotic overtones, haunts such diverse period pieces about martial rebellion as Mishima's *Yūkoku/Patriotism* (1965) and Yoshida's sublime *Kaigenrei/Martial Law* (1973).

But the masochism of Borneo Maya is quite evidently something else. It enacts a far less orthodox masochistic "resistance": her goal is to rebel—and survive to enjoy the fruits of rebellion. As we shall demonstrate below, the behavior of Maya in the whipping scene of *Nikutai no mon* thus demonstrates what I suspect to be a critical difference between the aesthetic politics of Suzuki's films and those of the *roman poruno* (and other *pinku eiga*) that *Nikutai no mon* greatly inspired.

Some attention to the aesthetic politics of the *roman poruno* is therefore warranted. A small subset of films unambiguously highlight the murder (and requisite terror) of female victims. But apart from this, the *roman poruno* tends to be structurally defined, across the board, by sequences in which an "innocent" female is dominated and sexually violated by a phallic agent (usually male) who "demonstrates" to the victim, by these means, some perverse principle of power. Certainly this is male domination, but, perhaps, in the very extremity and repetitiveness of these scenarios, some unspeakably destructive theorem beyond this. Obedience to phallic authority is compelled, whether through fear, pain, or—in the commercial/erotic idiom of these films—by instilling the victim with the sexual pleasure of being dominated. In most *roman poruno*, the victim derives an "unfettered" sexual pleasure from her torturer; the initially "cold" masochistic young woman depends on the sadist to realize her "true" desires,[47] a dependence that reinscribes female sexuality (and its rebellious potential) into the patriarchal order.

The ideological structure (or fantasy?) of *roman poruno*, and to a recognizable extent the *pinku eiga* genre, seems, as a rule, to follow a strand of modernism in violating the feminine on account of the latter's (imposed and facile) symbolic associations with the middle class, the domestic, and, paradoxically, the law. How, then, do we account for two so different, yet highly intellectualized allegories of individual resistance from the same studio—Suzuki's and the *roman poruno*? We may gain some perspective from Marcia Kinder's reading of the violent representations of the post-Franco art cinema in Spain, a culture steeped in an imagistic tradition of ritualized, aestheticized sacrifice. Kinder detects the continuity of an entrenched mythical subtext of female sacrifice even in the case of anti-authoritarian Spanish films where (to simplify a complex argument) the subtext is ideologically reoriented towards a female who is violated as an allegorical representative of a (politically) sterile post-war bourgeois regime.[48] Kinder grounds the almost sacral iconography of these violations in an Oedipal master narrative that is to some degree universal, to some degree uniquely Spanish. It disregards or disavows violence against the actual father figure while concentrating on the violation (e.g., "*sacrifice*") of the so-called "Phallic Mother"; that is, a repressive, stifling mother-substitute for the Patriarch who appears dominant in a disillusioned post-war society without The Father.[49] Taking into account the cultural differences, Kinder's Oedipal scenario seems broadly applicable to the *roman poruno*, but there are telling markers of difference in Suzuki's allegories of the familial-political. Although images of sacrifice do appear in Suzuki's films in certain contexts (for instance in the satirical Christian imagery of *Kenka erejii*), in general this is a body of work shaped by the worldview of not a "fatherless" child of war, but a war veteran with "eyes wide open"; and one who, moreover, believed that long institutionalized coding, not sacrifice, was the baseline structure of Japanese society. Suzuki's films focus, as always, on the historical continuities of Japan's active, not merely symbolic, hierarchies of power. (Recall that the commanders in *Shunpuden* are not so much dedicated fascists as hypocritical parasites of an unearned masculine, hierarchical privilege). The figure of the overbearing mother is entirely absent from these films apart from the satirically monstrous Mrs. Nomoto, who in the hard-boiled economy of *Yajū no seishun* appears as almost a caricature of Kinder's "Phallic Mother." Indeed, the only mothers who appear in Suzuki's films following the Wada period are the weak, defeated victims of the reactionary subcultures of *Oretachi no chi ga yurusanai* and *Kawachi karumen*. One cannot rebel against something that is not there. Instead, there are a plethora of corrupt, decrepit, irredeemably evil fathers and patriarchs who represent "the institution."[50] These must inevitably be done away with (like the lecherous mountain priest killed by Tsuyuko in *Kawachi karumen*), thus reminding us of the scenarios in the work of von Sacher-Masoch in which a complex route of resistance and suffering results in the expulsion of the father both inwardly and outwardly. On this basis—the absence of the mother and expulsion of the father—Suzuki's films are uniquely poised to avoid identification with a certain sentimental mother-son dynamic that figured in Japanese wartime popular culture and in the cinema; yet it also negates the *de rigeur* alignment with the righteous patriarch that featured prominently in wartime morale boosters,[51] and continued on into the popular "action" genres of the 1950s before attaining a political transmutation (via the New Left) in *erodokushon* such as the *roman poruno*. Suzuki's films, in contrast, may well illustrate Deleuze's witheringly anti-Lacanian position that "the only danger of the absence of the father is the return of the father."[52]

The revolt against the father is, I believe, the best context in which to understand the whipping scene of *Nikutai no mon*, with its young heroine enacting a rebellion against all father figures, from the *yakuza* to the myriad representatives of the "great American father." Although it is Sen and her gang who subject Maya to a fascistic, quasi-ritual punishment when latter willfully sleeps with Ibuki, their ultimate purpose is the demonstration of authority—its self-appointed freedom to act capriciously and hypocritically. This aligns the gang for all intents and purposes with the pimps and other patriarchal enforcers from which they supposedly seek refuge. The scene also functions as a distant reflection of the earlier, crucial sequence of the slaughter of the cow amidst a montage of lustful countenances. The butchering of the cow is a self-conscious exercise on the part of the filmmakers in a pure, undiluted cinematic sadism—far stronger than the *roman poruno* variations—from which all degrees of difference may be measured.

Maya, however, refuses to learn her "lesson." Seeing both Sen and society for what they are (venal), Maya knowingly accepts punishment and regards this suffering, in the manner of Theodor Reik, as the *price* or necessary condition of achieving the forbidden (Ibuki). Maya takes the punishment, first by laughing derisively, then by refusing her captors the satisfaction of a single scream of submission. Afterwards, she proceeds on the path of resistance by rejoining Ibuki. Unlike in *roman poruno*, Maya neither derives pleasure from her torturers nor allows them to extract any. Torture is the social cost of a path of desire that she herself has decided upon. Maya's masochism, far from suppressing a rebellious instinct, serves to justify and encourage rebellion: punishment is the point of no return for the rebel.[53] The struggle of resistance against social obstacles to the expression of carnal desire was, after all, the point of Tamura's original. The Suzuki version appreciates the struggle rather more than the endpoint. As Satō writes, for Suzuki the war veteran, "it was necessary to discover . . . a masochistic pleasure in . . . an experience that shook one's core,"[54] so Maya only discovers her heroism when she becomes a punished outlaw. In this allegory, Maya may be seen as the diegetic doubles of the filmmakers, a stand-in for a male, authorial masochism.[55] If there is any resemblance to the more "willing" female protagonists of *roman poruno* who "purchase" pleasure from their tormentors—that is, who desire the punishment *itself* rather than some ulterior objective—*Nikutai no mon* differentiates itself in terms of the politics of gender, by treating masochism as an inevitable social relation that is not *essentially* gendered and retains at least the possibility of resistance. On this point, it is illuminating to reiterate (see the text preceding note 21) the difference between Tamura and Suzuki's respective treatment of the story's narrative climax, the intercourse between Maya and Ibuki. In Tamura's original the sex is a violent demonstration of Ibuki's domination and Maya's submissive pleasure. Tamura writes, for example:

> He grabbed her legs suddenly, pushed them open, and tried to tear them further apart like ripping a frog to pieces. . . . Ibuki knew by intuition that his hatred wouldn't subside until he tortured this sassy girl through and through . . . The moan of pleasure that Maya's body emanated poured oil onto Ibuki's burning hatred . . . She experienced a fulfilled feeling for the first time. . . .[56]

In Suzuki's version, however, it is a determined Maya who instigates and demands sex from the (symbolically) near-comatose Ibuki. The latter is attractive to Maya not as a father figure but, explicitly, as the object of transference of her rather mild, incestuous feelings for her lost brother, one of the war dead. The film version negates Tamura's sadistic, allegorical utilization of the submissive female body, nor does the sex have the overwhelming character of violent male domination, though such desires cannot be far from Ibuki's subjectivity: the filmmakers cannot help mocking the latter's "Alpha Male" persona by intercutting military footage of rocket launches with the moment of Ibuki's erection. It has often been said that in the dominant Japanese cinema, men are the spiritual sufferers whilst women are physical sufferers. In Suzuki's version, as opposed to Tamura's, this is entirely reversed. Ibuki's persona is entirely physicalized (indeed, crippled) whereas Maya is a quester after spiritual and erotic transcendence. Of course, for Maya's quest of rebellion against the libidinal economy to bear fruit in a "true erotic reciprocity of equality based in mutual tenderness,"[57] her object of grand passion would have to be better than he is: which Ibuki, in Shishido's sly, self-mocking performance, certainly is not. The objects of Nogawa's affections in the subsequent *nikutai* films are even worse.

In sum, there is a very real sense in which the whipping sequence, a scene of exploitation for the film's critics, establishes Maya as the quintessential Suzuki hero. Hasumi argues that in her physical "vitality," Nogawa's characters are the equal of Suzuki's male *yakuza*; but this does not go far enough.[58] Unmarked by their neurotic identity crisis in relation to the father, she is by far their superior. We should not, however, pass over Hasumi's compelling speculation that "perhaps Suzuki refuses to recognize the difference between men and women."[59] We may even divine in this some measure of Studlar's claim, based on the feminine aspects of classical male movie stars, that "the combination of male and female into one figure suggests a fetishistic disavowal of sexual difference that functions as a defense mechanism . . . embedded in the female spectator's need to achieve some measure of fantasy control of the dominance/submission agenda of the patriarchy."[60] Ultimately, though, that fantasy (which may itself transcend gender) is experienced as insufficient.

Unfortunately, like the male "heroes" of the *yakuza* sequence, Maya's resistance remains compromised: her (incestuous) investment in heterosexual romance appoints Ibuki as the focus, crux, and goal of her rebellion. When the Alpha Male proves insufficient (in fact, is slaughtered by the pack), Maya's only route of dissent is through negativity: the refusal to survive.

Varieties of Cinematic Masochism

Since Suzuki's Japanese critics point to his realizations of gendered violence not as sadistic allegory, but as a visually sadistic mise-en-scène, we ought to propose at least a provisional distinction between a sadistic aesthetic and a masochistic one. Studlar analyzes the eroticized masochism of von Sternberg's mise-en-scène in order to evince certain distinctions between masochistic and sadistic cinematic style.[61] Taking into account their respective cultures of representation and star *personae*, the *Nikutai* Trilogy is remarkably parallel in its recurring textual features and masochistic narrative arrangements to the melodramas of Sternberg (e.g., *Morocco*, 1930), in which Marlene Dietrich's character experiences a variety of obstacles and reversals in her quest for an unworthy object of desire in an elliptical, fetishistic, and ironized visual milieu. In fact, the trilogy is far closer to these films than it is to the pure "masochistic" and "sadistic" scenarios explicated by Deleuze. The essence of the masochistic scenario is a sort of pact between a cold, cruel woman torturer who whips a complicit male "victim," who is, in fact, prompting the whole scenario; whereas in *Nikutai no mon*, we have a fairly warm ingénue being whipped by a fascist woman she despises in a scenario controlled by male filmmakers.[62] One could argue that these differences are the result of the film's being a palimpsest of the obsessions of, first, Tamura and, second, Suzuki and company, with the result being untranslatable according to the aesthetic/thematic economies of sadism and masochism. One could, alternately, appreciate its "popular modernist" orientation in presenting a free collage or pastiche of sadistic/masochistic scenarios for many purposes, political and otherwise, including the fetishistic "denial of difference" that Hasumi identified. I believe, however, that there are still considerable insights to be gained from theories of masochistic mise-en-scène, especially in countering certain fairly widespread assumptions of Suzuki's Japanese critics.

Studlar is persuasive in defining the masochistic aesthetic in the cinema as an aesthetic that reemphasizes, through various formal means, the masochism that has always been an important aspect of viewership. This methodology—which accords with the purpose of this book in pointing to Suzuki's films as definitive of the way that cinematic form conditions the interpretation of meaning—is not uncontroversial. Some contemporary film scholars, even while treating the interface between cinematic mise-en-scène and a particular cultural imagery of sadistic/masochistic tropes, have been more or less pointedly moving away from seeking a working correspondence between psychoanalytic theories of spectatorship and visual/textual interpretation. Kinder, for example, threads a delicate needle between Lacanian film theory (with its characteristic emphases on concepts of "suture" and phallic "lack") and Deleuze's theory of masochism in interpreting the post-Franco cinema's bald and graphic images of paedophilic rape and murder and the mutilation of body parts, including female genitalia.[63] Given the Spanish Catholic regime of images of noble self-sacrifice that served to disavow the ignoble operations of a series of brutal political regimes, Kinder identifies a strange (yet familiar) rhetoric that could be summed up as "sadism in masochistic clothing" or "sadism with a masochistic face":

> In contrast to Masoch's model, the masochistic aesthetic in Spanish cinema is always associated with Catholicism and/or fascism, and its language and formal conventions . . . are always used to disguise acts of violence that would otherwise seem more readily assigned to the sadistic aesthetic: in this way, sacrificial ritual is used to justify modern massacre.[64]

For Kinder, these images are "brutal, graphic, and ugly, highly fetishized and specularized."[65] If we were to apply Kinder's categories, the whipping scene in *Nikutai no mon* and similar scenes of gendered violence in Suzuki's films would suggest that the operative aesthetic is more akin to "masochism in sadistic clothing." That is to say, sadistic acts (of a much "tamer" nature than the "highlights" of 1970s Spanish cinema) are *fetishized* and *specularized* but, through aesthetics of absence, concealment, or temporal suspension, are precisely *not* so "brutal, graphic, and ugly"—in short, *not sadistic* in their visual economy. This is because they are elements of a properly masochistic cinematic fantasy, a kind of staged role play (or, in Deleuzean terms, a "contracted" performance) that works, *pace* Deleuze and Studlar, to instantiate a fantasy of resistance, however whimsical or disavowing; quite possibly in order to distance itself from the equally, but differently, fetishistic social spectacles based on sacrifice-as-political-disavowal that Kinder identifies. These sacrificial images could arguably be associated with the shadow of prewar fascism—as in, for example, Nitobe Inazō's Christianized resurrection of the *bushidō* ideal, or the infantilized spectacle of Ibuki, the disillusioned veteran who still drapes himself in the Japanese flag. Kinder's "faux masochism," in contrast, seems to represent a specific ethnographic perspective on sadistic/masochistic imagery and should not be interpreted as seeking to define the integrity and proper role of a sustained masochistic visual/rhetorical economy in the cinema that might carry its own distinct, if historically contingent, ideological effects.

Masochism and Sadism as Visual Rhetorics

For Studlar, then, sadism and masochism are distinguished by their respective narrative and visual economies, presentation and ordering of time, and strategies of description. Following a Foucaldian critique as well as Deleuze, she describes the patriarchal aesthetic of de Sade as controlling, quantitative and linear, exacting in its attempt at comprehensiveness and mastery. "Sade's language—demonstrative, imperative, and obscenely descriptive—creates a fantastic world based exclusively on the rule of reason. In this world, the mechanistic negation of Nature dominates in the routine . . . destruction of female victims."[66] It is, in sum, obsessively descriptive, graphic, and repetitive in its representation of gendered violence. Sadean discourse is thus a kind of perverse *bildungsroman* in which (as Deleuze defined it) both daughters and sons may be co-opted by the father into violating the mother, who is "the victim par excellence as she remains faithful to her nature"[67] (e.g., presumably, the feminine *qua* feminine). Though anarchic, this is the kind of rationalist "constructionism" (based on gendered subjugation) that Suzuki famously decried. "The Sadean discourse is denotative, unblinkingly 'scientific' in its obscene descriptions. . . . Numbers, not individuals, count . . ."[68] Textbook examples of this aesthetic in Japanese cinema are easily located throughout the studio *pinku eiga* of the 1970s, as in the capture below.

Everything here, from straight lines and angles to the endless repetitions/reduplications, corresponds to Studlar's description. The bloodspurting sword fight of Nikkatsu's *Otoko no monshō/Gambler's Code* (Matsuo Akinori, 1966) also obeys a sadistic economy, with every violent "penetration" (this time entirely between men) clearly displayed with a linear and somewhat boring precision.

If sadism benefits from a largely realist, temporally and spatially ordered mise-en-scène, the masochistic aesthetic is often oneiric and narratively obscure, like the shooting of the secretary in *Tokyo nagaremono*. Though certainly involving eroticized violence, Studlar identifies "the temporal core of masochism" as "the suspension of gratification manifested in games of waiting, surprise gestures of tenderness and cruelty, and masquerades that . . . delay consummation."[69] The erotics of masochism "obsessively recreate the movement between concealment and

Fig. 5.12. Sadism and Sexploitation: in Suzuki Norifumi's satire *Ero shogun to nijūichi nin no aishō / Lustful Shogun and his 91 Concubines* (Tōei 1972), a long shot captures dozens of concubines lined up in a row, tickled and then seemingly violated by serving woman with paintbrushes, on the orders of the shogun.

revelation, disappearance and appearance. . . ."[70] Its visual and narrative account of the sexual is therefore not only in the fashion of a masquerade, but often formally and metaphorically full of gaps and wholes. Because of these factors, the encounter with the nude body is usually masked in some way: Deleuze writes of von Sacher-Masoch's fiction that "we never see the naked body of the woman torturer; it is always wrapped in furs. The body of the victim remains in a strange state of indeterminacy except where it receives the blows."[71] A variety of strategies of "masking" the body (from costume to shadow to non-diegetic optical effects, as in Figure 5.3 above) are certainly a crucial aesthetic of *Nikutai no mon*. Such formal marks of difference from the studio's broader *erodokushon* genre carry the potential of a site of resistance, however fragile or conditional, to the dominant patriarchal tenor of post-war popular culture and film.

The Whipping Scene:
Spectatorship and Masochism as Visual Style

In contrast to the sadistic desire for intervention and penetration of the object by the subject, Studlar maintains that cinema spectatorship is masochistic in that "it depends on separation to guarantee a pain/pleasure structure."[72] The passive, sometimes overwhelming submission to cinematic pleasure only works, paradoxically, on the condition of an unbridgeable separation and distance. Crucially, Suzuki's definitive assertion of the *figurative/symbolic*, not the representational, capacity of the cinema is also predicated on the distance between screen and viewer. Perhaps spectatorial masochism may be a means to understand a fundamental alternation in Suzuki's films between critical distance and irony and, conversely, an awestruck absorption in aestheticized spectacles of light, color, and eroticism.

The notion of spectatorship as a submission to a powerful cinematic "other" carries the possibility of irony, which is not normally understood as commensurable with "submission" to a spectacle or work of art. For Studlar, irony consists of "self-awareness" even in moments of extreme passion.[73] The individual stands outside of himself, at a distance, as it were, even while suffering pain. "Ironic humor qualifies the melodramatic absurdity of masochistic posturing."[74] This relates not only to the dialectic of (specular) involvement and ironic withdrawal in Suzuki's films, but also their tendency towards the overtly artificial. In the aesthetic economy of masochism, narrative events are "related paratactically rather than causally as antecedent/precedent rather than cause/effect."[75] Rather than relying on the distribution of images according to classical continuity, it exploits the graphic match and other contiguities of juxtaposition based on sensory perception.[76] Studlar calls this *synesthesia*, the substitution of sensory elements for one another. Since *synesthesia* "permits . . . the forging 'of new multi-sensory meanings,'" this cinematic style tends toward an overload of sensory excess.[77] Narrative is "dissipated into spectacle."[78] Of course, such departures from the continuity system are only partial: the latter functions both as the engine of narrative and as the "scene" of disruption.

In seeking a "visual attitude" towards the representation of violence, *eros*, and the relation between them, the *nikutai* films work through a masochistic economy, at least as Studlar defined it. The only moment in *Shunpuden*, for example, which reveals the nude body of the heroine is a moment from Harumi's dream. In an extreme long shot, she casts off her clothes and runs free through the Chinese courtyard, retreating swiftly from the camera into a cloudy background as a symbol of freedom (Fig. 5.13).

In an earlier, potentially lascivious moment, a prostitute is forced to strip off her clothes and submit to a cold bath. However, Suzuki depicts her nudity in the background of an extreme long shot, in front of a vast desert plain and at the back of two recessed archways, while in the middle ground, gossiping prostitutes in their kimonos move about and obscure our view of the nude.

This "promise and refusal" of voyeurism is gently ludic, recalling the games of delay, revelation, and concealment by which Studlar character-

Fig. 5.13. Nakedness as Freedom: Harumi dreams of running free through an old Chinese courtyard (*Shunpuden*)

Fig. 5.14. Nakedness as Art: The female nude in the extreme background of an artfully composed, multiplanar social tableau (*Shunpuden*)

izes masochism. In the Suzuki aesthetic, however, the game goes on forever: there is no consummation, only the endless erotic play of art. In that respect, as in *Yajū no seishun*, the nude is integrated as only one compositional element of a multi-faceted canvas of extreme depth, encompassing landscape, architecture, costume, and an overtly "posed" and painterly framing. Kajiwara Ryūji opined that Suzuki's aesthetic was foreign to the modern "Japanese mind which thinks too easily of a sexually desiring, lascivious eroticism called 'nudity'" and that earlier filmmakers had avoided such compositions because they "feared misunderstanding."[79]

In both cases, the long shot and the extreme distance from the eroticized body are the most notable compositional elements. These qualities

Fig. 5.15. Masochism and Distance: Shigeyoshi Mine's "flattened depth" barely conceals the extreme distance between the camera and the hazily glimpsed nude body of Maya (*Nikutai no mon*)

Fig. 5.16. Masochism and Concealment: carefully placed shadows and non-diegetic green "masking" foreground the lack of visibility (*Nikutai no mon*)

are brought to a logical conclusion in the whipping scene at the climax of *Nikutai no mon*. Maya's nude and hanging body is portrayed in a series of three long shots, interspersed by close-ups (just as Deleuze theorized) of the precise sites of the blows (for example, the knees). This is followed by three skillful close-ups of Maya's twisted countenance from different angles as she is whipped, the sound of which is not presented according to a plausible rhythm, but all at once, like an avalanche. The final long shot captures Kimura's magnificent expressionist set of the bombed-out building interior, punctuated by strange (possibly non-diegetic) colored windows resembling stained glass. Within this composition, Maya's body hangs from the visible ceiling just off-center. Carefully placed shadows conceal her genitalia, buttocks and (usually) breasts. A non-diegetic translucent masking effect, which grows thicker and more greenish in hue in each of the three long shots, covers the frame on both sides of Maya's hanging body.

The mask has the effect of emphasizing Maya's body (the only unmasked part of the frame), but because of the camera's distance and the covering shadows, the mask ironically emphasizes what *cannot be seen*: it fetishizes not exposure, but concealment itself. In short, the scene displays every aspect of masochistic economy: the play of concealment; overt (non-diegetic) artifice; a montage based not on cause and effect but the escalation of impression and sensation, a visual and narrative confusion of pleasure and pain. Through the self-reflexive play of "masking," the film reemphasizes the fundamental separation of the viewer and the cinema screen, which, for Studlar, is the basis of (masochistic) pleasure, and which, indeed, makes the unique fascination of the cinema possible. Where the sadistic aesthetic would attempt to penetrate this distance, reveling in visual clarity and the voyeuristic capacity of the apparatus, the filmmakers turn to the opposite. Perfecting the mirror sequence from *Yajū no seishun*, the *Nikutai* Trilogy celebrates the polymorphic capacity of the film image to render *eros* abstract, to transmute the voyeurism of the body into the fascination of a diffusive and non-representational erotic mise-en-scène: in other words, into erotic art. By arguing the necessity of this transmutation, they are among the most distinctive of the erotic art films of the 1960s in their aesthetic politics of cinema's confrontation with the body.[80] While violence against woman, often mandated by Nikkatsu's scripts, is indubitably represented as erotic spectacle, it is also clear from above, as informed by the concept of masochistic irony, that this is increasingly a "spectacle" that acts like a modernist canvas, allowing, indeed insisting, on a critical perspective. The reality of sexual and gendered violence in Japanese society, especially in the period films of the trilogy, is invested with masochistic visual significance because that is essential to their political understanding. At the same time, the "image" of violence—frequently off-screen and as part of a complex masochistic fantasy—is clearly not as important a component as the female nude itself in the creation of an anti-representational erotic art. To clarify this, one might say that in Suzuki's political aesthetic, gendered violence must *not* be represented either as (graphic) realism or as melodrama; it is far preferable to recast screen violence, and the pleasure of the (heterosexual) male spectator, as a graphical abstraction, a problematic work of art suffused with masochistic irony. At the risk of appearing blasé—a consequence of the director's firsthand experience of violence as absurd—such abstraction recuperates violent representations, not as figures of ideological drama or of self-assured political demonstration, but as figures of discourse, ironic and critical.

Kawachi karumen's Rebellion without Masochism?

Although I have posited masochism in Suzuki's films as the structure of relation of the individual to society, *Kawachi karumen* (1966) appears as an attempt to imagine female resistance from without a totalizing masochistic scenario that is still, nevertheless, inevitably in the background. The director's collaboration with a younger *kumi*, developments towards activism in the political climate, and the film's contemporary setting may have all contributed to this. Nakahira Kō 's earlier *Getsuyōbi no Yuka/Monday Girl* (1964) provides an illuminating comparison to *Kawachi karumen*, as it is an extremely similar Nikkatsu picture, even more indebted to the French *nouvelle vague*, about a sexually liberated, young urban socialite who ends up murdering a patriarch. In Nakahira's version of the story, the protagonist's sexuality and serial affairs is presented as a problem, indeed a neurotic pathology, thus interpolating a fundamentally patriarchal viewpoint. By contrast, apart from humorous commentary on her provincial assumptions, *Kawachi karumen* is entirely non-judgmental of the sexual life of its protagonist, Tsuyuko (again played by Nogawa Yumiko). Perhaps more importantly, the character and subjectivity of Tsuyuko is neither reduced to nor principally determined by sexuality.

In the film, every level of patriarchal society, from homeless drifters to *zaibatsu* industrialists to promiscuous *yamabushi* (a mountain holy man whose presence is an allegorical indictment of the prewar episteme), attempts to subjugate Nogawa's robust heroine, but ultimately fail. Rape and an intolerable family situation brings Tsuyuko from rural Kawachi to the Club Dada in Osaka—the setting of a marvelous satire of crass *sarariman* culture—where she becomes a hostess (and *not*, for once, a prostitute). As she wades through a succession of professional and sexual relationships, Tsuyuko learns to participate in Osaka's libidinal economy only enough to make a living and flourish. The question is whether she will be corrupted; that is to say, whether she will be fixed as a commodity (as a kept mistress, fashion model, or porn actress) or whether, on the other hand, she will join the ranks of the exploiters.

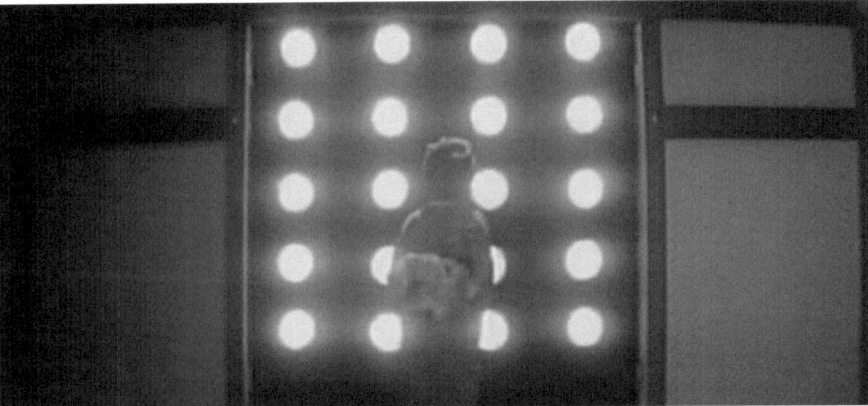

Fig. 5.17. Pornography's Threat in a Media Regime: on a porn set, non-diegetic flats resembling klieg lights literally close in on the heroine (*Kawachi karumen / Carmen from Kawachi*)

Despite the temptations of money and fame and a romantic/nostalgic attachment to her worthless small town sweetheart (Wada Kōji), she manages to avoid these pitfalls. While what we might call the "primary" masochism of "taking on" or contending with a series of painful, gendered social barriers, internal and external, remains in evidence across the trilogy, Tsuyu is the only protagonist to evade the "specific" forms of masochism (in all their complex interrelation with the gendered and coercive group dynamics of Japanese social tradition) that sometimes result from that wrenching and sometimes crippling struggle. To put it plainly, she avoids the trope of female self-sacrifice for the object of desire. In the end, she rejects—seemingly out of mere strength of character—all relations of dependency, even that of the heterosexual couple, which here is depicted as profoundly unstable. In this, Tsuyuko is stronger than her prewar counterparts.

Tsuyu returns to Kawachi as a rich woman, but when she finds that the predatory *yamabushi* has seduced her younger sister, she lures him to a waterfall and pushes him in. Tsuyu is haunted by this deed; but as she was haunted by the malevolent patriarch in life, what is lost? Who is to judge whether her action is unjustified? The studio removed Suzuki's ambiguous climax to the film, in which Tsuyu is, or imagines she is, sexually assaulted by the *yamabushi's* ghost. This may have been fortuitous: as it stands now, *Kawachi karumen* appears remarkably like proto-feminist empowerment, with Tsuyu's violent resistance metonymic for the militant activism that would soon preoccupy Japan's students and the *nuberu bagu* as well. However, we might also consider Suzuki's more pessimistic version as expressing that there is ultimately no such thing as 'successful' murder. Tsuyu is able to save her own family through violence, but other women may not be in a position to do so without reprisal. Lacking a political consciousness, Tsuyu's resistance does not change society—hence the returning ghost of patriarchy. Despite its provocative exploration of sexual politics, then, *Kawachi karumen* is ultimately *less* a political discourse then a semi-comic fantasy (not unlike screwball) of female success against the odds. Nevertheless, it is Tsuyu's nonconformist survival through a sense of self-worth that shines through the trilogy as a ray of potentiality.

CHAPTER 6

The Break

*(Tokyo nagaremono, Kenka erejii,
Sandanjū no otoko, Mikkō o-rain,
13-go taihisen yori sono gosōsha wo nerae)*

Introduction: The Suzuki Difference

I view the consecutive films *Tokyo nagaremono*, *Kenka erejii*, and *Koroshi no rakuin* (1966-67) as forming a "Trilogy of Violence" or better, to use the title of the middle film, an *Elegy for Violence*. All three works cover the same thematic ground: the foundational role of violence in the formation of Japanese masculinity. This "elegy" for violence is therefore a metonymical elegy for masculinity. This dissolution of a quasi-traditional, prewar concept of masculinity is perhaps the dominant social theme that recurs across Suzuki's many films.

Of course, the word "elegy" must be understood primarily as ironic. These films present "case studies" of men whose unwavering devotion to an imagined code of masculine conduct spells disaster for themselves and their communities. In these films, Japanese culture hypocritically encourages and enables this kind of fanaticism at every turn, while ultimately suppressing it in the name of social order.

The trilogy also contains some of Suzuki's most critical negations of genre and popular cinema. While *Tokyo nagaremono* vigorously pulls down the formal structures of the *yakuza* and *akushon* genres as they had been understood before 1966, it also holds out the possibility of a modernist, playful approach to the material, which brings violent spectacle to the cinema without reproducing the conventional ideologies that seek to justify such violence in the service of patriarchy or social control.

The "Violence" films also have a formal consistency that sets them apart from earlier exercises. The discontinuity effects of *Shunpuden* (1965)—the use of sound/image disjunction and non-diegetic graphic effects—are no longer exceptional in these films: they are essential. The films also share a strategic tripartite structure that emphasizes an accelerating pattern of repetition. Altogether, The Violence Trilogy sees the director's now tightly knit *kumi* reaching that point of stylistic maturation which I have called "The Suzuki Difference." Here are no more "halfway points," like *Irezumi ichidai*, that fairly safely embody the Nikkatsu *akushon* formula as a comprehensible narrativization of a given script, only to burst out in a privileged instant of stylized action. The Violence Trilogy retains only the deformed or hyperbolic, ironized "shards" of the old *akushon* formula, as if it was a glass that had been shattered to pieces and reassembled in a different order, or as a collage, with a plethora of new material pasted in. No longer could a Suzuki film be considered as roughly equivalent to the 1960s output of a Kurahara or a Nakahira. The Violence Trilogy is as distinct, in every way, as Ōshima's politico-cinematic provocations of 1966-67, and they appear, today, a good deal less dated.

Having used such terms as "stylistic maturity" throughout this book, I run the risk of indulging in a teleological or "progressive" reading of a directorial career, which, after all, has multiple points of historical and aesthetic interest. Although I want to forestall this objection, it is nevertheless important to remember what academic film scholarship does its best to make us forget: that academics *do* take a major role in judging, for a varied audience of readers, which films are worth viewing and reviewing. Critical judgment will never entirely be separated from analysis. This being said, my assertion of a "Suzuki Difference" is not *primarily* a canonical-aesthetic question of whether a deconstructive experiment like *Tokyo nagaremono* is in some sense superior to a taut, dynamic hard-boiled thriller like *Ankokugai no bijo* (1958). I merely assert that there *is* a difference of form between those earlier films and the films of the Violence Trilogy, though often it is as much a question of quantitative intensity as it is of qualitative change. The definition and significance of that difference is the purpose of this chapter. I have been tracing a development in a certain direction towards the "Suzuki Style" at its most radical point of divergence, or active differentiation, from Japanese film practice, especially in the context of studio genre. Hence, "The Suzuki Difference."

Amongst established film critics, there were signs of an implicit, anxious acknowledgment that there was indeed a "difference" to Suzuki's films of 1966-67. Up to this point, with the exception of *Eiga hyōron*, Suzuki had been the most critically ignored of 1960s directors. The critic Yamaguchi Tetsu, who loved Suzuki's *Kenka erejii*, excused himself for having "not had the opportunity to see a lot of his [previous] films."[1] *Tokyo nagaremono* was widely but negatively reviewed by the major magazines, more as a Watari Tetsuya vehicle than as a director's film, its stylistic eccentricities duly noted by an uncomprehending establishment: "... people fight each other ... in the style of ... pantomime often performed at the Nichigeki or Komageki [theatres].... The tone became all the more mismatched."[2] *Kenka erejii*, however, had its screenplay published in *Kinema junpō*.[3] With this film, Suzuki found himself on the critical map in a way that had eluded him even after the commercial success of *Nikutai no mon* (1964).

Forms of Reflexivity: Tokyo nagaremono

Is There a *Wataridori* in This *Mukokuseki*?

Tokyo nagaremono began life inauspiciously as another *kayō eiga* (pop song film), a movie meant to cash in on a popular tune. This was common practice at Nikkatsu: the title song to virtually any *akushon* vehicle would be released as a record featuring the vocal "talents" of the picture's male star. In this case, Nikkatsu took the music from an existing popular ballad and rewrote the lyrics and arrangement to suit a male vocalist.[4] A screenplay was then written by Nikkatsu stalwart Kawauchi Kōhan on the basis of the song before the project was handed over to the director. Nikkatsu marked *Tokyo nagaremono* as the film with which to make a star of Watari Tetsuya, a young contract player with a few supporting roles to his name. Nikkatsu hoped to re-establish the kind of star power, particularly over female viewers, that Kobayashi Akira had by reinventing Kobayashi's *Wataridori/Wanderer* (1959-1962) and *Nagaremono/Drifter* series (1960-61). The film was meant to be the first of a new *Nagaremono* series.

As the *Wataridori* series is subject to both satire and revisionism in *Tokyo nagaremono*, it is important to understand its character. Like the mustachioed prewar imitators of Chaplin, it is one of the more notorious examples in the Japanese cinema of wholesale iconographic borrowing from Hollywood. Though the stories were set in contemporary Japan and featured pickup trucks, greedy land developers and the like, Kobayashi occasionally rode a horse, fought with a bullwhip, and dressed in a cowboy hat, boots, and "tasselled" leather shirt.[5]

His costume may well be a direct recreation (Fig. 6.2) of Montgomery Clift's star-making outfit from *Red River* (released in 1948).

Nikkatsu being Nikkatsu, the publicity stills were more fantastic, and probably more important, than the films themselves. *Gitā o motta watari-*

Fig. 6.1. The Frontier as Fashion (1): Kobayashi Akira as a Japanese film star/pop singer in Western cowboy dress for the *Wataridori* series publicity (1959-62)

dori (Buichi Saitō, 1959), the first in the series, begins with Kobayashi in a far less ridiculous outfit and does not last two minutes before he loses his boots and dresses in a normal fashion—after which the film settles into an agreeable re-tread of Ishihara's biggest hit, *Akai hatoba/Red Quay* (1958). Evidently emboldened, Nikkatsu leaned heavier into cowboy fashion in *Daisōgen wataridori* (1960) and in subsequent pictures; but the more implausible cowboy accoutrements once again tended to be relegated to the more "evocative" opening or closing moments of these pictures. The *Wataridori* stories were nominally specific about their settings, including the supposed "frontier wildlands" of Shikoku and Hokkaido;[6] but this hardly explained the diegetic non-sequitur of Kobayashi's initial Americanized appearance. The fashion and action codes of these aspects of the series are purely iconographic, the fetishistic, exotic poster images of a commercial multi-media operation at work beyond the diegesis in the form of songs, magazines, etc.: an operation nearly indistinguishable from

Fig. 6.2. The Frontier as Fashion (2): Montgomery Clift's stylized "Frontier Youth" outfit in *Red River* (released 1948)

what Masumura satirizes in his *Kyōjin to gangu* (Daiei, 1958) in which candy is advertised to children through men in spacesuits and giant European wrestlers outfitted vaguely like cavemen. The novelty was the appeal, but this in turn determined the ephemeral nature of the *Wataridori* cycle. Kobayashi's Westernized fashion statement, showcased in easily digestible, escapist action pieces, was lucrative but short-lived.

Nevertheless, *Wataridori* had a great influence on the Nikkatsu "house style." With their dependence on artificial "cinematic" milieux and conventions derived from previous studio pictures and from Hollywood, the series gave rise to Nikkatsu's *mukokuseki* (borderless) action picture aesthetic, of which Kobayashi's costume is a striking example. Some of the jarring cultural juxtapositions in these films have led to the misleading notion that all or most of Nikkatsu's *akushon* pictures, because they were often set in such liminal spaces as harbors, dockyards, and Westernized Ginza bars, were also *mukokuseki;* that is to say, vague and disingenuous as to their location and socio-cultural context.[7]

Suzuki brought a sense of absurdity to bear on one film that is widely considered a *mukokuseki* exercise, *Sandanjū no otoko/Man With a Shotgun* (1961), an outdoors adventure that is notable, formally, for its charming (and probably cost-saving) use of extreme long shots to depict action sequences, favoring landscape over movement in a way that was unusual for Suzuki and Nagatsuka. This film may not have been designed to show up the absurdity of the *Wataridori* pictures, but in retrospect, it cannot escape that interpretation. As much as the *Wataridori* formula trades on the pleasures of generic repetition, I cannot think of any major studio film as *internally* repetitive, and doggedly so, as *Sandanjū no otoko*, which subjects the *akushon* formula to such a multiplication that it creates a kind of heightened, diegetic hyper-reality. The picture consists of a bar fight, followed by an unfinished duel, then a bar fight, then an unfinished duel, then a brawl, then a duel, *ad infinitum*. Guns are ubiquitous, with the characters constantly pointing them at one another, yet hardly ever firing—and when they do, they invariably miss.

Nikkatsu's *mukokuseki* postures seem to operate at a greater level of sophistication, however, when it comes to Suzuki's earlier success, *Mikkō o-rain/Undercover o-Line* (1960). A biting, sour, and fairly relentless portrait of crime reporters competing for a scoop, *Mikkō o-rain*'s morally bankrupt urban milieu and hard-boiled character delineations provoke ethical questions that echo those of the later *Tokyo nagaremono*. Nagato Hiroyuki (in one of his best roles) plays Katori, whose devotion to getting an exposé crosses every possible boundary: allowing him, for instance, to trap women in compromising positions and induce them into sex. Irony abounds, since the actions of Katori's naïve, principled rival are no less disastrous in their outcomes, while Katori's very consistency offers a partial redemption when he tries to protect a potential source even after she has vengefully tortured him. The urbane, cynical subculture of Tokyo's newspaper business resonates with Nikkatsu's *mukokuseki* orientation as it is represented in terms not much different from "journalistic" thrillers set in New York or London. *Mikkō o-rain* also highlights scenes of narrative interaction with several foreign characters—most of whom, to the film's detriment, are too grotesque to be taken seriously—who quite literally exist on the (maritime) borders and margins of the Japanese islands. Perhaps most interesting, from a film-historical perspective, is the dominance of an extravagant, if largely realist, visual style that baldly alludes to Godard and the *nouvelle vague*, with endless elaborate travelling shots and exterior location shooting (much of it on familiar Nikkatsu backlots). There is an unmistakable imitation of the infamous "driving montage" of *À bout de souffle* with its then-revolutionary disjunctions of sound and image. However distinctively Suzuki would use some of these tools in *Tokyo nagaremono*, the Godardian stylization of *Mikkō o-rain*, which is energetic and elegant when viewed in isolation, is contained by a rhetorical dynamic of imitation/adaptation that seems only to inhibit the Suzuki-*gumi*'s distinctive stylistic integrity without engaging the *nouvelle vague* in a conceptually provocative manner. Parody had been a feature of Suzuki's films since the earliest period, so there is some question as to whether the style of the film constitutes an enthusiastic borrowing or whether it parodies the very notion of stylistic borrowing at a time when it was becoming the height of fashion (e.g., the *Wataridori* series or Kurahara's outwardly Godardian *Kyōnetsu no kisetsu*).

It is fascinating to compare *Tokyo nagaremono* to both *Mikkō o-rain* and *Sandanjū no otoko*. The latter, as a narrative exercise, is equally as contrived and absurd as *Tokyo nagaremono*, and, indeed, makes even less room for Nikkatsu's familiar masculine sentimentality and melodrama. But *Sandanjū no otoko* does not carry over its absurdity to the *formal* register; that is, to the point where departure from convention and seemingly arbitrary form *become* the meaning of the film and perhaps (considering that the earlier pictures were far more popular in their day than was *Tokyo nagaremono*) its only justification. Just as there is a difference between the grand metaphors (or clichés) reproduced by mass culture and the creative, unconventional metaphors of path-breaking works of art, so there is a difference between the outlandish, yet formulaic, aspects of certain genre cycles (which are entirely disavowed in the *Wataridori* pictures) and *Tokyo nagaremono*'s self-conscious absurdity of style, narration, and montage. When compared to *Sandanjū no otoko* (or the sober *Mikkō o-rain*), much of the facetious tone of *Tokyo nagaremono* can be explained as a far more knowing, even "winking" acknowledgment of the manufactured postures of the *Wataridori* series and its spinoffs, exploiting their artificiality in order to dissociate spectacle from the conventional, commercial ideologies so typically attached to it, initiating a self-reflexive discourse on cinematic falsity itself.

Discontinuity in Action

Suzuki and Kimura Takeo began production on *Tokyo nagaremono* by rewriting the script, deciding for themselves where and how the protagonist would "drift." As is clear from the finished film, however, Watari's character is not really a drifter at all, and the film, despite an important,

Fig. 6.3. Discontinuity in Action (shot 1). LS: a pan right shows that Viper (*right*) is just behind Tetsu (*left*). Viper turns away for a moment to put a silencer on his gun (*Tokyo nagaremono / Tokyo Drifter*).

symbolic interlude in snowy Yamagata, is largely set within and about Tokyo itself. Suzuki remembers being "severely scolded" by Nikkatsu for the finished product, as the studio claimed that Watari was not shown to best advantage and could not be marketed on the basis of such a film.[8] A desultory sequel put paid to plans for a *Nagaremono* series.

Despite the studio's protestations, *Tokyo nagaremono* is still, recognizably, a Nikkatsu *akushon* picture. Yet this "genre" had no stylistic, tonal, or even narrative consistency beyond the *sine qua non* of action, accommodating the hardest of hard-boiled (*Kenjū zankoku monogatari*, 1964), just-plain-silly pastiche like Noguchi's *Dainippon koroshiyaden/Murder Unincorporated* (1965), or prestige romantic melodrama (e.g., Masuda Toshio's *Akai hankachi/Red Handkerchief*, 1964). *Tokyo nagaremono* is therefore a complex intertextual response to multiple generic conventions, including the somber *ninkyō* tale of loyalty and the far-fetched *Wataridori* phenomenon. As the common denominator is action, it is fitting to resume our examination of the "Suzuki Difference" with the novel approaches to filming action taken in *Tokyo nagaremono*.

The film's earliest action sequence demonstrates the inception of a bolder, intensive aesthetic of "discontinuity editing." It involves the hero Tetsu taking the wheel of the enemy's car. The scene features frequent and abrupt ellipses which, in terms of classical editing, are entirely dysfunctional, since they serve only to mystify the viewer about what has transpired between the break. In one shot, the car is on a road; after a shot

Fig. 6.4. Discontinuity in Action (shot 2). LS: Viper turns his head back in the direction of Tetsu. A non-diegetic, translucent, triangular mask covers the upper left portion of the frame (*Tokyo nagaremono*).

Fig. 6.5. Discontinuity in Action (shot 3). LS: Viper's POV of the empty field of snow in front of him—Tetsu has mysteriously disappeared.

of the passengers being tossed about, the car is now shown in the middle of a hitherto unseen stream. In the next shot it is back on land, in a quarry. Finally, the sequence abruptly disappears with a tranquil shot of a restaurant sign in Tokyo. It is never revealed how the heroes extricated themselves from the gangsters. Suzuki withholds both spatial and narrative clarity, seemingly for the sake of it.

A sequence involving a train track is even more radical. In the first shot, Tetsu is being pursued by his rival Viper Tatsu (Kawachi Tamio) across the snowy plains of Yamagata.

188 / NEGATIVE, NONSENSICAL, AND NON-CONFORMIST

Fig. 6.6. Discontinuity in Action (shot 5). LS of Viper on a rail overpass, while Tetsu is behind the cement pylon underneath the bridge. There are no visible means by which Tetsu could have climbed down. The non-diegetic mask now emanates from the lower left.

Fig. 6.7. Discontinuity in Action (shot 8). Extreme LS: an abrupt ellipsis. Viper is now also under the bridge, aiming his gun at Tetsu on the tracks in the foreground.

Exciting on its own terms, this bizarre action sequence contains narrative mysteries created by spatial non-sequiturs: how did Tetsu disappear (from a long shot) and reappear under the bridge (Fig. 6.6)? Why does Viper wait on the tracks for the duration of twelve shots before shooting? When did the painted red line, which guides Tetsu's measurement of his shooting range, suddenly appear?[9] It is not simply the case that Suzuki has more interest in expressive stylization than verisimilitude.

Fig. 6.8. Discontinuity in Action (shot (3)). MS: six shots later, Viper is still pointing his gun at Tetsu. He has not fired.

Fig. 6.9. Discontinuity in Action (shot 15). A notoriously unconvincing, tension-diffusing rear projection (or process shot) of the train supposedly bearing down on Tetsu.

The translucent masking over the lens, in select shots, has no expressive function and is nothing but distracting. In comparison to earlier *akushon* pictures, including *Yajū no seishun*, the train sequence plays like a deliberately orchestrated nonsense. It is impossible to understand Suzuki's filmmaking here as anything other than symptomatic of a "break," if not a "breakdown." Narrative coherence is frequently denied, diegesis is often ruptured, but more than this, local narrative and visual events are themselves fragmented. The twin essence of the *akushon* formula—the action

Fig. 6.10. Discontinuity in Action (shot 20). LS: after seven further shots Viper, still on the track, finally fires as Tetsu. The masking has by now become a translucent bar across the top of the frame.

Fig. 6.11. Discontinuity in Action (shot 21). Overhead LS of Tetsu, still on the tracks, running toward Viper with the train behind him. Tetsu drops to the ground at a non-diegetic red line and fires before the train roars past.

sequence itself and the martial, masculine superiority of the hero—are particularly subject to dismantling. One must conclude that *Tokyo nagaremono*'s attitude towards its genre is significantly negative. These qualities are, to be sure, a major reason why we still watch *Tokyo nagaremono* with fascination, when Nikkatsu's biggest contemporary hits are all but forgotten. It is only through this progressive establishment of a "freewheeling" dynamic between the viewer and the film's narration, a "loosening" of how they expect it to proceed, that an incredibly unconvincing rear projection shot (Fig. 6.9 above) purporting to show the train bearing down on Tetsu, can be considered as an amusing part of the film's ironic, hyperbolic texture rather than a dismal distraction.

This is in notable disagreement with Hasumi Shigehiko, the most prestigious of Suzuki's supporters within Japanese academia. Hasumi argues that when Suzuki cuts without strict regard for continuity (for example, when he cuts before the principal action of the shot is completed, as when Ōtsuka slaps Chiharu in *Tokyo nagaremono*), the purpose is to create tension by speeding up the tempo. It reflects, for Hasumi, "a consistent dedication to suspense and action."[10] For Hasumi, Suzuki's is categorically *not* an avant-garde artist even though he "achieve[s] avant-garde effects" (a suspicious distinction), and is certainly not parodic in his treatment of genre material.[11] But how can Hasumi accommodate the radical derangement of cause and effect in the Violence Trilogy, the editing of which incontestably represents a violation of normative practices relating to continuity and narration? Hasumi confirms the violations in regards to the director's "disordered" handling of images and symbols associated with weather and the seasons.[12] Evidently, Hasumi (who appears totally uninterested in the stylistic norms of the studio system) wishes to demonstrate a fidelity to action and "suspense" on a more idiosyncratic level. For most narrative theorists, however, "suspense" requires suspension of disbelief, a maintenance of faith in the film's diegesis. Especially in a film that is not obviously a work of fantasy, there must be at least a temporary acceptance that what is happening on the screen reflects a spatio-temporal plausibility in proximity to the viewer's own profilmic experience. Yet, what happens to narrative suspense when the universe in which it takes place and the conditions that we have assumed it to be governed by are suddenly undermined by the film itself? Satō Tadao gave a firsthand account of viewing the infamous sequence of the "collapsing red walls" in *Kantō mushuku* upon its original theatrical release. He recalled that "while the viewers were startled and absorbed by them, they could not help laughing at themselves for having been taken in by such abrupt histrionics."[13] This is hardly evidence of a "dedication to suspense" in any way in which we have previously understood the term; nor does it evidence much respect for Nikkatsu's established genre conventions. If Max Tessier is slightly overemphatic when he claims that "Suzuki's derision is aimed against a genre and a morality. . . . He denies any validity, any credibility to these clichés,"[14] Hasumi errs too far in the other direction. If Hasumi has a point in regard to the dramaturgy of *Yajū no seishun*, for example, his argument founders in regards to the Violence Trilogy that, he concedes, "disorders a ready-made genre."[15] The purpose of Suzuki's films is not to reify the genre forms of the classical studio narrative that they so deliberately depart from: it is to replace them with their own. *Tokyo nagaremono* in particular exemplifies these "new forms" in which a proper balance (or a reverse *imbalance*) of spectacle, narrative, and intellectualization of the material is restored. This certainly involves, as Satō discovered, a kind of a pleasurable, ironic distance achieved via artifice and the spectator's attempt to interpret that artifice: the spectator who, as Hasumi puts it superbly, "is trying to determine the proper distance."[16]

The argument that Suzuki is dedicated to a cinema of action and movement is far more defensible than the idea that he is interested in suspense. But what does Hasumi mean by "action"? Perhaps we can better understand, or profitably adjust, Hasumi's subtle and ambiguous usage by placing it in parallel with Deleuze's concept of the "action image" of the classical cinemas. The "action image" is rooted, for Deleuze, in the consistent imitation and maintenance of the human "sensory-motor schema"; that is, the reliable, uninterrupted linkage between perception, judgment, and action on the part of individuals within their environment. It is principally for this reason, and several others on which Deleuze elaborates at length, that the action image is viewed as the locus and definitive form of what he defines as cinematic realism, especially in a studio filmmaking context.[17] *Tokyo nagaremono* represents a purposeful violation of this paradigm as Deleuze sets it forth. This places Suzuki in closer proximity to the European art cinema and to "avant-garde" directors like Teshigahara and Kazuki Kuroi than Hasumi would care to admit. Not that Hasumi's reading is totally incommensurable with Deleuze. Hasumi sees the film's discontinuity as giving rise to a state of "pure action," a constant sensation of pure movement uninterrupted and uninhibited by elaborate cultural codes of symbolic gesture.[18] For his part, Deleuze sees extreme discontinuity of action, generally, as giving rise to a "pure" state of time as lived duration (or "time-image"), which is beyond a reductively sequential, or spatial, concept of time.

From this perspective, Hasumi's term "pure action" is radically different from Deleuze's classical "action image" in which the action is seen "as if through one's own eyes." Hasumi's term may be better understood as *kinesis*, for the purpose of which a high degree of spatio-temporal coherence is only a limitation. A truly intensive state of *kinesis* is something that, arguably, can *only* arise through the breakdown of such coherence.[19]

Where my reading principally differs with Hasumi, then, is in the negative consequences of pure action and disjointed spectacle for dramaturgy (what Hasumi calls "suspense") and for the viewer's consciousness of genre conventions. An excessive amount of generic awareness leads to an ironic and occasionally disenchanted view of "the ordinary product," something that works very much in favor of a more "knowing" film that communicates its own self-awareness to the receptive viewer. Even Hasumi, who concedes that Suzuki's films of 1966-67 are marked by "the spirit of rebellion" and a "self-destructive tendency," concludes that the director's investigation of cinema "finds out more limitations than possibilities":[20] in other words, a negative aesthetic. Still, it is rather too easy to interpret Hasumi as claiming that the "negative" stylization in Suzuki's films amounts to merely a set of devices relating to tempo which not only do not have to mean anything, but simply do not mean anything, even figuratively. But this would be to fundamentally misunderstand negativity. As Iser demonstrates:

> Negation may relate . . . to something preceding a statement. This does not mean that nothing is left of it. A poster stamped "performance cancelled" is still a poster, and is all the more striking. . . . So the indeterminacy of the text increases . . . Thus negativity turns out to be a basic constituent of communication. . . . *indeed can be regarded here as the structure bringing forth—at least potentially—infinite possibilities.*[21]

The climactic shootout of the film, in the Club Alulu, provides an excellent test case. It also adds a theatrical dimension to the fragmentation of the previous action sequences. This is boldly announced by a non-diegetic change of colored lighting *in media res* (Fig. 6.13).

Even more revealing is the theatricality of Kimura's nightclub set. Compared to the theatricality of *Hana to dotō*, this represents a bolder leap into self-reflexive artifice. But theatricality in Suzuki's films is never an end in itself. If Suzuki, who proudly cited kabuki as an influence, were to agree that movies would benefit from being viewed as spectacles, closer to stage presentations than to "happenings in the world," this still does not go far enough. Like discontinuity, theatricality must be used to reveal a cinematic "falsity." It must negate some aspect of cinematic practice that, in other hands, might be passed off as conventionally or consensually "real."

In the space of one shot, the already "ultra-stylized" climax degenerates into farcical incredulity. Tetsu and another gangster are perched behind evidently fake Greek columns that are not connected to anything. They are ludicrously small, not wide enough to conceal a human body, and

Fig. 6.12. Imposed Style (shot 1a). The nightclub set begins entirely black, then fades in as Tetsu enters the space; the donut-shaped sculpture insists on the non-diegetic provenance of the light sources.

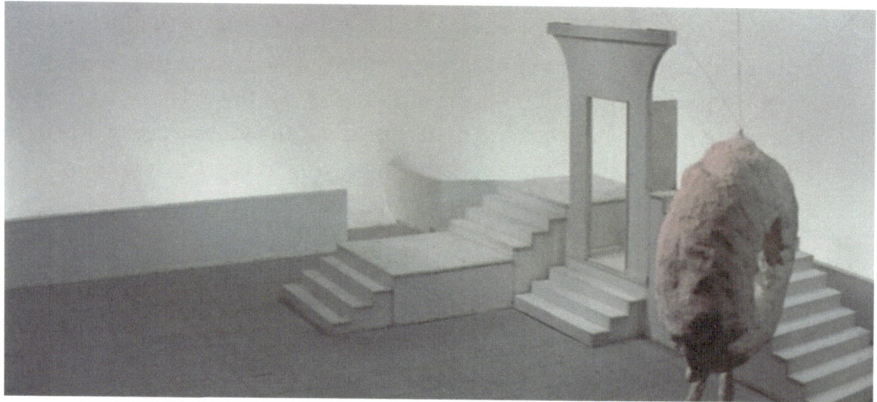

Fig. 6.13. Imposed Style (shot 1b). In the same shot, after Tetsu kills Ōtsuka (and four others), the lighting turns a blanket white, as if an orgasmic release of masculine violence.

scarcely more than fifteen feet apart from one another. And yet, Tetsu and the gangster shoot at one another twice from such a short distance away, with neither managing to score a hit. Tetsu then proceeds, for the duration of *several* shots, to use the column as protection from the whole gang's innumerable bullets.

What are we to make of this, if not genre self-parody? Hasumi's characterization provides no answer. Certainly, the shot plays upon the motif of surface and depth, appearance and reality, so evident throughout the

Fig. 6.14. Theatrical Style as Falsity

film. Even if one assumes that, within the diegesis, the columns are fake because they are leftover set pieces from a musical number, the characters *act* as if they are real; that is, adequate cover from which to evade bullets. The artificiality of the nightclub set, as a "stage" for the action, announces the artificiality of the film itself and its generic requirements (the climactic shoot-out). The fact that Tetsu's fighting prowess is visualized in the most unbelievable terms shows this up, too, as a masquerade. It is one layer of artifice upon another, masquerade upon masquerade, a *mise-en-abyme* from which nothing, except perhaps its dynamism, survives intact.

To conclude that the scene is a productive confusion of the diegetic and the theatrical probably errs too much on the side of diegetic. It is more

Fig. 6.15. Heroic Action as Dance: Tetsu throws his gun away, then leaps back onto it and shoots in three directions before his enemies can squeeze off a shot

accurate to say that the very possibility of authenticity in genre pictures is exposed as merely another rhetorical gesture—like Watari's pouting countenance, the snow-covered Yamagata landscape with its classical poetic associations, the evocative melancholy of the title song—and then dissolved within an aesthetic of falsity. This leads me to a point of agreement with Hasumi. Suzuki upholds an aesthetic of *surface*,[22] the knowing rhetorical gesture over the claim to truth. But in order to declare the primacy of surface, he must first reveal the falsity of the presumption of depth.

The Aesthetics of Iconicity

How can one characterize the formal "leap ahead" that the Suzuki-*gumi* accomplished between the films of 1963-65 and the Violence Trilogy of 1966-67? Hasumi is noticeably hesitant on this question.[23] We have already discussed the intensified discontinuity, the rhetoric of "falsity," and the breakdown of generic integrity. But we need to identify a deeper shift in Suzuki's formal address to the viewer which causes and conditions these formal strategies. The shift is one which, moreover, enables his films to break out of an ideological mode dependent on the righteous *yakuza* hero who, despite the corruption of *yakuza* and corporate society around him, still legitimizes Japanese patriarchy and its inherent violence.

I would characterize this new development as a reflexive aesthetic of *iconicity*. Reflexivity entails self-consciousness of filmic narration,[24] which will constitute the main strategy of *Koroshi no rakuin*. Yet *Tokyo nagaremono* offers a particular kind of reflexivity that contemplates directly the function of genre and stardom in the popular culture. It is this culture, after all, permeated on every level by the form of the commodity, that imposed these generic structures upon studio cinema. Iconicity is a vernacular, even populist form of reflexivity because it evolved not primarily out of avant-garde discourses, but from experimental temperaments working in a commercial cinema aimed (theoretically) at pleasing a knowing audience. Iconicity can be "populist" because it trades on a currency with which the mass audience is abundantly familiar: the iconography of stars and of generic objects (e.g., the cowboy hat). Audiences recognize such icons as meaningful entities, not just within a particular narrative, but applicable to multiple narratives and to the society that produces them. These commercial workings of iconography are evident in Kobayashi's "cowboy" persona-cum-fashion statement in the *Wataridori* advertisements (see Fig. 6.1). In *Tokyo nagaremono* the question becomes how and in what way the viewer's consciousness of iconography can be deployed for a greater range of artistic and critical (rather than simply commercial) purposes. It has an indubitable effect on *Tokyo nagaremono*'s largely negative representation of character subjectivity, marked by a cartoonish excess which is often typical of iconic discourse as opposed to naturalist discourse. It permits gender difference to appear as largely performative: masculinity is revealed not to have a basis in any authentic or "original" model, but in reference to culture and media.

What constitutes a particularly "iconic" visual discourse in a medium which automatically and universal deploys iconic signs? While some of the most informed theories of cinema and cinematic rhetoric, such as Trevor Whittock's, tend to treat film as composed of a system of literal representations of things in the world, other theorists of "visual representation," such as Nelson Goodman, argue that it is more a matter of learned/shared conventions of reference. I lean towards Gaylyn Studlar, and many others, in treating film images as morphological signs operating on a continuum of semiotic functions, with different film practices tending towards one or the other. Studlar treats the notion of "iconicity" thusly in her study of the films of von Sternberg, finding that the question of "iconic style" in the cinema involves "the effect of style on the cinematic sign's classification as indexical, iconic, or symbolic."[25] She is referring here to C.S. Peirce's famous tripartite division of signs into those that function on the basis of (1) natural, causal connections (indices), (2) perceptual (i.e., visual) resemblance (icons), and (3) those that are entirely dependent on conventional cultural association (symbols). André Bazin's theory of cinema emphasized the indexical; Eisenstein, to the contrary, insisted on a symbolic, "linguistic" function of the image as a mere "cell" or component of didactic montage. Studlar judges that neither stressed the iconic dimension: this was von Sternberg's great quality. "Von Sternberg remarked . . . that the perfect film of the future would be totally artificial."[26] Iconicity de-stresses the indexical function by virtue of an anti-illusionistic, artificial visual style. "Iconic relations do not value the illusion of authenticity . . . the reality of imagination is exalted over any presupposed objective reality."[27]

And yet, anti-illusionism was not exactly a "new discovery" for Suzuki, whereas I claim that the iconicity of *Tokyo nagaremono*, per se, was. This may be explained by the fact that Studlar acknowledges, but seems not to fully tease out, the relation between iconicity and intertextuality. In its everyday usage, the word "iconic" signifies "a person or thing regarded as representative of a culture . . . important or influential in a particular (cultural) context."[28] It is an image that stands for a powerful idea, and

Fig. 6.16. An Icon of the Genre: the gun "triply emphasized" by film style

this idea is loaded with cultural association for the ordinary viewer based on multiple textual experiences. As we shall see from the examples below, an iconic film practice can involve an excess emphasis on icons as cultural signs that are so overly familiar to the cinema audience that they detach themselves from a particular diegesis: in effect, they are clichés.

The iconic discourse in *Tokyo nagaremono* focuses, unsurprisingly, on the (exclusively masculine) iconography common to *akushon*, crime, and contemporary *yakuza* scenarios of the 1960s: guns, glasses, and suits. Working in a familiar generic context, Suzuki does not merely present, but "quotes" these abundantly well known genre elements rather than passing them off as a "natural" consequence of social representation, as a crime film invested in verisimilitude might do (for example, *Kenjū zankoku monogatari* or, for that matter, Suzuki's *Kemono no nemuri*).

A very clear example of "iconic quotation" is the extraordinary emphasis placed on the image of the gun in the first scene of *Tokyo nagaremono*. Trying to go straight, Tetsu has refused to fight a rival gang and has been savagely beaten for his trouble. In this monochromatic opening sequence, the battered Tetsu, unable to defend his own honor and virility, sees a gun lying on the ground and feels the temptation to reach for it. The gun is emphasized by a close-up loosely from Tetsu's POV (Fig. 6.16). So far, despite the familiar cliché of "the gun within arm's reach," this is not an unusually iconic visual rhetoric. With one of Suzuki's characteristic nondiegetic effects, however, the gun is depicted as glowing red against the monochrome background. To take matters still further, the glowing gun seems to be merely a children's toy.

This "commodity" form of the icon of the gun trades on the play of surface/depth and the motif of "falsity." Moreover, this *triple* emphasis on a cinematic icon (the pistol) promotes a consciousness of cliché that is very easy to achieve when Suzuki's artifice has "extracted" the sign from out of the diegesis.

By such means *Tokyo nagaremono* manipulates pop-cultural iconography for a number of ends: it characterizes pop culture as commodity-based and an endless, transient flux of sensory stimulation; it redirects the iconic husks of genre in the service of an ideological critique in a manner not so different from contemporary films by Godard (e.g., *Alphaville*, 1965).

The satirical potential of iconic discourse is clear from Suzuki's use of six extreme close-ups of sunglasses to introduce the sadistic *yakuza*, Ōtsuka (Esumi Eimei). The glasses are all that is requires to sum up this cartoonish patriarch: they are his armor and phallic signifier. Suzuki had already used this kind of iconic shorthand in *Sono gosōsha wo nerae: "Jûsangô taihisen" yori/Take Aim at the Police Van* (1960). The villain of that film, a sort of corporate "pimp" who murders his own prostitutes when convenient, hides his identity behind his sunglasses, again viewed in extreme close-up. When his glasses are finally torn off, the villain turns out to be the dignified, elderly father of the heroine, who is authentically horrified. What we remember of this earlier film—which in comparison to *Tokyo nagaremono* is almost too efficient in subordinating its technical polish and stylistic panache to serve the narration—is not the moral mystery at its heart concerning an aging prison guard's inexplicable and unswerving loyalty to a dishonest and foolish ex-con. Nor is it the way in which the white-coated guard (Mizushima Michitarō) is eternally moving forward, in frame after frame, like an inflexible automaton, strangely alien and out of step with every contemporary environment that he passes through, blundering destructively into one mess after another. What stays in the mind is, instead, the iconicity of the glasses and the metaphorical frisson of "coldness" (rather than "cool") that it gives off, evoking the frisson of the fetishistic murder of a prostitute (discussed in chapter 5) by the very same, sunglasses-wearing patriarch.

In *Tokyo nagaremono*, however, it is the iconic discourse of the movie hero, not the villain, that particularly enables a critical view of popular film culture. In the opening scene, Ōtsuka warns his subordinates about his formidable enemy, "Third Time Phoenix Tetsu," so-called because if anyone challenges him three times in a row, he will finally get angry. As Ōtsuka speaks, the monochromatic opening scene is interrupted by a three second, splashy color insert of the heroic Tetsu. Dressed in a yellow suit against a black background, Tetsu spins around and shoots off his

Fig. 6.17. Iconic Shorthand: for twenty-five minutes, the cold villain Ōtsuka is viewed only by extreme close-ups on his sunglasses (or else from the back of his head).

Fig. 6.18. The Action Hero as Commodity: Watari Tetsuya as "Third Time Phoenix Tetsu"

gun, accompanied by flashes of red, in three different directions. This brief color image has no diegetic status. It utilizes color spectacle not merely to "illustrate," but to "advertise" the hero in an iconic pose.

The black background, devoid of any location or depth, is indeed reminiscent of an advert. The character of Tetsu, before he is properly introduced in the narrative, has been defined according to a "trademark" fighting style (which reappears at the climax). The insert attempts to turn Tetsu (and actor Watari) into an instant icon like James Bond who can, among other things, be utilized in other narratives such as the anticipated

Fig. 6.19. The Libidinal Economy: the exotic sexual promise of Akasaka's neon signage

Nagaremono series. Viewed in a more ironic light, however, Suzuki presents a "hero," much like any other *akushon* hero, who is denied subjectivity, pre-packaged and reduced to a fixed, predictable commodity, and whose starring vehicle can therefore only escape its limits through ironization.

In fact, the film's representation of 1960s Tokyo posits a society under the thumb of advanced capitalism, visually and symbolically manifest through the ubiquity of advertising. The dominance of the visual culture of advertising represents the director's iconic discourse at its most critically prescient. In three montage sequences he portrays Akasaka—as well as Sasebo, where the American military presence is symbolically exploited—as a virtual sea of neon signage, each sign promising a more exotic and erotic product than the last.

One Akasaka cabaret sign is a cartoonish neon approximation of a nude girl; another club called The Casanova connotes a "Latin" sexual promise. The city life in "New Tokyo" is suffused with a commodity fetishism that conditions the identities of its inhabitants through the channeling and selling of libidinal energy. *Tokyo nagaremono* is probably the only *yakuza* film in which the narcissistic tough guys are seen to use and discuss the latest 1966 fashion in men's hair dryers, the "Light Punch." But the film mainly anticipates Guy Debord's *Society of the Spectacle* (1967) in preferring to observe the operations of the libidinal economy through the disorienting neon regime of the specular. The city's visual surface eternally promises fulfillment—that is, depth—for a price, but, as we shall see, there is nothing underneath. It is a society built on lies, or worse.

Modernity and the City: Surface and Death

The tripartite structure of *Tokyo nagaremono* is differentiated by location. The first and longest section of the film takes place in Tokyo. The second takes place in snowy Yamagata, where Tetsu has drifted, and the third in Sasebo. *Tokyo nagaremono* accelerates in rhythm with each part: the Yamagata section is less than half the length of the Tokyo, while the last section in Sasebo, centered around a barroom brawl, is short, frantic, violent, and, as a result of intercutting, fragmented.

The film's title sequence features a montage of the bright, touristic attractions of Tokyo circa 1966. A series of wipes display Tokyo Tower (finished 1958); the newly built *shinkansen* bullet trains; the new highway system connecting Southern and Western Tokyo; the Yoyogi Olympic gymnasium; the San-ai building of Ginza. Not one of these "monuments" had existed before 1955. This is the "New Tokyo," the product of massive urban redevelopment in preparation for the city's 1964 Olympic Games. There is no visual trace of prewar central Tokyo nor its *shitamachi* working class neighborhoods. By 1966, Suzuki was hard put to recognize the city of his own youth.[29] While the Olympics were an initial *succès d'estime*, the cost to the residents of Tokyo of this top down, high-handed, often corrupt urban renewal program soon became apparent.[30] Skyrocketing property values, which depopulated the "central city" of lower middle class residents,[31] furnish the mundane plot of *Tokyo nagaremono*, which concerns the struggle of two yakuza gangs to acquire an office building. The film could not be a more timely reflection on the effects of authoritarian redevelopment. Behind the bright, clean, commercial surfaces, there is despair. The glamour of the title sequence (typical of a Nikkatsu film) works perfectly as the opening "screen" underneath which is developed an ironic subtext. This is the image of Tokyo that the film sets out to negate: its own representation of the city, which doubles as a critical investigation of an era, is entirely structured by the visual opposition between "surface" and "what-that-surface-conceals." We cannot say "depth" because *nothing* lies behind the surfaces of Tokyo: nothing, that is, except death, which amounts to the same.

This opposition dominates Kimura Takeo's memorable realization of the film's major Tokyo interiors, the Club Alulu in Akasaka and the "Club Manhole" in the Shinjuku area. Club Alulu is a posh cabaret with an empty, cavernous interior bathed entirely in garish yellow. The depth and contours of the space are completely erased by the oversaturated coloration. The performance stage consists of a detached staircase beneath a free-standing door that, symbolically, leads to nowhere.

Fig. 6.20. Stage Door: the illusive, elusive space of the affluent Club Alulu

Visually, the Club is as elusive as its owner, the false-faced Boss Kurata (Kita Ryūji). All that can be seen is a hazy but lavish display of wealth and expanse, typical of the ageing patriarchy to which the club caters. Akasaka was famous for entertaining the ruling bureaucratic elite, and for this reason, Club Alulu is not, like other cabarets, a place for sexual titillation, but for the substitute erotics of conspicuous consumption.

As its name suggests, The Manhole Jazz Café, owned by the sadistic Ōtsuka, is a less dignified establishment. The main interior is glimpsed only briefly, in three shots lasting a total of 12 seconds, yet full of dynamism and movement. A crowd of teenagers dances madly around an unbelievably modish and garish space suffused with purple light (Fig. 6.21), while a dozen pipes, each painted a different pastel color, snake their way across it, even functioning as chairs.

Dripping with sexual suggestion, the Manhole is a place of frenzied excess. A promise of Dionysian violence seems to loom over the revels. The specter of death is communicated by the opposition of "surface" and "underneath." The pipes, like the club's suggestive name, challenge us to look beneath the surface, to "plumb" the depths: when Tetsu attempts to "penetrate" the interior, he is dumped into a dark grimy hole, the embodiment of abjection.

Here, Tetsu finds the corpse of the last honorable businessman in Tokyo, the elderly Yoshii (Hino Michio). His death, in this place of nothingness, signifies the ascent of "New Tokyo" and its corrupt and venal rulers.

What is it that links the libidinal leisures of the 1960s (the dancing teenagers) to the promise of violence? Since *Tokyo nagaremono* returns

Fig. 6.21. Club Manhole: Youth, Sexual Suggestion and the Commodification of Excess

Fig. 6.22. What Lies Beneath: through "The Manhole" and into the Abject

obsessively to *yakuza* aggression against women (Kurata's murder of the secretary, Ōtsuka's abuse of Chiharu, Tetsu's coldness), it is perhaps this which provides the link. Sexual mores may have loosened, but the gendered power structure remains its old, oppressive self.

It is an open question whether the nihilism of *Tokyo nagaremono* represents the world-view of its makers or a moral criticism of the shallowness of the 1960s, an awareness that there *should* be a depth that is lacking. *Tokyo nagaremono* is characterized by this ambivalence, or perhaps, by a spirit of investigation. The second section, in quiet, traditional Yamagata, represents Tetsu's search for "depth" in Japanese cultural tradition. Yet this is represented as a false hope. Tetsu liaises with the local

Fig. 6.23. Women and *yakuza:* the threatened Chiharu travels across Japan to find her boyfriend; on an opposite-moving train, he cannot bring himself to reach out to her

oyabun, whose residence resembles those of the Edo-period *daimyo* (provincial lords). Kimura Takeo exploits the recessed paneling of Tokugawa architecture to suggest an infinite depth that is equated with tradition. The solemn, rigid formality of the *oyabun* and his environment suggest that in its own way Yamagata, reminiscent of an age of duty, aristocracy, and self-sacrifice, is just as deathly and alienating as Tokyo. Because of his youth and post-war situation, historical depth and rituals cannot take a hold over Tetsu. If the "honorific" behavior of the *yakuza* can be said to take two forms—the form of ritual and the form of violence—then Tetsu can only express his fanatically dutiful nature through the latter.

In contrast with Yamagata, the Sasebo section is dominated by a humorous Western saloon brawl reminiscent of *Destry Rides Again* (George Marshall, 1939). A *reductio ad absurdum* of the *Wataridori* series, this section takes place entirely in the realm of intertextual reference and movie iconography. The search for "truth'" is abandoned in favor of an ecstatic reinvestment in cliché, the more foreign, the more liberating. Even this section, however, ends on a sour note which brings us back to where we started: the betrayed Tetsu returns to confront Tokyo and its rulers in a frenzy of righteous violence.

Tears of Betrayal: A Generation without Fathers

The contemporary milieu of *Tokyo nagaremono* situates a conflict between generations and competing versions of masculinity. The "story" of *Tokyo nagaremono*—that of a young *yakuza* betrayed by a boss (*oyabun*) whom he loves like a father—reiterates the theme of the *necessity* of betrayal.

Betrayal is necessary not only because of Kurata himself—affable on the outside, utterly devoid of morality on the inside—but because of his social context. Betrayal is simply the reality of contemporary *yakuza* life: "That's how it goes," shrugs Kurata. In contrast, the (media) stereotype revolves around principle and ritual. While the rituals (overwhelmingly prominent in Tōei's *ninkyō eiga*) maintain the illusion of a functional patriarchal family, Suzuki's film stresses the Oedipal structure of the *yakuza* and links it to advanced capitalism, that great new determining factor in Japanese life, which, like the Oedipal scenario, is based on competition. Kurata tries to escape the logic of succession: confusing institutional power with virility, the father must kill the son in order to avoid the truth of his own obsolescence. His failure to do so is the cause of his own death. Suzuki—and perhaps Kawauchi, whose original script included the betrayal theme—accomplished in 1966 what Standish credits to the director Fukasaku in the early 1970s: "an antithetical position . . . presenting masculinity beset in a world devoid of an archetypal patriarch."[32]

The masculine star image of Montgomery Clift was a visual, and I would argue ideological, model for up-and-coming Nikkatsu stars like Kobayashi and, later, Watari. Steven Cohan has analyzed Clift's image as that of the "boy who wants to be a man." With this image, the post-war studios could trade on the "erotic appeal of these young actors . . . underscoring their alienation from the screen's more traditional representations of masculinity,"[33] while still theoretically upholding that tradition. For Clift in *Red River* (Hawks, 1946/8), there is still a heroic father (John Wayne), however cracked or bigoted, to look up to and compete with. In Japan, however, Tetsu's generation, born during wartime, is a generation without fathers, and Kurata's impotent faithlessness is the proof. As Satō reported, "It is commonly said in Japan that women have become stronger because men have lost all confidence in their masculinity due to Japan's defeat."[34] Thus, Tetsu must set out on his wandering quest to locate a social and sexual identity within the post-war landscape, a quest doomed to failure.

Of course, the yakuza's betrayal of "values" in favor of capitalist greed had been a "complaint" of the *yakuza eiga* since its beginning, but Suzuki's 1966 take has the ring of historical truth. "1960 marked a turning point . . . [after which] the yakuza distanced themselves from rightist violence. . . . They were less violence specialists . . . and more economic beings that dealt in corruption."[35] The business advisors Kumamoto (Chō Hiroshi) and Fujimura (Kiura Sazō) represent a new "managerial" class of *yakuza* deal-makers who effortlessly destroy Tetsu where legions of gunmen have failed. They appeal to Kurata's financial security—his place in the *system* as opposed to the "family." *Tokyo nagaremono* brings us to the endpoint in the evolution of the *yakuza* as one functional cog in the corporate wheel. In *Koroshi no rakuin*, the gang structure itself vanishes, subsumed into a vast, technocratic, semi-legitimate "Organization."

This split between a pragmatic patriarchal machine and an idealized, honorific Japanese masculinity is not in itself particularly original; but it interestingly determines Suzuki's representation of three generations of masculinity in seemingly inevitable conflict. As always in a Suzuki film, betrayal by the father is an allusion to the war. At about 70, Boss Kurata represents the architects of Japanese imperialism. Tetsu is in his twenties and thus a member of the post-war generation for whom imperial Japan is not even a memory, no less "legendary" than the samurai nostalgically evoked in post-war *chanbara*. Without personal experience to the contrary, Tetsu finds the legend more appealing than the fact of his own situation.

There is an intermediary generation between these two represented by the ex-*yakuza* drifter "Nagareboshi" (Shooting Star), memorably played by the falling Nikkatsu star Nitani Hideaki. Nitani was born in 1930, but his lined face and practical clothes, contrasted to the youthful, fashionable Watari, make him appear much older. "Shooting Star" represents Suzuki's own generation, those that suffered in the Pacific War. He is a melancholy and disillusioned character, forever warning young Tetsu not to put too much trust in his elders. When Shooting Star makes statements such as, "I don't want him to know the tears of having been betrayed . . . but he has to go down that road just once, by himself," it is clear that his *yakuza* backstory is a flimsy cover: he is referring, at least metonymically, to the betrayal of Japan by its leaders during the war. The film's only true *nagaremono*, Shooting Star no longer belongs to any social structure. Like his directorial alter ego Suzuki (note the identical roman initials "SS"),[36] he has seen through it all. "SS" is the ideological focal point of the film: possessed of the demoralizing truth, his wisdom can only be expressed in negative terms: "I don't want him to know . . .". Most importantly, Shooting Star's lonely, secure masculinity is the measure of Tetsu's labored pretense. It is still based on toughness and martial prowess—this is Nikkatsu *akushon*, after all—but it does not exclude giving, caring, tolerance of insult, or fluidity of sexual preference. In this 1966 film, the sexual identity of this secondary protagonist can only be referred to in code,[37] but the relationship between Tetsu and "SS" seems to be characterized more by homoerotic tension than by conventional homosociality. Shooting Star's attraction to Tetsu results in the latter's ambivalent and suspicious attitude towards him. The only legitimate father figure to Tetsu and his generation, he is also the most off-limits because of that Oedipal disavowal of "incest" from which Tetsu suffers more than anyone else.

Violence, Commodity, and Masculine Crisis

In contrast to the easy-going Shooting Star, Tetsu is perpetually sulky and irritable. Suzuki has said that the key to this character is his stiff, unnatural gait, an imitation of John Wayne.[38] Tetsu is as uncomfortable in his own skin as he is with others. He seems happy only when playing cards with strangers, or when sitting with his girlfriend, but *only* on the condition of distance. At one point, Chiharu expects Tetsu to accompany her to her room; instead, Tetsu rolls up his car window, and with this barrier safely established between them, drives away from her with an affectionate wave. The pronounced masochism of Chiharu does not mitigate the fact that Tetsu has a neurotic fear of female sexuality and struggles to contain a misogynist impulse.

This is hardly without cinematic precedent. Cohan detects "an uncomfortable feeling about romancing women central to Bogart's persona as a tough guy . . . with his 'toughness' functioning as a mechanism of sexual regulation . . . of . . . hegemonic masculinity."[39] This may be overstated, but it suggests how Tetsu is problematically aligned to an older generational ideal of masculinity and thus to the "hysterical" containment of the feminine for which Suzuki's films relentlessly satirize the martial tradition. Tetsu is not much different from the impotent Kurata who, when given an opportunity to shoot his bitter enemy Ōtsuka, instead shoots the sexually threatening young secretary.

At the same time, Tetsu's reactionary masculinity is at odds with the new libidinal economy. As Stephen Barber writes, Tetsu is "the sole inhabitant who refuses to participate in that sexual regime."[40] But Barber does not notice the neurotic ambivalence of this revolt against commodification. Tetsu's iconic baby blue suit, perpetually clean and immaculate no matter what violence is going on, recalls the costume of Cary Grant in *North by Northwest*, in which Grant plays an advertising executive. As Cohan interprets, "The male adaptation of commercial fashion signified the unorthodox—but . . . economically advantageous—absorption of masculinity into consumerism . . . as both a producer and product of the advertising industry."[41] Cohan's thesis serves to explain *Tokyo nagaremono*'s emphasis on adverts for male hair dryers.

Fig. 6.24. Masculinity and Commodity Fetishism: Tetsu tries the "Light Punch" male hair dryer

Tetsu's performance of prewar masculinity belies his interest in clothes and hair. Tetsu does not need to prove his fighting ability—that is a narrative given—but he has something to prove about his sexual identity. Why does he put on the masquerade of having a girlfriend whom he loves like a mother, but does not desire? Heterosexual desire has evidently been sublimated, and substituted, by a commodity-based narcissism that is necessarily auto-erotic. Tetsu's fanatical embracement of "honorific" male violence is a pathological overcompensation for a widespread source of male angst in the libidinal economy of the early 1960s.[42] Despite his sulkiness, Tetsu's fanatical morality is not inner-directed but other-directed, a conformist type derived from media and pursued with a single-mindedness that only shows up the existing masculine ideal as an absurd performance, neurotic at base and disastrous in consequence.

Tetsu begins the film as a lonely man and ends it even lonelier. In the final sequence, he looks out upon a sea of Akasaka cabaret signs advertising sexual promise.

After his cathartic orgy of violence, has Tetsu finally accommodated himself to his environment? It is difficult to imagine a solution to his identity crisis. He has rejected monogamy, yet heterosexual promiscuity has never been an option. Is Tetsu capable of adjusting to Shooting Star's non-conformist life of homoerotic bonding? Or will the narcissism of the urban *flâneur*, punctuated by bouts of libidinal violence, suffice? It appears not, for the final shot of the film shows Tetsu walking off in the opposite direction, drifting away from the bright lights of Tokyo once again.

The classical studio star system depended on a rhetoric of authenticity,

Fig. 6.25. Urban *Flâneur?* The lonely Tetsu looks over the sexualized, neon cityscape of Tokyo (*Tokyo nagaremono*)

a "guarantee" to viewers that a star was more or less just as he appeared in his films.[43] Extending the aesthetics of iconicity to both Nikkatsu stardom and its commodity culture, *Tokyo nagaremono* shows up the façade of authenticity in a movie that, for the studio and critics, was all about the creation of a star. Moreover, the rhetoric of youthful sincerity had a deeper resonance in Japanese post-war cinema. The clean-cut, romantic heroes of countless post-war *chanbara* were exemplars of ideological and moral purity (*makoto*), which had roots in the Meiji and prewar culture of militarism. Tetsu represents a fetishization of *makoto* taken to similarly violent extremes. Considering the uncanny similitude between Tetsu and wartime youth such as the *tokkōtai* (*kamikaze*) pilots, who were promoted to the nation (both during and since the war) as pinnacles of *makoto*, it is a meaningful critique that comes to full fruition in *Kenka erejii*.

Kenka erejii: *The Contexts of Violence*

Violence and Absolutism in *Kenka erejii*

Kenka erejii is about Kiroku (Takahashi Hideki), a young man in secondary school in the 1930s who is preternaturally drawn to fighting. The more sexually frustrated he becomes, the more he channels his libido into violence. One day he catches a glimpse of ultranationalist revolutionary Kita Ikki, and later learns of the February 1936 revolt of the young officers inspired by Ikki, which led to the assassination of several government officials and the execution of the revolutionaries. Inspired by the incident, Kiroku rushes off to Tokyo to join the biggest fight of all: the war in China.

Both *Tokyo nagaremono* and *Kenka erejii* are films about young fanatics, but the latter explicitly represents the coming-of-age of Suzuki's war generation. It was scripted by the leftist director Shindo Kaneto, a naval veteran like Suzuki, and then drastically rewritten by the director before filming.[44] Given such a pedigree, it is impossible to view the film without reference to the fate of patriotic servicemen during the war era of 1932-1945.

Suzuki's colleague Shinoda has said that he set out to answer, "How can . . . absolutism take hold in any individual?"[45] *Kenka erejii* contemplates just that, in the form of a *bildungsroman* devoted to one student's idealistic and self-imposed devotion to martial training. By the 1930s, Japanese servicemen and their families had been shaped by decades of state propaganda and social ideology meant "to encourage soldiers to plunge to death as an honorable act and for the people not to object to their sacrifice."[46] The 1890 Imperial Rescript on Education, an infamous attempt at social engineering by the Meiji oligarchs, ordered that a young person "should sacrifice oneself courageously for the country by guarding the Imperial Throne."[47] The nation's children were thus ordered to perform a samurai-esque "duty unto death" to an almighty god (the emperor) who had only been declared to be such the previous year. Yet two victorious wars and the rise of Japanese nationalism served to naturalize this initially alien ideology by the turn of the century. Militarism in textbooks, school songs, and in state-sponsored Shintō reached every household.[48]

After three generations of such ideology, the period 1932-1945 saw not only casualties in battle, but various forms of self-sacrifice which strike us today as fanatical: military operations which were expected to fail simply in order to make heroes of the fallen servicemen (e.g., the "Nikudan" Incident of 1932, the Battleship Yamato);[49] *seppuku* in situations of military failure, an infrequent practice widely praised by war propaganda;[50] and *gyokusai*, or mass suicide charges by Japanese troops in hopeless situations such as the struggle for Attu Island (1943). Most infamous of all were the *tokkōtai* pilots of 1944-45, essentially a "forced voluntary" corps of servicemen and recent university graduates trained to smash bomb-holding planes into enemy ships. In truth, many Japanese servicemen (including Suzuki and many of the *tokkōtai* pilots themselves) were neither fanatical nor interested in self-sacrifice. *Kenka erejii* sets out to tell the pre-history of the servicemen who were. As many have pointed out, it is an attempt at the loose autobiography of a generation. But the film is

Fig. 6.26. Violence and Genre Cinema: Kiroku is cajoled into violence in front of a (fake) poster for a silent Fox Western (*Kenka erejii* / *Elegy for Violence*)

not only meaningful in historical reference: it is, simultaneously, a broad critique of the ideology of genre cinema and its representations of martial heroism, sexuality, and the war itself.

What, specifically, do *tokkōtai* pilots, Phoenix Tetsu, and juvenile delinquent Kiroku have in common, according to Suzuki's films? Surprisingly, *Kenka erejii* contains few references to the emperor, the *kokutai* ("the whole nation as one family") and other by-words of early Shōwa nationalism. Instead, it relates the deeper psychological and mythical underpinnings of a culture that promotes male violence and martial prowess to the point of death. The question boils down to the significance of "fighting"; I shall therefore examine some major contexts of "fighting" in *Kenka erejii*.

Violence and Sexual Purity

Whereas Tetsu is functionally virginal, Kiroku is explicitly identified as a virgin harboring an unrequited love for Michiko, the daughter of his innkeeper. As Richie memorably writes, "his girlfriend is far too pure to do anything, and he hates himself for masturbating . . . a life of violence seems to be the only answer."[51]

The idea of a "virginal" soldier was both a wartime ideal and, often, a literal fact, since many servicemen had barely finished school. It is linked to a mythic ideal of masculinity unsullied by sexual contact with the feminine in both pre-modern and wartime culture. Sexual repression had always been an underpinning of the *giri/ninjō* (duty versus emotional inclination) narrative archetype that formed the structure of kabuki and its ancestors, *chanbara* and *ninkyō* narratives.⁵² But Standish asserts a special "underlying text" in wartime popular discourses—including the morale-boosting films of Inagaki, Ozu, and others—of a seemingly "hysterical" *machismo* and the rejection of the feminine: "the father figures become almost iconical virgin symbols (as in a reversal of a Christian virgin birth) of an ideal patriarchal male purity."⁵³ Standish has also valuably examined how 1950s war-retro films depicted the "purity" of the suicide pilots who must overcome female attachment to do their duty.⁵⁴

Standish's invocation of a Christian influence on this "virginal masculinity" is fortuitous, as both Kiroku and Michiko in *Kenka erejii* happen to be Christians and the film itself is replete with Christian imagery and symbolism. Christianity, viewed critically as the immediate context of Kiroku's sexual repression, may be an allegorical shorthand for a wider national pathology. Considering the influence of Christian intellectuals such as Tanabe Hajime and Nitobe Inazō, author of the epochal *Bushidō* (1899)⁵⁵, an integral connection existed between Japanese militarism, pre-war Christian ideals of martyrdom, and the reckless romantic idealism of wartime intellectual culture.

As soon as *Kenka erejii* has quoted the wartime motif of the "virgin soldier," it undermines it. The "pure" Kiroku is as much a compulsive masturbator as he is a compulsive fighter. The film's comedic emphasis on masturbation paints the ideal of (martial) masculinity as not only narcissistic, but literally auto-erotic. Kiroku's "love" for Michiko is actually pure lust, which, having no outlet, stokes itself into masturbatory fury through the language and forms of romantic idealism. In a culture of denial of the

Fig. 6.27. "Sex" and the Middle Class: Kiroku masturbates by playing piano with his member (*Kenka erejii*)

body, Kiroku is too buttoned up to touch Michiko or propose anything of an amorous nature. He can only express lust by writing in his diary about romantic and spiritual longing for Michiko, after which writing he typically gets an erection and must go out and fight to blow off steam. The famous scene in which Kiroku masturbates on Michiko's piano conflates unconquerable biology and the *bourgeois* forms of culture through which desire was customarily channeled.

Violence and Militarism

Other issues of interpretation are not as clear as the issue of sexual repression. Critics have widely disagreed on an ideological reading of the film's central motif of youthful brawling. While Tony Rayns, among others, argued that fighting in the film—which Kiroku considers as "training," for what he does not know—is about "the making of a model fascist,"[56] Satō and Ian Buruma are less judgmental of the protagonist's violence. The film, writes Buruma, "is literally an elegy . . . to the innocent violence of youth. It is a nostalgic yearning for the period in life when one can be self-assertive . . . before the hammer of conformity knocks the nail back in."[57]

For years, I was unable to quite make out the nostalgic film that Buruma claims to have seen. His interpretation views male biological aggression as one thing, and the patriarchal manipulation of it as another. But close textual reading finds youth violence and war violence drawn so close together that they appear to be the same. The 16-year-old Kiroku does not simply engage in schoolyard fisticuffs, he joins the school equivalent of a club for militant ultranationalists. The students imitate the pompous speeches and written declarations of military commanders, even, on one occasion, summoning fighters with an ancient gong. They wear club insignia replete with war symbols (a major aspect of actual military culture).[58] And rather than using the weapons of school-sanctioned martial arts (i.e., bamboo *shinai*), the students use hidden razor blades and construct hand-made spikes made from the metal cleats of their track shoes.

Kiroku's fighting has serious consequences: expulsion, delinquency, and, eventually, enlistment in the army. Moreover, *Kenka erejii* dwells obsessively on the bodily damage sustained in Kiroku's fights, visualized graphically and often in extreme close-up. Cleats are driven through one character's cheek; Kiroku bites off an ear. The student fights occupy an uncomfortable grey area between brawling and actual combat to the death. The boundary is indeed unclear when we consider the extreme youth of so many enlisted servicemen in the Pacific War.

Kiroku's obsession with fighting is clearly an allegory of the militarist culture of his elders. Kiroku's club leader is both an ideologue and a coward who manipulates the junior members into fighting in his place. This is a blatant satire of wartime military hierarchies. The fact that the character is called Takuan, the name of the priest who legendarily trained Miyamoto Musashi, is an additional swipe at both martial myth and popular film culture.[59]

Despite all this, I cannot dismiss entirely Buruma's critical intuition of a sort of materialist/nihilist reading of the film's emphasis on sheer physical energy and its outlet in play. Kikuo is a believer, but the film undercuts his belief system at every turn—in part by reducing grandiose ideology to a basic, real stratum of play (violent, masculine as it may be). The order of play, paradoxically serious as it becomes, is evident when Kikuo's father shows up at school to discipline him, only to be seen proudly sporting a borrowed police uniform. In Kiroku's case, "war play" appears inseparable from the explosive combination of thwarted sexual energy and instinctive youthful adventurism. For Suzuki's reactionary heroes, ideology is everything: but from the critical distance of the film itself, ideology may be sufficiently reducible to biology to be, occasionally, undermined by it. But not for long. The adult world and the demanding, deathly hand of the Law of the Father is always on the horizon: scarcely less dangerous, and more sinister then Kiroku's war games, despite, or perhaps because of, its surface of sobriety and sacrifice. In the end, what *Kenka erejii* concedes to biology is fleeting, like youth itself. This seems to be why the perpetually "hot" Kiroku, after his meeting with Kita Ikki and his journey towards enlistment, is surrounded by the coldness of snow as he restrains himself from going after the desperate, hysterical Michiko.

Violence and Patriarchy

The reality of war is brought home in that final sequence, in which Michiko runs away from the Kiroku who, resolved to remain undistracted by female attachment, does not follow her. Outside in the snow, Michiko is framed in a close-up, while in the background a troop of young soldiers are rushing along the narrow road, heading to war. They are pushing her up against a barbed-wire stockade fence (another instance of war iconography). Two further troops march by, after which we find Michiko lying prostrate in the snow. She has either been trampled underfoot or, like femininity itself, violently shunted aside in this unforgettable allegory of the brutality of militarism.

Fig. 6.28. Between a Rock and a Hard Place: Women Under a Militarist Patriarchy. Michiko shunted aside and trampled by columns of rushing troops (*background*) (*Kenka erejii*)

This finale is prescient in contextualizing the ambivalence of male violence in a patriarchal society. The Japanese military state, from the 1880s to 1945, was explicitly predicated on the conflation of the family sphere and the sphere of political authority; filial piety was equated with duty to the emperor as father of all, and many servicemen took this to heart.[60] Recalling the 1936 revolt of the young officers, met with incomprehension and rage by the emperor in whose name they revolted, *Kenka erejii* depicts wartime relations between youth and patriarchy as anything but harmonious. As Kiroku's fighting prowess grows, he challenges the authority of his club *senpai*, his school teachers, principals, even his military training officer. The naïve Kiroku assumes that the basis of authority, indeed the basis of all social relations, is strength. In response to his challenge, Kiroku is punished and expelled; his father confronts him, supposedly in order to reign in his wildness. Instead, the father's indulgent attitude only encourages Kiroku to continue on this path. The very patriarchy now disturbed by Kiroku has instilled in him these ideals.

As in *Tokyo nagaremono*, patriarchy is both arbitrary in its wielding of authority and deeply contradictory at heart. The conflict is one of honor versus order, or social control at odds with a long history of idealized male competition. When Kiroku meets the stiff and pompous headmaster (Tamagawa Isao) of his new school in Aizu, a region that is proud of its samurai past, the headmaster points to some archaic calligraphy on the wall which allegedly declares the virtue of something like "appropriateness." But when Kiroku wreaks havoc with the Aizu kendo club, the headmaster becomes as childishly indulgent as Kiroku's father: he digs out his old kendo *shinai* and challenges Kiroku to a practice duel. Brushing away his subordinate's objections about the "inappropriateness" of this behavior, he asserts, "One must be a man above all." Clearly, the bureaucratic demand for order is only skin-deep. Underneath, the ordinary man understands, and even longs for, Kiroku's violent nature. While youth play at being virile soldiers, the adults wish to become children again. Japanese society is in arrested development.

Violence and Romantic Idealism

Kiroku lives in a world of ideological fantasy. In one scene he is sitting on the right of screen with his diary while Michiko plays piano on the left. On the *shōji* behind Michiko is a bizarre, non-diegetic pattern of swirling light. Kiroku gets an erection, looks out the window, and stiffly walks off to the right. As Kiroku thrusts open a set of doors, the area outside the house is bathed in a blinding white. Kiroku boldly strides into this haze, through which the viewer makes out a wooded area where two students are waiting for him.

As Kiroku begins to fight them, the oversaturated whiteness begins to fade away, but instead of clarity, the shot dissolves into a close-up on Kiroku's diary, expressing his desire for Michiko. This is followed by two further shots of Kiroku fighting. During the second shot, the camera suddenly flash-pans back into the house to rest on a *shōji* through which Kiroku enters, looking happy and refreshed. How could he have moved so quickly from one place to the other?

Fig. 6.29. Violence and Sexual Fantasy (shot 1): Kiroku fighting in an orgiastic white haze. Reality or masturbatory fantasy?

Fig. 6.30. Violence and Sexual Fantasy (Shot 4a): a fade-in from Kiroku's diary to Kiroku, continuing his fight outside

Fig. 6.31. Violence, Fantasy, and False Time (Shot 4b): the same shot finds Kiroku impossibly entering the house after a flash-pan to the left

As he sits down, the framing duplicates that of the first shot, but there is now no swirling pattern behind Michiko, only blackness. The scene's audacious non-diegetic lighting, oversaturation, and spatial impossibilities give it a dreamlike quality. Why does Suzuki cut back to Kiroku's diary? Is the fight scene only a fantasy in Kiroku's head? Or is the diary an expression of his romantic thoughts during an actual fight? Did Kiroku actually leave the room to masturbate, while the film shows us fighting as a non-diegetic metaphor? It is impossible to decide between these in Kiroku's "borderless" fantasy world where libidinal energy translates to romantic/martial idealism.

One could make the argument that wartime Japan was similarly trapped in a haze of ideological fantasy. This was as true of the intellectual culture as it was of the nation's optimistic military commanders:[61]

> In 1943, the major journal of Japan's romantic movement, *Cogito*, which became colossally tied with ultra-nationalism, was launched. *Les liaisons dangereuses* between the intellectual . . . community and ultra-nationalism . . . were forming. Of critical importance is the emphasis on aesthetics . . . which pilots projected onto their . . . patriotism, using it to justify their sacrifice as a . . . beautiful act.[62]

For Emiko Ohnuki-Tierney, these idealistic servicemen sought an "aesthetics . . . of life." They were also, like Kiroku, mostly single, teenage men.

Kiroku's "reason" for fighting is every bit as phantasmagorical as that of the *tokkōtai* pilots. Kiroku challenges another student on the streets of Aizu by asking a question: What should a man do if he is in the middle of a street and a bus comes toward him? The student answers that he would step aside. Kiroku begs to differ: "If you're in the street . . . whether it's a bus or a tank, you should boldly go forward." Kiroku's naïve idealism has transformed the socially accepted militarism of his time, which was rigorously conformist, into a fanatical, non-conformist religion of strength, impossible to practice on a social scale. His creativity, unhampered by knowledge or experience of the social and material realities of the adult world, takes militarism one step further from reality and drags the culture along with him.

Violence and Aesthetic Iconography

The importance of aesthetics to the patriotic idealism of Japanese servicemen is no doubt the reason why *Kenka erejii* begins with a montage of dynamic, pulsating nature imagery: ominous clouds in the sky, a rushing mountain stream,[63] and rolling seas.[64] These had been romantic symbols of Japanese nationalism from Meiji onwards.

Ohnuki-Tierney has chronicled how social agents manipulated this ancient iconography for nationalist purposes, capitalizing on the operation of *méconnaissance*, by which the various meanings of complex cultural symbols could be conflated together or substituted for one another in the service of a state-sanctioned ideological program. For example, cherry blossoms, which in Heian literature mainly signified youth and love, were gradually transformed into something amenable to the military regime: "falling

Fig. 6.32. Natural Imagery and Martial Training: Kiroku (*kneeling foreground*) receives training from a self-proclaimed 'master' (*left-of-center*) in a mountain glade. Such iconic compositions would have been familiar to viewers of martial arts and *chanbara* films such as the *Miyamoto Musashi* variations.

like a beautiful cherry petal" was the metaphor the Japanese state used to promote the sacrifice of soldiers "for the emperor *qua* state."[65] Countless servicemen in the Pacific War would console themselves with the idea that their death would be aesthetically beautiful "like falling cherry petals"—one of the commonest phrases in the writings they left behind.

Kenka erejii manipulates the iconography of cherry blossoms to illustrate, succinctly, this trifecta of nationalism, idealized masculinity, and the rejection of the feminine. Kiroku is taking an evening stroll with Michiko through the cherry trees, with the camera tracking through the luxurious blossoms above to represent their POV. Thus far the blossoms preserve their ancient connotation of youth and courtship. But when Kiroku touches Michiko's hand for the first time, disaster ensues. Suddenly his ultranationalist club leader appears from under the cherry blossoms, signifying their transformation into icons of male martial valor. The leader denounces Kiroku for having contact with a woman. In a panic, Kiroku pushes Michiko aside and runs toward the leader, a jump cut signifying his crisis of values. Kiroku pretends Michiko is his sister. When the leader discovers the lie and declares a feud between them, he smacks the cherry tree with his sword. The falling petals seem humorously to signify the collapse of Kiroku's romantic idyll and his choice of fighting over women. It is a turning point for the worse. It is also a tour-de-force of cinematic metaphor, with the blossoms transitioning from one symbolic cultural

Fig. 6.33. Symbolic *Méconnaissance:* falling cherry blossoms (once a symbol of courtly romance, later of death and self-sacrifice) disrupt Kiroku's courtship

association to its opposite, and thence to a more original, context-specific objective correlative of Kiroku's divided psyche.

Kenka erejii submits imperialist iconography to the same ironic treatment given to advertising and mass culture in *Tokyo nagaremono*. At one point *Kenka erejii* makes an explicit link between the two regimes: while Kiroku is sneaking out to fight a battle, Suzuki cuts away to a non-diegetic cartoon illustration of a Western cowboy.

Concluding Remarks

The Violence Trilogy drives a wedge between youthful male violence and the repressive violence of patriarchy, while at the same time maintaining that they are both informed by the same mythic and gendered structures of thought. Certainly the filmmakers admire youthful non-conformism: but it must be founded on negative ethics and not on idealism. Kiroku is a dupe of repressive ideology and will die in the war; Tetsu is eternally lonely. The transition from naïveté to the disillusioned (and equally lonely) competence of Shooting Star *must* count as a form of wisdom, if not positive growth. What is worse is to be caught in the middle between innocence and experience, like the wretched protagonists of Suzuki's subsequent three films. Only a transformation of society's gender dynamics (as we shall find in part in *Koroshi no rakuin*) holds out better hope.

Is it possible to escape the grip of a society's consensual reality, even when it turns delusional? What is the role of the cinema itself, with its representation of eroticism and violence, in this process? Normatively, cinema reflects consensus, and the *yakuza eiga* did so despite its subject of rightist rebellion. In Suzuki's first two Violence films we see the formation of an alternative practice. One alternative is to visualize the hidden repressions unacknowledged by patriarchy concerning the sexual basis of violence, in the hopes that cinema might possibly exorcise it (a mass catharsis). Simultaneously, though, Suzuki amongst others in the 1960s proposed a non-cathartic possibility: an advanced cinematic ethics of living and dying without delusion. This answer lay in attacking the spatial, temporal, and narrational systems by which a consensual "reality" is reified on the screen.

Tokyo nagaremono crosses the line between a classical "action" cinema of continuity and narrative pleasure to a differential "new wave" cinema based on the possibilities of discontinuity and non-diegetic gesture. Sometimes the film is balanced on that line (for example, the aforementioned car chase preserves a constant screen direction), allowing many scenes to be appreciated in two ways, one for the twisted progress of Tetsu's journey, one for the humor and excitement of loose, kinetic variations of visual narration. Yet Suzuki's practice also begins in earnest to deploy the use of "superfluous" spectacle that depends not on diegesis, but on iconicity, for comprehension. During the barroom brawl, a spectacle of comic excess, a lady in French can-can dress is hanging from the rafters. A grizzled sailor on the floor looks up to take a peek under her dress, but a gallon of white cream suddenly descends on his head. The hypertextual reference is the slapstick pie fight, but here the motif becomes scatological. It is also a diegetic impossibility, while Kiroku's fight, discussed above, heaps a spatio-temporal impossibility on top of this. Bending "gags" such as these to purposes at once satirical and reflexive, the filmmakers announce their determination to break the rules.

CHAPTER 7

The Hinge

(Koroshi no rakuin, Pisutoru opera)

Negativity and Surrealism

Koroshi no rakuin/Branded to Kill is a film in negative. At one remarkable moment in this 1967 film, four long shots of the Tokyo cityscape are *actually* shown in negative, that is to say, the negative film stock is displayed on the screen rather than the expected "positive" footage.

True to the preoccupations of *Tokyo nagaremono* and Suzuki's self-proclaimed destructive tendency,[1] *Koroshi no rakuin* portrays 1960s Tokyo and the "progress" ideology of the economic miracle in a highly "negative" light. Throughout this film, the massive, unpopular, authoritarian urban renewal program before and after the 1964 Tokyo Olympics is shown to have resulted in a stark, empty wasteland of concrete.

Suzuki's oppositional struggle for a radical freedom of cinematic expression not only negates post-war Tokyo, but the film itself, ideologically and formally. The reception of *Koroshi no rakuin*, a "quota quickie" scripted, planned, and shot in a few months to fill a hole in Nikkatsu's release schedule, was also resoundingly negative, resulting in the end of Suzuki's studio career and the virtual burial of the film by its own studio. Nikkatsu president Hori Kyūsaku famously called the film "incomprehensible" while *Eiga geijutsu* complained that "we do not go to the cinemas to be puzzled."[2] All these negativities would be only incidental, a mere accident of reception, if the film text itself was not so proleptically dedicated to a negative aesthetic on multiple levels. This being so, parallels between the aesthetic of destruction within the film and the social destruction *of* the film have become inevitable: each paradoxically contributes to the other.

In its defiant non-conformism and non-diegetic surrealism, its deliberately avant-garde tenor, its increasingly radical gender critique, and its concern to negotiate skepticism and nihilism in an ethics of death as the crux of relation between the individual and society, *Koroshi no rakuin*

/ 223 /

Fig. 7.1. Cinematic Negativity (shot 1): the negative film stock of a disorienting, aimless pan across an apartment high rise on redeveloped *yamanote* (Western) side of Tokyo (*Koroshi no rakuin / Branded to Kill*)

Fig. 7.2. Cinematic Negativity (shot 3): right pan with a rushing Shinkansen bullet train, a symbol of economic progress through technology (*Koroshi no rakuin*)

positions itself as a critical culmination of The Violence Trilogy. It is the apotheosis of his studio career as it related to the central concerns of the great Nikkatsu genres: *akushon*, *hādo-boirudo*, the *yakuza eiga*, even the burgeoning cycle of *nikutai* sex pictures. The film and its notorious history also solidified Suzuki's fandom and his high reputation in many quarters, while creating a kind of aesthetic and ideological template for Suzuki's later, independent career: including, most obviously, for *Pisutoru opera* (2001), a direct sequel. In that sense, the most nihilistic film ever produced by Suzuki and Nikkatsu stands out as the most productive, even positive

Fig. 7.3. Cinematic Negativity (shot 4): moving in the same direction, a fourth negative pan shot across the roof of Yoyogi Gymnasium, the iconic centerpiece of the 1964 Olympic Games (*Koroshi no rakuin*)

link between past and present; the hinge interposed between two sides of a vast filmography and all that it represents.

The first portion of this chapter discusses how Suzuki extends his overarching theme of the dissolution of Japanese masculinity to a consideration of studio filmmaking itself, establishing an "ideological complicity" between post-war society and the "masculine" crime thriller, and undermining that very ground. Masculinity and generic iconography are alike related to a third term, the entrenchment of post-war capitalism. The second section likens the formal construction of *Koroshi no rakuin* to a whirlpool, an ingenious *mise-en-abyme* of endless self-negation, an extreme but appropriate device for a film that crystallizes a genre based in death. I will chart various formal and structural "movements" of negativity such as *invisibility*, *reversal*, and *interruption*. A third section understands the significance of Suzuki's negative aesthetic—especially its lynchpin, discontinuity editing—with some reference to the film theory of Deleuze, and relates it to a decisive, transnational moment of departure from the classical cinema: the period 1966-1967.

By way of an introduction, however, I want to touch upon the principal aesthetic well-spring of the picture's negativity. While the 1967 *nuberu bagu* films of Yoshida expounded a form of existentialism and those of Ōshima channeled Brechtian theatre,[3] Suzuki responded to cinema's political and representational crisis of the late 1960s by a profound return to a different branch of the prewar avant-garde: French and Japanese surrealism. Suzuki has assented to the label of surrealism and this is only fitting considering surrealism's formative influence on the post-war hard-boiled fiction and *film noir* that had in turn inspired Nikkatsu.[4] But it is *Koroshi no rakuin* that channels surrealism most directly as a springboard for an attempt to break (or else destroy) the boundaries of narrative film practice.

While mindful of the Japanese surrealism (*chōgenjitsushugi*) of the Taishō era, *Koroshi no rakuin* shows the direct influence of the cinema of Buñuel. Daisuke Miyao agrees with me in noting the film's homage to *Un Chien Andalou* (Buñuel and Dali, 1929): a close-up of an eyeball pulled out of its socket by a criminal optometrist.[5] Suzuki may also have seen *L'âge d'Or* (1930), which played in Tokyo art theatres in the 1960s and excited the attention of film magazines and younger directors.[6] Whether consciously or not, *Koroshi no rakuin* synthesizes the genital symbolism of the former Buñuel film with the scatological motif of the latter one. In *Un Chien Andalou*, the heroine's underarm hair famously disappears and reappears as a moustache. Both are, of course, metonymies of pubic hair. In *Koroshi no rakuin*, Hanada (Shishido Jō), the psychotic protagonist, shoots his wife (Ogawa Mariko) in the breast and vagina. Her corpse falls into the toilet and her black hair is flushed down.

This abject scene of gendered violence sets up a surrealist transformation that reveals the pathology of Hanada's misogyny; in a later scene, as he enters a restaurant bathroom, he encounters a disfigured man flushing a toilet which is filled with black hair rather than feces. Hanada backs away in utter panic as the voice of his dead wife cries "We are beasts!" on the soundtrack. It is Hanada's reactionary terror of the (gendered) body, in all its biological functions, that drives him to kill, to negate.

This return to surrealism did not occur in a cultural vacuum, but

Fig. 7.4. Surrealism and Abjection: hair-as-feces links gendered violence and body horror

Fig. 7.5. Surrealist Transformation: feces-as-hair and the horror of the (gendered) body (*Koroshi no rakuin*)

within the ferment of the 1960s Tokyo avant-garde.[7] The screenwriter and novelist Abe Kōbō had formed a surrealist club at Tokyo University in the 1950s. Miryam Sas briefly contemplates the surrealist influence on the playwright/filmmaker Terayama Shūji,[8] whose play *Kegawa no mari/ Mari in Furs* (1967) utilizes the feminine, metamorphic symbol of the butterfly that is applied so memorably to the character of Misako in *Koroshi no rakuin*.[9] Kazuki Kuroi's briefly seen *Tobenai chinmoku/Silence Has No Wings* (1966), the only theatrical release in Japan which can be confidently said to have *pre-dated* the non-diegetic avant-gardism and discontinuity aesthetic of *Koroshi no rakuin*, was also dominated by a butterfly metaphor and also demonstrated a surrealist bent.

Like these avant-garde works, *Koroshi no rakuin* related a surrealist spirit of social rebellion and radical alterity to the ferment of the New Left leading up to the mass student demonstrations of 1968. Suzuki was, as ever, mindful of Taishō culture. When encouraged by his assistants (Yamatoya Atsushi and Tanaka Yōzō) in the Guryū Hachirō circle that wrote and produced *Koroshi no rakuin* with him, he chose Taishō surrealism as his meeting point with the agitational leftism of 1967.[10]

The importance to Japanese surrealism of the "negative aesthetic" cannot be emphasized enough. Takiguchi Shūzō called art "an act of destruction . . . to fulfil the aims of poetry."[11] The poet Kitasono Katsue viewed surrealism as the material and skill employed to produce a "vacuum tube," that is, "nothing at all. . . . The work that leads to this vacuum is the essence of art."[12] Sas reminds us that Kitasono's term for "vacuum" (*shinkū*) is also the Buddhist term for "the void." The writings of

Fig. 7.6. Butterflies and the Avant-Garde: surrealism and metaphors of femininity in *Tobenai chinmoku*

Fig. 7.7. The Butterflies of Death: *Koroshi no rakuin*'s desiccated butterflies associate radical femininity and radical negativity

the Buddhist-educated Koga Harue, who promoted surrealism as a form of liberating "self-extinction," illustrates how French surrealism's negative aesthetics were quickly, if inaccurately, interpreted by many Japanese artists according to the Buddhist theology of nothingness,[13] another resource which Suzuki had at his disposal.

The 1920s poet Kanbara Tai declared that "there is no poetry, no painting, no music. What exists is creation only. Art is absolutely free. The freedom of its form is absolute. . . . Nerve, reason, sense, sound, smell, light, color, desire, movement, pressure . . . there is nothing that does not fit the content of art."[14] In this declaration of the radical freedom of artistic subjectivity, representation and generic distinctions collapse not only into a democratic heterodoxy, but devolve into fundamental sensible and tonal relations. *Koroshi no rakuin* is a similar exercise in "getting back to basics," a devolution of film narration into deceptively "crude" forms with a minimum of continuity in time and space necessary for viewers to comprehend the trajectory of the protagonist. This looseness has the effect of emphasizing "pure" sounds and images (the pure *sonsigns* and *opsigns* of Gilles Deleuze). On this level of spectacle, the impression of spontaneous experiment is essential, yet deceptive. Nagatsuka's low-key lighting is highly complex even when welded to a "free-for-all" compositional strategy that displaces the classical "centered" representation of characters and actions in favor of shots of feet at the top of the frame, or heads at the bottom. A surrealist ethic of impertinence enables the film to push transnational hard-boiled fiction to a point of *sine qua non*, a collapse of generic and narrative integrity into the sensible and metaphorical.

As Miyao and Anthony Antoniou have noted, *Koroshi no rakuin* is also steeped in the history of surrealism's Franco-American descendent, the *film noir*. Of all Suzuki's films, *Koroshi no rakuin* is most explicitly referential to the American crime films. Particular scenes, including the murder of Mami Hanada, not only utilize low-key lighting effects but "quote" such iconic visual motifs of *noir* as the back-lit silhouette of a killer walking down a long corridor.

Most importantly, the film extends the generic and iconic reflexivity of *Tokyo nagaremono* to a new level of metatextual or hypertextual reference, unheard of for a studio film of 1967: as Hanada looks out on the Tokyo cityscape, he begins to believe that he can become Japan's Number One Killer

Fig. 7.8. Iconicity of *Noir* (*Koroshi no rakuin*)

and take over the criminal Organization that is hunting him down. A rather nasal yet masculine American voice is suddenly heard on the soundtrack, crying "I'm Champion!" again and again. The voice cannot help but remind us of Kirk Douglas' *Champion* (Robson, 1949), a determined and physically unstoppable boxer who is also a morally shiftless, worthless bum. Like the Douglas character, Hanada will also meet his well deserved end in a *noirish* boxing ring at the end of the picture. Douglas's prizefighter found his *noir* equivalent, barely a year later, in Richard Widmark's legendary portrayal of petty crook Harry Fabian from Dassin's *Night and the City* (1950). Fabian is another big-dreaming, morally compromised, and ill-fated loser. The point being made is that Hanada, for all his lethal talent, is also a loser, his ambitions nothing more than pipe dreams; and what is more revealing, that he is playing a losing game.

Criminality, Ideology, Satire

Hanada Goro: The Performance of Japanese Masculinity

Koroshi no rakuin distils the many varieties of Nikkatsu *akushon* into a cold, basic scenario about a heartless, murderous thug whose deluded, egoistic quest for underworld supremacy ends in his own death. The charm, magnetism, and attraction of the amoral "gangster as tragic hero" is replaced by the often comical pathos and neurosis of Shishido's antihero Hanada.[15] In place of the cool professionalism and statuesque physical stoicism of *ninkyō* heroes Takakura Ken and Tsuruta Kōji, Tōei's biggest stars of the 1960s, Shishido's Hanada communicates an ugly, brutal masculinity. This repellent protagonist, anticipating the ugliness of criminal life in Fukasaku's *jitsuroku* (true account) gang films of the 1970s, wipes the "shine" off of the cinematic *yakuza* in order to show the "seam." In *Yajū no seishun*, Shishido had occupied a grey area between "law and order" (the hard-boiled detective) and lawless perversity. Here, he embodies a brutish, perverse criminal incarnate, without decency or excuses.

The first thing one notices about Hanada, as he climbs into a limo in the second shot of the film, is that he is constantly playing a role. Every component of his visual persona is a cliché, a reflexive gesture. His expensive black suit never gets dirty; his black trench coat signifies professionalism and coldness. Most notable are the outsized sunglasses, always a significant motif in a Suzuki film. They communicate a cruel, inviolate remoteness and the self-assertion of power. Hanada expects to be looked

Fig. 7.9. The Protagonist as Demon: the killer wreathed in smoke as he sniffs boiled rice

at and attended to (without saying a word), but will not lower himself to be seen looking back. With his oversized glasses, puffy, scarred cheeks, and a pasty complexion overemphasized by the harsh top lighting of his close-ups, Shishido looks like a folkloric demon (*oni*).

Hanada's performance of himself as a virtually unsocialized, inhuman killer is a façade that will be stripped away with clinical detachment by the filmmakers, as Hanada falls in love and becomes "only human" after all. This humanity—in the form of a paranoid, lovesick wreckage inciting, by degrees, the viewer's pity and scorn—departs as quickly as it arrives, as Hanada, unable to stand his own weakness under the harsh light of society's patriarchal structures of judgment, turns to murdering women and embroils himself in a sadomasochistic duel with his superior in order to prove himself.

Nevertheless, Shishido imparts to this character, in visual terms, a peculiar variety of sexual charisma. Semi-nude for nearly half of the film, he projects the dangerous attraction of a snake or a wolf. Hanada's wife Mami confirms his monstrosity: "My husband is a terrifying (*osoroshii*) man," she says with obvious sexual relish. The opening sequences insist on Hanada's highly repressed and exclusively fetishistic sexuality, centered on his addiction to the smell of boiled rice. In one sequence, Hanada is sniffing rice as his nude wife emerges from the shower. Thanks to the rice, Hanada suddenly stands "erect" and chases after her. The sex scene between the newlyweds is a *reductio ad absurdum* of the ideological determination of sexuality. Through his rice fetish, Hanada is literally "steeling himself" for playing his role, a performance for Mami, for the viewer, and

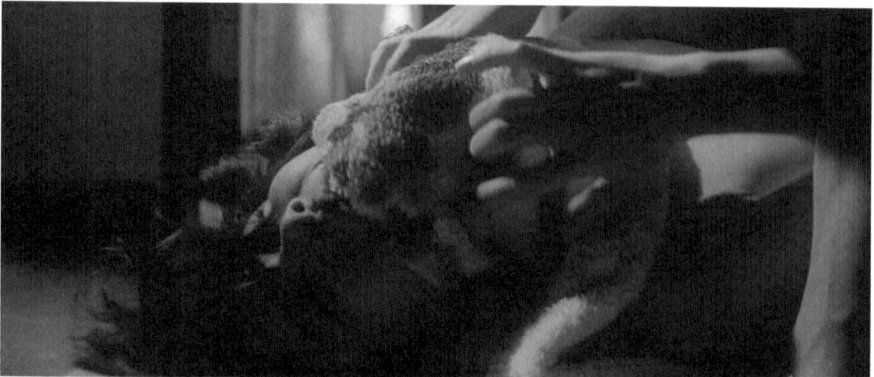

Fig. 7.10. Sex and Subjugation: out of control smothering and savage blows *almost* terrify the irrepressible Mami

for himself. Brutality is the only aspect of intercourse which seems to galvanize Hanada. Mami is the objectified, subjugated target of blows and of penetration from Hanada as the active, sadistic male.

Hanada's energy is passionless and noncommittal: the "impenetrable" male never risks losing control of the situation (as he will shortly do with Misako). Sex is an obligatory ritual of the containment of the feminine. Yet Hanada's comical dependence on rice sniffing in order to get up the willpower for intercourse is a humorous negation of his posture of strength. When Hanada hides out in Misako's apartment and she, unlike Mami, denies him his rice, Hanada breaks down like a sulking, histrionic child, bringing about the loss of control that the male "professional" fears most.

One of Suzuki's notorious "open metaphors," Hanada's rice sniffing is perhaps, among other things, a nostalgic reversion to adolescent sexuality and to Japan's past. Ohnuki-Tierney extrapolates the modern symbology of rice from its ancient, sacred status as a sustenance crop: "the aesthetics of rice lies in its luster as well as in its whiteness and purity.... Motōri Norinaga ... discerned the superiority of Japan ... in the superiority of its rice and cherry blossoms."[16] Within a dehumanized urban milieu, the smell of boiled rice may signify for Hanada the mythical space of rural, hometown (*furusato*) Japan. Since Hanada's childhood would have been in the 1940s, therefore displaced by the war, the *gestus* of the boiled rice may evoke a naïve longing for the prewar, rural, implicitly imperial past that characterized much of post-war studio cinema.

Masculinity as Capitalism

The most important aspect of Hanada's character is his all-consuming competitiveness. This is perhaps the principal motif of the film: the *ethos* of competition as an allegory for Japan's transformation into a player in global capitalism. The whimsical obsession of the killers with their "ranking" is, among other things, reminiscent of the life of the 1960s *sarariman*, forever caught up in anxious relations with superiors and inferiors. Hanada's hypersensitivity to position, to judging whether a man is better or worse than he, becomes more and more acute, drowning out sex and relationships. By the end of the film, Hanada literally murders the possibility of anything else in his life when he "accidentally" shoots his only love, Misako, in a wild attempt to defeat Number One. So, in the social equation, may one succeed (temporarily) in capitalism's game of life, yet lose all else in doing so.

Hanada's fetishistic professionalism is established in comparison to his alcoholic partner Kasuga (Minami Hiroshi) who has lost his confidence and can barely hold a gun. Kasuga obsesses over his violation of the assassin's code: "Drink and Women Kill a Killer." Compared to the unspoken, situational, but elaborate code of honor in the *ninkyō eiga*, the "code" at work here is a piece of crude, essentialist masculine posturing. It constitutes nothing more ethical than an imaginary prescription for self-preservation achieved at the expense of the Other (the female) who signifies a loss of boundaries. A killer must never lose control, especially through sex: to break this abstemious code is considered by other killers not only as proof of incompetence, but, paradoxically, as loss of virility. Kasuga's "impotence" is expressed with a brilliant metaphorical economy by his manner of stopping short with the car. When Hanada slaps his old friend with pained contempt, this is the final humiliation for Kasuga, who no longer feels himself to be a "man." Honorific redemption through suicide seems the only way out. Gun in hand, Kasuga takes a running leap down a dark underpass at the end of which waits killer Number Four. The oft-seen tunnel or underpass, a negative symbol of industrial development with obvious sexual connotations, becomes the film's dominant metaphor for the (perceived) loss of masculinity.

After executing Kasuga, the smartly dressed Number Four (scriptwriter Yamatoya Atsushi) turns around, walks a few steps, and drops dead from Kasuga's bullet. After death, he pulls his immaculate white coat over his own head. This superbly Brechtian gesture is essential to the argument

Fig. 7.11. In the Tunnel: the downward slide of masculine competition

of the film. Violence is not reducible to male competition on a biological level, but operates within a ritualized ideological system that compels behavior regardless of personal impulse. In this final "case study" of the "Violence Trilogy," the divorce between naturalism and ideology represented by Kasuga is also channeled through the conflict of worldview between Hanada and Mami. The only character in the film more interested in survival than death, Mami views humanity, not unreasonably, as purely bestial. But Hanada is attached to a vision of human/corporate "progress," a dream of beating the odds and becoming Number One. At the moment of Hanada's professional "high point," when he has ingeniously defeated five Organization agents at the harbor, the "left-handed" dream of success in the criminal "business" is metaphorized in the form of an American aircraft carrier passing by, while jaunty pop music plays over the soundtrack: the Japan of the economic miracle and its disavowing fantasy of regeneration through American-style capitalism.

Training for Power

When Hanada holes up in Misako's apartment, unable to leave for fear of Number One's sniper bullet, the latter passes up countless opportunities to kill Hanada, preferring to call him on the phone and offer advice ("you need protein"), or to belittle him with droll, suggestive remarks. Number One's cat and mouse game with Hanada begins to resemble not a duel, but the master-apprentice training of countless *chanbara* films (e.g., the many versions of *Miyamoto Musashi*). Number One, who is "well endowed" with

Fig. 7.12. Political Allegory: Who Is Number One?

extraordinary techniques, is a nightmare vision of the patriarch, the castrating father/master who cruelly demands more than the child/apprentice can live up to. "This is the best position for you," he says as Hanada bends down, his posterior in sight of Number One's crosshairs. The disavowed homoerotic subtext here is not incidental. In a contemporaneous exploration of the erotics of male violence, the protagonist of the 1968 British film *Performance* appears to fire a gun into the camera lens itself (Fig. 7.13) as he proclaims, "I am a bullet," thus reinforcing his "hardness."

In both films, the fetishism of maleness is elevated to a way of life through the practice of violence, which is a *jouissance*: an erotic substitute for heterosexual intercourse, from which both protagonists either abstain or attempt to transform through sadism; and for homosexual contact, which both men will not allow themselves except through the substituted form of violence. But in *Koroshi no rakuin*, as Number One decides inexplicably that he and Hanada must eat, sleep, and even struggle to use the toilet together before they can resolve their duel, the homoerotic dynamic is played as a *reductio ad absurdum* mockery of the gangster, as the two killers farcically enact the rituals of heterosexual marriage.

Nevertheless, the relevance of the dictum "I am a bullet" becomes clear when Number One espouses his philosophy of the professional killer. "I smell women," he complains at one point. The comment leads to the following dialogue (which, interestingly, does not appear in the published script):

> NO. 1: Should we talk about women to stay awake? You were in love with Misako?

Fig. 7.13. I am a Bullet (The Fetishization of Violence): in *Performance* (1968/70), after being flagellated by a male ex-lover, the semi-nude Chas (James Fox) kills him with a bullet fired into the lens

> HANADA: There's no love for people like us. We can't love women.
> NO. 1: And yet you loved Misako.
> HANADA: Even for a killer, it was impossible. She was my weakness.
> NO. 1: Yes, a very human weakness. A killer is someone who cannot be humane. He must be dispassionate. A killer is someone who is beyond loneliness and isolation.

This dialogue illustrates a number of things. First, that there is no ideological distance between Hanada and Number One, the antisocial Lone Wolf and the Corporate Leader. Satō attempted to explain the attraction of the somewhat reactionary *ninkyō* films for leftist students: "we have entered an era in which the assault on a big organization by a small group in the name of justice is no longer doomed to failure."[17] *Koroshi no rakuin*'s social satire, a variant of the politics of the *nuberu bagu*, turns Satō's opposition of lone wolf versus institution on its head. The man hunted by the Organization wants to lead it; the man at the top is profoundly more alone than the loner. They are motivated by the same ideology of gender. In this sense,

Koroshi no rakuin offers a more sober political analysis than Wakamatsu's activist portraits of antisocial violence, such as *Okasareta hakui/Violated Angels* (1967). This far less populist film, which sets out to offend and dehumanize its audience, appoints a lone serial killer as a sort of political scourge of the *status quo* viewed in exclusively feminine terms (his victims). In *Koroshi no rakuin*, "the Organization"—the mirror of mainstream social organization—is simply the psyche of the individual Japanese male (Wakamatsu's killer) given absolute power and writ terrifyingly large.

"The Organization" is the negative mirror of all institutional power, and their torture of Misako makes explicit the ingrained misogyny that extends downwards from the ruling classes. The scene is not presented to the audience directly but in the mediated, impersonal, and self-reflexive form of an 8mm film presented, instructively, by Number One. Hanada watches the film as both fascinated voyeur and captive audience, and in this manner the scene cannot help but cast a negative reflection on gendered violence in genre cinema.

In the 8mm film, several middle-aged, well-dressed men from the Organization watch from the safety of a glass booth, both voyeurs and remote controllers of the action.

They are gazing at a naked Misako tied to a pole, the ultimate patriarchal totem. An automatic blowtorch on a robot arm is then applied to Misako's breasts and hair, transforming her into a bandaged, de-sexed, neutralized walking corpse. Note the unbridgeable distance between the staging and mise-en-scène of this torture and that of Maya in *Nikutai no mon*. This is a literal and sadistic negation of the female carried out

Fig. 7.14. Reluctant Voyeur: Hanada despairs at the unbridgeable distance between himself and the screened violence (*Koroshi no rakuin*)

Fig. 7.15. The Discreet Charm of the Bourgeoisie: Organization leaders operate torture devices from a glass booth

as a reflex of institutionalized misogyny. The scene spares no one from uncomfortable complicity: not the *yakuza*, not the legitimate (male) world of business, not the makers and viewers of genre films.

The philosophy of Number One also reveals the most final negation: the rejection of the human in favor of the robot.[18] A killer must not need love or emotion, sleep or food. In order to achieve this "inhumanity" Hanada puts himself into a noose that will strangle him if he falls asleep.

This sort of painful, masochistic male training is the recipe for competitive success as well as the ultimate protection from the feminine: the final phase of masculine identity viewed as a search for almost supernatural "hardness" stretching back to wartime ideology. Theweleit famously described a German cultural analogue to this:

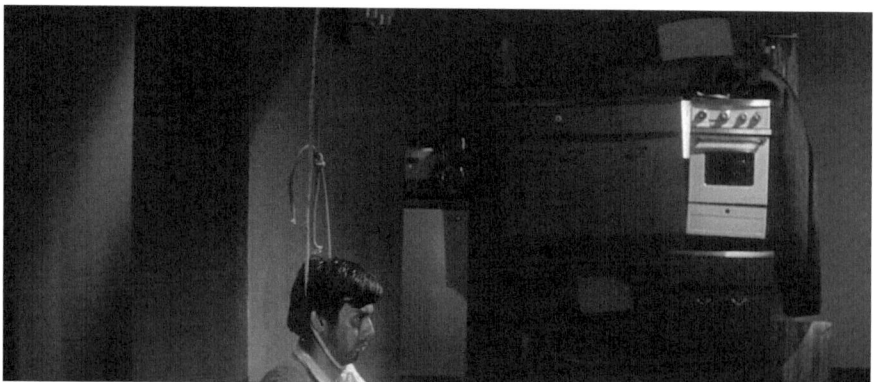

Fig. 7.16. Training for Power: in extreme pursuit of "hardness"

> The person is split into an inner realm, concealing a 'numbly glowing, fluid ocean' and other dangers; and a restraining external shell, the muscle armor, which contains the inner realm the way a cauldron contains boiling soup. The bubbling contents wants to get out. . . . The political 'order' holding the Metropolis in check also appears to have the same function of the body armor that 'bottles up' his own seething interior . . .[19]

Hanada and Number One thus carry male performance to its logical conclusion. But, like the film itself, this very extremity is the ironic route by which a social critique is achieved. The possibility of the negation of this masculine ideal appears only because the film has visualized, through these crystallized, fantastic gestures, its utter absurdity and futility.

Hanada has internalized the insane psychological demands of Japanese patriarchy well before the narrative begins; and yet *Koroshi no rakuin* is not a scenario of patriarchal succession. Hanada can only defeat his opponent through suicide. The dream of success remains elusive, even (or especially) for the talented. You cannot beat the system; that is, the Organization. Its ultimate victory is in drawing out its most capable individuals (Hanada, Misako, Number One) in order to eliminate them in the name of stasis. Hanada's decision to play "the game"—his deluded belief that he has a chance at winning—is the one and only cause of his downfall. The affair with Misako is viewed by Hanada as a nightmarish distraction from his *raison d'être*, but it may actually be a road not taken. Misako's unpredictability powerfully breaks her out of her role as a projection of male anxiety, representing not only a radical independence from social mores and patriarchal oppression, but the freedom of choice itself. She is superior to Hanada on the basis of the longstanding, Buddhist cultural admonition against attachment. She is also positioned as another directorial alter ego: both derive a masochistic view of life from the omnipresence of death. "Where will I pin you?" she asks, comparing Hanada to her butterflies. But Hanada has already been trapped, pinned down, and dissected, with ironic detachment, by Suzuki's film. The inscrutable Misako is, like Suzuki's film, like reality, in a continual state of flux: not even her obsession with butterflies remains constant, and her stubborn survival belies her touted death wish. But Hanada, like Suzuki's post-war Japan, remains trapped in his dark tunnel, struggling towards the light while, paradoxically, pushing farther into darkness that will, eventually, submerge both characters.

The Varieties of Negative Structure

Genre, Structure, and Farcical Negation

Up to this point my chapter is in broad agreement with Watanabe Takenobu's analysis of *Koroshi no rakuin*, although I have emphasized the political and directorial intentionalities that Watanabe deliberately ignores in his search for a general essence of Nikkatsu *akushon*.[20] Watanabe views the film as a reflexive film about genre, a "maximal accumulation" of the mythic/generic elements familiar to Nikkatsu viewers,[21] yet pushing them towards abstraction and pure visual interest.[22] This is true, but it is important to recognize that the film, by its negative design, cannot be bounded by generic constraints or even, finally, narrative ones. Some of its most striking features, such as framing, are quite unrelated to genre—or narrative—while others are recognizably oppositional.

Nearly every *yakuza* and crime thriller of the 1960s, including Suzuki's, progresses in a linear fashion that suggests fate towards a climactic duel or battle. *Koroshi no rakuin* corresponds to this structure and yet confounds it with a profound circularity. The story begins with former No. 7 killer losing his confidence because of a woman, taking to drink, and finally sacrificing his life to kill a high-ranking assassin. The story ends with the former No. 3 Killer losing his confidence because of a woman, taking to drink, and sacrificing his life to kill a higher-ranking assassin. The Organization's dystopic operation will thus go on repeating itself.

Circularity does not, nevertheless, prevent the film from making up a structural triptych. The film falls neatly into three thirty-minute segments, and like a creature that swallows its own tail, the final segment enacts the satirical negation of what has come before. The first segment is in every way a setting up of milieu and character. Hanada does his job, sleeps with his new wife, and meets Misako. In the second segment, "everything goes crazy": Hanada is pursued by the Organization, shot by his wife, and falls for Misako. It is important to note where the segment ends. Following the murder of Mami, Hanada picks up the professional pieces and faces off against the Organization. This shootout at the Tokyo docklands, though distinctive as an action set piece, is nevertheless structurally predictable. It stands for the climax of so many studio action films, which typically come to an end at this point, but for a short coda. Hanada has wiped out the rival gang and has wrapped up his love problems unhappily. This is precisely the point at which Shishido's more conventional vehicle, *Koruto wa ore no pasupōto* (1967), ends.

But at *precisely* this moment, Number One reappears on the scene and initiates a third segment of the film that is superfluous in narrative and structural terms. The possibility of a final duel on the spot is dangled before us four times. Rejecting the pleasures of closure, however, the film carries on in the form of the interminable cat-and-mouse game between Hanada and Number One. Although this portion of the film carries the satirical "sting," narratively it is a mere repetition of the second segment. Again Hanada starts off with confidence, descends into paranoia, is tested by his love for Misako, and picks up the pieces and fights back in a second and final climax. The difference between the two segments is that Hanada appears to die in the film's final moments. And this is a crucial difference. The film repeats the second segment in order to negate it, killing off Hanada to reveal the "truth" of the duel: nobody beats the system and survives. This is not the truth of Tōei's *ninkyō* hero, who masochistically accepts the system by accepting imprisonment;[23] it is simple annihilation.

As *Koroshi no rakuin* rehashes its own and every other 1960s crime narrative, history, as Marx observed, is played first as tragedy and then as farce. This is the best possible summation of *Koroshi no rakuin*. The expressionist violence of the second segment gives way to the utter absurdity of the third. Compare the treatment of Misako in these respective parts. In the second, Hanada has a nightmarish sexual encounter with Misako, suffused with the dread of death, in an apartment full of desiccated butterflies. The third segment portrays a washed up, drunken Hanada pining for the lost Misako. An overhead shot finds him an abject, pathetic figure, kneeling face down on the floor before a small pile of butterflies,

Fig. 7.17. Negativity as Farce: the breakdown of Hanada's masculine ideal as comic-pathetic spectacle

tossing them up in the air and letting them fall on his head as he whimpers "Misako! Misako!" It is perhaps the most ridiculous moment of a sublimely absurd film.

The centrality, in crime thrillers, of the male homosocial union is also devolved into farce. As Hanada and Number One establish a tedious routine of eating, sleeping, and using the toilet together, Number One also suggests that, *ostensibly* for security, they must keep their arms linked at all times. When the two go out, arm and arm, to a restaurant, their adoption of the postures of marriage comically provokes the postman, the passersby, and potentially many of the viewers of the period.

Negative Movements: Invisibility, Disappearance, Reversal, Interruption

Thus far I have identified the narrative and ideological structure of *Koroshi no rakuin*. Yet we need to identify the formal markings and varieties of what I have called Suzuki's negative aesthetic. For it is principally through mise-en-scène and montage that this film differentiates itself from the formal economy of Nikkatsu *akushon* and indeed from the classical studio cinema as a whole. Several distinct strategies of "negative movement," such as invisibility, disappearance, reversal, and interruption, accomplish in themselves the reversal of the classical cinema, which was defined by narrative and visual "comprehensibility" and was precisely what Nikkatsu President Hori, after seeing this picture, was motivated to reinforce with the firing of Suzuki.

Koroshi no rakuin is remarkable for its time in insisting upon the lack of visibility of the characters and main actions in a scene. Invisibility is appropriate as a narrative metaphor: Hanada cannot see what goes on behind the scenes (the Organization), nor, indeed, can he use his eyes to separate reality from fantasy (Misako). Invisibility mounts to a paradoxical presence in the "sniper duel" sequence between Hanada and Number One. A large portion of the montage emphasizes the "phantom presence" and the disembodied/mediated voice of Number One, who represents another negative power that is particularly germane to montage: *disappearance*.[24] Hanada cannot see or determine the enemy's position, yet is himself under surveillance at every moment; wherever he goes, Number One can (impossibly) see him, an excessive visibility that invokes the panoptic.

Especially in this sniper sequence, large objects such as walls and partitions block the camera's view of the characters.

If this is only mildly distracting, the constant reframing of character action and movement calls blatant attention to itself. Here, flash pans in

Fig. 7.18. Blocked Up: the frame bisected by a moveable partition while the head of the frustrated protagonist is barely glimpsed (*bottom left of center*)

all four directions steal the center of the frame away from the protagonist. At other moments, the camera pans away from Hanada, anticipating his future movement in the same direction; when Hanada arrives back in the frame, however, the result is askew: it might contain only his head at the bottom of screen, or his feet at the top.

These framings represent a new variant of the active, reflexive camera which had appeared in the earlier sex scene in Hanada's apartment, asserting its own mobile POV as it prowled through empty spaces. In both sequences, an unusual number of shots emphasize, either by fixed framing or panning, *the lack of action* going on in a given space, or the disappearance of a character from his or her expected position.

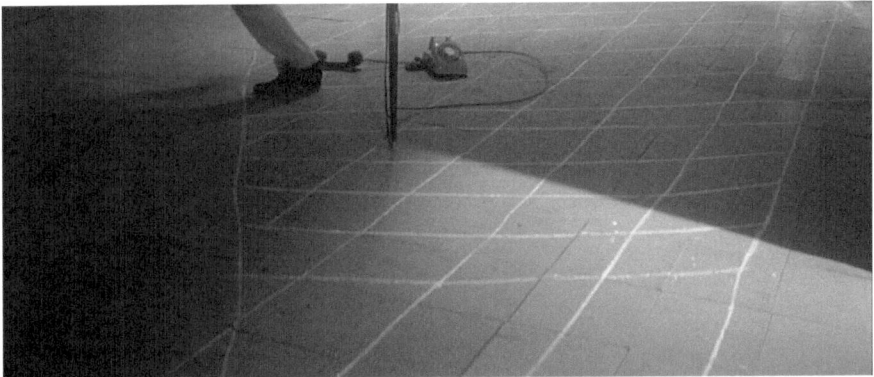

Fig. 7.19. Deframing: a composition with Hanada's feet flashing across the top of the frame

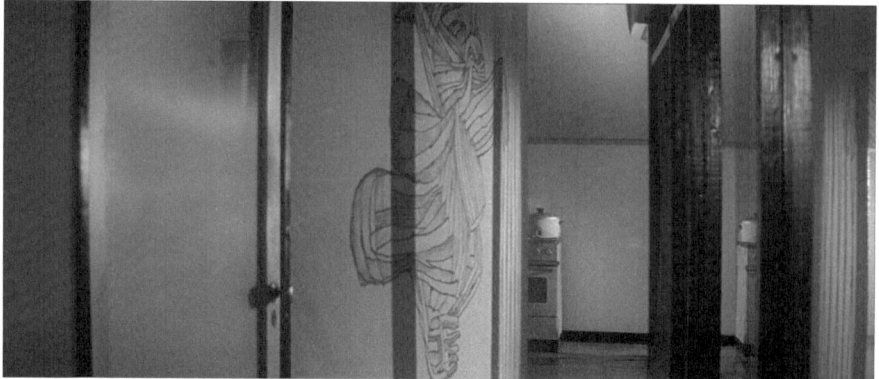

Fig. 7.20. Empty Space and the Moving Camera: four extended, elaborate tracking shots, which locate neither actions nor characters

With these provocative strategies of denied visibility, the camera becomes a more independent presence than the Japanese cinema had yet experienced. David Melville writes that "Suzuki has rebelled constantly against the 'compulsion to create worlds that do not acknowledge that they are being watched.'"[25] What the denial of visibility accomplishes, paradoxically, is the implied "visibility" of the camera itself. This virtual appearance of what cannot appear (the camera) is a profound and unmistakable negation of the classical style, especially given that the gesture seems to lack any figurative dimension. *Koroshi no rakuin* seems to me to aspire to transcend, if not negate, not only the iconic reflexivity of *Tokyo nagaremono*, but even the freest conception of cinematic metaphor. It is the moving camera's equivalent of the "unmotivated cutaway" from a narrative sequence that Bordwell declared "absolutely forbidden" in the Classical Hollywood cinema.[26] The camera declares unorthodox agency in the shaping of events: is it interfering in or creating the narrative? The notion of a closed diegesis, so often tenuous in a Suzuki film, dissolves here into *mise-en-abyme*. This self-reflexivity extends beyond the camera to other formal strategies such as the new and intensive use of non-diegetic graphics. At the film's exact midpoint, Hanada is obsessed with his inability to kill Misako. Several rows of illustrated feminine symbols—butterflies, birds, and rain—invade Hanada's close-up, occupying in succession the top, bottom, and sides of the frame. Hanada reacts in dismay: but what, in terms of diegesis, can he be said to be reacting to?[27]

The chiaroscuro patterning of Nagatsuka's low-key lighting creates a constant play between visible and invisible areas of the frame. Even when natural light is abundant, as in the daytime sequences in Misako's apart-

Fig. 7.21. Non-diegetic Style and Satire in the '60s: Hanada dismayed by cartoon illustrations of femininity

ment, Nagatsuka uses a direct and undiffused spotlight as the key light source in several shots. Often this encourages the eye to wander over to a shining point of light on an object or area of the frame that is not relevant to the action; again, problematic visibility.

The final scene in the gymnasium is lit entirely by weak spotlights which make it impossible to determine Hanada's position from shot to shot. Eventually, Hanada steps into the spotlit boxing ring and makes himself a target. Betting on the visibility that his sunglasses will afford him when the lights go out, he uses the tactic of becoming visible in order to spot the location of "invisible" Number One.

Fig. 7.22. Excess Visuality: spot lighting on an area of the room with no narrative function

Fig. 7.23. The Allegory of Excess Visibility: the sunglass-wearing Hanada utilizes his own visibility and a trick of the light

As this finale demonstrates, the motif of withheld visibility relates to other varieties of negative movement, notably that of reversal. In the sniper sequence, the position of Hanada and Number One had become increasingly reversible, with the camera adopting both POVs. This in turn led to the aforementioned reversal of love and death between the assassins as they adopted the habits of a married couple. In the end, Hanada turns the tables on Number One, but seemingly only at the price of his own death, the final reversal.

In the nightmare sequence in Misako's apartment the movement of reversal evolves into the trope of *interruption*. Both characters try to express physical love for one another, but on each occasion, one attempts to kill the other instead. This leads to several infamous scenes of *coitus interruptus* between the rapine Hanada and the murderous *femme fatale* (Fig. 7.24). The tough guy cannot handle these overt and symbolic displays of uncanny female power, however, and starts to fall apart: thus the film accomplishes the most significant reversal, that of gender and power, passivity and activity.

Discontinuity as Difference, Aesthetic, and Ethos

Time and Technique in the Modern Cinema: Deleuze, Buñuel, Suzuki

In *Koroshi no rakuin*, the breakdown of the flawed hero is accompanied by the chaotic, spatially indeterminate action that had been developing in

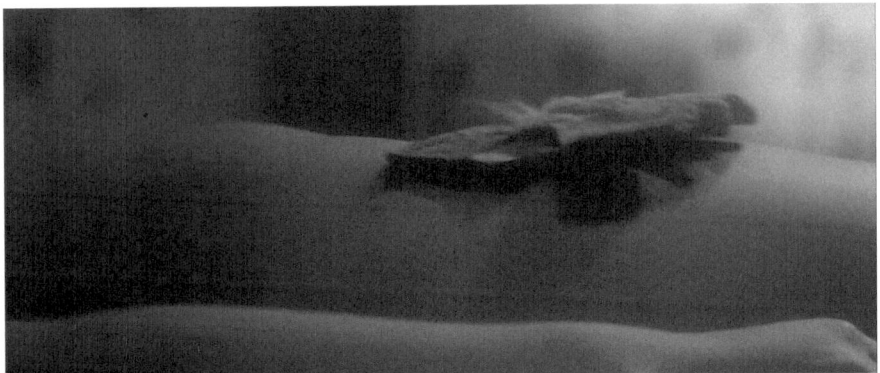

Fig. 7.24. Uncanny Femininity: a "dead" butterfly floats onto Misako's crotch and terrifies Hanada as he attempts to have intercourse with her

Suzuki's films since *Rajo to kenjū* (1957). More than ever, this aesthetic emphasizes not only visible discontinuities between adjacent shots, but incongruities of sound and image in a single shot. For instance, while Hanada and Misako are having a conversation on the film's soundtrack, they are situated at different points of a large public square.

This strategic use of "discontinuity editing" is the lynchpin or hinge of Suzuki's mature films.[28] I do not know whether Nikkatsu's ubiquitous editor, Suzuki Akira—who surprisingly was not assigned to either *Tokyo nagaremono* or *Kenka erejii* after dozens of collaborations with Suzuki in the past—was personally inclined to encourage these developments, or whether he was gradually co-opted by a confident directorial vision, itself

Fig. 7.25. Disjunction of Sound and Image: a conversation on the soundtrack from an "impossible" spatial distance

bolstered by the radicalism of Guryū Hachirō. It is most likely a combination of both, and in any case only matters for the appreciable results. *Koroshi no rakuin* showcases this editing practice in its most differential form; I argue that it raises this "discontinuity aesthetic" to a new level of (hitherto unrecognized) conceptual significance. Suzuki's contemporary, Gilles Deleuze, who also did his formative work in the late 1960s, employed the term "time-image" in order to theorize the transition from classical cinema to a post-war modern(-ist) cinema and to situate this within a comprehensive formal taxonomy of the semiotic practices of narrative cinema generally. The *time-image* signifies, specifically, a direct "image" or representation of time. This primarily entails "false continuity and irrational cuts" deployed to violate the system of classic continuity editing that imitates the human sensory-motor schema and subordinates cinematic time as merely the measure of logical movement through space.[29] By subordinating spatial representation to temporal structures, the possibilities of cinematic expression are multiplied as new configurations of "irrational" cutting proliferate. Whereas editing in most narrative film serves the interest of spatio-temporal continuity, consider the blatant spatial and temporal "falsity" of the following juxtaposition from *Koroshi no rakuin*. In the first shot, Hanada spots Number One outside his apartment window, on the top of a church tower in the distance.

Fig. 7.26. Discontinuity Aesthetics (shot 1): Number One on the bell tower

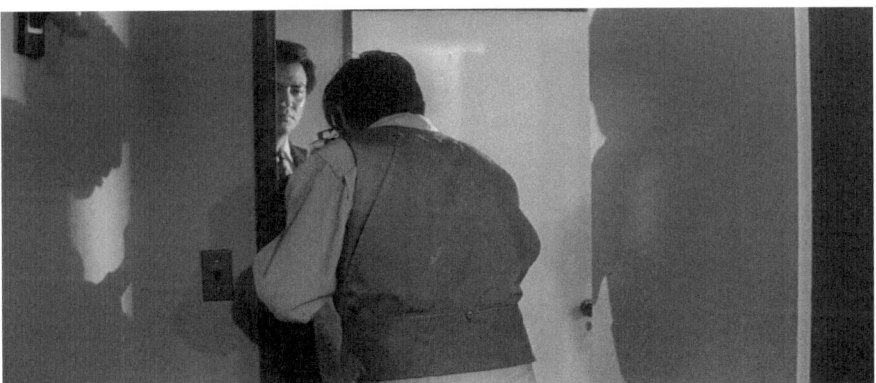

Fig. 7.27. Discontinuity Aesthetics (shot 2): Number One in the apartment

In the second shot, Hanada jumps up from the window, turns, and runs out of his apartment door. However, a second later, he returns to the apartment followed by Number One, whose gun is trained on the protagonist's head.

How could Number One have crossed the distance from the church tower to the apartment complex hallway in the four seconds of time that have passed from the end of Shot (1) to his appearance in Shot (2)? It is in some sense "impossible," and such impossible or "false" narrative events, achieved through editing, typify the kind of cinema that is pursued in *Koroshi no rakuin*. This is, moreover, just one kind of cinematic sign among many that are at play here and each of which, as Deleuzean theory informs us, constitute a modern cinema in a slightly different way.

Why turn particularly to Deleuze, or for that matter any Western theorist, to understand *Koroshi no rakuin*? First, Deleuze sought to ground and condition cinematic meaning in the semiotics of a medium in which, beyond narrative and representation, time and space themselves are constituent elements. He was able to introduce into film criticism a new range of "meaning effects" that parallel what Suzuki and certain other directors of that era (e.g., Teshigahara) were working through in their distinctive film practices; ultimately corresponding, in Deleuzean terms, to new forms of distinctly "cinematic" thought. Second, whereas Hasumi considered the break between the silent cinema and one of synchronized sound to be the most fundamental, Deleuze is more congenial to Suzuki—and other practitioners of characteristically urban/cosmopolitan modes of representation such as hard-boiled—because he identifies the Second World War as the decisive break in cinema history. "The post-war period . . . greatly increased the situations which we no longer know how to react to, in spaces which we no longer know how to describe.... deserted but inhabited... waste ground, cities in the course of demolition and reconstruction."[30] No one understood better than ordinary Japanese the experience of staring helplessly at bombed-out spaces or indeterminate, faceless, de-historicized remains. Such conditions demanded an altered scheme of representation.

Finally, Deleuze's account of modern cinema specifically emphasizes the centrality of "discontinuity"—exactly of the sort we find in the Violence Trilogy. He isolates a transnational continuity, at once reflexive and ethical-political, of post-war cinematic innovation in this regard, from Buñuel to Welles to Godard. Since Deleuze ironically failed to reckon with the insights of Japanese filmmakers who, unlike Ozu, began their practice after the war, this leaves fallow ground for the contemporary scholar on which to supplement, internationalize, and revise his work in reference to those insights.

What is the fundamental distinction between the classical and modern? In the classical cinema, Deleuze argues, "the setting described is presented as independent of the description which the camera gives of it and stands for a supposedly pre-existing reality." However, in the modern cinema of false continuity, "it is now the description itself which constitutes the sole decomposed and multiplied object.... Those pure descriptions... develop a creative and destructive function. In fact, [such] descriptions... constitute their own object."[31] Thus the modernist cinema defines itself as one of "description" rather than, primarily, representation.

In a cinema of irrational and discontinuous juxtapositions, the image becomes in a sense simplified: the "image itself is the system of relationships between its elements," that is, "pure" optical (and sonic) elements that are no longer anchored and constrained by continuity. Such optical and sound descriptions, which Deleuze detected in Ozu's much debated "still life" and "pillow" shots, are only the most basic signifiers of modern cinema's "pure descriptions." The further category of *chronosigns* gives us a tool by which to better relate the originality of *Koroshi no rakuin*'s arrangements of narrative time to those of various European filmmakers who were notably *en mode* in Japanese film circles at the time.

Chronosigns depict complex time relations in the cinema through the invocation of multiple, simultaneous "presents." Deleuze is somewhat vague as to how "simultaneous presents" may be represented through cinematic technique, but fortunately gives concrete examples from the later films of Buñuel. The surrealist is considered to have evolved from a harsh naturalism towards *chronosigns* that could be identified by "the subjection of the image to a power of 'repetition-variation'."[32] Sometimes Buñuel uses such repetition-variation to represent time as cyclical rather than linear.[33] *Koroshi no rakuin* is also perfectly circular; but in Deleuze's rigorous taxonomy, cyclical time is not enough to accomplish the break with classical cinematic continuity. Repetition in the late films of Buñuel, for Deleuze, presents not cycles of time, but paradoxes of simultaneity. In *Phantom of Liberty* (1974), a little girl is reported as being lost by her parents even though she is right beside them the whole time: "she has never stopped being there and will be found again." In *Belle de Jour* (1966) "the husband's final paralysis does and does not take place."[34] In *Zigeunerweisen*, similarly, the extramarital affair does and does not take place. But it is the newlywed sex scene in *Koroshi no rakuin* that is one of the more stunning cases of a "complex present tense" in the cinema of the 1960s.

In this sequence, one can sense how far that Suzuki (and his collaborators) had moved in a direction similar to the semiotic that Deleuze has described. Let us compare it to the similarly fragmented, disorienting "flashback" montage of *Kagenaki koe* (1958), in which expressionist canted angles and rapid cutting allow certain briefly seen actions (e.g., the bar girl's sadistic play with a slaughtered pigeon) to "leap out" of their station in the progress of the narrative and "hang," as it were, in the viewer's consciousness. Nevertheless, the viewers will not as a rule question the diegetic status of these distorted images, nor their distance from extracinematic "actuality." This is because they are fairly clearly marked as presenting a subjective memory, a recollection-image representing a relatively well defined section of narrative time; that is, a few hours in which a set of would-be killers await their chance to act. In the sex scene between Hanada and Mami, in contrast, one cannot determine whether the various sex acts are represented in chronological order. Did they occur in close succession, or were they repeated over a long period of time? It is impossible to know how much time, hours or days, have passed. Not only this, but moments of the before(s) and after(s) of intercourse are intercut with the sexual acts themselves, including moments of crucial narrative exposition. The scene also contains close-ups of Misako, with whom Hanada has become sexually obsessed. Misako is clearly not in the house at the time(s) of the intercourse, but Hanada has met her before, and he will meet her again in the house at the end of the sequence. Are these shots, then, memories, fantasies, or moments of the future? Without the ability to discriminate, they may be seen as a paradox of simultaneity. "It is the simultaneity of points of present, these points breaking with all external succession, and carrying out quantic jumps between presents which are doubled by the past, the future, and the present itself."[35] Through discontinuity, each shot becomes a "present" in and of itself rather than a point in an orderly succession of events. We have little choice but to consider the various sex acts on screen as each equally and irreducibly "present." A linear succession of shots ceases to signify the linear succession of narrative time. This in turn discourages the viewer's faith that there *is* a linear order of diegetic events, independent of its formal description, to be represented. Indeed, this sequence of "pure description" cannot or will not represent anything *beyond* description (such as, i.e., an independent linear, diegetic thread).

There is nothing comparable to a sequence of this kind or intensity in the 1967 films of Suzuki's universally esteemed colleagues, Imamura and Kurahara, nor fellow journeymen like Nomura or Hasebe.[36] Space in the modern cinema becomes transformed: the new spaces, writes Deleuze, "cannot be simply explained in a spatial way. They imply non-localizable relations" that can only be understood as "direct presentations of time. . . . A chronic, non-chronological time which produces movements necessarily 'abnormal,' essentially 'false'."[37] The function of montage in this descriptive system is ultimately that of "decomposing time relations" rather than composing them, in order that *"all possible movements emerge from it."*[38] Suzuki and his collaborators were in the vanguard of this transformation.

In the "simultaneity" that achieves a cinema of "pure description," so far as that is possible, *Koroshi no rakuin* locates, at last, a place for Suzuki in the grand academic narrative of film history. History inevitably highlights as exemplary the practices of some contemporaries over others. The pioneering uses of iconicity (in *Tokyo nagaremono*) and "falsity" (*Koroshi no rakuin*) exemplify key elements of a global transformation of cinematic form in the mid-1960s: a broadening of the formal parameters of narration in the sphere of popular cinema towards a cinematic performativity or "staging" that could reach "beyond" narration and beyond *diegesis* in describing a course of events that is still, in *some* important sense, fictional. The year 1967 saw parallel developments from filmmakers internationally, from Theodore J. Flicker's satirical *The President's Analyst* to Godard's *Week-end* (one should also mention Ossie Davis's *Cotton Comes to Harlem* as a remarkable analogue, though it came later). It is impossible to recognize and productively link these important transnational developments according to a narrative of directorial "influence." But it is equally important to recognize that a "historicist" narrative focusing on the transnational networks of film production and reception of the 1960s (from which Suzuki, like Flicker and Davis, remained largely excluded), is only a part, though an important one, of the answer. We must also isolate the conceptual and philosophical linkages and the politics of representation that became possible: possible because they were already latent in the semiotics of cinema and were finally given form, to some extent independently, by different filmmakers working in different cultural traditions and modes of production.

From Discontinuity to Nihilism: Welles and Suzuki

Koroshi no rakuin's complex time relations are not only relevant as a kind of analogue to the complexity of subjective experience in its negotiations of present and past, sense, memory, and desire. They have other, far reaching, consequences for social representation: the notions of truth and falsehood, judgment and relativism in the cinema and without.

For Deleuze, the words "truth" and "falsity" as applied to the modern cinematic practice relate not to questions of morality or even veridical truth but purely and simply to the logical sequencing of space and time (the imitation of the human sensory-motor schema). However, the consequences or "powers" that emerge from "false" continuity are another matter: they allowed certain directors of the 1960s to represent the world as constituted by ontologies and moralities that were alternative to what the classical cinema had proposed. This is what Deleuze calls "the powers of the false," an aspect of his *chronosigns* that speaks broadly to the sense, in Suzuki's films, of radical removal from any extra-cinematic constitution of "reality." Narration in the classical cinema of representation "claims to be true" by virtue of its grounding in "legal connections in space and chronological relations in time"; that is, the human sensory-motor schema.[39] Through irrational cuts and other techniques, the modern cinema "frees itself from the claim to be true, and becomes fundamentally falsifying."[40]

One of the consequences of this transition from "truth" to infinite varieties of "falsehood" has to do with character and identity. Because of the descriptive worlds to which they belong, characters in the modern cinema are no longer marked by fixed qualities: the character has an infinite capacity for change, variation, constant metamorphosis. With reference to Nietzsche and the films of Welles, Deleuze calls this quintessential modern protagonist "a forger" because he is always lying, either to himself or to others. The careening, survivalist protagonist of Imamura's *Nippon konchūki* may be seen as a nascent example. Because lacking in essence, the "forger" can be reduced to "a product of pure descriptions." Cinematic description is all that can be said to exist of the character. The two female assassins in *Pisutoru opera* (2001) are a full-flowered archetype of this, as they "jump cut" from one attitude or emotional state to its opposite. This suited Suzuki admirably, for as Hasumi noted of Nogawa Yumiko, "Suzuki's favorite actors use a physical approach, not a psychological one."[41] The lead performances in *Kagerō-za* and *Pisutoru opera* are notably comprised of no more or less than broad theatrical, or creatively physical, gestures.

The character as pure description can also be seen as an outgrowth of the *consciousness* and *multiplication of cliché,* which Deleuze considered as the first sign of the break-up of the classical cinema and its rhetoric of realism.[42] Under this new regime of character, *Tokyo nagaremono* presents a self-reflexive caricature (Phoenix Tetsu) of the hero/fighter of Nikkatsu popular cinema, who was already a sort of homogenization, for mass audiences, of two sources: the sexually attractive "good bad teen" of Nikkatsu's *taiyōzoku* (Sun Tribe) films and the "chivalrous" gangsters and samurai of Tōei studios. Takahashi Hideki's Kiroku is, similarly, a humorous diminution of the post-war cinema's nostalgically "pure" (*makoto*) and strait-laced youth, while the character of Hanada does the same for the reassuringly professional criminal of Nikkatsu's hard-boiled films, going from impregnable to pathetic and back again in his deluded quest to be "Number One."

Another inestimable consequence of the "powers of the false" is that a cinema of discontinuity no longer sets up "a structure of judgment"; that is, a moral and ideological standpoint, embedded in the narrative, from which the characters are judged ("crime never pays," etc.). *Koroshi no rakuin* does not interpolate its viewers into the patriarchal structures of judgment which drive Hanada to madness; the viewer is kept at a critical distance *precisely* through the use of discontinuity and other non-diegetic gestures. Even in the alienated, but essentially realist, mise-en-scène of hard-boiled films like *Koruto wa ore no pasupōto* (1967), the viewer maintains a certain empathetic and ideological closeness to the protagonist. This entertaining hard-boiled thriller, directed by Nomura Takashi, is often evoked by apologists for Nikkatsu (e.g., Schilling) as evidence for the claim that there was little or no textual or philosophical difference between Suzuki's films and Nikkatsu's ordinary product. But considering that it was made by every one of Suzuki's key collaborators (Kimura, Mine, Suzuki Akira, with Shishido as the star), and is *directly* imitative of previous Suzuki films (for example, the "car demolition" montage from *Tokyo nagaremono*), such arguments are invalid. It is probably hopeless, in any case, to describe with any useful specificity exactly what constituted Nikkatsu's "house style"; one cannot even say that an embarrassing exercise in youth-pandering such as Masuda Toshio's *Ore ni sawaru to abunaize/Black Tight Killers* (1966) is "typical" of it. In emulating the style of various predecessors, *Koruto wa ore no pasupōto* is sometimes formally clumsy, sometimes charming, but it reifies the hard-boiled *ethos* of the "principled" stoic male professional just as clearly as *Koroshi no rakuin* deconstructs it. Its often elliptical editing and fluid, breezy stylization is not as *conceptually* provocative as *Kutabare gurentai* (1960), let alone *Koroshi no rakuin*, since it functions mainly as an underscore to both narrative and ideology. The most notable discontinuity, for instance, appears at the beginning of the picture to highlight or embellish the theme of professional rivalry. The same theme governs an unconventional use of shot-reverse shot in a scene of dialogue on a barge. Rarely interrupting the pleasures of identification and narrative drive, *Koruto wa ore no pasupōto* may exhibit a certain tension between its unapologetic stylization and the generic expectations of viewers who had not yet seen a film like *Tokyo nagaremono*; but there is little sense of tension between its form and (narrative) meaning, particularly in regards to character. If the "structure of judgment" of classical cinema, which is perfectly evident in the *akushon* vehicles of Ishihara Yūjirō, for example, is not wholly in operation here, neither is there the distance between the patriarchal protagonist and the viewer that could evade ideological determination and permit an ethically subversive reading. But it is impossible to maintain such an empathetic proximity to an inconstant protagonist like Goro Hanada who might be suddenly confronted by rows of cartoon butterflies. At such moments, the interpretative distance and questioning attitude of the viewer of Suzuki's film is forcible and inevitable.

The absence of judgment that arises from such detachment results in a cinema of "nihilism" often attributed to Welles, but equally attributable to the mature films of Suzuki. As Deleuze writes, with blithe confidence, "the true world does not exist, and if it did . . . if it could be described . . . it would be useless, superfluous."[43] As "pure description" replaces the camera's supposedly "indexical" view of the world, the viewer is urged to question whether a "real" world beyond our symbolic description is a necessary or desirable postulate at all. Again, this has consequences for character. In this Nietzschean paradigm, a "truthful" man is idealist, judgmental, constructionist: precisely what Suzuki (in *Shinema '69*) had famously denounced. Phoenix Tetsu is just such a man, and therefore a disaster for all those around him. This is also true of the purity-obsessed lovers of *Akutarō-den*. A more extreme example is Ishihara Yūjirō's holier-than-thou brother in Nakahira's *taiyōzoku* classic *Kurutta kajitsu* (1956), who runs a speedboat over a would-be girlfriend who has been in some vague sense unfaithful to him. In place of such men who stand for "law" and "higher values" over life itself, Welles and Suzuki give us protagonists who cannot be judged by conventional standards. Judgment itself is revealed as "an infinite sham" in *Le Procès/The Trial* (1962) (which also relies heavily on discontinuity editing).[44] Without a moral anchor, either human or divine, the only thing that remains in this view of the world are "bodies which are forces, nothing but forces." The world is therefore without a center, and the film style represents that de-centering as such. Welles, in particular, opposes exhausted and spent forces, which desperately appeal to the will to dominate, to changeable, variable forces which are constantly reinventing themselves, thus representing "the goodness of life itself."[45] This is an evident reading of Suzuki's *Oretachi no chi ga yurusanai* (1965), which contrasts two brothers, a reckless, querulous, joyful ne'er-do-well and a stoic, successful, secretive, miserable *yakuza*. It is inevitable that the latter must sacrifice himself for the former: the act, like the film itself, implies no judgment on the younger brother's irresponsibility. This "renewable" kind of personal energy may also be linked to artistic will. Nevertheless, all these forces/personae are "forgers," liars, falsifiers, and a common link between them, according to Deleuze, is the natural necessity of betrayal. Betrayal is fundamental to Suzuki's films even beyond the standard requirements of Nikkatsu's crime pictures and melodramas: betrayal by the boss in *Tokyo nagaremono;* by Nogawa's lovers in the *Nikutai* Trilogy; by the bewitching youth in *Pisutoru opera;* by Mami, by the Organization, by the world-system itself in *Koroshi no rakuin*. As in *Tokyo monogatari* (1953), among other masterpieces, there are forms of betrayal that cut deeper into the particular "soul" of modern life than the predictable corruption of the institutions that claim the right to govern us.

At the very least, *Koroshi no rakuin* subjects Japanese social hierarchies to a kind of reductive, materialist, negative analysis in the manner of Welles. Beyond the ideological fanaticisms which are often so fragile, beyond the paranoiac search for security, lies the universal, exhausting refusal to acknowledge the decline of one's powers. But in showcasing weak antiheroes who are ultimately incapable of change, the nihilism of *Koroshi no rakuin* poses a conflict of *two* exhausted powers (bad hero and bad bosses), without a "life-affirming" power in sight except for Suzuki himself, the artist who thrives on negative energy.

A Negative Ethics: Koroshi no rakuin *and* Pisutoru opera

If *Koroshi no rakuin* dwells reflexively on narrative, time, and subjectivity, it also reorients all this as a perspective on the ethical problems that routinely confront the protagonists of Suzuki's films. Like the films of Ozu and Kurosawa, they do not skirt the ancient question of "how to live." But due to its negative character, the substance and form of "wisdom" in *Koroshi no rakuin* would have been all-but-unrecognizable to those earlier Japanese masters. What *Koroshi no rakuin* teaches us, I think, is simply the reality principle, that which continually eludes the ill-fated Hanada. This is not at all to assume that Suzuki's films find "reality" to be positively comprehensible. John Gray, the eminent skeptic and anti-humanist, assures us that "the deepest contemplation only recalls us to our own unreality.... To see ourselves [thusly] is to be awake, not to reality, but to a lucid dream." Gray reminds us that the Chinese sage Chuangtzu used the metaphor of a butterfly—just as Misako does—in order to illustrate a state of "having dreamt of dreaming more lucidly."[46] This, sometimes, must pass as the only means of escaping the blindest delusions.

Koroshi no rakuin's skeptical vision of truth is to embrace the real through negation, principally by insisting on the unreality of its own medium, the cinema. In a 1968 interview for *Eiga geijutsu*, Suzuki demonstrates this caste of thought to his former Assistant Director, Sone Yoshitada: ". . . my method is to construct 99% falsity. When I've done that, I can have a glimpse of an instant of truth."[47] His cinema exalts the primacy of arbitrary form, rhetorical mannerism, and non-diegetic gesture in the genre film over (direct) sociopolitical representation, the emphasis of the early *nuberu bagu*. Classical cinema, for its part, sought to verify and "naturalize" the truth of abstract ideals and propositions; but, as Deleuze understood, modern cinema abandons these criteria of judgment in favor of relativism and negation. In *Koroshi no rakuin*, beliefs and ideals appear to be little more than death-traps, laid by civilization itself, to snare the excessively socialized ego. Following surrealism, the film exalts the "innocent" dreams of the unconscious, full of violence and desire, over the constructed aspirations of civilization. Professionalism is just one of the social illusions that it stretches on the rack; the principal target of attack may be the "ideal" itself, the phantasmic construct of thought that Japanese cultural and social organization had imposed on subjective experience, with little regard for the empirical. The Pacific War is never a stone's throw away from the textual "consciousness" of any Suzuki film. Here, the ranks of the assassins are like the rigid hierarchies of the military, which strive to construct something orderly, something "positive" out of the chaos and insanity of annihilation. Hanada may be willing to sacrifice everything to be Number One, but it is difficult to find anything more than absurdist pathos in the way in which he, like Donald Duck, carries on in the most frenzied and ridiculous manner in his refusal to compromise with the knowledge that loss and death is the inevitable course of the pursuit that he has chosen.

Hanada is incapable of willful change, a spent force, magnificent in his decline, but literally exhausting himself to death before our very eyes. The spark that sets Hanada's downfall in motion is the butterfly that lands on his gunsights, causing him to miss a target. This may be the hand of fate, or a Buñuelian "bio-psychic impulse" relating to his fatal attraction to Misako.[48] *Kinema junpō*'s Iijima Tetsuo and Shirai Yoshio interpreted the film this way, asking, "Is it their own weakness whether a *yakuza* loves a woman or not?"[49] But this is a red herring. The fact remains that it is Hanada's only *strength*, the killing prowess honed by years of egoistic competition, that keeps him on the path to self-destruction. Nature, gendered as feminine in the form of the butterfly, is merely that which reveals the lie.

Even so, this does not quite clarify *Koroshi no rakuin*'s ethical position in relation to a national culture that has been forever branded with an over-determined, frequently doctored imaginary of eroticized martial valor and honorific, self-willed death. Is there a compensatory glory, or heroism, to fatal defeat? It is not a simple matter for any Japanese film to negate, without qualification, a longstanding cultural *ethos* that has many subtle shades and variants. Both Mizoguchi (*Genroku Chūshingura*, 1942) and Kurosawa (*Kagemusha*, 1981) negotiated a relatively humane revision of honorific martial sacrifice. Nor is there a nation state today, even in Europe, that does not routinely assert and depend on the sacrifice of the "honored dead" for the greater good of its polity. On the other hand, Mori Ōgai reminded us—as did Shakespeare—that there is nothing more uncertain than *posterity*—which is all that a suicide has left.[50] In keeping with my readings of *Kenka erejii* and the reductive materialism of modern cinema's archetype of the "forger," I find little in *Koroshi no rakuin* that offers an antidote to nihilism.

As Aaron Gerow reminds us, there are at least two kinds of "lack" or "emptiness" at play in Japanese cinema. Both are of ethical consequence in the representation of culture and nation, and both have been considered, in certain discourses, as forms of *nihirisumo* (nihilism).[51] There is an abrasive, modern emptiness "radically opposed to ideological signification" and self-consciously negative in its relation to society;[52] and a more traditional one—a nexus of the concepts of *ma* (empty space) and the Buddhist-inflected *mu* (non-existence)—which is easily associated with both *nihonjinron* ("Japaneseness") and with the "suicidal honor" that was demanded of Pacific War servicemen. But when it comes to the interpretation of an open-ended text like *Koroshi no rakuin*, or any similar offshoot of Japanese surrealism, how is it possible to distinguish the two? Even in the case of the modernist variety, moreover, it is not always easy to distinguish "nihilism" from the merely antisocial or dissentient when the difference between these attitudes is so often a matter of one's own cultural position.[53]

In the indeterminate space, then, between the transcultural nihilism of modernism and a specific cultural tradition that (even in its martial aspects) absorbs "foreign ideas" remarkably well, can Hanada's struggle be seen as anything more than a cautionary tale? *Pisutoru opera* (2001), a film that combines the discontinuity editing of *Koroshi no rakuin* with the action montage of *Tokyo nagaremono*, the "colourism" aesthetic of *Yumeji*, and the gag structure of the old Asakusa comedy revues, provided Suzuki with an opportunity to revisit this question. But the end result, I find, is a (formally masterful) revisionism that introduces new cultural variables into the equation while only marginally clarifying the same, essentially ethical, question of its predecessor. This belated sequel imagines a deliberately fanciful, indeed unbelievable, subculture in which everyone is, to venture a pun, just dying to be killed. One assassin stabs himself; another smiles in death; still another carelessly strides into ongoing traffic. It is therefore ironic that, in this version of the story, Hanada himself has survived the events of *Koroshi no rakuin*, only to be reduced to a nostalgic, crippled old braggart who never ascended to the reins of power. Despite this "reality check," *Pisutoru opera* reassesses the ideology of martial competition and the possibility of heroism through the prism of a female assassin—a strictly autoerotic lesbian—who moves up in the ranks of the Organization. (Suzuki chose a professional volleyball player, Esumi Makiko, for the lead in order to convey with accuracy, as it were, a distinctly feminine physical prowess).[54] This central conceit removes the strictly "masculine," and some (though not all) of the dynamics of domination-submission from the equation.

Esumi's "No. 3 Killer" calls herself "Stray Cat," which is one of the film's many intertextual convergences, in this case with Hasebe Yasuharu's *sukeban* or "girl boss" films of the 1970s.[55] Stray Cat contrasts her "felinity" to the blind loyalties of a dog; but she herself is hardly independent from Japanese martial tradition. Indeed, in her visual association with sacred mountain streams, household deities, and rural/traditionalist domestic architecture, she seems to have "sprung" fully formed out of a prewar cultural imaginary. This mythical substratum of Japanese nationalism is everywhere evident,[56] less obviously ironic than in *Kenka erejii*, but far more mediated and filtered through aesthetics—as indeed is universally true of our own national and cultural identities. In contrast to the uncompromising, desolate urban modernity of *Koroshi no rakuin*, *Pisutoru opera* seems, on some level, to legitimate a return to an aestheticism of Japanese mythic iconography without necessarily endorsing the *content* of the myth. Gerow follows a long post-war tradition in asserting the "pernicious relationship between aestheticism and nationalism in Japanese thought and culture."[57] I remain doubtful that Suzuki, for all his skepticism, would credit any necessary connection between the two that would condemn outright the idea of the aesthetic. *Pisutoru opera* does not simply invoke the forms of prewar, and often pre-modern, art: it transforms them by means of non-diegetic video graphics. For example, the mythic "bridge of souls" (as also seen in *Zigeunerweisen*) is often evoked, but is surrounded above and below by a luminescent orange glow. To some extent these videographical gestures achieve both the figurative openness and the quasi-Brechtian ideological distance discussed in previous chapters. Furthermore, there is an equal aestheticism associated with the film's "villainess" (Yamaguchi Sayoko), whose flair for cosmopolitan costumery, cynical self-centeredness, and cultural "code-switching"—as signified by her use of English expletives—distances her, and the film, from the equation of aestheticism and Japanese nationalism.

In contrast, the heroine's own relation to Japanese martial myth is practically unmediated. Having killed her female rival and various other sources of sexual temptation, and having easily defeated the naturally treacherous Hanada, Stray Cat becomes "Killer No. 1" and promptly commits suicide. Since no one can, now, take the title away from her, Stray Cat, unlike Hanada, is at least successful in her mission. Her avoidance of failure only returns us, after a series of culture clashes and post-modern deviations, to the older, unresolved question: the ethical interpretation of self-willed death. Only a monologue concerning Mishima Yukio—that notorious aestheticist of masochism and the martial tradition—seems to point the way towards a more skeptical wisdom that is mindful of the "association of suicide [in] Japan . . . with the motivations of an irrational leadership."[58] An old gun seller (Katō Haruko) describes an absurd

Fig. 7.28. Aesthetics of Death: In a gun battle amid pastiche recreations of aesthetic tradition (including Greek columns and *butoh*), the famous photograph of Ground Zero appears (*Pisutoru opera / Pistol Opera*)

dream about trying and failing to sew Mishima's decapitated head back on his shoulders. Despite all the fearful political continuities on display in Suzuki's films, the gun seller's "lucid" dream (*pace* Gray) reminds us that, ultimately, we cannot go back: what is sundered cannot be restored. Stray Cat's darkly playful vitality is not enough to overcome her (rather canine) fidelity to myth; but then again, the amoral cosmopolitanism of Sayoko (who continually describes herself as "tired") is hardly a positive alternative. We need to come to terms with our myths and our love of art—in all its glorious amorality—without being overwhelmed by them. The climactic shootout in a theater, reminiscent of the hall of mirrors in Welles's *Lady from Shanghai*, interpolates into every baroque and overcrowded shot of gunplay a creative, non-diegetic pastiche on disparate artistic traditions: Greek colonnade and ruined statuary; "dark paintings" of European Baroque and Romantic masters such as Rubens; the iconography of the Buddhist hells (incorporating dancers reminiscent of *butoh*); humorously ersatz images of macabre clichés such as hanging skeletons; and, shockingly in terms of its relation to these aesthetic objects, the infamous photograph of Hiroshima's Ground Zero.

In Suzuki's body of work, aesthetic will—in the form of a differential cinema—is often the only redemptive factor, and thus we obsessively return to the association of the aesthetic with death. As Alan Wolfe writes, trenchantly:

> A. Alvarez considered that even in the face of modern technological destruction, it was possible and desirable . . . to either 'forge a language which would somehow absolve or validate absurd death' or to find a language appropriate to this 'dimension of unnatural, premature death.'[59]

What if, unlike Hanada or Stray Cat, we wish to survive, to be a proteus rather than a narcissus? Can we interpret *Koroshi no rakuin*, if not *Pisutoru opera*, as holding out a hope that material realities may ground us just enough so as not to be carried away by ideology and myth? Perhaps not, for materiality as a form of reality testing is elusive and totally negative. The reality of sex, which in the *nikutai bungaku* and in many of the *nuberu bagu* films was sufficient to confound institutional power and its organization of our subjectivity, is shown here as infinitely corruptible by social constructs of gender. Like Mami Hanada, the modernist *auteurs* of the *nuberu bagu* overestimate the "reality" of the senses and underestimate the power of ideology; critics certainly read such tendencies into Imamura's rural "originary" societies and Yoshida Kijū's female protagonists.[60] If Hanada represents the Quixotic failure of civilization, Mami represents the failure of biology.

How can we improve on Mami's belief that we must embrace our own beasthood in all its sex, violence, and mortality, without involving these in models of social aspiration as the mythic-fetishistic underpinnings of organized power? How can we live the Dionysian life of anarchy without slipping into brutish tyranny, the dominance of the few? *Koroshi no rakuin* puts the question in these terms. If it has an answer, it is a negative one, and it is surely located in the radical individuality of Misako, who is the character most associated with nihilism and surrealism. In a slightly complicated move, surrealist imagery in *Koroshi no rakuin* is also used to express the paranoid nightmare of patriarchy. But the nightmare shakes our grip on the so-called reality. Patriarchal ideology is shown up for what it often is: an erotic fantasy of domination which society has mistaken for the natural order of things. The surrealism of Buñuel—which in its riposte to Christianity and bourgeois hypocrisy sometimes appeared as the Sadean wish-fulfillment of an "entitled" patriarchy (*L'âge d'Or*)—is reconstituted in the form of Misako as a frighteningly liberated force.

But Misako herself is continually hovering on the verge of self-willed death. Misako's suicidal bent suggests that we cannot interpret *Koroshi no rakuin* as recommending survival at all costs. It is decidedly not life-affirming. If there is a positive wisdom to the film, it is meant to save us from delusion, not from annihilation, which is inevitable. Sooner or later, whether through war, crime, or exploitation, society will turn on the individual. There is no escape. But whereas the violence and self-destruction of Hanada, like the martial tradition he represents, is thoroughly ideological, the violence of Misako comes from a place of radical subjectivity. It is an indecipherable nexus of the antisocial (rebellion against imposed gender constructs), the biological (sexual sterility, which may be either the result or cause of her social rebellion), and something having to do (á la Wolfe) with her eroticized, masochistic appropriation of the inevitable; that is, death. Despite all this, it is surprising that Misako's negativity leads to death, but also somehow, like Hamlet's, permits exactly what Hanada and his protégé Stray Cat seem to lack: the capacity for change.

A truly negative morality such as Misako's rejects such notions as the obligation to die for a political cause. Perhaps the best remembered moment from *Pisutoru opera* is the soliloquy of Sayoko on nationalism:

> In the movie *Karumen kokyō ni kaeru*, when I saw the Rising Sun spread out, fluttering in the midst of two dancers who were obsessed with America, I cried and cried. Afterwards, in a dream, I saw fireworks over those two, and they burst: the Rising Sun, the Stars and Stripes, the Tricolor, Union Jack, one after another spread out in the blue sky, but all the flags, each one, were smeared with blood, with mud, with shit. . . . I use unspeakable words, but really these stinking, stinking flags full of blood, full of slime, full of decaying flesh burned in the sun and fell as if rotted. Germany, Russia, Italy, Spain, Canada; not one upright flag.

This sublime outrage is more than a fashionable nihilism of the 1990s, coming as it does from a director and war veteran who, in his personal life, often revealed an emotional commitment to the Japanese flag.[61] We may be inclined to attribute its sentiments to the scriptwriter, Itō Kazunori (of the *Kōkaku Kidōtai/Ghost in the Shell* series), but we should recall that none of the sublime women in Suzuki's films, from *Kantō mushuku*'s Hanako to the suicidal Misako, have any truck with nationalism or any "transcendental" ethos at all. Why should Sayoko? In its imaginative, empathetic crossover of both gender and ideology, this is a cinema that is free to discover what even its "creators" cannot, precisely by means of its distance from them— and from the viewers.

We can safely reject, then, the transcendental myths of *giri* as anything other than a delusion for Suzuki. We may also hold in suspicion the eroticized *personal* loyalties that laid the initial, medieval foundations of Japanese martial idealism. One recalls the poor fate of *Hana to dōto*'s Manryū, while even the loyal Shooting Star ends up betraying his former "*kōhai.*" This does not entail, nevertheless, that it is necessarily foolish to choose to die for *something*, that is to say, that survival is a supreme, and not a contingent, value. If *Koroshi no rakuin* teaches anything, then, it is perhaps that we should use our death wisely. Either route—reality testing

Fig. 7.29. Aesthetics of Nihilism: The chic cosmopolitan Killer wears a flag while declaring all flags to be muddy, bloody, and "full of shit" (*Pisutoru opera*)

or ideological fantasy—terminates in death, but it is more empowering to escape delusion. This frees up the time that is given to us *before* death, for instance, to lose ourselves in passion. As the director said in a famous interview, ". . . it is better to be asleep. That way you can do what you want. That blissful Japan really lives."[62] Passion, which in its carnal form is too much subject to the entropy and compromises of lust, can endure in the forms of dream, eroticism, surrealist artistic expression.

Koroshi no rakuin's wisdom treads a fine line, and is easily corruptible. Is it possible to escape ideology and the mark that the socializing process leaves upon our desires? Never entirely. There is no way out, but our ability to tolerate our situation is located in dreams and in a process of endless negation and self-negation, a marshalling of pleasure towards difference, a strategy of resistance for the soul.

CHAPTER 8

The Double

(Zigeunerweisen, Kagerō-za,
Yumeji, Hishū monogatari,
Rupan sansei: Babiron no ōgon no densetsu)

"No Need for Causality"

During his decade of cinematic exile, Suzuki met regularly with former "Guryū Hachirō" screenwriter Tanaka Yōzō for a game of Go while discussing how to make "a new kind of film."[1] The discussions resulted in the collaboration of an ex-Nikkatsu creative team to produce two films in rapid succession, *Zigeunerweisen* and *Kagerō-za/Mirage Theatre* (1980-81).[2] Suzuki and his producer conceived of *Yumeji* almost ten years later, and at that time declared the films a "Taishō Trilogy."

After the critical and commercial failure of *Hishū monogatari*, Suzuki was less acceptable to what remained of Japan's commercial film industry than ever before. The Taishō films were produced independently thanks to the intervention of a third key figure: Arato Genjirō. Arato was an actor/manager who had been active in the heyday of *andogura* (underground) theatre in the late 1960s. He was connected to associates of Suzuki such as Tanaka, Yamatoya Atsushi, and director Fujita Toshiya (star of *Zigeunerweisen*),[3] who had made for themselves a dual cultural identity as producers of Nikkatsu *roman poruno* and self-appointed representatives of the political avant-garde within the film industry. The entrepreneurial Arato acquired money to finance a very low budget film; without him, the second chapter of Suzuki's 50-year cinematic project would not have been possible. Unable to find any corporate or independent cinema willing to screen the completed film of *Zigeunerweisen*, Arato resurrected a strategy of the influential "Red Tent" theatre troupe—so-called because they bypassed commercial exhibition by staging productions in a tent—when he created an inflatable dome near Ueno Park.[4] This functioned as the sole venue for the film's exhibition until ground-level enthusiasm led to an expanded release and to shocking financial and critical success. In many ways, the dream of the cinematic independents of the Japanese *nuberu bagu* had been realized by Suzuki Seijun, their most marginal of associates.

I have argued in this book that over the course of his forty-three feature films made before *Zigeunerweisen*, Suzuki's film practice and mark of "authorship" is located in the development of an oppositional and "differential" image practice from within the studio system—and yet reliant on the tools of that system and on its populist address. But in the 1980s, Suzuki was given the opportunity to reassert and justify his once discredited signature practice at Nikkatsu—and yet compelled to readjust that practice to suit a very different era and a different mode of production, namely, the independent art film in Japan. It was no longer a case of excess stylistics atop a formulaic narrative—rather, we are confronted, for the first time, with a "Suzuki-esque" conception of the totality of (independent) film production. Of Suzuki's later work, the Taishō films are best suited to conclude our study, for they self-consciously represent, as we shall see, a reassertion, a summation, and a stock-taking; a definitive return to a multivalent past viewed metonymically as personal, aesthetic, cultural, and national.

While the Late Suzuki fits comfortably, almost exemplarily, into the recognized guise of the global art cinema auteur who had come into being in the 1950s as a result of transnational art cinema exhibition, the continuities, nevertheless, between the Nikkatsu and Taishō films are so trenchant that each has come to partially define the other. Suzuki's independent career utilized his newly privileged status, what Pierre Bourdieu would call the position of the "consecrated artist" (or auteur),[5] to defend a concept of cinema that his films had long struggled to express. Both halves of his career amount to a "minor" cinema, a self-defined counter-cinema that differentiates itself—by opportunistic adjustment to internal norms and cultural change—from what exemplifies the "institutional." In the role of art cinema practitioner, Suzuki was encouraged to demand the viewer's questioning of the possibility of representation and the relation of image to narration.

Koroshi no rakuin and *Hishū monogatari* had presented an aggressively contemporary mise-en-scène, an apocalyptic historical present that, like the sublime Misako, was as exhilarating as it was dangerous. But the Taishō Trilogy's return to the past seemed to catch another *zeitgeist*, a national mood of introspection and, to some extent, acceptance of history. But its sense of past is revisionist and critical, rejecting notions of cultural "wholeness" and uniqueness in favor of an unstable yet liberating duality.

In attempting to solidify a "new" film aesthetic as a means, ironically, of engagement with the past, the Taishō films drew partly on the motifs of *Kantō mushuku* (1964): dream and reality, the haunting of the past, the stubborn persistence of prewar patriarchy and its traditional concept of masculinity. At the same time, they adapt literary works by the eminent Taishō-period writers Izumi Kyōka and Uchida Hyakken.[6] Thus, they engage not with the historical past of the Taishō era, but a more subjective, fragmented, and multiple sense of "pasts" deriving from cultural, literary, and cinematic self-reflection. Many, not always congruent, aspects of Japanese cultural and artistic inheritance are represented in these films, whether originating from the Heian period or from the 1920s themselves. Suzuki's Taishō films are not adaptations so much as interventions into this artistic paternity that they both court and anxiously evade. On one level, they picture the popular historical imaginary of Taishō as ordinary Japanese see it: consumerism, speed, Westernization, and eroticism; on another level, ironically, their vision of Japan's *modan* era is dominated, visually and otherwise, by the spectre of pre-modern culture and belief. Given this choice of focus, the films more or less embrace the broadly anti-realist strand of the hybrid art and literature of the Taishō era, which was antagonistic to the dominant, naturalist *shōsetsu* ("I-novel"), with its narrowly phenomenological approach. It was also antagonistic to the Socialist realism of the leftist intelligentsia. This "new phase" of Taishō art had applied successive waves of European artistic influence—German idealism, Victorian gothic, Expressionism, and, finally, Surrealism—to the purpose of revitalizing the Japanese traditional arts.[7]

Given these dialectics of ancient and contemporary, Western and Japanese, I shall begin this chapter with a discussion of Suzuki's allegorical use of ghosts (so central to pre-modern culture) and Doubles in *Zigeunerweisen*: the Ghost being a "transitional" metaphor of the multiple past identities of both Japanese culture and the self. Crucially, as we shall see, the Ghost and the Double also allegorize Suzuki's own conception of cinema and its "fundamental illusions." This, in turn, leads to a consideration of *Kagerō-za*'s engagement with theatre and the trilogy's search for an ideological position between the pre-modern tradition and the 1960s avant-garde.

Allegories of the Past: The Ghost

Suzuki told Isoda and Todoroki that his conception of a ghost (*yūrei*) was that of a being who shifts from one world to another, always on the margins.[8] On one level this accords with longstanding "strongly held [Japanese] beliefs in the reality of the dead,"[9] predicated on the "notion of coexistence of the world of the living (*kono-yo*) and the world of the dead (*ano-yo*)."[10] It is exactly at this point, however, that *Zigeunerweisen* parts company with the conventional Japanese ghost story. The structure of post-war ghost pictures, like its literary antecedents, was dependent on the traditional notion of "the grudge" (*urami*) as the kernel around which the narrative unfolds. In Nanboku's kabuki masterpiece *Yotsuya kaidan/Ghost Story of Yotsuya* (1825), the quintessential Japanese ghost story of the last two centuries, a man mistreats and murders his wife: he is then haunted by her hideous ghost. The "grudge" imparts structural and ideological causality to the ghost tale. As in the Noh theatre, there is always a reason or grievance that ties back the dead to our material world.[11] But Suzuki remarked that he had a pet theory about ghosts: there was "no need for the causality."[12] In other words, ghosts may haunt the living for no understandable reason. This fundamentally reorients the Japanese ghost tale, and I find the Taishō Trilogy's treatment of the ghost to be largely allegorical. In conversation with Ogawa Tōru, for instance, Suzuki became uncomfortable with the use of the term "mysticism" to describe *Zigeunerweisen*. "Well, should I do the next one as naturalism?" he taunted Ogawa.[13] The condition of being "stuck between two worlds" should not be understood purely supernaturally,[14] but as a metaphorical condition of being stuck between past and present. "Past and present" in the context of the Taishō Trilogy refers to the "present" of the Taishō moment looking back on a pre-modern past. But this kind of allegory in a Suzuki film always extends to the self-reflexive, as cinema is already, and always, simultaneously "past" and "present" at the moment of each viewing. When Suzuki asserts "no need for causality," we can take this as a characteristic cinematic manifesto. The Taishō films are a catalogue of spatio-temporal discontinuity, dysfunctional ellipses, ruptured diegesis, and "impossible" POVs. Narrative continuity is stretched to a breaking point beyond which, at moments, "another world" of cinema thus appears on the screen, or haunts the familiar along its edges, threatening to break through.

The post-war ghost film and *kaiki eiga* (horror film) was defined in the 1950s, ideologically and industrially, by Daiei's "ghost cat" thrillers and by Nakagawa Nobuo's innovative thrillers for Shintōhō, such as the box office success *Tôkaidô yotsuya kaidan/Yotsuya Ghost Story in Tokaido* (1959).[15] Nakagawa followed this with *Jigoku/Inferno* (1960), a film which, rather like Suzuki's films, captured the fascination of younger audiences and critics while ignored by the critical establishment at large. Both *Zigeunerweisen* and *Jigoku* feature a doppelganger, in any case a popular motif of post-war horror; both feature one actress playing two different, but physically identical, women; both feature a mysterious, demonic character who is clearly the alter-ego of the repressed male hero.[16] But when we examine the ideological function of such devices, a different picture emerges. In *Jigoku*, the doubling of the hero's slain fiancée and his sister serves a clear purpose apart from suggestions of incest: it also provides the guilty, suicidal hero with a reason to live. In *Zigeunerweisen*, the double illustrates the mental instability of the protagonist and allegorizes not only the existence of multiple temporalities in our consciousness, with fantasy and memory intertwined, but the paranoiac "doubleness" of culture in the Taishō period, a notion which dominated intellectual discourses at the time.[17]

Nakagawa's horror films are centered around that fear of female sexuality which Suzuki's films often uncover. But sexuality in Nakagawa's films is configured, predictably, in the form of temptation readily yielded to. Outside of the Christianity of *Kenka erejii*, temptation is not integral to Suzuki's cinematic world. Sexuality in *Zigeunerweisen* is uncanny in itself, estranged from the everyday, an aspect of that other world which, unlike Nakagawa's portrait of hell, is not necessarily worse than our own. Hence, the protagonist has fleeting fantasies, or unreliable memories, of sex with various women. Similarly, Nakagawa's narratives of displaced guilt presume a concept of sexual immorality and its consequences. The hellbound protagonist of *Jigoku* is guilty of nothing except illicit, premarital sex. Nakagawa passes off the suffering of this character as a matter of karmic retribution, an iron moral law. The Taishō Trilogy could not be more different in its sexual politics. Suzuki is concerned to achieve exactly what he praised Ōshima for doing in the notorious *Ai no korida/The Realm of the Senses* (1976): ". . . Ōshima has denied the existence of immorality . . . Starting from [that] hypothesis, he has reduced it to a legal problem."[18]

Having said that, the post-war ghost film—not Nakagawa's but also those of directors like Toyoda Shirō—does share with Suzuki an aesthetic that is heavily reliant on color.[19] Nakagawa explicitly acknowledges the inspiration of pre-modern visual painting and theatre, with red light sources, red filters, and various kinds of graphic art representing hell, and pale blue used to represent ghosts and animated corpses.

The "haunting" scene in *Zigeunerweisen* calls up these traditional aes-

Fig. 8.1. The Colors of Hell: blue light filters signify the dead while red filters signify the denizens and torments of the Eight Hells (Nakagawa's *Jigoku*)

thetic associations, and yet differentiates itself. At the beginning of the film Nakasago, an amoral writer played by Harada Yoshio, aggressively courts a geisha named Oine (Ōtani Naoko). But, a year later, the protagonist Aochi (Fujita), a teacher, finds that Nakasago has married a woman named Sono who is Oine's virtual double. Nakasago abandons Sono just after they have a child. Because of this, Aochi visits Sono at his friend's house. In this scene the visual rhetoric of the ghost picture comes fully into play, especially in regards to the use of light and color. The sequence begins with a long shot of Sono alone inside her house and looking into the camera, which is situated on the outside. Sono is in the extreme background, but also in the center, framed by a doorway, the border between worlds. Sono makes an "inviting" gesture and the lights go out (Fig. 8.2).

The next shot is a reverse angle of Aochi stepping through the doorway inside the house, but now the lights are on again, a spatial-temporal confusion typical of Suzuki. Behind Aochi, the front door slides closed by itself, as if quoting a horror cliché. The next shot is a backlit silhouette of Aochi wandering down a dark corridor, with only a pale blue light illuminating the extreme background of the shot.

This blue light is not used, as in Nakagawa or Toyoda, to illuminate a ghostly body like that of Sono. Instead it falls on empty space (Fig. 8.3): space itself is rendered uncanny. In this same shot, the lights in the hall briefly reappear and dim again, as does a strange red lantern that flares in and out. Unable to find Sono, Aochi wanders through darkened spaces for several shots, until the lights rise again on an empty room dominated by a screen painting of a peacock, a traditional symbol of masculine power that

Fig. 8.2. At the Doorway: the lights dim themselves at Sono's gesture (*Zigeunerweisen*)

may indicate the "absent presence" of Nakasago in the house. Again, the red lantern flashes in sync with the brief reappearance of the shot's key light source, as if the key light is meant to be a diegetic light source (the lantern). However, the light that rises and falls in time with the lantern is *not* filtered red (Fig. 8.4). Here is an extraordinarily original deployment of what Deleuze called the "powers of the false."

After two lateral tracking shots of Aochi moving through a dark hallway, he turns around in panic with his lighter, only to see the faces of three Kamakura beggars (Fig. 8.5).

We learn later that these blind beggars may have killed each other, and this brings to the scene another allegorical element, that of the outcast and the social abject which the buttoned-up Aochi is evidently afraid of. In the next shot, the beggars have disappeared, but the wood-paneled wall of the hallway in front of the camera mysteriously collapses, revealing Aochi from the reverse angle of the previous shot.

The wall in front is now glowing, with the suggestion of fire behind it, a clear indication of "hell." Sono stands in the place where the beggars stood previously. The film then cuts to the face of Sono appearing over

Fig. 8.3. The Blue Light of Haunting: empty space made uncanny (*Zigeunerweisen*)

Fig. 8.4. Cinema in a False Light: a "diegetic" red lantern flashes in the darkness, but it is non-diegetic white light that illuminates the space

Fig. 8.5. The Return of the Oppressed: Aochi glimpses the three beggars in the ghostly house

Fig. 8.6. Interior: Hell

Fig. 8.7. Beguiled by a Fox? Aochi struggles to define the uncanny Sono

Aochi's shoulder as he murmurs, "I was once deceived by a fox [*kitsune*] at night."[20]

This sequence abruptly cuts away to another time and place: Sono cooking a hot-pot filled with uncanny masses of *konnyaku*, a traditional shellfish that, according to Rachel DiNitto, is "used repeatedly in the film to represent sexual tension."[21]

The scene of "haunting" contains a great deal that was conventional for ghost films of the 1950s: the symbolic use of red and blue light, a ghostly appearance in the mirror, dreamlike erotic promise, the invocation of the flames of hell. Even the use of the abject (the beggars) has a corollary in Nakagawa's films. But the treatment of genre material here is highly revisionist: the reflexive conflation of diegetic and non-diegetic light sources owes far more to Suzuki's own practice than to ghost films. The latter, as Keiko McDonald has suggested, usually strive to render the fantastic "convincingly"; that is, with verisimilitude rather than obvious artifice.[22] Indeed, *Zigeunerweisen*'s play of light gives way to a play of space when Sono and Aochi, in a moment of sexual promise and confusion symbolized by the *konnyaku*, impossibly switch their positions in the room.

The cinematic "powers of the false" (moments of spatial and temporal "impossibility") themselves represent the uncanny, which forces us

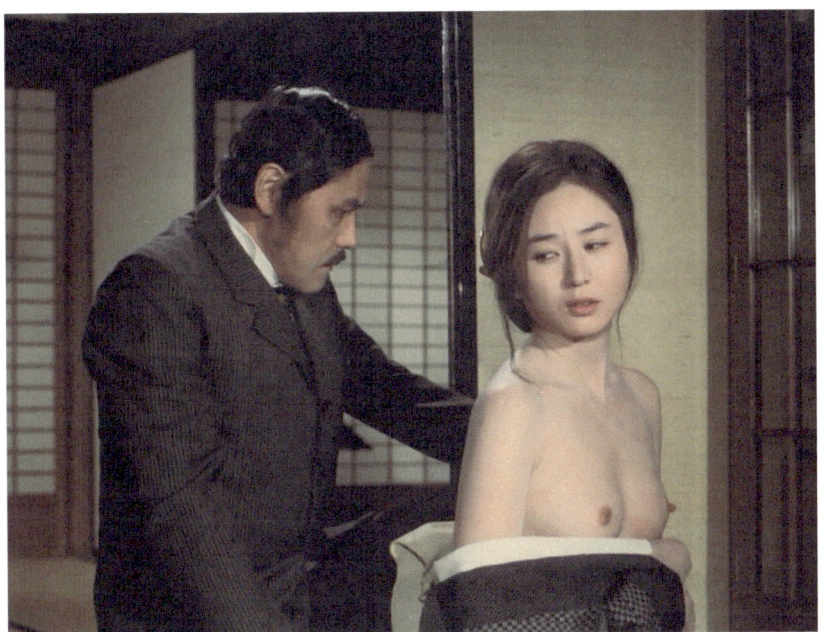

Fig. 8.8. Representation Breaks Down (in the face of female sexuality) (shot 1)

Fig. 8.9. Representation Breaks Down (shot 2): jump cut to Sono in a different room and pose

Fig. 8.10. Representation Breaks Down (shot 3): cut back to Aochi, apparently watching Sono but seated in a totally different area of the sitting room from shot (1)

to consider the concept in more than mythological terms. Aochi wonders whether Sono is a fox, a ghost (*obake*), or a *doppelganger* of Oine (both roles are played by Ōtani Naoko). But if the house is "haunted," who is throwing stones at the roof while Sono is cooking in the same room with Aochi? The only other candidate is Nakasago, but he is not yet dead: thus we return obsessively to problems of temporality. Further, how much of the uncanny mise-en-scène is the product of Aochi's imagination, which can only account for what it does not understand by reference to Japanese mythology? Should we read all manifestations of the supernatural as images of Aochi's subconscious, or as a purely cinematic expression of his mentality, itself representative of Taishō thought? The film's visualization of the supernatural is not simply structured by "hesitation" as to whether supernaturalism can possibly exist, an approach which Todorov described as being at the heart of fantastic narrative.[23] The viewer is confronted with a far more radical epistemological uncertainty which infects the whole of the film, denying us the means to choose between fragmented supernatural narrative, unconscious projection, or cinematic self-reflexivity. Ghost, fox, sprite, double, dream, cinema?

Social allegory is also invoked here, establishing a crucial difference between Suzuki and his genre predecessors. Sono's strange behavior in the scene may be the result of her loneliness and cruel abandonment by Nakasago. But the montage of "haunting" equates her metonymically with the beggars: a middle class Taishō housewife related to the socially dispossessed. This is a sentiment which Japan's first "gothic" writer, Izumi Kyōka, had expressed.[24] Sono, as a loyal wife, mother, cook, long-suffering victim, embodies every pre-modern stereotype of the Japanese feminine as articulated by the *ryōsai kenbo* ("loyal wife, good mother") social code of the Meiji patriarchal order. In this sense, the film clearly subjects long-standing mores of domesticity to a process of eerie defamiliarization.

One way of understanding this gesture is to return to the question of generic causality: who is haunting who, and why? The elliptical narrative provides no clear answers. In *Tōkaidō yotsuya kaidan* (1959) and in hundreds of similar variations, the protagonist mistreats a wife or lover for the purposes of money, social status, or lust. As in the *yakuza* film, the sense of being torn between social advancement and a domestic woman is understood in terms of *giri* and *ninjō*. *Zigeunerweisen*'s narrative renders this dichotomy totally irrelevant. But more important is the ideological placement of the feminine. Colette Balmain considers whether the female ghost in post-war horror films can be seen as a figure of patriarchal resistance,[25] but she does not address this moral causality. Arguably, the male protagonist of the ghost story is haunted specifically because he has failed to appreciate women who fulfill the roles that patriarchy has prescribed for them: that is, the "loyal wife, good mother" ideal. The admonition against lust, from Nanboku to Nakagawa, serves to reaffirm the gendered status quo. The only victor in such a scenario is neither man nor woman, but the ideology of *on*, or enforced social obligation. The post-war horror film tends to reify the continuity of prewar gender roles and the ideology of selfless social/familial obligation. But *Zigeunerweisen*, as we have said, rejects the causality of "the grudge." After Nakasago dies, the geisha Oine is left alone with Sono's child, Toyoko. Toyoko "speaks" to her dead father at night and even demands that Aochi return Nakasago's books and records (including the titular Sarasate recording). When Aochi does so, he finds Oine speaking of her undying, jealous love for Nakasago. "He never cared about me. . . . He knew I loved him, but he went back to her." She is speaking from the experience not of Oine, but of the dead Sono. She claims that she wants the child to belong to her instead of Nakasago, and appears to have a mental breakdown over this. Oine/Sono claims to have a grudge against Nakasago, but in this perverse "inversion" of the ghost story Nakasago is never the victim of haunting: Oine/Sono end up haunted *by* him—through the agent of his daughter—without any cause beyond Nakasago's preternaturally malicious desire. It is only Nakasago's reticent alter-ego, Aochi, who will be "haunted" by these women. Nakasago and Aochi represent, respectively, the pre-modern and "modern" manifestations of the same patriarchal ideology. But whereas Nakasago is radically individual, a dismissed professor, itinerant philosopher, a hedonist and a criminal, his alter-ego is a professor of German and a teacher at a major military academy: a reluctant cog in the wheel of the Taishō machine, a representative of the university-educated, bureaucratic "mandarin" class which mandated the nature and direction of change (or lack of change) at the turn of the century, often despite the strenuous resistance of the lower classes. Perhaps for this reason, he is haunted by the "abject."

Zigeunerweisen challenges patriarchy, but unlike Shindō Kaneto's *Onibaba* (Tōhō, 1964), it does not speculate an imagined pre-modern site of resistance for women. In Suzuki's satire of tradition, Oine becomes a woman eaten up from the inside by a pre-modern masochism. Like Harumi in *Shunpuden*, she is destroyed by her romantic attachment to the neglectful Nakasago, the embodiment of a pre-modern masculinity that refuses to die. In terms of the allowed social roles of the feminine in prewar discourse, Oine journeys from one extreme to the other. She begins as a geisha, which for many Taishō intellectuals was a kind of nostalgic exemplar of spiritual and sexual freedom, based on a life of entertaining and ephemeral attachment. She ends up, like Sono, an isolated widow, so spiritually dependent on her late husband that it has poisoned her relationship with the child. A radical social critique emerges in which marriage and the family structure are defamiliarized as a powerful but intolerable continuity in a period (Taishō) that popular discourse associated with unstable change and modernization.

What is most extraordinary is the fact that Aochi, the middle-class male protagonist, is *himself* "haunted" by Nakasago's out-of-control performance of sexual domination. Aochi cannot escape this all-consuming male desire that he himself shares.

If Suzuki's focus, in the Nikkatsu films, was on the post-war dissolution of Japanese masculinity, the greater energy of *Zigeunerweisen* lies, accordingly, not in the theme of "haunting," but in the allegorical doubling of the male characters.

Allegories of the Modern: The Double

Suzuki's use of the *doppelganger* was mandated by Uchida's source novella, but it is important to recognize that the Double, unlike the female ghost,

Fig. 8.11. Erotic Grotesque Nonsense: the ghostly Nakasago grips Aochi's chin suggestively as he demands Aochi's bones

has not been a figure of cultural import since the beginning of recorded history in Japan. Rather, the Double should be viewed as the product of Meiji era cross-cultural fertilization. John Orr has characterized the reappearance of the Double in Nineteenth Century European culture as a process of Othering particular to Romantic literature, a manifestation of anxiety about its own project: "The Other has become . . . the phantom which cannot finally be accommodated in the romantic utopia of an organic and pantheistic world. The Other is a hallucination of romantic disorder, an effigy of disintegration."[26] In Meiji and Taishō Japan, European romanticism was enthusiastically imported by major writers such as Mori Ōgai, Kyōka, and Uchida.[27] Just as the European Other resists the organic unity of the Romantic imagination and therefore functions as a destructor, so the uncanny female Other of Uchida and Kyōka cannot be fully accommodated into the rationalistic Meiji order, nor, finally, into the crude transcendental order of the Shōwa imperial state. This is *despite* the fact that popular imperial discourse traded on nativism and irrationalism. The suicide of the literary giant Akutagawa Ryūnosuke in 1927, Uchida's friend and the alleged model for the character of Nakasago, was symbolic of the "demise" of modernism in Japan.[28] The Robot Maria in Fritz Lang's *Metropolis* (UFA,

1927) is modernism's ultimate female "effigy of disintegration," a figure of revolution, disorder, and sexuality uncontainable by patriarchy nor, ultimately, by her creators. Like Robot Maria, Suzuki's Sono/Oine is similarly let loose on the Taishō middle class; yet the bourgeois-patriarchal order notoriously reified at the end of *Metropolis*, and here represented by Aochi, implodes upon contact with a female agency and sexuality that literally "disorders" its version of reality.

In modernist cinema, as Orr notes, the Double is not only the disordered image of the middle class but also "a technical fact" of the cinematic apparatus. That is to say, the Double may be the female abject of patriarchy, but in terms of cinema it is also the immediacy of the cinematic viewing experience interrupted or "haunted" by the mediation of a mechanical "Other" like Robot Maria: the camera itself.

The proliferation of *doppelgangers* also applies to the relationship of Aochi and Nakasago. Both are representatives of Taishō, but Nakasago's empowerment is configured in terms of "cultural capital" (the pre-modern past) while Aochi's is economic (his bourgeois academic status). Aochi wears impeccable tweeds while Nakasago wears a tattered black kimono. Yet a binary opposition between the two is not adequate. Nakasago is not so much a remnant of the Japanese past as a romanticized representation of it in the mind of the modernist author Aochi (a thinly-veiled alter-ego of Uchida himself).

Aochi's social existence is solidly middle class. Therefore he is separated or alienated from his own unstable imagination and from the abject inherent in Japanese folk culture (Nakasago and the beggars). His institutional status, appearance, and marriage of convenience to a *modan* girl all seem meant to mediate desire while his Europeanized *châtelet* insulates him, as if it were an ivory tower, from Japan. This identity is a shackle for Aochi; he has none of the freedom of movement and freedom from commitment that Nakasago enjoys, and in a familiar *nuberu bagu* scenario, it represses him sexually. Non-linear images of the women in his life appear with subliminal rapidity, as if Aochi's respectability has displaced sexual activity to "another" realm (*kono-ya*) of the visual only. Aochi "views" his desires vicariously through the actions of Nakasago, at once seductive and violent towards women. Here again is the inherent reflexivity of the cinematic Double. Nakasago is, more or less, Aochi's Id. But, like the cinema viewer, Aochi is an outwardly passive "watcher" of the erotic and violent spectacle of Nakasago, the identity that must be kept at a distance. Accordingly, the film's breakdowns in spatio-temporal continuity occur when Aochi observes Nakasago. For example, in Kamakura, Aochi sits nearby as Nakasago grabs Oine.

Fig. 8.12. Violence at a Distance (shot 1): Aochi discreetly gets up, but turns back to gaze at Oine's "seduction"

Fig. 8.13. Violence at a Distance (shot 2): the vampirical Nakasago moves to kiss (or bite?) Oine's neck, but is distracted by something off-screen

Fig. 8.14. Violence at a Distance (shot 3): Aochi, who was standing in front of the lovers in shot (1), is now a distant figure on the sea-cliff in the background

It is clear that Aochi's gaze serves to "authorize" Nakasago's behavior at the expense of Oine, to whom Aochi himself is attracted. But at the same time, as in the cinema, a distance must be kept for the "enjoyment" to remain vicarious and controlled.

Aochi's guilty indulgence in his alter-ego Nakasago becomes an existential crisis that strands him somewhere between Japan's past and (capitalist) present. In Orr's Freudian reading of the Double as Other, the impossible desire to repeat the past, that is, the attempt to bridge "a gap between past and present in which nothingness intercedes," is equaled by the desire to escape that very same impulse.[29] Aochi needs to return to, or *repeat*, the pre-modern imaginary which informs his sexual desire, while at the same time preserving his social identity by escaping it: a cycle of unbearable separation, repression, and compulsive "reliving [of] certain events and re-seeing certain images in an endless . . . replication."[30] This process reduplicates the personal past in the form of the cultural past and vice versa. The more Aochi's bourgeois humanism pulls him away from the abject sexuality of Nakasago, the more his sanctuary crumbles around him. Not only does he come to believe that his ultra-consumerist wife is

Fig. 8.15. The End

sleeping with Nakasago, but Aochi himself ends up stranded between two worlds which are metaphorized (as in Uchida's neo-gothic stories) as the living and dead, the past and the present, or the real and the imagined; that is, memory and fantasy. Aochi encounters Nakasago's child on a bridge, where she tells him, "my father is alive. You think you're alive, but you're dead. Give your bones to me as promised!" The horrified Aochi attempts to turn and walk away, only to find, in the film's final act of discontinuity, that he is staring at Toyoko on a beach, standing beside a boat covered in a funereal bouquet of white flowers.

Is Aochi "literally" dead, or has he been emotionally and spiritually dead all along, while the socially liberated "soul" (*tamashi*) of Nakasago remains very much alive? In this "new age" of commodity and the machine, are we all, perhaps, living the life of the phantom?

The Double, as in *Metropolis*, enables a critique of desire under capitalism. As Orr has written, commodification may result in the kind of "split personality" that bedevils Aochi, leading to a "loss of selfhood" in "the contradiction between economic and cultural capital. Here the dominant fear is the fear of being petrified into the fixed value of a commodity. The

Fig. 8.16. What Price (Male) Freedom? The crimes of the rakish, attractive Nakasago are laid out for the viewer—or is it a fantasy of the protagonist?

image of the double is the . . . lure of a multivalent desire which cannot congeal into a market price."³¹

Even though the bourgeois Aochi is a normative point of identification for the author, director, and the 1980s viewer, *Zigeunerweisen* stacks its deck in favor of the transgressive and murderous Nakasago. But why? This cannot be the simplistic distinction between institutional patriarch and violent "lone wolf" that is rejected in *Koroshi no rakuin*.

Just as there is no longer a "morality" to haunting, there are no clear moral demarcations between Aochi and Nakasago: ". . . evil remains the supreme form of moral transgression but . . . it generates mere banalities."³² Both envision the same transgressions, and the only difference between them, on the diegetic level, is that between vision and action. If the hypnotic Nakasago embodies the indulgence of the male cinema viewer in violent but lavishly aestheticized spectacle, Aochi is the spectator's guilty prurience. It follows then, that Aochi may represent a post-1960s liberal guilt at being taken in by cinema, if, for "cinema," we understand the gendered and violent discourse of Nikkatsu and other genre cinemas. By forgiving Nakasago and punishing Aochi, the filmmakers evidently do not want to make the male spectator feel guilty, but to make him honest: not disavowing, but accepting. And yet, if the film addresses the male spectator in this way, the question arises: what form should this "acceptance" of our anti-social (and often violent) desires take? This is a crucial question for the Suzuki project in this phase. Clearly Suzuki did not make such an unconventional picture as *Zigeunerweisen* in order to accept and reproduce those linear, patriarchal structures of desire that fill the studio genre pictures against which he famously rebelled?

Violence and Evanescence: Representing the Past

Zigeunerweisen aligns with Charles Shirō Inouye's view that Japanese culture alternates between two deep ideological structures. The first, which can be called evanescence, involves "the order of the here and now," the appreciation of the ephemeral as best epitomized by the Floating World of the Edo period middle class, with its worldly but transient pleasures. The second is "the order of the transcendental" first introduced by religious and elitist martial philosophy. This exerted a hegemony over culture in the Meiji era in the form of emperor worship, essentially forced on culture from the top down through the Imperial State; so much so that Edo pleasures of tea, kabuki, and the geisha were re-imagined as "universal values" in the intellectual culture of the late empire.[33] Inouye credits the entrenchment of the transcendental order as a prime factor in Japan's imperial disaster. It should be no surprise that Suzuki's negative aesthetic prefers the realm of the "here and now" to a facile transcendentalism. An establishment figure paranoiacally obsessed with the "other realm," Aochi represents transcendental thinking but is pursued by ephemeral imagery of desire and fear. His interpretation of reality—the consensual reality of the middle class—is undermined by a cinematic representation of "the here and now" in the form of repetition and the sense of "simultaneous presents" discussed in chapter 7.

With his wandering in search of pleasure, violence, and spectacle, Nakasago is not Aochi's opposite but his mirror image. The filmmakers added a motif to the story in which Nakasago says that, despite his philandering, he actually despises human flesh and prefers the "pure" and everlasting pleasure of bones. This is Nakasago's own desire for transcendence—sexual and patriarchal tyranny viewed as pure aesthetics—but the film will disabuse us of it. Nakasago decisively returns to the order of the "here and now" upon his lonesome, drug-addled death, an apotheosis of the *nagaremono* ideal surrounded by a rapid montage of cherry blossoms

Fig. 8.17. Miraculous Transformation: cherry blossoms, defamiliarized by non-diegetic color, as multivalent symbols of death/change/ephemerality

and Mt. Fuji in the throes of miraculous transformation, accompanied by expressive non-diegetic color changes and nonsensical folk chanting (see Fig. 8.17).

The scene, which mixes the national mythology with commonplace notions of *zazen* enlightenment, is metaphorically a "fireworks" display of the Suzuki Difference. Nakasago's death/enlightenment/return to the "here and now" returns us to the question of cinematic reflexivity. While alive, Nakasago espouses the idea that bones and ashes can turn red if they soak up the blood of a dying man. The impressionable Aochi becomes convinced that this is true of Nakasago's own ashes, only to be told by Oine that the ashes are, in fact, just plain white. This is a critical point at which material reality cuts through the dreamlike grip of the transcendental. It suggests that the only possible articulation of "reality" must come from *outside* the cultural/aesthetic universe that the film represents: that is, it must come from an "authorial" intervention. Suzuki's own ironic voice intrudes on the soundtrack at the moment of Nakasago's enlightenment, making critical comments like "Not finished yet?"

Perhaps the possibility of "accepting ourselves," and the violent fantasies that cinema fulfills for us, can only be actualized not through the "regressive" milieu of studio genre, but through *Zigeunerweisen*'s "new kind of film," which, after all, differentiated itself from the mainstream on virtually every level, even that of distribution. Just as its allegories of ghosts and doubles are allegories of the cinema, Suzuki's films are always defining and defending their particular cinematic practice even in the midst of its realization. The self-reflexivity that attends the concept of the Double translates into something like aesthetic self-exaltation, an inward-turning cinematic will to power. As Orr puts it:

> Despite its obvious powers of illusion, the camera still records 'nature' in its broadest anthropological sense. But [in] the modern cinema . . . [r]epresentation becomes a will-to-power and the figure of the double one of its vital legacies. . . . Refusal to recognize this is itself but a romantic failing.[34]

The "independent Suzuki film" thereby declares its difference from a major strand of the 1960s *nuberu bagu*. Among that movement's apparent cultural aims—not counting those, like Wakamatsu, who sought a "primitive" image of irrational violence—was an image practice that would enable an *Escape from Japan* (Yoshida, 1964); a subjective or epistemic break with an internalized history of Japanese authoritarianism that both encouraged and neutralized violent dissent (we see this in the long cultural tradition of rebellion from the Right). Diverging from this tendency, Suzuki and his purely predatory antihero Nakasago take it that the past is as indispensable as it is irretrievable. The past is desire, all the more so for being "past" and thereby forbidden (or made abject) by modernity. Cinematic representation as a will to power takes that desire as its object. In the Taishō Trilogy, you suppress the past, in the name of humane rationality, at your own risk—it will come back to haunt you. The question of a "cinematic ethic" then becomes one of how to *destabilize* the representation of "pastness"—the achievement of Suzuki's next film, *Kagerō-za*— with the result that power no longer recognizes its usual tools. Images of (male) desire are reinserted into the politics of the image, but on the condition of sacrificing entirely the cinema's claim of having a privileged relation to the "actual"—the documentary impulse which the *nuberu bagu* had interrogated but never abandoned.[35] The ethical and political problem of narrative cinema is not, in the end, the existence of abject male fantasies of empowerment through violence, but their fetishistic claims to representation and truth.

A New Kind of Film: From Narrative to . . . What?

At one point in *Zigeunerweisen*, Aochi and Nakasago listen to a record of Pablo Sarasate playing his own composition, *Zigeunerweisen*. Nakasago points out that Sarasate's voice can be heard on the record, but that no one can make out what he says. The gesture invokes discourses of the technological uncanny and holds out broader metaphorical implications. In the form of the voice on the record, the past is still present, as is the trace of an intentionality and an aesthetic will; but it is also profoundly "illegible." This scene is later paralleled by the visual prominence of the record player in a notable tracking shot through Nakasago's haunted home.

On one level, we interpret Nakasago's strange "survival" after death in the light of the equally ambivalent "survival" of Sarasate on the record.[36] But the record seems also to problematize or literally to "haunt" the act of representation. Is Suzuki's vision of Taishō, despite a mise-en-scène cluttered with period artefacts and spaces, a mere phantom?

Harootunian generalizes that "thinkers and writers responded to Japan's modernity by describing it as a doubling that imprinted a difference between the new demands of capitalism . . . and the force of received

Fig. 8.18. The Phonograph as Technological Uncanny (*Zigeunerweisen*)

forms of history and cultural patterns . . ."³⁷ DiNitto argues, further, that this sense of "doubling" in *Zigeunerweisen*, also impinges on the possibility of representing history: "The past is not necessarily missing for Suzuki, but if it can be apprehended, it is only through this slippery double structure."³⁸

This holds true for *Kagerō-za* (1981), a visual catalogue of period-specific artefacts and practices (jazz, imported dance and dress styles, railway carriages, antique rifles, Taishō anarchism) as well as mythological objects and settings (stone bridges, theatre masks, clay dolls). The film does not set out to represent history but to discourse upon a historical imaginary. *Kagerō-za* re-emphasizes formally what was nascent in *Zigeunerweisen*: a radical negation of narrative (and therefore historiographical) causality and a privileging of cultural symbols that are excessively "mediated," that is, mediated through prewar art forms such as theatre, dance, and painting. By denying the possibility of an "unmediated" original or an organic, causal and therefore knowable route to "pastness," it literally and figuratively refuses a stable "image" of the milieu.

Just as I previously extended DiNitto's conclusions by arguing that Suzuki's allegories of the phantom and the double are also allegories of cinema, so the Taishō Trilogy does not confine itself to the problem of representing history, but questions the possibility, even the desirability, of representing any form of narrative at all. In Suzuki's late films, representation is always unutterably *other* to what it represents, and that may be their strongest legacy. When an onscreen red lantern flashes and the light that appears is not red, *Zigeunerweisen* challenges the representation of "the actual" (physical reality) on the level of the shot. Irrespective of relation to a historical or personal past, *Kagerō-za* deploys montage specifically to challenge the integrity of a clear succession in time, for Suzuki had long since posited that such integrity is false. Such a strategy has negative consequences for the conventional "cinematic present" as well, for it refuses the very function of montage, which is to render the inherent instability of our sense of the present into a continuous past: a narrative. Montage in *Kagerō-za* instead maintains, like the voice on the Sarasate record, a mysterious and alluring illegibility.

Reading the progression of an "illegible" image/montage practice from *Zigeunerweisen* through *Kagerō-za* to *Yumeji* (Suzuki's 1991 fantasia on the life of the Taishō painter Yumeji Takehisa), one is struck by the fact that it was not the endpoint of the journey, but the exploration itself, that has proved of lasting cultural value. *Zigeunerweisen* was a milestone in Japanese cinema history: *Yumeji* was somewhat overlooked; *Kagerō-za* was, in every way, in-between. Certainly *Yumeji* is in some sense the culminating "achievement" of an extraordinarily autonomous image practice, a permanent "leaving behind" of classical narration in favor of a catalogue of surrealist happenings and associations. A teleological, "progressive" reading of this practice is therefore tempting but, finally, reductive. Our investigation of Suzuki's cinematic "pasts" is not necessarily best served by *Yumeji*, which, despite a tone of cheerfully absurdist amorality that makes it a very attractive entrée into the entire trilogy, is broadly considered as Suzuki's *sine qua non* rejection of narrative cinema: its "maximal point" of aesthetic differentiation. Perhaps this is due to an atmosphere of tonal unrestraint (*à la Tokyo nagaremono*) that is unusual to the gothic "mode"; or perhaps the frequent disappearance of even a baseline of visual continuity—with only the flirtatious chatter of Yumeji (Sawada Kenji) to assure us, definitively, whether we are in Tokyo or Kanazawa—allows other undisguised structures to come to the fore. These include a broadly allegorical, facetious "gag structure" that depicts erotic obsession and masculine ego-fragility through Yumeji's frustrated attempts to produce a nude painting of his female object of obsession. Though it is an inescapable cliché, one must acknowledge that here at last, in *Yumeji*, is a "cinema of painting": not only because Yumeji's works appear non-diegetically on a wooden post or the side of a boat, or because the film itself turns out to be a meditation on one particular painting ("The Evening Primrose").

So dominant is the regard for "painterly composition"—albeit in a generous sense that incorporates some quantity of cinematic movement—that while the absurdist narration makes it impossible to treat death seriously (including that of Harada Yoshio's undead Wakiya, a clownish debasement of Nakasago), the alienated "bucolic" visual metaphors of slaughtered cows and mangled crows have, truly, the opposite effect. *Yumeji*, unlike its predecessors, appears fundamentally uninterested in maintaining a critical/ideological distance from its subject, Yumeji's artistic practice. It is true that Yumeji Takehisa's lazy libertinism, unoriginal aesthetic pronouncements, and masculine privilege need to be, and are, humbled by his encounters with the uncanny. But when his mysterious paramour finally, unambiguously offers her body to the painter, he humbly, respectfully declines and paints her kimono instead, achieving the distance of aesthetic sublimation.

In spite of *Yumeji*'s "total," even "Romantic" commitment to a cinematic, admittedly revisionist, variation on Taishō aestheticism, its two predecessors—in all their continuities with the Nikkatsu years—have better claims to represent the legacy of Late Suzuki. *Kagerō-za*, particularly,

Fig. 8.19. The Cinema of Painting: Yumeji's works appear non-diegetically on surfaces (*Yumeji*)

builds on *Zigeunerweisen*'s dualities through a negative and reflexive mode that depends on the viewer's familiarity with and expectation of narrative in order to refuse it. It marks out, in other words, a sliding, morphological, in a word *transitional* film practice, lying somewhere between *Tokyo nagaremono* and the Japanese avant-garde, between tradition and radicalism, narrative and spectacle. It is a vision of independent cinema not as the binary, theoretical opposite of studio practice, but as an unending questing after the (cinematic) encounter in all its multiplicative facets and uncertainties, in its ironic juxtaposition of prior cinematic modes, and in its excesses and departures from them. *Kagerō-za* is to the past and future of Suzuki's film career what Taishō is to Japan's past and future: a retrospective negotiation. The textual features and contours of *Kagerō-za*'s "newness," in other words, continues and inevitably rereads Suzuki's negative aesthetic of the representation of the past.

Non-Narrative and Un-Knowing

Returning to Suzuki's oft-quoted remark about a cinema which can be likened to the joys of sleeping and dreaming,[39] *Kagerō-za* represents human behavior and understanding as wrapped, to use a well-known Buddhist phrase, in a cloud of unknowing. Removed from any obvious narrative context, the image takes on the multiplicity of meaning to which, in Suzuki's established anti-realist philosophy, it is essentially suited.

What does *Kagerō-za* offer in place of narrative? The film may be best described as "happenings," a series of images and events which are anchored by the perception and reaction of the central character, *shinpa* playwright Matsuzaki (Matsuda Yūsaku). What little continuity is offered to us is rooted in the ubiquity of a perceiving subject. Some few onscreen events (for example, the second Mrs. Tamawaki appearing to watch the funeral procession of the first Mrs. Tamawaki) do not appear to be from the POV of Matsuzaki, but he is never, spatially, distant from these events, and some of them are probably in his mind.

Matsuzaki is orbited by a limited number of characters whom he observes, framed in a limited number of *transitional* and historically indeterminate settings in Tokyo and Kanazawa: a stone bridge, a flight of steps to a shrine, a country road; and at the beginning, some fleeting, feverish spaces of the modern city that are entirely owned by the *zaibatsu* (big conglomerate) fat cat Tamawaki (Nakamura Katsuo). Dialogue often accompanies these images, but of a special kind: the characters, anticipating the cinema viewers, constantly question the meaning and ontological status of visual events and propose explanations that are unsatisfying both to Matsuzaki and to the viewer. Nothing penetrates the cloud of unknowing, which is perhaps why Matsuzaki as a protagonist is uniquely passive and reactive. Things happen to Matsuzaki; he never initiates an action or clearly takes a position. He is constantly gazing, with a wide-eyed stare, at the actions of others, constantly responding to their questions and telegrams. At two crucial points, when Matsuzaki may (or may not) have had sex with Tamawaki Shinako (Ōkusu Michiyo), and when he may (or may not) have attempted a double suicide with her, the body of Matsuzaki is literally being "pulled" into position by an invisible force, a *deus ex machina*, which forcibly acts upon Matsuzaki's chronic, intellectualized non-participation in events, possibly in accordance with his inner desires.

Given the loose causality and often baffling ellipses which crop up between and within individual scenes, we are continually tantalized with the possibility of a diegesis, of a narrative connecting disparate events, only to be disappointed. Taking into account disjunctions between sound and image, only roughly half of the edits in the film can be said to establish a conventional narrative continuity. Viewers may attach themselves, desperately, to certain conventional deployments of mise-en-scène such as the long sequence shots of extended dialogue between Matsuzaki and Madame Mio. These are only further "enticements" to play the erotic game of narrative.[40] The viewer is frequently given intimations of narrative events that may have happened off-screen. We are told that the first wife of Tamawaki was German, and that he forced her, in an outrageous patriarchal crime, to take on the hair color, skin color, and eye color of an ordinary Japanese. But where is Ine? Is she dead (as reported by the hospital staff) or alive (since Matsuzaki and the viewers have seen her)? If Matsuzaki has seen a ghost, is this indeed "a story of ghosts and grudges," as Tamawaki satirically characterizes the film that he is in? If so, whom does Ine have a grudge against? What is her relation to the second wife, Shinako, who is seen bringing flowers picked from the local cemetery to Ine's hospital bed? *Kagerō-za* builds up the possibility of erotic narration—a question and answer structure—only to frustrate it; the "real" structure in place here is incapable of, and uninterested in, answers. As we have contended of Suzuki's past practice, the negation of narrative meaning is also, in a sense, the multiplication of narrative and meaning.[41] In place of one narrative, there are images of multiple possible narratives; but as new possibilities branch off at every point, the viewer must despair of the Aristotelian sense of "knowing," that is, of constructing a master causal chain. This would be tantamount to mastery over the image, and *Kagerō-za* refuses us this conventional pleasure. With sound and image divorced from spatial and temporal continuity, we return to a "primitive" or "magic" spectacle observed through the tatters of narrative; yet for all this, the human interest generated by the gestures and interaction of the actors does not disappear.

The Structure of *Kagerō-za*

Various traditional arts, from *ikebana* flower arrangement to the Noh theatre, partake of the tripartite structure called *jo-ha-kyū*. The structure has various aesthetic interpretations relating to rhythm and other qualities. The avant-garde filmmaker Katsu Kanai claimed that this unified triptych is a form of cosmological allegory, with one part representing "heaven" or divinity, one part representing earth or nature, and one part representing man.[42] This pattern applies neatly to the tripartite structure of *Kagerō-za*. Each section is roughly forty minutes. The first, taking place in Tokyo, may be said to represent humanity, especially in its focus on relationships of erotic attraction, romantic attachment, or marriage. The second part, on the rural outskirts of Kanazawa, enacts a discourse of nature. The third part, an amateur stage performance, represents the marriage of art and the divine through the theatre.

Of these, perhaps the discourse of nature is most surprising for a Suzuki film. In Kanazawa, Matsuzaki's interaction with others is on country roads and foggy marshes, nebulous boundaries between land and sea. Here he encounters the earthy, lusty anarchist played by Harada Yoshio. Suzuki's treatment of anarchism—a notable strain of Taishō political culture and perhaps the closest to what we can make of Suzuki's politics—is as ambiguous as the film itself.[43] Harada's character walks along an old dirt road and stops to urinate in a beggar's cup.[44] The beggar, however, looks nearly identical to Harada's character, perhaps visualizing an ambivalence. Certainly, the figure of "the anarchist" in this film is associated with symbols of the bodily and the transient, including, for instance, some vulgar clay figures that the anarchists and freemasons ceremonially smash. The anarchist separates the discourse of nature from the discourse of tradition.

Tradition, itself, is divided between the folk customs, which Matsuzaki encounters in Kanazawa (epitomized by the *matsuri*, or village festi-

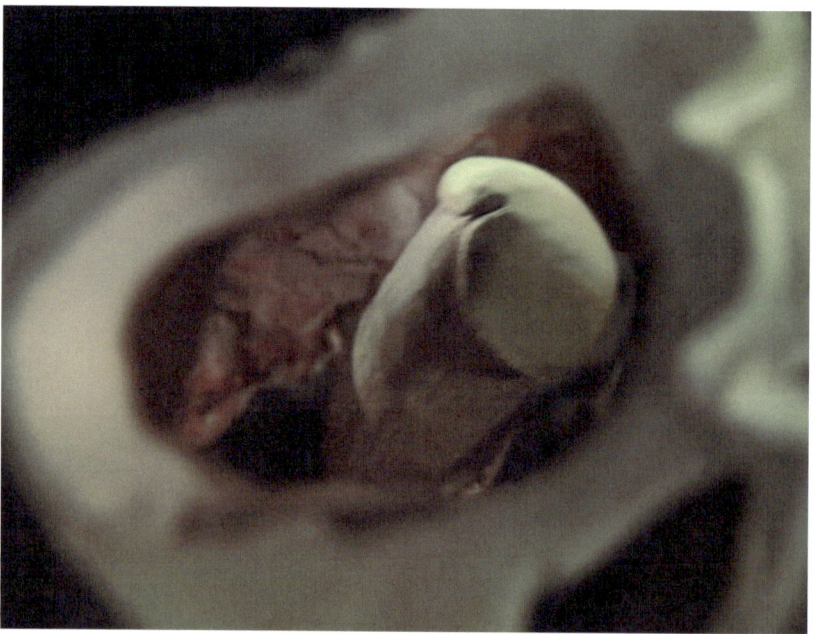

Fig. 8.20. Anarchism and Earthiness: a solemn ceremony in which anarchists view and then smash traditional clay figures, inside of which lie smaller, vulgar sculptures, for example a penis, or a man being swallowed by a vagina (*Kagerō-za* / Mirage Theatre)

Fig. 8.21. The Consequence of Power: the haunting corpses of birds on Tamawaki's estate (*Kagerō-za*)

val), and the hierarchical-authoritarian social continuity represented by Tamawaki, the cynical industrialist who is visually associated with Tokyo and would as soon erase tradition as he erases nature with his ubiquitous hunting rifle.

These two "branches" of the tradition might be reductively configured as patriarchy and as a mythic structure older and deeper than patriarchy, one ambiguously centered on the symbol of female sexuality.

Hybridity, Ideology, and Magical Transformation

The third part of the film consists of Matsuzaki viewing a lengthy theatre performance put on by itinerant children in a Kanazawa warehouse. The performance contains loose and freely imaginative renderings of various forms of Japanese classical theatre, including kabuki, *bunraku*, and the four major branches of *minzoku geinō* (ancient folk performance). *Shinpa*, the "modernized" Meiji theatre, is conspicuously absent. The performance loosely synthesizes these multiple theatrical forms to create new aesthetic ideas, but it is still, clearly, a pastiche, as is obvious from the fact that the first two acts are performed by amateur children.[45] Pastiche was as important to avant-garde theatre of the 1960s as it had been to the Asakusa popular theatre of Suzuki's youth, which Miriam Silverberg theorized as a form of "cultural montage."[46] It relates this sequence to the "Red Tent" theatre in which Arato had participated, given to creative representations of Noh and other classical forms.[47] Here, Suzuki and Arato capitalize on the inherent intertextuality of pastiche: as the play is utilized to retell the story of Tamawaki and his wives in a theatrical idiom—a story which *Kagerō-za* has given us mere glimpses of—it becomes a reflexive comment on the film and its structure, and hence on the cinema in general. The play is an avatar of the discourses of the film: the rejection of realism; the ideological relation between art (theatre) and the sacred; and the positioning of women within that relation.

In *Zigeunerweisen* the sound of theatrical clappers is heard over the soundtrack of scenes which had nothing to do with the theatre, thus transforming the "mimetic" into the theatrical. *Kagerō-za* reverses that procedure: cinema explores the limits of theatrical expression and, indeed, extends the theatrical in a particular direction: the cinema's capacity, through editing, to convey uncanny transformation.

Fig. 8.22. Miraculous Transformation (II): Shinako turns into a life-sized *bunraku* puppet in the middle of the performance (*Kagerō-za*)

Suzuki has often been said to use theatrical effects in his films, derived largely from his beloved kabuki. In certain respects this is accurate: the manner in which the sets fall away, like theatrical flats, in *Kantō mushuku* and *Zigeunerweisen*. The long held and almost frozen poses of the action hero in *Irezumi ichidai* and *Tokyo nagaremono* resemble the dramatic tableaux of the hero in the Edo-based *aragoto* style of kabuki performance.[48] *Irezumi ichidai* stages its major action sequence in a long corridor, down which the camera tracks from a high angle; this allegorizes the *hanamichi*, the corridor down which the kabuki actor would enter and exit, posing along the way.

In their practice of mise-en-scène, however, Suzuki's films are not theatrical in any conventional sense, avoiding the kind of frontal, proscenium staging that Burch has written about in regards to Taishō cinema.[49] Suzuki's Nikkatsu films increasingly emphasized de-centered angles of framing and spontaneous, "incomplete" compositions (*Koroshi no rakuin*). The major exception, ironically, is the plain, frontal handling of *actual* theater performances in several films. While *Kagerō-za* also employs a frontal angle during the children's performance, it thrillingly compromises this very aesthetic by breaking the fourth wall that proscenium staging

Fig. 8.23. Breaking the Wall: stage and backstage dynamically interacting in the same frame, from the POV of the audience (*Kagerō-za*)

implies. The children in the audience are as much a part of the performance as the children onstage and at one point rush onstage themselves. More importantly, the film cuts from its frontal coverage of the stage to diagonal compositions that show both the stage and the backstage wings at once, revealing Shinako, formerly a viewer of the play, in the wings and interacting with the onstage players.

The male characters, in contrast, are not allowed onstage, thus gendering both the performance and its ideological thrust. The audience members—a dirty *yakuza* with an artificially high-pitched voice and a dwarf who, between shots, morphs into Suzuki's favorite actor Tamagawa Isao—actively prevent Matsuzaki from getting on stage. As for Tamawaki, when his patriarchal crimes are depicted by the children onstage, he shoots his rifle at them in a hysterical reassertion of phallic power, which the children then "magically" incorporate into their performance as if it had been anticipated.

From these examples one gleans a "participatory" theatre, long cherished by the avant-garde of the 1960s and designed to break the distance between the stage and the passive audience in moments of politically and aesthetically destabilizing "engagement."[50]

Fig. 8.24. "Hysterically Phallic" Capitalism: Tamawaki shoots off his rifle "from the hip" at anything resembling the feminine or natural

Even more crucial is the relation posited between avant-garde and classical theatre. David G. Goodman has explored the notion of a "Return of the Gods" in Japanese avant-garde theatre,[51] describing a theatre that intended to be "rooted in tradition," that would reject the "secular realism" of *shingeki*, and yet not "for the purpose of a religious revival. . . . but as a process to liberate Japanese ghosts, i.e. Japanese gods as a symbol of Japanese archetypal, aesthetic, socio-psychological heritage . . . not to affirm them, but to acknowledge and negate them."[52] *Kagerō-za* adapts precisely this aspect of the avant-garde theatre which was already critical to Suzuki's film project: the deep structures of representational power both within and without. It is no poor description of Suzuki's cinema to say that it is meant to visualize such structures (including ritualized violence) "not to affirm them, but to acknowledge and negate them." *Acknowledgment*, however, is far from uncomplicated. *Kagerō-za*'s discourse of theatre again questions whether there is a necessary relation between the sacred, which manifested itself in the "Transcendental Meiji Order" and its revival of concepts of sacrifice and suicidal honor, and the aesthetic, which in the history of kabuki traded heavily on represented violence. Can the two be separated? Does the film wish to interrogate the role of art in transmitting the claims of myth throughout modern Japan, or does it simply revel in these colorful, dynamic, and "magical" theatrical forms through which religious belief is made visible, perhaps expiated in the process, and, certainly, transmuted back into dream?

The gods do indeed return in the third act of *Kagerō-za*, replete with theatrical icons of the divine. Japanese *kami*, the *yuki onna* (snow witch), *kitsune*, *obake* and the *deus ex machina*—an essential element to kabuki performance—all make an appearance.[53] The first part of the performance is a kabuki, and yet the children soon put on crudely wrought, highly creative masks, a perfect example of the hybrid aesthetic. In this third act, the operative tradition is *bunraku*. However, it is Shinako who now appears on stage as a live puppet manipulated by a *kurogo* (puppeteer) in a red mask whose voice identifies her as the *deus ex machina*. Since the *kurogo* is usually clothed in black, the red color of the puppeteer's mask associates her with violence, as in all Suzuki's color films, but also with passion: Matsuzaki's fanciful sex scene with Shinako involves a red thread proceeding from his crotch, a Buddhist icon of desire.

Various wild events then occur before Matsuzaki's eyes. The ghostly character of Ine appears above the stage, connected to a transom, and flies out into the audience towards Matsuzaki. This is the technique of *chunori*, one of the great *keren* (or techniques) of kabuki and largely reserved for the appearance of supernatural beings. This is an important gesture in many ways. There is no attempt to hide the stage mechanism of the transom, so that Ine's flight might seem supernatural within the film's diegesis; on the contrary, the mechanism is excessively transparent. When cinema possesses so many technologies of illusion, *Kagerō-za* prefers, self-consciously, the artifice of stage technique.

The representation of *chunori* is accomplished in three shots.

The stage artifice of *chunori* is overlaid with blatant cinematic artificiality. Cinema transcends the theatrical experience, but not in the direction of verisimilitude: quite the opposite. The second shot of Ine (Fig. 8.26) is remarkable in its dual capacity as frozen time and as false time (i.e., discontinuity). It is cinema's transformation of time and space that is upheld, and yet can *only* be upheld through the abandonment of the sacred cows of realism and continuity. Small wonder that Tamawaki looks directly into the camera and laughs, "It's nothing like *shinpa*, is it? Preposterous!" If one were to choose a pair of shots (that is, a single cut) to represent the "Suzuki Difference," the anti-realist spectacle of Ine's flight from the stage would do nicely.

Fig. 8.25. Cinematic *Keren* (shot 1): backward track from a Long Shot of the stage as Ine descends on a transom towards Matsuzaki in the audience

Fig. 8.26. Cinematic *Keren* (shot 2): close section of Ine's upper body as she passes over Matsuzaki. However, in this shot Ine is no longer in motion, but stationary

Fig. 8.27. Cinematic *Keren* (shot 3): a continuation of Shot (1). Ine is still in motion (i.e., she has never stopped)

Fig. 8.28. Backdrop: Shinako (*extreme background, right of center*) willfully brings down the entire makeshift theatre in a spectacular collapse

In this third act, the distance between audience and performance breaks down to such an extent that the performance literally annihilates itself. After having been apparently possessed by her demonic puppeteer, Shinako straightens her posture as if she has been freed; but a mysterious dissolve follows, after which Shinako is still standing in roughly the same position. But something has changed nevertheless; Shinako abruptly turns around and runs straight through the theatre backdrop; her exit pulls down the backdrop and then, spectacularly, the entire stage.

Kagerō-za portrays the woman in classical theatre as a manipulated object; but Shinako escapes in a spectacular negation. The discourse on gender and cultural tradition is not quite ended, though. Behind the theatre, Shinako lowers herself into a tub of water, seemingly intent on drowning. As she does so, thousands of bladder cherries (*hōzuki*), which are funereal symbols but also, allegedly, crude forms of pre-modern contraception, emerge from under her skirt to cover the surface of the water. Matsuzaki attempts to follow Shinako into the tub, but he is held back by the powers of the *deus ex machina*, now revealed as a female witch or deity who appeared earlier in the film as an old seller of bladder cherries. She explains to Matsuzaki, "I have no need of men's souls." It is only Shinako's death that the deity demands. Nevertheless, Matsuzaki fights her power and plunges his head into the pool, seemingly committing suicide.

Sacrifice, Shamanism, and Female Gods

What is this archaic deity that governs the theatre, and is both hostile and not hostile to women? The malicious force is gendered as female seemingly in order to clarify that the mythic structure revealed here is not the patriarchy represented by the capitalist Tamawaki. Tamawaki urges Matsuzaki to commit suicide with his unfaithful wife; but the deity is not interested in love suicide, only in female sacrifice.

Chikamatsu, the great "poet" of the love suicide, typically presented a narrative of a merchant class hero torn between a wife and a mistress. The protagonist resorts to suicide because of the pressures of society. At risk of oversimplifying the sublime Chikamatsu, we may interpret that the love suicide, while declaring the lovers' anti-social emotions (*ninjō*), is also an indirect means by which patriarchy attempts to control what it absolutely cannot control: adultery. In *Yari no Gonza/Gonza the Spearman*, later filmed by Suzuki's friend, Shinoda (Shōchiku, 1986), a husband is unwillingly pressured by society into killing his wife and her lover.

But matters are still more complicated in *Kagerō-za* by its historical context. The motives of Shinako and Matsuzaki are not those of Chikamatsu's heroes. As Matsuzaki points out, he and Shinako are strangers with nothing to bind them together but erotic attraction. It is only due to the "transcendental" imagination of Meiji/Taishō culture, as filtered through the works of Izumi Kyōka, that they conceive of an irrational desire to commit suicide together. Inouye believes that in Kyōka's Meiji-era stories, ". . . women are objects of sacrifice . . . tempting yet nurturing, they are pitifully oppressed while being divinely powerful. Kyōka's sympathy is with them . . . But . . . [his] inner peace is predicated on [their] . . . unimaginable suffering."[54] But so, it seems, was the average *shinpa* play of the time. Suzuki's film reflects their sinister implications: whereas in the kabuki ghost story, the female ghost avenges her own murder, Ine's grudge, seemingly directed towards the innocent Shinako, is nothing more than unrequited love for the monstrous Tamawaki. It is typical of Suzuki's films to insist on what no audience would like to accept; that is, the profoundly amoral irrationality, even injustice, of attraction.

And yet the film intervenes in Kyōka's sexual politics—which were *highly* progressive for their time[55]—through the heroism of Shinako. She instructs Matsuzaki that "a woman is not so weak as you think," and this dialogue is repeated by the female *deus ex machina*. Unlike Ine who remains jealous beyond the grave, Shinako is largely immune to the allure of masculine power (Tamawaki). Her "affair" with Matsuzaki begins as deliberate provocation, an act of resistance. And yet, like an "object of sacrifice" in Kyōka's original, Shinako must die for defying the social order, hence her (apparent) desire to draw Matsuzaki into a lover's suicide.

What cultural inheritance has motivated Shinako towards suicide rather than survival? Two conceptual readings are possible, both of which are intimately tied to the sacred origins of Japanese theatre, the form through which *Kagerō-za* has presented its argument.[56] The first reading emphasizes a notion of sacrifice that goes deeper than the social mechanisms of patriarchy, returning to its sacral origins as the offering of a slaughtered precious object to the deity for the protection of the community. And yet, is it really possible to read the concept of sacrifice in the history of Japan, whether as ritual or as myth, as categorically and functionally distinct from patriarchy?

The second essential concept is that of shamanism. Benito Ortolani grounds the origins of Japanese theatre in sacred rituals surrounding shamanism, a practice which penetrates further back into Japanese pre-history than the patriarchal *uji*, to a period in which the female shamans were, in fact, the possessors of political power.[57] A prominent type of female shaman was the medium who negotiated between the "other realm" of the spirit and the world of men (as in *Rashōmon*). Hori has also argued that, like sacrifice, shamans become particularly important in times of local crisis. Ortolani emphasizes the theatricality of the female shaman's divine ecstasy: "The encounter of shamaness [and] *kami* happens . . . in the middle of theatrically suggestive, sometimes comical or erotic actions. When angry, vengeful powers are concerned, it may occur during terrifying high points of the rhythmic dances."[58] The shaman entertains divine guests, some of them distinctly unkind.[59] Shinako's fatal dance also involves a radical transformation of body and spirit leading to the return of the gods.[60]

Scholarly accounts of Japanese shamanism conspicuously lack any reference to the death of the shaman. This complicates our reading of *Kagerō-za*, which must be understood in the complex cultural nexus that relates shamanism/magical transformation to gendered sacrifice, which is not essentially patriarchal, but often suborned to it. What seems clear is that Shinako has carried out an active resistance to patriarchy through adultery, but in the process has channeled, Faust-like, an archaic female deity. Although this deity is explicitly not patriarchal, she seems to demand a price for social resistance. Nevertheless, the female-as-shaman seems to ensure that women, and not men, have the power to effect or prevent fundamental change. In Imamura's later *Narayama bushikō/Ballad of Narayama* (1983), a rural matriarch engineers the death of an adulterous daughter-in-law. Is such an act done in the virtual *imago* of patriarchy—hence the female adulteress is the object of greater wrath—or is it purely in service of a coercive, transgendered communal order based inherently on false promises? Although *Kagerō-za* may speak of humanity's fundamental entrapment in a hostile universe, we also return, in the end, to a social reality that Suzuki has emphasized in the past: the cost of resistance is high, in fact, fatal. In a modern era where even the powerful shamaness is subject to male authority, how can resistance manifest itself? In the world of *Kagerō-za*, female resistance turns back upon itself in the form of the love suicide. Even in rebellion, how can one escape the closed interpretative circle of ideology? Yamane Sadao is correct to write that "to watch *Kagerō-za* is to be bewitched by a dangerous beauty"; in other words, to be seduced into a trap. In the end, what has killed Shinako (and Matsuzaki?) is *transcendental thinking*—the kind of thinking that welded religious belief to the existing social structure even in marginal communities, from pre-historic Yamato up until the Pacific War. But its sacred roots also, unquestionably, power a revisionist theatre/cinema that can hold this very discourse and reveal these cultural operations.

The Crystalline Images of Cinematic Memory

Gilles Deleuze's concept of the crystal sign (*hyalosign*) identifies a particular *species* of the modern (post-war) cinema, associated, for instance, with the films of Orson Welles. But it is also a foundational semiotic of what we (though not Deleuze) typically refer to as modernism. It concerns the indiscernibility of the "real" and the "imaginary," broadly understood. In visual narrative, the result is that the diegetic and temporal status of the image is constantly called into question. *Hyalosigns* allow us to appreciate *Kagerō-za* as a remarkably, ironically lucid exemplar of the evolution of dream-images and memory-images in modern cinema. For Deleuze, flashbacks and dream sequences (as in, e.g., *Kagenaki koe*) were still integrated into continuity and linked to the sensory-motor-schema of classical cinema. Crystal signs represent a further evolution because they render a narrative cinema wherein the real and imaginary, though theoretically separable, are "confused": more precisely, there is a "perpetual exchange" of real/imaginary in which the status of any given point is in question. Among other things, this indiscernibility results in cinematic formal arrangements which finally recognize the complex temporal relations that govern everyday perception and, therefore, subjectivity. In order for human beings to be able to recognize and assign value to the objects that they perceive in the ever-flowing present, memory must be actualized at each present moment, so that the past in the form of memory (which is virtual or "imaginary") and the present (which is actual, but unrecognizable without recourse to the virtual, that is, memory) coexist.[61] One could argue that *Koroshi no rakuin* anticipated Deleuze's theory in the infamous "butterfly" sequence wherein the viewer becomes unable to distinguish between Hanada's reality and mentality, between diegetic and nondiegetic, linear time and circular time. The feverish Hanada, in this scene, cannot register or *remember* events properly, and this is what calls up a realm of fantastic, abstract imagery. When we engage in "attentive recognition" of what we perceive, the past in the form of recollection becomes a decisive factor in our effort.[62] Conversely, if we *cannot* remember—if our act of recognition is not successful—this opens the doors to a realm of virtuality: "The actual image ... does not link up.... It rather enters into a relation with genuinely virtual elements, feelings of *déjà vu* ... dream images.... fantasies or theatre scenes."[63]

Zigeunerweisen already witnesses the impossibility of a simple "actuality" image when an abrupt cut reveals Sono suddenly standing halfnaked in a different part of the room than in the previous shot, striking the spirited pose of a dancer or female shaman (Fig. 8.9). This image fulfills the "absolute reversibility" of the actual and the virtual, the real and the imagined. Because of the presence of Aochi as perceiver, we are tempted to classify the image as his fantasy; but in the Taishō Trilogy's chronically discontinuous mise-en-scène, there is no criteria by which to mark this image as "less actual" than its surrounding images. Each successive image, no matter how strange, is equally actual and virtual, believable (in terms of the film) and unbelievable.

Kagerō-za also operates according to a "crystalline" regime. The three ghostly appearances of Ine before the eyes of Matsuzaki may be fantasies, hauntings, or stagings; they are crystal signs by virtue of the fact that none of these explanations—these attempts to code and delimit the image—are determinable; each appearance is really none of these things, but purely indiscernible. The final ten minutes of *Kagerō-za* presents a more complex example in the form of a reflexive manifesto on the necessity of a dreamlike, crystalline cinema. This begins with an abrupt cut after Matsuzaki has plunged his head into the tub of water, seemingly committing suicide

Fig. 8.29. In the Realm of the Virtual: obscenely violent paintings replace the backdrops for a scene on a moving train

with Shinako. But the scene then changes to Matsuzaki on a moving train, propositioning a pretty girl. Outside of the train windows, however, instead of scenery, are sections of obscene paintings.

We cut to Matsuzaki standing alone on a Kanazawa street with another obscene painting in the background. In two discontinuous shots, Matsuzaki appears in front of the mural holding a decorative spyglass.

As he looks through it towards the camera, there is a cut to another scene. Matsuzaki and Madame Mio are speaking in what resembles her Tokyo hostel, except that the *shōji* are now covered in obscene paintings. These paintings, some genuine and some fabricated, depict horrific gendered violence in the Edo-period style of woodblock prints and illustrations, specifically locating a tradition of violence in art. Mio claims that Shinako died not with Matsuzaki, but her husband Tamawaki: suicide or murder? Matsuzaki responds by reciting a verse taken from the Kyōka story: "Since I saw my lover in a dream, I have depended on dreams." Mio opens the letter that was sent to her to find exactly this verse, written by Shinako.

There is an abrupt cut to a scene between Matsuzaki and the anarchist and then a return to Matsuzaki in the street, gazing through his

308 / NEGATIVE, NONSENSICAL, AND NON-CONFORMIST

Fig. 8.30. Imaginary Signifier: Matsuzaki on the "street" views different scenes and locations through a spyglass

spyglass. The next shot, from his POV, is a zoom through the open doorway of a house.

Shinako enters, crossing in front of Ine who stands motionless. Two close-ups of a rather triumphant Shinako follow, one a profile, the other a frontal angle. The next shot is of Shinako sitting in the background right, in front of the painted walls and on a painted platform. In the foreground is Matsuzaki, watching this scene with his back to the camera. A second Matsuzaki emerges from this first, immobile Matsuzaki.

The doubles bow to each other (Fig. 8.32); then the second sits with his back to Shinako. This ability to "see oneself" is a form of death, according to the freemason who told just this sort of story to Matsuzaki earlier. The last shot of the film is a close-up of Matsuzaki sitting in this position and facing the camera as he discusses his death in the future tense.

In this unique sequence of film, the painted walls and surfaces convey an artifice which barely mediates the horrific events they represent, removing them from an (unstable) diegesis and towards the realm of abstract expression. Matsuzaki being a writer, after all, the sequence

Fig. 8.31. The (Virtual) Realm of the Dead: Shinako and other casualties of society appear in a ruined house from Matsuzaki's POV

Fig. 8.32. The Double as Death: Matsuzaki (from the street) watches himself watching his double as the latter joins Shinako in an erotic/deathly union

Fig. 8.33. Whither the Present? Shot (1): Matsuzaki on a Kanazawa street viewing another scene from his spyglass

metaphorizes the act of artistic creation, operating here as a specifically non-diegetic engine of difference. But the sequence also foregrounds perception, particularly the "arranged" perception of a filmmaker and his camera. Shots of Matsuzaki gazing through the spyglass frame or initiate the other scenes that occur, as if he is a director/photographer "recording" what he has choreographed. Our interpretation must therefore recognize the double nature (actual and virtual) of perception that is a key to Deleuze's crystalline image. The scenes that he "views" (the conversation with Mio, for instance) might have happened in an "actual" world, but they are recollected/reimagined/recreated in the virtual form of a purely cinematic expression; hence the presence of a "lens."

It is a mistake to think of these scenes as occurring in a present tense, as if Matsuzaki and his lens were passively recording, like a documentary, some given reality as it happens before his eyes. Since Matsuzaki is perceiving scenes involving himself, the scenes must in some sense be recollections. Madame Mio's story recounts past events, but they are events

Fig. 8.34. Whither the Present? Shot (2): Matsuzaki is viewing himself in Tokyo discussing what happened in his "future" after he left Kanazawa

which took place after the third act of the film; that is, in some sense in Matsuzaki's "future."

There are (notional) geographical shifts between scenes: a train, then Tokyo (Mio), then Kanazawa (the anarchist), with Matsuzaki "perceiving" all these things from the Kanazawa street near to the theatre where he *appeared* to have drowned. The past, which is always virtual, is simultaneously actualized with the presumed "present" of Matsuzaki's act of perception; the "virtual" future is also actualized at that moment, either as expectation or fantasy that may never become actual, or as an actual future which has not happened yet. In that case, Matsuzaki's "knowing" present is impossible: the present therefore "disappears."

The most we can say about this temporally indiscernible sequence, therefore, is that Matsuzaki is in the act of recording, reviewing, or recreating either something that happened (in memory) or something in his mind, in order to represent it aesthetically. The scenes, then, must be memories represented in the form of fantasy or pure artistic expression; or, they may be fantasies cast in the form of fictitious recollections. *Kagerō-*

za's independent creation of a "crystalline cinema" denies any means by which to judge.

Death Twenty-Four Frames Per Second

Why does Matsuzaki end up apparently committing suicide with a woman he barely knows? *Zigeunerweisen*'s portrait of uneasy cultural transition and *Kagerō-za*'s double suicide as a romantic return to the symbolic order of a mythic past have their analogues in European art cinema. Similarly, Matsuzaki's double suicide, even as a historical symbol of a Japanese "absolutism of the spirit," is inseparable from a Taishō-era cultural awareness of European "romantic love" (as recognized in *Kenka erejii* and *Akutarō-den*). John Orr argues that in Antonioni's films the crisis of modernity "lies in its failure to create new values which match the progress in technology we use in everyday life . . . If there is little to replace absolute value in the modern world, desire does not replace love. Yet already love is a conception which belongs to the past."[64] The gesture of love suicide both represents and distorts an increasingly archaic "past." Yet Taishō democracy and consumerism put nothing in place of nostalgia for that past. The now capitalist patriarchy offers only a hypocritical continuity based on a virtual, commodified tradition. Apart from negating this, the trilogy's only answer to an ongoing crisis of values is to revisit the past in the pleasurable form of art pastiche, yet in full knowledge that Japan's answer, in the Shōwa period, was reactionary militarism.

Through his romantic suicide (real or imagined) Matsuzaki goes through an inverse variation of the prewar past. Like Tetsu in *Tokyo nagaremono*, he wishes for an impossible return to the past because stymied by ill-fitness to the environment around him. Tetsu lets himself go through a tirade of savage violence in order to repair his relationship to Tokyo, to feel at home in this spatial environment. Matsuzaki goes through the inverse—suicide or a *zazen*-like "blowout" or extinction of the mind—in order to have a *rapprochement* with time rather than space. While *Tokyo nagaremono* ironically revises studio genre material, Matsuzaki's "melt down" represents the *nouvelle vague* and *nuberu bagu* protagonist, from Godard's *Pierrot le fou* (1965) to Cammell and Roeg's *Performance* (1968), from Masumura's *Kyōjin to gangu* (Daiei, 1958) through the destructive sexual epiphanies of Ōshima's *Ai no korida*, a film which Suzuki claimed should be seen by the whole world.

Yet the indiscernibility of the "real" in cinema profoundly affects this question. Does it matter whether Matsuzaki has "actually" committed suicide, or is actuality less important than the fact that Matsuzaki's beliefs and desires lead him to romanticize this backward looking act? On one level, the distinction between actuality/agency and expressive representation matters a great deal in Suzuki's films. They consistently present it as necessary, even desirable, to call forth even our most dangerous desires in the act of cinema viewing. This abject "desiring" in the safety of the cinema is akin to dreaming, and the last thing this director wants is the policing of dreams. The problem, in reference to aesthetics, begins when society institutionalizes desire within a symbolic order; hence the necessity of a counter-institutional cinema.

Viewed in this light, Matsuzaki's "artistic experience" of love suicide may be perfectly commendable: indeed, he is much happier in the denouement than in the "real world" where Tamawaki has mobilized both desire and the traditional arts. Matsuzaki critiques the magical theatre performance, which retells the story of Tamawaki's crimes, by saying, ironically, that he does not go in for "realism." When fantasies of violence and gendered subjugation appear in genre cinema as an industrial mandate, they create a false (ideological) image of reality; but Suzuki's non-diegetic cinematic artifice justifies itself as an acceptable, indeed necessary space within which to relive our abject desires. The "Suzuki difference," then, appears as an ethical imperative: it is necessary to be "false," to be "impertinent."

Coda: The Other Suzukis

The conclusions above hold true, I think, for nearly all of the cinematic encounters between Suzuki's modernist practice and the Japanese historical imaginary. We should, however, be cautious of too unitary a reading of a long, unpredictable career. This book has, necessarily, emphasized the continuities of a directorial practice as a textual (not an empirical) phenomenon, a way of reading the intentionality of that most highly constructed of aesthetic forms, the cinema. Such continuities, ironically, are the principal signposts of the process of negative differentiation from all other film texts. But when we consider, firstly, the insights of fifty years of deconstructive criticism, and secondly, the director's own insistence on an open, evasive signification and on the "doubleness" of all our mental and cinematic reckonings of reality, we must concede that there can be no one single or superior construal of Suzuki's film practice—no one Suzuki the auteur—just as there is no one reading of his films, ideological or otherwise. The diversity of approaches that I have taken in this book have already revealed—or indeed *created*, since I grant that function to criticism—a certain duality to Suzuki's aesthetic; that is, two related readings that are subtly alternate, among many other readings. I shall therefore, as something of an epilogue, consider a "Suzuki" who is distinct from the one I have presented heretofore, a one more urgently related to our current, post-filmic media environment. One such was invoked in the discussion of nihilism in *Koroshi no rakuin*; but it is particularly in Suzuki's most reviled film, *Hishū monogatari*, his "unsuccessful" comeback to the Japanese cinema, that this divergent reading seems to come to the fore.

Hishū is a disgusted satire of post-war modernity—and television in particular—that proved to be savage beyond the bounds of popular and critical taste. A textile corporation starts with an image of luxury golfing clothes for women, then proceeds to mold an actual woman—the hardworking young golfer Reiko (Shiraki Yoko)—to fit that image. Having her play golf in a bikini for the camera is only the beginning. A modern youth with no direction other than to grab at celebrity, Reiko at first cooperates with the corporate patriarchs in her own commodification. Her professionalism and craftsmanship elevate her above a degrading context. But later, as she becomes a celebrity on TV—on which every show devolves into a beauty contest—she almost willfully begins to suffer at the hands of the viewers and "fans." Once again, in the masochistic aesthetic, it is punishment that not only demarcates, but truly creates, the individual. In a final bid to squash her self-confidence and bring her back down to the level of the group, the viewers subject Reiko to violation and, then, prostitution. Only then is she "fit" to be sacrificed. What begins as corporate manipulation expands to discover the deep pathology of the "ordinary," to which the corporations offer up celebrities as a sacrifice and distraction. Reiko is no hero like the *Akō gishi*—this is a quotidian universe devoid of ideal types— but she is unquestionably a martyr who is suited to her times.

This is why the viewers must bring Reiko "down to their level," for in an age of televisual narcissism, why should our martyrs/victims be any different than ourselves? The all-consuming, Moloch-like nihilism of *Hishū* suggests that there are at least two Suzukis, just as there are two Kurosawas, the maker of *jidai-geki* period films and *gendai-geki* (modern) social dramas. In Suzuki's world, the "period film" is not defined by narrative setting—which might as well be contemporary—but by an aesthetic frame of reference to a pre-modern world view. In the Taishō and *yakuza* films, *Nikutai no mon* and *Pisotoru opera*, this historical imaginary functions as the site of masochistic play and abject spectacle that exorcises our demons. The "Second Suzuki" is the maker of devastating social satires:

Fig. 8.35. Suzuki's Homage to Dreyer: Reiko as Jeanne D'Arc (*Hishū monogatari / A Tale of Sorrow*)

Hishū, Koroshi no rakuin, Shunpuden, Kawachi karumen (despite its survivalist ending). Both types of films utilize a reflexive and negative aesthetic: the difference between them is, possibly, the difference that Deleuze proposed between negativity as disavowal and negativity as destruction. Disavowal, in the "period films," creates a dreamlike alternate reality in which the cruelty of history and our conditioned, cruel desires can be refashioned, so as to leave the spectator in a position that is, ideally, both honest and bearable. But the satirical films follow Honda Ishirō's *Gojira* (1954) in obliterating everything in their path, including, symbolically, the viewer. Rejection predominates: are our desires ultimately as irredeemable as the society that exploits and suppresses them? The question of which mode is more trenchant is undoubtedly relative to the viewer's historical situation and intellectual context.

Finally, there are, of course, other readings of Suzuki that I have not emphasized for reasons of space and argumentative focus. Some might wish to emphasize his skills as a narrative artist more than I have done: for this book has appreciated Suzuki as the antagonist of conventional cinematic narration. To be sure, Suzuki's films (except *Yumeji*) are not free associative collages. Created within a popular idiom, they depend on the tension between narrative and other structures as a source of pleasure and stimulation. However, this book has proposed a set of readings of Suzuki related to a central (modernist) core of the operations of negativity and the recognition of difference. When we encounter Gaudi's Sagradia Familia Cathedral in Barcelona, we must first account for its extraordinary material and conceptual difference to all Christian architecture before or since.

Should we choose to later dwell on the Augustinian piety that informed Gaudi's worldview and has much to do with Catholic intellectual tradition, this in no way diminishes the fact and significance of the Sagradia Cathedral's manifest difference. "Augustinian piety" does not explain the great influence of Gaudi's work on the Spanish surrealists. From out of the edifice of tradition, Gaudi carved the unique. What I have done here, in the case of Suzuki, is to account for a similarly irreducible difference: for that is ultimately his contribution to the history of the cinema. Compared to Lubitsch or Renoir, Ozu or Kurosawa, films like *Tokyo nagaremono* and *Kagerō-za* are hardly triumphs of narrative art. Rather, they are triumphs of audiovisual art that is narrative *among other things*. The formal and conceptual economies that I have investigated in these chapters—discontinuity, fetishism, figuration, iconicity, theatricality, the fantasy scenarios of masochism, and the polysemic, non-diegetic gesture—all contributed to a revisionist cinema of spectacle that had to be divorced from the narrative and indexical assumptions of the classical cinema in order to re-establish an ethical and *intentional* autonomy.

In their manner of critically redressing the post-war balance of spectacle and narrative, the films of Suzuki hold a value in film history that is readily related to its era (the era of *Week-end*, *Performance*, and *Easy Rider*) and yet close to unique. As a cultural influence, moreover, they have a central place, along with manga, in the evolution of whole sectors of the Japanese cinema: the evolution from *narrative-as-continuity* to *narrative as successive iconographical units*. The ongoing reign of television anime,[65] where a constant recycling of familiar visual, narrative, and mythological clichés replaces the need for a reality effect, seems to have fulfilled this evolution only to create another crisis of the image—an endless cycle of ironic repurposing followed by emotional reinvestment in hollow clichés.

Suzuki's under-evaluated contribution to the *Rupan sansei/Lupin the 3rd* series (1969-), culminating in the feature *Babiron no ōgon densetsu* (1986), inevitably contributed to, yet offers a proleptic critique of, this media future. In an outlandish sequence, Rupan and Zenigata motorcycle across the utterly grotesque face of a three-dimensional Times Square billboard (advertising cigarettes?). The subtext is another satire on American commercial spectacle, behind which lies homelessness and rundown hotels with aged African-American clerks. But the film's real target of irony is now all the more recognizable, not only from TV *anime* but from our popular cinema's inescapable obsession with "canon" and "shared universes," which are, among other things, baldly acknowledged exercises in multimedia "franchise building." Suzuki's *Rupan* accomplishes a *reductio ad absurdum* of anime's fetish for "mythologizing" by randomly attaching mythic signifiers to unsuitable objects (rather like the changing colors of *Kutabare gurentai*'s stuffed dog). Thus, Madison Square Garden (built c. 1964), it turns out, is actually the ancient Tower of Babel thanks to the meddling of some cupidinous extraterrestrial deities. This picture, like its far less original *anime* brethren, identifies our perpetual, problematic return to the pleasures of myth and grand narrative, which are universal. The reign of cliché (and commodification) need not be. This, perhaps, should be a point of departure for a further, and reoriented, investigation into Suzuki's place in the history of film and media cultures.

Appendix
A Complete Filmography for Suzuki Seijun, Director

ABBREVIATIONS: Scr: writer; Pro: studio or production body (line producer given in parentheses); M: musical composer or director; Ed: editor; Ph: director of photography; Pd: production designer; O: other production staff

nota bene:
- Only theatrical releases are included in this filmography. Television and video productions are omitted.
- Features listed here from 1956 to 1957 carried the directorial credit of "Suzuki Seitarō." Films from 1958-2005 were credited to the director's assumed name, Suzuki Seijun.

1956

Minato no kanpai: shōri wo wagate ni (勝利をわが手に港の乾杯)/*Harbor Toast: Victory is in Our Grasp* aka *Victory is Mine*

Cast: Mishima Kō, Maki Shinsuke, Minami Sumiko, Amaji Keiko, Sugai Ichirō, Sano Asao, Ashida Shinsuke. Scr: Nakagawa Norio, Urayama Kirio. Pro: Nikkatsu (Asada Kenzō). Ph: Fujioka Kumenobu. Ed: Kondō Mitsuo. Pd: Satani Teruyoshi. M: Hirakawa Hideo. O: Kurahara Koreyoshi (asst. dir.). Japan, 21.3.1956.

Plot: Pop song film. A tale of brotherly sacrifice. Shinkichi (Mishima), a former sailor, has trouble with his brother Jirō (Maki), an up-and-coming jockey. Jirō runs after the mysterious Asako (Minami) against Shinkichi's advice and gets into trouble with a shady figure who may be her pimp, Osawa (Ashida). Soon Osawa is blackmailing Jirō into taking a dive in a major race, but after much complication, Jirō rides to victory. Osawa beats up Jirō and tries to kill him; Shinkichi intercedes and Osawa is killed. Shinkichi asks Asako to look after his brother as the cops come to arrest him. He looks out on the ocean one last time.

Umi no junjō (海の純情)/*Pure Emotions of the Sea* aka *Innocent Love at Sea*

Cast: Kasuga Hachirō, Kobayashi Jūshirō, Takada Toshie, Kō Tomoko, Akemi Kyōko. Scr: Norimasa Mayumi, Tanabe Tomomi. Pro: Nikkatsu (Mogi Ryōji).

Ph: Nagatsuka Kazue. Ed: Suzuki Akira. Pd: Yagyū Kazuo. M: Eguchi Yoshi. O: Takeda Kazunari (asst. dir.). Japan, 7.6.1956.

Plot: Pop song film. Handsome sailor Hachirō (singer Kasuga), on a whaling vessel headed for the Antarctic, is pursued by a geisha (Akemi) but loves the captain's gentle daughter Kazue (Takada). The captain (Kobayashi) is beset with a poor catch and a fractious crew. Upon returning, Kazue spurns Hachirō over a misunderstanding; after a suicide attempt, Hachirō finds himself falling for the shipping company boss's daughter Mitsuyo (Kō), but this arouses the jealousy of a higher-ranking shipmate who slanders Hachirō. The ship goes out once more, but Mitsuyo disguises herself as a sailor. The captain kills a whale but fractures his bone in the process; Hachirō takes over, successfully, as harpooner. On land again, Mitsuyo approaches Kazue and clears Hachirō's name so that he and Kazue can be together.

Akuma no machi (悪魔の街)/*Demon Town* aka *Satan's Town*

Cast: Kawazu Seizaburō, Sugai Ichirō, Yumi Asuza, Ashida Shinsuke, Hisamatsu Akira. Scr: Shiraishi Gorō (based on a novel by Matsumura Motoki [aka Shiki Ichirō]). Pro: Nikkatsu (Yanagawa Takeo). M: Kosugi Taichirō. Ph: Nagatsuka Kazue. Ed: Suzuki Akira. Pd: Satani Sanbei. Japan, 12.7.1956.

Plot: Two convicts escape from prison, a *yakuza* boss (Sugai), and his cellmate (Kawazu), in reality an undercover cop. As the former re-involves himself in horse race fixing and other *yakuza* activities, a game of feint and double feint, suffused with questions of loyalty, is played out. Eventually, as the boss goes on a spree of violence, the undercover cop must protect a girl (Azusa) he is smitten with and help the police apprehend the *yakuza* on a ferry.

1957

Ukikusa no yado (浮草の宿)/*Inn of the Floating Weeds* aka *Floating Inn*

Cast: Nitani Hideaki, Kasuga Hachirō, Kimuro Ikuko, Abe Tōru, Yamaoka Hisano. Pro: Nikkatsu (Mogi Ryōji). Scr: Yamazaki Gan. M: Eguchi Yoshi. Ed: Suzuki Akira. Pd: Satani Teruyoshi. O: Takeda Kazunari (asst. dir.). Japan, 9.1.1957.

Plot: Pop song film. A young yakuza (Nitani) in Yokohama is manipulated by his boss (Abe) into killing a rival and going to prison for five years. Upon his return he finds that his girlfriend is the boss's mistress. While distracted by the sister (Yamaoka) of a crooner (Kasuga), the hero is eventually drawn into a shootout with his reckless boss.

Hachi jikan no kyōfu (8時間の恐怖)/*Eight Hours of Horror*

Cast: Kaneko Nobuo, Nitani Hideaki, Shima Keiko, Nakahara Keishichi, Tone Harue, Fukami Taizō, Misuzu Eiko, Uemura Kenjirō, Kondō Hiroshi, Hara

Hisako, Minami Sumiko. Pro: Nikkatsu (Asada Kenzō). Scr: Tanada Gorō, Tsukiji Rokurō. M: Niki Takio. Ph: Nagatsuka Kazue. Ed: Suzuki Akira. Pd: Satani Sanbei. O: Takeda Kazunari (asst. dir.). Japan, 8.3.1957.

Plot: A storm and flood stops a train dead in its tracks for eight hours. The passengers try to leave by bus in the perilous weather, but a young mother with a baby disappears in the process. The other passengers, including a student (Nitani), an elderly couple, and a compassionate bar hostess search for her. The suicidal mother is found but the baby has become ill and all depends on an ex-doctor (Kaneko) who is a convicted murderer. He wants to reform, but the bus on its rural journey is also boarded by two *yakuza* thugs who have pulled a heist. The bar hostess lures one gangster into the woods and into a bear trap; the other commandeers the bus only to run across a police truck. The passengers finally band together in the ensuing chaos, and the gangster falls off a mountain road along with all the loot.

Rajo to kenjū (裸女と拳銃)/*Nude Girl With a Gun* aka *The Nude and the Gun* aka *The Girl and the Gun*

Cast: Mizushima Michitarō, Shiraki Mari, Sugai Ichirō, Shishido Jō, Minami Sumiko, Nitani Hideaki. Pro: Nikkatsu (Asada Kenzō). Scr: Tanabe Tomomi (from a short story by Washio Saburō). M: Hara Rokurō. Ph: Matsuhashi Umeo. Ed: Suzuki Akira. Pd: Chiba Kazuhiko. O: Takeda Kazunari (asst. dir.). Japan, 7.12.1957.

Plot: Newspaper crime photographer (Mizushima) follows an anonymous tip about drug smuggling to a seedy cabaret. As an erotic dancer (Shiraki) performs, a shot rings out. During the chaos of fleeing bodies, the photographer hooks up with the dancer and goes to her apartment. She steps out for cigarettes, and the hero finds he is locked in the room with a concealed corpse. The police lieutenant (Shishido) is inclined to believe the hero's innocence, and as he seeks to clear his name he meets a professional woman who is a dead ringer for the cabaret singer. Is she the same woman? His erotic obsession leads him into the secretive smuggling operation of a crime lord (Sugai) operating out of a Buddhist temple. He ends up shanghaied on a ship with the mysterious girl, who is the kingpin's wily mistress. The police attack the boat; the mistress is killed in the escape, but it transpires that she has sabotaged the kingpin's escape boat, which blows up.

1958

Ankokugai no bijo (暗黒街の美女)/*Underworld Beauty*

Cast: Mizushima Michitarō, Shiraki Mari, Kondō Hiroshi, Abe Tōru, Takashina Kaku, Ashida Shinsuke. Pro: Nikkatsu (Nishihara Takashi). Scr: Saji Susumu. M: Yamamoto Naozumi. Ph: Nakao Watarō. Ed: Suzuki Akira. Pd: Sakaguchi Takeharu. O: Takeda Kazunari (asst. dir.). Japan, 25.3.1958.

Plot: Professional criminal Miyamoto (Mizushima) is released from jail and recovers stolen diamonds from his hiding place in the sewers. In order to help his ailing ex-partner Mihara (Ashida), Miyamoto arranges to sell the diamonds to the *yakuza* boss (Abe) for whom he took the rap five years ago. When the boss attempts to steal the diamonds, Mihara swallows them in desperation before falling to his death. The grieving Miyamoto attempts to look after Mihara's spunky sister Akiko (Shiraki), who rebuffs his advances. Akiko models nude for her callous boyfriend (Kondō), a perverted sculptor of store mannequins. The *yakuza* use the sculptor to stealthily extract the diamonds from the dead man's corpse. When Miyamoto finds out, he beats the craven sculptor, further alienating Akiko. When the gang arrives on the scene, Miyamoto hides the diamonds in the breast of the mannequin. A hunt for the right mannequin ensues across the city, with Miyamoto one step ahead until the gang kidnaps Akiko and threatens to roast her in a steam bath. A complex gunfight in the basement of a beauty parlor ensues in which all the villains are killed. Miyamoto and Akiko are now potentially a couple, but does she really want the older man?

Fumihazushita haru (踏みはずした春)/*The Spring That Never Came* aka *The Boy Who Came Back*

Cast: Hidari Sachiko, Kobayashi Akira, Asaoka Ruriko, Abe Tōru, Nitani Hideaki, Noro Keisuke, Shishido Jō, Tonoyama Taiji, Takashina Kaku, Hisamatsu Akira. Pro: Nikkatsu (Takagi Masayuki). Scr: Terada Nobuyoshi, Okada Tatsuto (based on a novel by Fujiguchi Tōgo). M: Hayashi Hikari. Ph: Yamazaki Yoshihiro. Pd: Chiba Kazuhiko. Ed: Suzuki Akira. Japan, 29.6.1958.

Plot: A worker (Hidari) from "Big Brothers and Sisters," an NGO that tries to rehabilitate juvenile delinquents, is attached to the case of an angry teen Nobuo (Kobayashi). She is drawn like moths to a flame to the sexual danger of his personality, and is induced to go to drinking with him at a Jazz Hall and eventually to a love hotel. Subsequently, the vicious thugs surrounding the hero put her in danger. Nobuo's sweetheart (Asaoka) is also preyed on by the gang, who drug her and try to rape her. Violent confrontation between Nobuo and his associates put him in dire straits with the law, but eventually the BBS woman's reckless, unprofessional infatuation proves, ironically, to be the support that he needs.

Aoi chibusa (青い乳房)/*Blue Breasts* aka *Young Breasts*

Cast: Watanabe Misako, Kobayashi Akira, Odaka Yūji, Nitani Hideaki, Inagaki Mihoko, Ōmori Yoshio, Chō Hiroshi, Ozawa Shōichi, Noro Keisuke. Pro: Nikkatsu (Yamamoto Takeshi). Scr: Suzuki Keigo, Tsuji Yoshio (from a short story by Ichijō Akira). M: Hiraoka Seiji. Ph: Nagatsuka Kazue. Ed: Suzuki Akira. Pd: Nakamura Kimihiko. O: Takeda Kazunari (asst. dir.). Japan, 8.9.1958.

Plot: The fiancée (Watanabe) of a wealthy man begins to worry about his younger son Hiro (Kobayashi), who shows signs of juvenile delinquency and reckless behavior towards his girlfriend. When she attends the art exhibition of an amateur painter (Nitani), she has a bizarre vision of a young woman being raped by an assailant in the deserted shack depicted in the painting. When the girl becomes pregnant, the older woman's concern draws her into the world of Hiro's dodgy associates, including an unstable nightclub owner (Odaka) who may be responsible for the girl's current pregnancy. She is sexually attracted to both the painter and the ne'er-do-well, but as it turns out, it is the upstanding painter who has not only targeted Hiro's girlfriend, but had raped Hiro's "stepmother" in the deserted shack years before.

Kagenaki koe (影なき声)/*Voice Without a Shadow*

Cast: Nitani Hideaki, Minamida Yōko, Takahara Toshio, Shishido Jō, Ashida Shinsuke, Kaneko Nobuo, Noro Keisuke, Chō Hiroshi. Pro: Nikkatsu (Iwai Kaneo). Scr: Akimoto Ryūta, Saji Kan (based on the novel by Matsumoto Seichō). M: Hayashi Hikaru. Ph: Nagatsuka Kazue. Ed: Suzuki Akira. Pd: Sakaguchi Takeharu. Japan, 22.10.1958.

Plot: Switchboard operator Asako (Minamida) hears a murderer on the telephone but the authorities fail to catch him. Asako is fond of a reporter (Nitani) covering the case but marries a businessman (Takahara) who, in economic desperation, becomes connected with a shady character Hamazaki (Shishido) and his dubious connections (Kaneko, Ashida). When Asako—whose ears are well trained to the point of being supersensitive—realizes that Hamazaki was the murderer on the phone, her life descends into nightmare, with Hamazaki turning up dead and her husband arrested. The reporter, though constantly sidetracked by new evidence, eventually precipitates the revelation of the real murderer.

1959

Raburetaa (らぶれたあ)/*Love Letter*

Cast: Tsukuba Hisako, Machida Kyosuke, Nagai Franku (aka Frank Nagai). Pro: Nikkatsu (Asada Kenzō). Scr: Ishii Kiichi (based on a novel by Matsuura Takeo). M: Mamiya Yoshio. Ph: Kakita Isamu. Pd: Yagyū Kazuo. Japan, 15.1.59.

Plot: A young pianist at an Osaka nightclub, Kozue (Tsukuba), has exchanged love letters for years with a man she met once in the mountains. The letters have now mysteriously stopped, and the nightclub owner (Nagai) continues to offer his affections, but she is profoundly unmoved. The two agree that she must visit her one-time lover to find closure. Once there, she finds him loving but surprisingly different in some respects. It turns out that the man she has found is the brother of her dead lover (played by the same actor, Machida). The brother was responsible for most of the love letters. Shocked, Kozue runs back to Osaka where a decision looms as to which of her suitors she will accept.

Ankoku no ryoken (暗黒の旅券)/*Passport to Darkness*

Cast: Hayama Ryōji, Tsukuba Hisako, Shiraki Mari, Okada Masumi, Sawa Tamaki, Ashida Shinsuke, Kondō Hiroshi, Noro Keisuke. Pro: Nikkatsu (Asada Kenzō). Scr: Takaiwa Hajime (based on the short story by Washio Saburō). M: Kosugi Taichirō, Kawaba Koichi. Ph: Nagatsuka Kazue. Pd: Sakaguchi Takeharu. Ed: Suzuki Akira. O: Takeda Kazunari (asst. dir.). Japan, 19.5.59.

Plot: A television variety show highlights the marriage of jazz trombone player Ryōji (Hayama) and his hastily acquired bride (Sawa), even paying for their honeymoon. But she disappears before the train even departs the station. The confused trombonist becomes desolate and drunk, but later finds that his wife was in fact strangled upon her return to their home. Under suspicion, Ryōji plunges into a hidden Shinjuku underworld of drugs, sleaze, and corruption in search of the murderer; hazy memories of a certain bar which he visited when he was drunk seem to hold the key. It turns out his wife was involved with covert heroin smugglers, and with the help of a sympathetic woman (Okada) and a conflicted nightclub singer (Shiraki), a businessman-cum-heroin wholesaler (Kondō) is revealed as the murderer.

Suppedaka no nenrei (素っ裸の年齢)/*Age of Nudity* aka *The Naked Age*

Cast: Akagi Keihachirō, Hidari Bozuken, Hori Kyōko, Fujimaki Saburō, Takahara Toshio, Tamamura Shuntarō. Pro: Nikkatsu (Sasai Hideo). Scr: Seijun Suzuki, Terada Nobuyoshi. M: Watanabe Michiaki. Ph: Fujioka Kumenobu. Ed: Suzuki Akira. Pd: Sakaguchi Takeharu. O: Takeda Kazunari (asst. dir.). Japan, 8.9.1959.

Plot: The fast lives of motorcycle-riding delinquent teens at a coastal resort which attracts all sorts, including a sage hobo (Hidari). One teen Ken (Akagi) leads a gang of younger compatriots who like to gather in an abandoned U.S. military barracks along with Ken's lover (Hori). The hero dreams of being a sailor, and in financial desperation attracts trouble for the gang by pulling a scam on a local *yakuza* operation. Ken's girlfriend is frightened and leaves him just as one of his gang brothers (Fujimaki) makes off with the money. Ken pursues him by motorcycle but, in an excess of speed, falls to his death off the high cliffs.

1960

Jûsangô taihisen yori: sono gosōsha wo nerae (13号待避線よりその護送車を狙え)/*Take Aim at the Police Van* aka *Target: Prison Truck from Sector 13*

Cast: Mizushima Michitarō, Shiraki Mari, Watanabe Misako, Ozawa Shōichi, Ashida Shinsuke, Abe Tōru, Uchida Ryōhei, Hiromatsu Saburō, Fukuda Toyo, Chō Hiroshi, Noro Keisuke. Pro: Nikkatsu (Mōgi Ryōji). Scr: Sekizawa Shinichi (based on a story by Shimada Kazuo). M: Kawabe Koichi. Ph: Shigeyoshi Mine. Ed: Suzuki Akira. Pd: Sakaguchi Takeharu. O: Takeda Kazunari (asst. dir.). Japan, 21.1.1960.

Plot: A prison guard, Tamon (Mizushima), finds himself suspended when his prison truck is hijacked: two convicts are assassinated by a sniper. Tamon compulsively investigates, starting with the connections of another prisoner, petty thief Gorō (Ozawa) to whom the warden is sympathetic. The trail leads to Gorō's stripper girlfriend (Shiraki), then to the escort agency to which she belongs, which is run by a woman, Yuko (Watanabe) in place of her ailing father (Ashida). A prostitute is shot by an arrow as Tamon investigates. It turns out that the agency's shady lieutenant (Abe) and his associates are undercutting the madam by taking orders from a mysterious crime lord, Akiba, who operates an illicit ring of teenaged girls beneath the "respectable" agency. Goro is working for them but he and his girlfriend get shot when the latter impulsively tries to communicate with Tamon. Tamon corners the unknown Akiba and his gang in a train yard: the crime lord turns out to be Yuko's ageing, "respectable" father. Though genuinely horrified, she impulsively tries to defend him from the police; but as he tries to escape his foot gets caught in a split rail and he is run over by a train.

Kemono no nemuri (けものの眠り)/*Sleep of the Beast*

Cast: Nagato Hiroyuki, Ashida Shinsuke, Yamaoka Hisano, Yoshiyuki Kazuko, Kusanagi Kōjirō, Kusonoki Yūko, Noro Keisuke, Nishimura Kō, Ozawa Shōichi. Pro: Nikkatsu (Mizunoe Takiko). Scr: Ikeda Ichirō (based on a short story by Kikumura Itaru). M: Kaburagi Hajime. Ph: Mine Shigeyoshi. Ed: Suzuki Akira. Pd: Nakamura Kimihiko. O: Takeda Kazunari (asst. dir.). Japan, 9.4.1960.

Plot: An aged, respectable *sarariman* (Ashida) is forced into retirement by his pitiless employers. Upon his brief disappearance, his daughter and a crime reporter (Nagato), who is drawn to her, stumble upon a complex crime syndicate involving drug smuggling and the leader of a popular religious cult. When the father abruptly turns up, it becomes clear that he is part of the syndicate. In the ensuing chaos of painful revelation, he burns the syndicate headquarters down and commits suicide.

Mikkō 0-rain (密航0ライン)/*Undercover 0-Line* aka *Clandestine Zero Line* aka *Smashing the 0-Line*

Cast: Nagato Hiroyuki, Odaka Yūji, Shimizu Mayumi, Nakahara Sanae, Takashina Kaku, Noro Keisuke, Tamamura Shuntarō. Pro: Nikkatsu (Ashida Shōzō). M: Kosugi Taichirō. Ph: Mine Shigeyoshi. Ed: Suzuki Akira. Pd: Chiba Kazuhiko. O: Takeda Kazunari (asst. dir.). Japan, 25.6.1960.

Plot: A saga of rival crime reporters. One (Nagato) is unscrupulous and exploitative, the other (Odaka) not. The former's aggressive tactics, including sexual manipulation, arouse the ire of a female drug madam (Nakahara) and threaten the safety of his sister (Shimizu); but in the end, both reporters find themselves trapped aboard a freighter of lowlife foreigners participating in drug smuggling and contraband. The protagonists survive after much death and destruction, but the cynical reporter has not changed his ways.

Subete ga kurutteru (すべてが狂ってる)/*Everything Goes Wrong* aka *Everything Goes Crazy* aka *The Madness of Youth*

Cast: Kawachi Tamio, Ashida Shinsuke, Yatsu Ryōko (aka Nezu Ryōko), Nakagawa Shinako, Naraoka Tomoko, Itō Takao, Ueno Koichi, Hatsui Kotoe. Pro: Nikkastu (Asada Kenzō). Scr: Hohikawa Seiji (based on a short story by Ichijō Akira). M: Miho Keitarō, Maeda Norio. Ph: Hagiwara Izumi. Ed: Suzuki Akira. Pd: Chiba Kazuhiko. O: Fujiura Atsushi (asst. dir.). Japan, 8.10.1960.

Plot: Jirō (Kawachi) is an angry high school graduate with no direction. He is ashamed that his mother (Naraoka), a war widow, has been the longtime mistress of a well-meaning businessman, Nanbara (Ashida). As a result, Jirō almost pathologically equates female sexuality with money. Nanbara treats Jirō like a son but it is no longer reciprocated. Jirō's upstanding friends work laborious jobs for little pay and no benefits, and so he gravitates towards a criminal youth gang. Their informal *modus operandi* is to find teen girls, seduce or sometimes rape them, and then prostitute them for cash. One girl attached to the gang, the free spirited but guilt-ridden Tani (Nezu), is attracted to Jirō and takes his virginity; but he responds to her with contempt and indifference. Tani's friend Etsuko is desperately looking to pay for an abortion without informing her upstanding boyfriend, a student protest leader, about the pregnancy. Increasingly in trouble with the law, Jirō directs Etsuko to try to sleep with, or at least blackmail, Nanbara. This leads to a confrontation between Nanbara and Jirō. The teen savages Nanbara for his generation's failures, including the war, but degenerates into pure rage, nearly beating Nanbara to death. He and Tani go on the run with a stolen car—which the hapless teen fatally crashes.

Kutabare gurentai (くたばれ愚連隊)/*Go to Hell Youth Gang!* aka *Fighting Delinquents* aka *Go to Hell Hoodlums!*

Cast: Wada Kōji, Hosokawa Chikako, Azuma Emiko, Kondō Hiroshi, Ozawa Eitarō, Takashina Kaku, Shimizu Mayumi, Utsumi Toppa, Kameyama Yasuhiro, Hiromatsu Saburō, Nezu Ryōko, Ozawa Naoyoshi. Pro: Nikkatsu (Koi Eisei). Scr: Yamazaki Gan (based on the story by Hara Kenzaburō). M: Ōmori Seitarō. Ph: Nagatsuka Kazue. Ed: Suzuki Akira. Pd: Satani Teruyoshi. O: Nishimura Shōgorō (asst. dir.). Japan, 23.11.1960.

Plot: A reckless tycoon (Kondō) kills a painter in a hit-and-run accident. The tough street kids for whom the painter was an adoptive father are in dire straits. The inept retainer (Takashina) of the ancient Matsudaira Klan of Awaji Island appears to claim one of the kids (Wada) as the lost heir to the *daimyō* clan. The clan is kept together by a stern, traditionalist matriarch (Hosokawa), but as she fights to keep the young, swinging, rock'n'roll-loving hero to stay and accept his responsibilities, the two develop great affection for one other. Unfortunately, the tycoon wants to buy off the Matsudaira lands for commercial development, aided and abetted by the matriarch's swindling brother (Ozawa) and the tycoon's mistress (Azuma), who turns out to be the hero's estranged mother. The hero vows to "win back" his mother without abandoning the clan or giving in to the corrupt cartel.

1961

Tokyo kishitai aka ***Tokyo naito*** (東京騎士隊)/*Tokyo Knights*

Cast: Wada Kōji, Shimizu Mayumi, Nezu Ryōko, Minamida Yōko, Ozawa Shōichi, Kaneko Nobuo, Azuma Emiko, George Ruika, Saga Zenpei, Kondō Hiroshi, Kijimi Ichirō, Yanase Shirō. M: Ōmori Seitarō. Pro: Nikkatsu (Koi Eisei). Scr: Yamazaki Gan (based on the story by Hara Kenzaburō). Ph: Nagatsuka Kazue. Ed: Suzuki Akira. Pd: Nakamura Kimihiko. O: Takeda Kazunari (asst. dir.). Japan, 1.2.1961.

Plot: Kōji, a student at an international school, is thrust into the position of a *yakuza* boss when his father, whom he thought was in the construction business, suddenly dies. Kōji would rather play soccer and study music while a rival gang naturally takes advantage of the power vacuum to horn in on the clan's territory, with the help of Kōji's unreliable lieutenant (Kaneko). Kōji is attracted to a daughter of the rival clan but it soon transpires that the rivals had his father killed. Kōji's love interest calls the police and her father is exposed, leading unexpectedly to his suicide in the face of his daughter's disillusionment. Kōji pursues a normal life.

Muteppodaisho (無鉄砲大将)/*Reckless Boss* aka *A Hell of a Guy*

Cast: Wada Kōji, Sagawa Mitsuo, Shimizu Mayumi, Ashikawa Izumi, Hayama Ryōji, Sugai Ichirō, Hatsui Kotoe, Noro Keisuke, Ozawa Shōichi, Chō Hiroshi. Pro: Nikkatsu (Kubo Keinosuke). Scr: Nakanishi Ryūjō, Matsuura Takeō (based on the short story by Ichijō Akira). M: Kaburagi Hajime. Ph: Nagatsuka Kazue. Ed: Suzuki Akira. Pd: Matsui Toshiyuki. O: Takeda Kazunari (asst. dir.). Japan, 16.4.1961.

Plot: Members of a high school karate club find themselves up against a band of local *yakuza* punks. Eiji (Wada) meets and falls for Yukiyo (Ashikawa), but her boyfriend Gorō (Hayama) works, unwillingly, for a *yakuza* front corporation. The *yakuza* boss also desires Eiji's mother, a bar hostess, while a *yakuza*'s daughter falls for Eiji. Despite his jealousy, Eiji gets involved against the *yakuza* when they plot against Gorō's life. Some of the criminals are arrested, but Yukiyo and father are kidnapped. In a rescue from *yakuza* headquarters, Eiji and the karate students are put to the test.

Sandanjū no otoko aka ***Shotto gan no otoko*** (散弾銃の男)/*Man With a Shotgun* aka *Man With the Hollow-Tipped Bullets*

Cast: Nitani Hideaki, Ashikawa Izumi, Odaka Yūji, Minamida Yōko, Tanaka Akio, Noro Keisuke, Gō Eiji, Sano Asao, Saga Zenpei. Pro: Nikkatsu (Iwai Kaneo). Scr: Ishii Kiichi, Matsuura Takeo. M: Ikeda Masayoshi. Ph: Shigeyoshi Mine. Ed: Suzuki Akira. Pd: Satani Teruyoshi. O: Higuchi Hiromi (asst. dir.). Japan, 4.6.1961.

Plot: An unnamed man with a shotgun (Nitani) climbs a remote mountain and into the camp of a lumber operation. He finds that the lumber chief's bar hostess and mistress is wearing a pearl necklace that belonged to his own girlfriend. It transpires that she had been raped and killed. After teaming up with the disrespected local sheriff and the latter's sister (Ashikawa), he soon becomes sheriff himself while contending with a smuggling cabal (led by Sano) that kills the former sheriff and even their own boss. The sheriff tracks them from mountain to ocean and the perpetrators are eventually killed or arrested.

Tōge wo wataru wakai kaze (峠を渡る若い風)/*The Wind of Youth Crosses the Mountain Pass* aka *The Wind-of-Youth Group Crosses Over the Mountain Path* aka *New Wind Over the Mountain Pass*

Cast: Wada Kōji, Morikawa Jun, Shimizu Mayumi, Hatsui Kotoe, Fujimura Arihiro, Kaneko Nobuo, Kondō Hiroshi, Aoki Tomio, Chō Hiroshi. Pro: Nikkatsu (Yanagawa Takeo). Scr: Morimoto Yoshihiro, Takeda Ichirō, Takahashi Nīsan (based on the novel by Himeda Yoshirō). M: Ōmori Seitarō. Ph: Isayama Saburō. Pd: Chiba Kazuhiko. O: Higuchi Hiromi (asst. dir.). Japan, 27.8.1961.

Plot: University student Shintarō (Wada) loses his job at an underwear factory, receiving underwear instead of severance, and so he peddles them in the countryside. He encounters a traveling theatre troupe which includes the lead performer's daughter, Misako (Shimizu). He therefore gets involved with this community of show people, good and bad, while various local *yakuza* (Kaneko, Kondō) get involved. The show goes on even after the death of its lead, but the troupe moves on and Shintarō, regretfully, does not go with them.

Kaikyō, chi ni somete (海峡、血に染めて)/*Bloody Channel* aka *Blood-Red Water in the Channel*

Cast: Wada Kōji, Hayama Ryōji, Hanabusa Yuriko, Hisamatsu Kōsuke, Shimizu Mayumi, Gō Eiji, Hatsui Kotoe, Yamaoka Hisano, Hijikata Hiromi, Tamamura Shuntarō. Pro: Nikkastu (Sasai Hideo, Ashida Shōzō). Scr: Tanada Gorō (based on stories by Ōmura Takehiro). M: Ōmori Seitarō. Ph: Mine Shigeyoshi. Ed: Suzuki Akira. Pd: Nakamura Kimihiko. O: Higuchi Hiromi (asst. dir.). Japan, 1.10.1961.

Plot: Adventures of a young coast guard trainee who is posted to his own home town. There he deals with all sorts of problems, from mundane criminality to local eccentrics, but nothing so painful as his tougher elder brother, a sailor (Hayama) who has become linked to a smuggling operation involving the trafficking of foreign refugees. In the face of his younger brother's contempt, and after the death of a young girl, the sailor defends his brother against the horde of smugglers in an elaborate action set piece finale involving the coast guard's pursuit of the pirate ship.

Hyakuman doru wo tatakidase (百万弗を叩き出せ)/*Million Dollar Match*

Cast: Wada Kōji, Noro Keisuke, Sawa Michiko, Kaneko Nobuo, Watanabe Misako, Yamada Goichi, Hirata Daizaburō, Abe Tōru, Tamamura Shuntarō, Saga Zenpei, Chō Hiroshi, Kiura Yūzō, Yanase Shirō. Pro: Nikkatsu (Ashida Shōzō).

Scr: Itō Naohachi (from a story by Yagi Yasutarō). M: Okumura Hajime. Ph: Mine Shigeyoshi. Ed: Suzuki Akira. Pd: Nakamura Kimihiko. Japan, 1.12.1961.

Plot: Two young friends Kinji and Tōkichi (Wada and Noro) leave their rural island for Tokyo, in order to pursue their dreams of being professional boxers. They almost immediately meet some *yakuza* who operate a gym: Tōkichi stays with the yakuza, Kinji does not. The latter passes a boxing tryout associated with rising pro boxer Iino (Hirata). The gym's manager (Kaneko) taps Kinji to replace the difficult Iino, but his first match turns out to be against Tōkichi. Kinji wins, but both are troubled and drown their sorrows, with Kinji falling for the bar waitress. In the meantime, Iino has become a champion, while Tōkichi goes to jail for assaulting him. Soon, Kinji fights Iino for the national title and wins.

1962

Hai-tein yakuza (ハイティーンやくざ)/*Teen Yakuza*

Cast: Kawachi Tamio, Hatsui Kotoe, Matsumoto Noriko, Sugiyama Toshio, Matsuo Kayo, Hara Keiko, Kiura Yūzō, Sano Asao, Hisamatsu Kōsuke, Yanase Shirō. Pro: Nikkatsu (Tomoda Jirō). Scr: Yoshimura Nozomi, Okuzono Mamoru. M: Ibe Harumi. Ph: Hagiwara Kenji. Ed: Suzuki Akira. Pd: Chiba Kazuhiko. O: Endō Saburō (asst. dir.). Japan, 20.6.1962.

Plot: A fatherless student (Kawachi) and his friend Masao (Sugiyama) live in a dangerous neighborhood, working at a cycling track associated with the *yakuza*. He becomes sick of the local gangs when the lame Masao is seduced into their ranks. He gets involved in a brawl at a Tokyo shopping arcade. When the police arrive it transpires that the boy has unwittingly neutralized the local *yakuza* boss. Needing to support his mother (Hatsui) and sister, he accepts gifts from the shop owners to protect them from the *yakuza*, thus becoming an unwitting bodyguard. Because of this he is soon arrested for "extortion," branded as a "high school *yakuza*" news item, and ostracized by the very same neighborhood. The *yakuza* take their revenge and force him into a knife fight with Masao. Masao repents, however, and betrays the *yakuza* operation to the police.

Ore ni kaketa yatsura (俺に賭けた奴ら)/*Those Who Bet on Me* aka *The Guys Who Bet on Me*

Cast: Wada Kōji, Hayama Ryōji, Kawachi Tamio, Shimizu Mayumi, Minamida Yōko, Shiraki Mari, Takashina Kaku, Sano Asao, Tatsuya Fuji, Hiromatsu Saburō, Yanase Shirō, Chō Hiroshi. Pro: Nikkatsu (Yamamoto Takeshi). Scr: Ogawa Ei, Nakano Akira. M: Ōmori Seitarō. Ph: Mine Shigeyoshi. Ed: Suzuki Akira. Pd: Sakaguchi Takeharu. O: Higuchi Hiromi (asst. dir.). Japan, 9.12.1962.

Plot: A truck driver (Wada) has an overweening ambition to be a pro boxer. But he and his trainer (Hayama) and their buddies have to contend, in typical fashion, with low-level *yakuza* enforcers harassing the local gym. Complications ensue involving the *yakuza* culture of fight gambling leading up to the hero's big debut. In the meantime, he is also troubled by the promiscuous manager's wife (Shiraki) while having to choose between an ex-girlfriend (Shimizu) and a nightclub singer (Minamida).

1963

Tantei jimusho 2-3: Kutabare akutō-domo (探偵事務所 23 くたばれ悪党ども)/ *Detective Bureau 2-3: Go to Hell Bastards!* aka *Detective Office 2-3: Damn the Villains!* aka *Detective Bureau 2-3: Down With the Wicked!*

Cast: Shishido Jō, Sasamori Reiko, Shin Kinzō, Kaneo Nobuo, Kawachi Tamio, Hatsui Kotoe, Sano Asao, Hoshi Naomi, Uenoyama Koichi, Kusonoki Masako, Hijikata Hiromi, Itō Toshiaki, Nomura Takashi, Chico Roland. Pro: Nikkatsu (Ashida Shōzō). Scr: Yamazaki Gan (based on the short stories of Ōyabu Haruhiko). M: Ibe Harumi. Ph: Mine Shigeyoshi. Ed: Suzuki Akira. Pd: Sakaguchi Takeharu. O: Higuchi Hiromi (asst. dir.). Japan, 27.1.1963.

Plot: The deliriously complicated hard-boiled adventures of a tough private eye Tajima (Shishido)—hindered by his inept male secretary (Hijikata) and an eccentric crime enthusiast (Hatsui)—as he is initially hired to protect an ex-con (Kawachi) who knows too much and has become a walking target. Tajima seizes the opportunity to pose as an (actually deceased) ex-con himself in order to infiltrate the murderous gang of an impotent old fox (Shin) who smuggles contraband from U.S. military bases and is connected to a powerful corporate leader. Tajima fends off the police chief (Kaneko) while becoming involved with the boss's mistress (Sasamori), whose own father, it turns out, had been killed by the boss. The two of them must escape from an underground garage set aflame.

Yajū no seishun/*Youth of the Beast* aka *Wild Youth* aka *Wild Beast of Youth*

Cast: Shishido Jō, Esumi Eimei, Kazuki Minako, Kobayashi Akiji, Kawachi Tamio, Shin Kinzō, Kaneko Nobuo, Watanabe Misako, Gō Eiji, Yanase Shirō, Kijima Ichirō, Shimizu Masao, Suzuki Mizuho, Kiura Yūzō, Tamamura Shuntarō. Pro: Nikkatsu (Kubo Keinosuke). Scr: Yamazaki Tadaaki, Ikeda Ichirō (based on the novella *Hitokari* by Ōyabu Haruhiko). M: Okumura Hajime. Ph: Nagatsuka Kazue. Ed: Suzuki Akira. Pd: Yokō Yoshinaga. O: Watanabe Noboru (asst. dir.). Japan, 21.4.1963.

Plot: A policeman and a showgirl are dead in what is reported as a love suicide. Meanwhile, a black-clad, violent stranger (Shishido) causes trouble in Asakusa until the crime family of Nomoto (Kobayashi), running a sleek, technologically advanced drug operation takes notice. They decide to hire him; so does the rival gang of Onodera (Shin) after he beats them all up. Soon he is playing both sides. The boss's wife (Kazuki) wants to hire him to discover the identity of Nomoto's powerful "7th mistress." The stranger, we soon learn, is Mizuno, a disgraced ex-policeman seeking to find the killer of his old partner. He has to keep the criminals from learning this, including his loyal but bestial new partner Minami (Esumi). Mizuno's investigation of Nomoto leads to Nomoto's brother Hideo (Kawachi), a sadistic pusher who is gay and extremely sensitive about his mother, who was a prostitute during the war. Nomoto catches his wife and beats her; he catches Mizuno, first immolating his fingernail and then stringing him up. Onodera performs a suicide attack on Nomoto which frees Mizuno. Minami is shot by Mizuno even while killing Nomoto for Mizuno's sake. Mizuno tracks down Nomoto's mistress (Watanabe), who turns out to be the chief of the operation as well as the ex-wife of Mizuno's old partner. As Mizuno discovers using a tape recorder, it was she who murdered the husband and the young girl. Mizuno engineers a situation in which Hideo attacks the mistress and slices her face. Following this act of savage vigilante "justice," he leaves the tape recorder for the police and flees the scene towards an uncertain future.

Akutarō (悪太郎)/*The Bastard* aka *The Young Rebel* aka *The Incorrigible* aka *Bad Tarō* aka *The Unimaginable One*

Cast: Yamauchi Ken, Izumi Masako, Tashiro Midori, Ashida Shinsuke, Noro Keisuke, Sugiyama Hajime, Sano Asao, Takamine Mieko. Pro: Nikkatsu (Takagi Masayuki). Scr: Kasahara Ryōzō (based on the novel by Tōkō Kon). M: Okumura Hajime. Ph: Mine Shigeyoshi. Ed: Suzuki Akira. Pd: Kimura Takeo. O: Endo Saburō (asst. dir.) Japan, 21.9.1963.

Plot: A schoolboy at the beginning of the Taishō era cannot help but act on his libidinous urges. He is expelled from his school in Kobe for an aborted romance with a priest's daughter and sent to a rural school in Toyōka. There he instinctually rebels against the school authorities (Ashida), whose oppressive disciplinarian tactics fail to entirely subdue him. He martials other boys to his instinctual rebellion, while falling passionately in love with and attempting to elope with innocent local girl Emiko (Izumi). But she will not leave her hometown to accompany him to Tokyo, where he sets off on his destiny as a writer.

Kantō mushuku (関東無宿)/*Kantō Wanderer*

Cast: Kobayashi Akira, Itō Hiroko, Itō Yūnosuke, Tonoyama Taiji, Matsubara Chieko, Nakahara Sanae, Noro Keisuke, Abe Tōru, Hirata Daizaburō, Takashina Kaku, Esumi Eimei, Chō Hiroshi. Pro: Nikkatsu (Asada Kenzō). Scr: Yagi Yasutarō (based on the serialized novel *Chitei no uta* by Hirabayashi Taiko). M: Ikeda Masayoshi. Ph: Mine Shigeyoshi. Pd: Kimura Takeo. Ed: Suzuki Akira. O: Kuzuu Masami (asst. dir.). Japan, 23.11.1963.

Plot: Schoolgirl Tokiko's father is Boss Izu (Tonoyama), a failing *yakuza* competing with his sworn brother Yoshida (Abe) for a construction contract. Tokiko (Matsubara) is smitten with Izu's right-hand man Katsuta (Kobayashi) while her girlfriend Hanako (Nakahara) attaches herself to Yoshida's punk, Diamond Fuyu (Hirata). But Katsuta's brutish gang brother (Noro) takes Hanako to a rural suburb of Tokyo and sells her into sexual slavery. Ashamed of his degraded gang, Katsuta vows to buy her freedom, but this brings him back into contact with a woman who fascinates him, Fuyu's older sister Mrs. Iwata (Itō Hiroko) and her husband, Okaru-Hachi (Itō Yūnosuke). Both are professional con artists. Katsuta appears to forcibly seduce Mrs. Iwata and then gambles against Okaru-Hachi with the money meant for Tokiko. Mrs. Iwata warns him against this but in the end helps her husband win. Later, Boss Izu pushes the frustrated Katsuta into dishonorable ways of making money. Katsuta takes a gambling job to support the Izu gang but kills two gamblers in a meaningless quarrel. Knowing that he is headed for jail, Katsuta attacks Yoshida and forces him under threat to submit to Izu. But when Katsuta places himself under arrest, Yoshida does the opposite and convinces Fuyu to assassinate Izu. When Fuyu does so he finds that Hanako, now a geisha, is Boss Izu's new lover and climbing her way up the ladder of influence. Apart from Hanako, all parties end up trapped: Mrs. Iwata in her loveless marriage and Katsuta in jail.

1964

Hana to dotō (花と怒涛)/*The Flowers and the Angry Waves*

Cast: Kobayashi Akira, Kubo Naoko, Matsubara Chieko, Tamagawa Isao, Kawachi Tamio, Yamauchi Akira, Takashina Kaku, Takizawa Osamu, Fukae Shōki, Saga Zenpei, Misaki Chieko, Chō Hiroshi. Pro: Nikkatsu (Yanagawa Takeo). Scr: Abe Keichi, Kimura Takeo, Suzuki Seijun (uncredited). M: Okumura Hajime. Ph: Nagatsuka Kazue. Ed: Suzuki Akira. Pd: Kimura Takeo. O: Kuzū Masami (asst. dir.). Japan, 1964.02.08.

Plot: Kikuchi (Kobayashi), a dissident young *yakuza*, rescues the young Oshige (Matsubara) in the countryside from an arranged marriage with an elderly *yakuza* boss. What to do now? They flee to Tokyo in the 1910s where Kikuchi takes work as the lowest of construction laborers. His passion for the girl has long since cooled, whereas sparks fly between Kikuchi and a spirited geisha Manryū (Kubo) whose tales of colonial Manchuria make Kikuchi dream of freedom and escape. Unfortunately a *yakuza* assassin (Kawachi) and a detective (Tamagawa), himself attracted to Oshige, are closing in. Hiding his past, Kikuchi does his best not to get involved in the struggle between the labor union and the strike-breaking local *yakuza* boss (Takizawa), but is pulled, out of comradeship, back into violence. The proud Manryū saves him from death by submitting herself to be stripped by the *yakuza* boss. On learning that the hired assassin is involved in an uneasy truce between the *yakuza* and the construction company that employs the laborers, Kikuchi tries to intervene. He gets blamed for the truce's failure, beaten and disfigured with a metal chain by the unscrupulous company boss of the construction crew (Yamauchi). Just before he learns that Oshige is pregnant, he kills this boss, who had conspired to murder him. Kikuchi tries to escape to Manchuria with Oshige but everybody, including Manryū, is following him. The assassin kills Manryū instead of Kikuchi; as the ship departs, the policeman lets Kikuchi go, but only at the cost of preventing Oshige from joining him. As the film ends, Kikuchi does not know what to do next.

Nikutai no mon (肉体の門)/*Gate of Flesh*

Cast: Nogawa Yumiko, Shishido Jō, Kasai Satoko, Ishii Tomoko, Tominaga Misako, Matsuo Kayō, Wada Kōji, Tamagawa Isao, Chico Roland, Noro Keisuke. Pro: Nikkatsu (Iwai Kaneo). Scr: Tanada Gorō (based on the novel by Tamura Taijirō). M: Yamamoto Naozumi. Ph: Mine Shigeyoshi. Ed: Suzuki Akira. Pd: Kimura Takeo. O: Kuzū Masami. Japan, 31.5.1964.

Plot: It is the summer of 1946 in ruined, bombed out, desolate Tokyo. Living conditions are abysmal; everyone fights for food; so many women are now prostitutes, many hocking themselves to the American occupiers while controlled by the local *yakuza*. The returned, disillusioned ex-veteran Corporal Ibuki (Shishido) successfully robs a U.S. military base. Injured, he hides out with a clique of prostitutes run by Komasa no Sen (Kasai). Loosely connected to the *yakuza*, this group of women has maintained a certain autonomy, but only at the cost of obeying Sen's rules: never sleep with a foreigner and never sleep with a man for free. To disobey is to be savagely beaten by other girls. The newest recruit is Borneo Maya (Nogawa), a country girl who lost her brother in the war, was pimped by the *yakuza* and then raped by an American. The girls are happy to have Ibuki around, but it becomes clear that one of them will break the rules. Kimono-clad prostitute Michiko (Tominaga), suffused with nostalgia for her hometown, sleeps with Ibuki for free as well as a commuter who reminds her of her husband. Maya reluctantly betrays this secret and Michiko is beaten, her hair shaved off, and expelled. The innocent Maya takes part in the beating after jealously noticing Ibuki's erotic delight at the spectacle of Michiko's nudity. In this spiral of corruption, Maya spitefully seduces an African-American priest (Roland) who has been trying to bring her to church. In a night of drunken revelations, Ibuki drapes himself in the Red Sun while Sen, who apparently cannot have an orgasm, becomes increasingly jealous over him. Later that night, Maya determines to sleep with the near-comatose Ibuki. They have a moment of carnal pleasure and agree to meet later to flee from Tokyo. When Sen finds out what has happened, they string up, beat, and torture Maya, who refuses to give in. Sen and the others tell the *yakuza* that Ibuki is carrying a stash of loot and stolen penicillin. They cooperate with the American Military Police to waylay and shoot him down in the hopes of grabbing the loot, but it turns out that what Ibuki has been carrying is not loot, but the remembrances of a fallen friend. In an ambiguous ending underneath the American flag, Maya says in voice-over that she would rather die than try to survive in this corrupted, venal culture of Occupied Tokyo.

Oretachi no chi ga yurusanai (俺たちの血が許さない)/*Our Blood Will Not Forgive*

Cast: Takahashi Hideki, Kobayashi Akira, Hase Yuri, Hosokawa Chikako, Matsubara Chieko, Ozawa Eitarō, Inoue Shobun, Takashina Kaku, Midorikawa Hiroshi, Noro Keisuke, Yanase Shirō, Hiromatsu Saburō, Chiyoda Hiroshi,

Tomio Aoki, Matsuo Kayo, Chō Hiroshi, Tamamura Shuntarō. Pro: Nikkatsu (Takagi Masayuki). Scr: Takemori Ryuma, Itō Michiko, Hosomi Katsuhiro (based on a novel by Matsuura Takeo). M: Suzuki Tadanori, Ikezawa Hiroshi. Ph: Mine Shigeyoshi. Ed: Suzuki Akira. Pd: Kimura Takeo. O: Kuzū Masami (asst. dir.). Japan, 3.10.1964.

Plot: A prominent *yakuza* (Midorikawa) is assassinated at his home. Before dying, he begs his wife (Hosokawa) not to let his two sons go the way of the *yakuza*. In this she seemingly succeeds. The grown up Shinji (Takahashi), is a happy, dynamic good-for-nothing who skips his job whenever possible and has a propensity for brawling. One day an aged *yakuza* (Inoue) contritely confesses to the two brothers that he was their father's assassin. This inflames Shinji, and after one fist fight too many and the loss of his job, Shinji is tempted to turn to the *yakuza* way. His brother Ryōta (Kobayashi), secretly a lieutenant of the *yakuza* boss Naniwada (Ozawa) beats him up in anger at this idea. Ryōta begs the boss to spare Shinji from the tattooed life, to no avail. Ryōta's girlfriend (Matsubara) also confesses that she is actually a plant for, and probably a mistress of, the suspicious boss. She is soon murdered, and Ryōta faces off against the boss while trying to keep Shinji from joining in and getting blood on his hands. The old assassin joins Ryōta's side; both are shot in the melee. Shinji searches for his dying brother in vain.

1965

Shunpuden (春婦傳)/*Story of a Prostitute* aka *Joy Girls*

Cast: Nogawa Yumiko, Kawachi Tamio, Tamagawa Isao, Ishikawa Tomiko, Imai Kazuko, Wakaba Megumi, Kaji Kentarō, Ozawa Shōichi, Hatsui Kotoe, Fujioka Jūkei, Mori Midori, Matsuo Kayo, Takashina Kaku, Izumi Hideaki, Hisamatsu Kōsuke, Chō Hiroshi. Pro: Nikkatsu (Iwai Kaneo). Scr: Takaiwa Hajime (based on the story by Tamura Taijirō). M: Yamamoto Naozumi. Ph: Nagatsuka Kazue. Ed: Suzuki Akira. Pd: Kimura Takeo. O: Kuzuū Masumi (asst. dir.). Japan, 27.2.1965.

Plot: Harumi leaves occupied Shanghai after savaging a lover who has jilted her. She has been hired as a "comfort woman" for the Japanese army on the Manchurian front. She and the other prostitutes are expected to provide "sexual relief" for hundreds of ordinary servicemen in the daytime, then consort and sleep with the officers at night. The adjutant to the general (Tamagawa) treats Harumi with brutal rapacity. Harumi is deeply ashamed about her body's response to the adjutant's love-making; she has fantasies of rebellion against him and tries to enact them by having sex with the adjutant's insecure orderly, Corporal Mikami (Kawachi), himself the victim of the adjutant's abuses. Mikami ambivalently rejects her attentions. Harumi cannot comprehend why grown men like Mikami accept this kind of domination from those of higher rank. A demoted officer, Uno (Kaji), an intellectual and possibly a former communist, is also a target of abuse. Because of constant unrest and

PLA (People's Liberation Army) activity in the Chinese village near to the base, the battalion officers inflict brutal punishment on both the Chinese and the soldiers who try to desert. Harumi is romantically attached to Mikami but enraged by how he treats her despite his obvious attraction. The two eventually sleep together, although Mikami is near-impotent. Another prostitute, Shinako (Imai) has high hopes for an arranged marriage with one of the Japanese farmers in the territory, only to return, desolate, after discovering that her intended is severely mentally handicapped. During a night attack by the PLA, Mikami is knocked unconscious and left for dead by his comrades in the trenches. Harumi courageously rushes through the bombs to save him, and when she cannot, lies down beside him. They are both captured by the PLA and find some of the Japanese deserters amongst them, including Uno, who invites them to join the PLA and march to safety. Harumi is overwhelmingly in favour of survival but Mikami is sick with the thought of joining the Chinese rebels. The unsympathetic Uno abandons them in disgust. As the Japanese approach, Harumi tries to leave Mikami behind and save herself: but she is unable to abandon him. The two go back to the base where Mikami is scheduled for a quick court martial and execution, ostensibly because he became a "deserter" when left for dead; in reality the adjutant is having his revenge. The PLA attack the base; in the ensuing defeat of the Japanese, the couple has a final chance at freedom, but as Mikami decides to blow himself up, Harumi inexplicably runs towards him at the last moment; they are both killed. The other prostitutes, looked after by an older Korean woman (Hatsui), decide they must try to survive this war at all costs.

Akutarō-den: warui hoshi no shita de mo (悪太郎伝　悪い星の下でも)/*Stories of Bastards: Born Under a Bad Star* aka *Story of Akutarō: In Spite of an Unlucky Star*

Cast: Yamauchi Ken, Hatsui Kotoe, Izumi Masako, Nogawa Yumiko, Hirata Daizaburō, Azuma Michie, Noro Keisuke, Benisawa Yōko, Yoko Tayōko, Tatara Jun, Chō Hiroshi, Yanase Shirō. Pro: Nikkatsu (Takagi Masayuki). Scr: Kasahara Ryūzō (based on the novel by Tōkō Kon). M: Okumura Hajime. Ph: Nagatsuka Kazue. Ed: Suzuki Akira. Pd: Kimura Takeo. O: Kuzū Masami (asst. dir.). Japan, 25.8.1965.

Plot: A student named Suzuki (Yamauchi) grows up on a poor farm in Hirano, near Osaka, in the early 1930s. He industriously delivers milk to save up for a good high school. An acquaintance, Mishima (Hirata), is punished for taking an evening walk with a girl, while at the same time a member (Noro) of the school "public morals" committee is making love with Mishima's cousin. Out of a sense of righteousness, Suzuki challenges this hypocrite to a fight. Meanwhile he is attracted to Mishima's younger sister (Izumi), but a teenage temptress, Kazuko (Nogawa) is attracted to him. He liaises with the latter at an inn, only to find his own father, a compulsive gambler, being beaten by the local *yakuza*. The younger Suzuki impulsively attacks them and must then go into hiding. After another inevitable scrap with the gamblers, Suzuki is arrested, then bailed, and has to quit school, thus destroying his dream of academic success. When he accidentally comes upon the wedding of the girl he loved, Mishima's betrayed sister, he repents and leaves the village to find a new way of life.

Irezumi ichidai (刺青一代)/*A Generation of Tatoos* aka *One Generation of Tattoos* aka *Tattooed Life* aka *The White Tiger Tattoo* aka *Life of a Tattooed Man*

Cast: Takahashi Hideki, Hananomoto Kotobuki, Izumi Masako, Itō Hiroko, Yamauchi Akira, Takashina Kaku, Komatsu Hōsei, Odaka Yūji, Noro Keisuke, Matsuo Kayo, Kawazu Seizaburō, Hino Michio, Chiyoda Hiroshi, Chō Hiroshi, Saga Zenpei. Pro: Nikkatsu (Sugiyama Nobutaka, Takagi Masayuki). Scr: Naoi Kinya, Hattori Kei. M: Ikeda Masayoshi. Ph: Takamura Kuratarō. Ed: Suzuki Akira. Pd: Kimura Takeo. O: Kuzū Masami (asst. dir.). Japan, 13.11.1965.

Plot: In the 1930s, the *yakuza* have decided to rub out the killer White Fox Tetsu (Kobayashi). Tetsu's younger brother Kenji (Hananomoto), an art student, follows his brother and shoots the would-be assassin. The bitter Tetsu must now take Kenji with him on the run; they flee to a port town in Western Japan in the hopes of getting to colonial Manchuria, but are swindled by Yamano (Komatsu), who is both a con man and an informal agent for a Manchurian land development cartel connected to local government and to the *yakuza*. Hiding his *yakuza* tattoos, Tetsu gets work with a sympathetic construction labor foreman (Takashina). Tetsu shyly flirts with Midori (Izumi) the forward sister of the company boss (Yamauchi), whom Tetsu does not trust. It is actually the boss's company manager (Odaka) who is untrustworthy, getting payoffs from the local *yakuza* while trying to marry Midori. He tries to frame Tetsu for his own collusion but is unsuccessful. Meanwhile, Kenji has developed an obsession with the boss's wife (Itō), who views him bathing one day. He wants to sculpt her nude body; tensions emerge forthwith between the older couple. It turns out that the boss is an understanding soul who wants to help Tetsu, but when the manager uncovers Tetsu's *yakuza* past, the brothers must flee from the law. Tetsu tells Midori that he is a no good *yakuza* who cannot live a decent life. Unfortunately Yamano, who has been helping the *yakuza* boss (Kawazu) try to muscle in on the construction contract, spots Kenji on his way to see the boss's wife one last time. This leads to Kenji's death at the hands of the *yakuza*. Tetsu is now free to reveal his tattoos and resume the life of a killer in a stylized, operatic finale of vengeful massacre. Tetsu goes off to jail and says goodbye to Midori; at least his brother, he says, died for love.

1966

Kawachi karumen (河内カルメン)/*Carmen from Kawachi*

Cast: Nogawa Yumiko, Wada Kōji, Kawachi Tamio, Sano Asao, Kuwayama Shōichi, Kusunoki Masako, Saga Zenpei, Miyagi Chikako, Matsuo Kayo, Hino Michio, Itō Ruriko, Ōtsuji Shirō, Noro Keisuke. Pro: Nikkatsu (Sakagami Shizuo). Scr: Miki Katsumi (based on the novel by Tōkō Kon). M: Kosugi Taiichirō.

Ph: Mine Shigeyoshi. Ed: Suzuki Akira. Pd: Kimura Takeo. O: Kuzū Masumi (asst. dir.). Japan, 7.2.1966.

Plot: In a rural village in the old province of Kawachi, high school girl Tsuyuko (Nogawa) is smitten with the son of the local factory owner Akira (Wada), but when he makes a pushy sexual overture one day on the road, they part—and Tsuyuko is seized and raped by two passing thugs. She finds no comfort at her family home in the mountains: her mother, in full knowledge of her defeated father, is in a superstitious and sexual thrall to a *yamabushi* (Kuwayama), or traditional mountain holy man. Tsuyuko leaves home without looking back and after an ellipsis we discover her as a hostess in Osaka's Club Dada, where she is repulsed by the antics of the drunken *saririman*. One night she gets drunk and (apparently) sleeps with one rather pathetic middle-aged worker at a credit union, Kanzo (Sano). Her girlfriends tell her to make herself a mistress of a wealthier man, but when Kanzo foolishly loses his job out of obsession with her, the pitying Tsuyuko takes him in. Soon, she becomes attached to a modeling agency run by Yōko (Kusonoki). She leaves Kanzo and briefly moves in with Yōko but, as a small town girl, is not prepared for the latter's sexual advances. She departs as a somewhat worldlier woman and begins a relationship with a painter (Kawachi). She hesitates to become a mistress to his patron, a worldly, elderly magnate (Saga) who is smitten with her. At this point, however, Akira re-enters her life. Somewhat impoverished, Akira dreams of getting enough money (by any means) to build his own *onsen* (hot springs resort) and Tsuyuko is sucked into the dream, until it becomes apparent that Akira has made a deal with the magnate to covertly make pornographic films of Tsuyuko. Furious and appalled, but moved by Akira's desperate situation, Tsuyuko appears to make love to him as requested. But the disillusion is permanent, and the next day she leaves him. Nevertheless, the magnate soon dies and leaves a fortune to Tsuyuko. She returns home only to find the *yamabushi* sleeping with her younger sister. With no other recourse, Tsuyuko lures him to a waterfall in the hopes of pushing him in: he slips, and she lets him die. She is initially hysterical; but life goes on.

Tokyo nagaremono (東京流れ者)/*Tokyo Drifter*

Cast: Watari Tetsuya, Kita Ryūji, Matsubara Chieko, Nitani Hideaki, Esumi Eimei, Kawachi Tamio, Tamagawa Isao, Chō Hiroshi, Go Eiji, Yoshida Takeshi, Hino Michio, Kiura Yūzō, Tamamura Shuntarō. Pro: Nikkatsu (Nakagawa Tetsurō). M: Kaburagi Hajime. Scr: Kawauchi Kōhan (Suzuki Seijun and Kimura Takeo, uncredited). Ph: Mine Shigeyoshi. Ed: Inouye Chikaya. Pd: Kimura Takeo. O: Kuzū Masami (asst. dir.). Japan, 10.4.1966.

Plot: Tetsu (Watari) is the young lieutenant of the doting, fatherly *yakuza* Boss Kurata (Kita), who has attempted to go straight. Kurata's unprincipled rival Ōtsuka (Esumi) uses this as an opportunity to steal a new office building that Kurata wants to buy from the honorable businessman Yoshii (Hino). Ōtsuka begins his reign of terror by beating up Tetsu, who is not allowed to fight back, murdering Yoshii, and attempting to kidnap Tetsu's oft disappointed and somewhat masochistic girlfriend Chiharu (Matsubara). Tetsu prevents Ōtsuka from forcing Kurata to sign over the deed to the building, but in the ensuing struggle, Kurata fires his gun on a sexually threatening young secretary. With both sides fearing exposure for these murders, Kurata's slippery *consigliere* (Chō) proposes a truce on the condition that Tetsu leaves town for the sake of peace. Tetsu therefore drifts away from his home and his girl out of loyalty to Kurata. In snowbound Yamagata, Tetsu stays with the local *oyabun*, a Kurata ally, but is hunted down by assassin "Viper" Tatsuya (Kawachi). Their presence in Yamagata incites a local gang war that causes suffering to all concerned. Tetsu's life is saved by an ex-*yakuza* drifter who was betrayed by Ōtsuka, nicknamed "Shooting Star" (Nitani). Shooting Star, who seems drawn to the unfriendly Tetsu, warns the younger man not to trust his *yakuza* bosses, including Kurata. Sure enough, Kurata inexplicably accepts a lousy deal with Ōtsuka that leases him the office building in return for killing Tetsu and pimping Chiharu out to Ōtsuka. After Tetsu survives a half-hearted assassination attempt, the vengeful hero returns to Tokyo and, in an orgy of violence, wipes out both the Kurata and Ōtsuka gangs. Kurata, disgraced, slashes his own wrists. The stage is set for Tetsu to reclaim Chiharu and Kurata's gang: instead, he callously declares that it is unseemly for a drifter to walk with a woman, and walks away from the neon haze of Tokyo, a loner by choice.

Kenka erejii (けんかえれじい)/*Elegy For Violence* aka *Fighting Elegy* aka *Born Fighter* aka *Elegy for a Quarrel*

Cast: Takahashi Hideki, Asano Junko, Kawazu Yūsuke, Kataoka Mitsuo, Onda Seijirō, Tamagawa Isao, Miyagi Chikako, Sano Asao, Noro Keisuke, Katō Takeshi, Chō Hiroshi, Kayama Aiko, Hino Michio, Matsuo Kayo, Midorigawa Hiroshi. Pro: Nikkatsu (Ōtsuka Kazu). Scr: Shindō Kaneto, Suzuki Seijun (uncredited) (based on a novel by Suzuki Takashi). M: Yamamoto Naozumi. Ph: Hagiwara Kenji. Ed: Tanji Mutsuo. Pd: Kimura Takeo. O: Kuzū Masami (asst. dir.). Japan, 9.11.1966.

Plot: In the mid-1930s, Kiroku (Takahashi) is a Catholic student at Okayama Middle School who cannot seem to stop fighting with his peers. His violent energy has something to do with his hormones and lust for Michiko, the daughter of the innkeeper with whom he lodges. Kiroku idealizes Michiko's virginal purity but has no outlet for his sexual attraction other than creative masturbation. At school, he joins the OSMS group, a patriotic and mock-military student association. The hypocritical, cowardly club president Takuan (Kawazu) manipulates the others into doing his fighting for them. He denounces Kiroku for being seen with a girl, Michiko. This precipitates all out war between Kiroku and the club, using such savage home made weapons as shoe cleats. Kiroku is aided by another student, the self-proclaimed master of martial arts Turtle (Kataoka), who "trains" him in painful endurance. With Turtle encouraging his rebellious streak, Kiroku duels with the local military instructor. The school brings in Kiroku's well-to-do father (Onda) to reign him in, but the father can't seem to help indulging what he sees as a youthful competitive spirit. Turtle tries to reason with the school administrators but ends up shooting at them with dried beans. Kiroku is expelled and packed off to a school in rural Aizu, which is proud of its samurai tradition. Soon Kiroku is fighting the entire kendo team in a nighttime guerrilla battle that resembles actual warfare. The school headmaster (Tamagawa) should punish Kiroku, but instead condones his fierceness: "One must be a man above all." One winter day, Kiroku glimpses the silent, grim ultranationalist revolutionary Kita Ikki, and this seems somehow to change him. Michiko travels across the country to visit Kiroku, confessing to him that she believes herself to be frigid. The "mature" Kiroku must reject attachment to a woman as detrimental to his martial spirit. As Michiko trudges home in the snow she appears to be knocked down by an implacable column of soldiers on their way to China. Kiroku, meanwhile, learns of the 1936 Tokyo revolt of young ultranationalist officers inspired by Kita, and is inspired to join the biggest fight of all: the war.

1967

Koroshi no rakuin (殺しの烙印)/*Branded to Kill*

Cast: Shishido Jō, Annu Mari, Ogawa Mariko, Nanbara Kōji, Minami Hiroshi, Tamagawa Isao, Yamatoya Atsushi. Pro: Nikkatsu (Iwai Kaneo). Scr: "Guryū Hachirō" (Suzuki, Yamatoya Atsushi, Kimura Takeo, Sone Chūsei, Tanaka Yōzo, Okata Yutaka, Yamaguchi Seiichirō). M: Yamamoto Naozumi. Ph: Nagatsuka Kazue. Ed: Suzuki Akira. Pd: Kawahara Sukezō. O: Kuzū Masami (asst. dir.). Japan, 15.6.1967.

Plot: Goro Hanada (Shishido) is ranked as Japan's Number 3 assassin. He returns from his honeymoon to meet his boss, Yabuhara (Tamagawa), who represents the shadowy "Organization." During the meeting, Hanada's wife Mami (Ogawa) starts cheating with the boss, while Hanada indulges in his addiction to the smell of boiled rice, which sexually arouses him. Hanada's assignment is to escort a mysterious passenger to Nagano. Hanada's partner Kasuga (Minami) has lost his ranking due to alcohol and women. During the trip, Kasuga is killed when he loses his nerve, but Hanada manages to kill the No. 2 assassin, while the mysterious passenger (Nanbara) reveals himself to be an excellent shot. On the way back, Hanada is picked up by Misako (Annu Mari), a mysterious woman who kills birds and claims that she wants to die. At home, Hanada violently makes love to Mami but thinks of Misako. Hanada carries out three ingenious assassinations for Yabuhara. Misako hires him to do a fourth job, but he misses the target when a butterfly settles on his gunsights. Hanada's career is now in ruins; when he returns home his wife shoots him. Wounded, he staggers to Misako's apartment, a nightmarish place covered with dead butterflies. Hanada tries to rape Misako, but the latter is hardly defenseless, and both of them attempt to kill each other. Misako says she loves Hanada, who panics and runs away, devastated by his inability to kill her: has he lost his professional detachment? Hanada tracks down his wife Mami, who was ordered to kill him by the Organization, which is linked to an international diamond smuggling scheme with political implications. Hanada murders his wife, then discovers that Misako was kidnapped and tortured by the Organization for failing to kill him. Hanada fights and kills five operatives, but then comes face to face with his former passenger, who turns out to be the phantom Number One Killer. Over several days, the two try to kill each other with sniper rifles, and Hanada begins to crack under the pressure of Number One's cat and mouse game. Eventually, Hanada overcomes his emotions and fights back, desiring to become Number One himself. In an empty boxing ring, Hanada and Number One shoot each other, and Hanada accidentally shoots the bandaged, invalid Misako when she appears on the scene. Hanada falls out of the boxing ring, whether alive or dead we cannot tell.

1977

Hishū monogatari 悲愁物語/*A Tale of Sorrow* aka *A Story of Sorrow and Sadness* aka *Sad Story*

Cast: Shiraki Yōko, Harada Yoshio, Enami Kyōko, Okada Masumi, Sano Shūji, Asao Koike, Noro Keisuke, Tamagawa Isao, Wada Kōji, Nakaya Noboru, Ashihara Kuniko, Matsuo Kayo, Shishido Jō. Pro: Shōchiku (Asada Kenzō, Kajiwara Ikki, Kawano Yasuhiro, Fujioka Yutaka, Nomura Yoshiki). Scr: Yamatoya Atsushi (based on a manga by Kajiwara Ikki). M: Miho Keitarō, Tomi Taiichirō. Ph: Mori Masaru. Ed: Suzuki Akira. Ph: Kikukawa Yoshie. O: Saitō Nobuyuki (asst. dir.). Japan, 21.5.1977.

Plot: A corporate conglomerate hits upon the idea of creating a female celebrity golfer as a way of selling a new line of sporting clothes. They recruit down-and-out sports agent Miyake (Harada) *pour cherchez la femme*. He selects a young, unknown pro-golfer, Reiko (Shiraki), who lives with her kid brother. Working under the best hired professionals, Reiko struggles to better her game and prepare for a major golfing tournament in just a short time. Her faith in and attraction to her agent supplements her innate self-confidence and work ethic. She does well in the tournament and wins the next one, albeit demonstrating a certain undue arrogance; she finally sleeps with Miyake. The process of becoming a media celebrity now begins. She poses on a golf course in a bikini and appears on endless, sexist television talk shows. She gathers a fan base. But her growing discontent with her endlessly profit-spinning corporate managers finds a somewhat perverse outlet: an overenthusiastic fan/neighbor (Enami) whose attentions Reiko had high-handedly rebuffed. During a drunken car ride home with Miyake, who pushes her to play against a European champion, Miyake hits the same neighbor and injures her leg. The neighbor can now blackmail Reiko into all sorts of favors, of which open access to her house is just the start. Reiko takes no rational action to escape this woman's clutches, as if her suffering is a masochistic rebellion against her patriarchal bosses. With the neighbor making a shambles of Reiko's career, Miyake is asked to intercede but is ineffectual; Reiko has lost all trust in him. Her brother suffers a messy upbringing as well; life seems to take place in a sort of time warp wherein it takes on the appearance of a pre-war childhood. Reiko allows her tormentor, and now the local neighbors as well, to trash her home and physically abuse her person. At a hellish party, in which the neighbor admits that she threw herself in front of Reiko's car on purpose, the locals and their children throw Reiko to the floor and strip her nude. The neighbor prostitutes Reiko to her own husband. Reiko, reaching the bottom of celebrity debasement, sleeps with the husband willfully, and the neighbor becomes jealous. Reiko's kid brother finally has had enough of these perversities and suddenly kills everyone in the house, not only the neighbors but an "innocent" stalker/fan (Noro) who happens to be there as well. As if in an unspoken pact between the two siblings in which Reiko must die as a martyr, her brother shoots her and torches the house.

1980

Zigeunerweisen (ツィゴイネルワイゼン)

Cast: Fujita Toshiya, Ōtani Naoko, Harada Yoshio, Ōkusu Michiyo, Tamagawa Isao, Maro Akaji, Kimura Yūki, Makishi Kisako, Sasaki Sumie, Tamaki Nagamasa, Kiki Kirin. Pro: Cinema Placet aka Cinema Purasetto (Arato Genjirō). Scr: Tanaka Yōzō (based on the novella *Sarasate no ban* and the story "Yamakata bōshi" by Uchida Hyakken). M: Kawachi Kaname. Ph: Nagatsuka Kazue. Ed: Kamiya Nobutake. Pd: Kimura Takeo, Tada Yoshito. O: Yamada Sumio (asst. dir.). Japan, 1.4.1980.

Plot: A woman washes up dead on a Kamakura beach, and a wandering intellectual named Nakasago (Harada) is implicated. He tells his friend, the narrator/protagonist Aochi (Fujita) that she committed suicide. As the two of them hang about Kamakura, Nakasago aggressively courts a geisha named Oine (Ōtani), whose resistance breaks down. A year later, Aochi finds that Nakasago has married a woman named Sono who is Oine's virtual double. Nakasago abandons Sono just after they have a child. Because of this, Aochi visits Sono at his friend's house and has the uncanny experience of being haunted either by Sono herself, or by something or someone else. Months pass. Aochi is bothered by the absent presence of Nakasago: the strange behavior of his ultramodern wife (Ōkusu) and the testimony of a dying sister-in-law lead Aochi to fear that Nakasago is sleeping with his wife. It transpires that Sono has died during a fever outbreak and Oine is taking care of Sono's child. Nakasago himself apparently has died on one of his wanderings, although Aochi seems to meet him again. One day a surprisingly cold Oine visits Aochi to tell him that Nakasago's daughter is communicating with Nakasago in her sleep, and that the latter had demanded some books and records that Aochi once borrowed (including the titular record by Pablo Sarasate). Aochi denies it, but is compelled to visit Nakasago's house once more; while there, he cannot be sure whether Oine's personality and memories correspond to Oine or Sono. Leaving, Aochi meets Nakasago's child on a bridge. She tells him that Nakasago is alive and he, Aochi, is really dead. Aochi tries to turn around, but finds himself confronting the child again, this time on a pier full of votive candles, with a wreathed funeral boat lying underneath.

1981

Kagerō-za (陽炎座)/*Mirage Theatre* aka *Heat-Haze Theatre*

Cast: Matsuda Yūsaku, Ōkusu Michiyo, Nakamura Katsuo, Kaga Mariko, Kusuda Eriko, Harada Yoshio, Ōtomo Ryūtarō, Azuma Emiko, Itō Hiroko, Tamagawa Isao, Maro Akaji, Sano Asao, Esumi Eimei, Kiki Kirin. Pro: Cinema Placet aka Cinema Purasetto (Arato Genjirō). Scr: Tanaka Yōzō (based on the short stories *Shunchū* and *Shunchū gokoku* by Izumi Kyōka). M: Kawachi Kaname. Ph: Nagatsuka Kazue. Ed: Suzuki Akira. Pd: Ikeya Noriyoshi. O: Kuzū Masami (directorial collaboration), Shiraishi Kōichi (asst. dir.). Japan, 29.8.1981.

Plot: *Shinpa* playwright Matsuzaki has a series of surreal encounters with a tycoon (Nakamura), and two women outside of a hospital. Sometime later he meets his patron—the same businessman, Tamawaki. One of the women is Tamawaki's recently married second wife Shinako (Ōkusu), who Matsuzaki appears to make love to. The other woman is apparently Tamawaki's first wife Oine (Kusuda), who was allegedly bedridden at the time Matsuzaki claims to have encountered her, and is now deceased. Matsuzaki is drawn into Tamawaki's world of decadence and wealth as a passive observer. He receives a mysterious communication from Shinako asking him to come to Kanazawa and join her in a double suicide. Still knowing nothing about Shinako and her motives, Matsuzaki is incredulous but fascinated. Despite much intimation that Tamawaki knows about this (intended) affair and that Matsuzaki is in danger, the playwright goes to Kanazawa. On the road he meets an itinerant anarchist (Harada) who has kidnapped a wealthy socialite as a political statement, but now has become attached to her. Matsuzaki attends a freemason ceremony in which the participants solemnly pass around cheap clay figures, then look inside the clay figures to find smaller, obscene figures inside. They then smash them. The chief freemason (Ōtomo) tells Matsuzaki that his son has died mysteriously in the process of jealously spying on his girlfriend. The son saw her meet another man who turned out to be himself, his own double. Matsuzaki has an uncanny erotic encounter with Oine; things come to a head when he finds Tamawaki and Shinako at a local amateur theatre production. The children putting on the performance mysteriously reveal Tamawaki's past through staged recreations: they reveal how he drove Oine insane by forcing her, a German woman, to take on the eye and hair-color of a Japanese woman; and how Shinako has tried to rebel against his tyranny through adultery. Confused by these uncanny happenings, Tamawaki urges Matsuzaki to commit suicide with Shinako and leaves. During the performance a mysterious female deity seems to emerge who demand's Shinako's life. Shinako leaps from the stage, destroying it entirely, and seems to drown herself in a tub of water. Matsuzaki fights the deity in order to reach Shinako and also seems to plunge himself in the water. Is Matsuzaki dead or alive? We see him as he converses with various characters, to whom he explains that it was Tamawaki who died with Shinako, not himself. However, nothing is certain: in the last scene, Matsuzaki sees himself (his double) join with Shinako, the very scenario of death that the freemason had imparted to him.

1985

Kapone ōi ni naku (カポネ大いに泣く)/*Capone Cries a Lot*

Cast: Hagiwara Kenichi, Tanaka Yūko, Sawada Kenji, Emoto Akira, Laurie Belisle, Chuck Wilson, Randy Rice, Kiki Kirin, Bengaru. Pro: K enterprise; Nippon Columbia/System Japan/Shōchiku (distributor) (Nakamura Kenichi, Okuyama Kazuyoshi). Scr: Kimura Takeo, Yamatoya Atsushi (based on the novel by Kajiyama Toshiyuki). M: Inouye Takayuki. Ph: Fujisawa Junichi, Takada Akira. Ed: Suzuki Akira. Pd: Kimura Takeo, Maruyama Yūji. O: Takahashi Masaharu (asst. dir.). Japan, 16.2.1985.

Plot: In the 1930s, a geisha (Tanaka) who was involved in an adulterous affair is forced to wear the tattoo of an octopus on her back as a kind of punishment. She develops a love for a young touring actor (Hagiwara) who wants to be a *naniwabushi* performer. They run away from those who claim to possess them and take a ship to San Francisco. Despite the actor's desire to perform, the couple's lack of funds shortly determine that they become a beggar and a prostitute, respectively. They meet a third immigrant Gorō (Sawada) who wants to stage their act at a posh nightclub; *naniwabushi* does not go down well, so the actor does variety acts dressed as a samurai. Al Capone's Chicago operation wants to move in on their new home, San Francisco's Chinatown. Unfortunately, the three immigrants are involved in their own, local, illicit liquor production. Their downward path against this opposition takes them to Chicago, where the geisha dies in a car accident, Gorō dies from eating poisonous *fugu*, and the actor performs *seppuku* with the help of his American girlfriend.

Rupan sansei: Babiron no ōgon no densetsu (ルパン三世 バビロンの黄金伝説)/ *Lupin the Third: The Legend of the Gold of Babylon*

Directors: Suzuki Seijun, Yoshida Shigetsugu. Voice cast: Yamada Yasuo, Kobayashi Kiyoshi, Masuyama Eiko, Naya Gorō, Inoue Makio, Katsusei Asaki, Shimazu Saeko, Shiozawa Toki, Carousel Maki aka Karūseru Maki. Pro: Tōhō/ Nippon Television/Yomiuri Telecasting (Takei Hidehiko, Sano Kazushichi, Katayama Tetsuo). Scr: Yamatoya Atsushi, Urasawa Yoshio, Monkey Punch (based on the mangas of Monkey Punch). M: Ōno Yūji, Suzuki Seiji. Ph: Ishigaki Tsutomu. Ed: Tsurubuchi Masatoshi. O: Aoki Yūzō, Owashi Hidetoshi, Yanagino Tatsuo (animation directors). Japan, 13.7.1985.

Plot: Another animated adventure of master thief *Rupan sansei*/Lupin III, his gang of compatriots, his amorous rival Fujiko, and pursuing police detective Zenigata. Lupin is in New York City chasing down clay tablets that have surfaced, somewhere in the city, indicating the location of the original (golden) Tower of Babel. A homeless old lady appears to leave Lupin a candlestick and a Babylonian word as clues to the mystery. Meanwhile, Zenigata assembles a squadron of international policewomen to arrest Lupin. Back in Europe on the Orient Express, Lupin and the police suffer a helicopter attack from the Italian mafia, led by the son of Lucky Luciano, who also wants to find the tower; Lupin escapes. His visions of the old woman lead to the Middle East and to a statue of a winged lion, which Fujiko snatches away. Now Lupin must return to

New York to help Fujiko escape the mafia. It turns out that aliens, who travel by means of Halley's Comet, are making off with the tower. They had greedily tried to take it in ancient times, but fumbled the pick-up operation. The tower fell back on Earth to rest under what is now Madison Square Garden. Lupin chases the airborne tower but the gold is ground up and destroyed in the atmosphere, where it will stay.

1991

Yumeji (夢二)

Cast: Sawada Kenji, Mariya Tomoko, Harada Yoshio, Ōkusu Michiyo, Miyagi Chikako, Miyazaki Masumi, Hirota Reona, Bandō Tamasaburō, Hasegawa Kazuhiko, Yo Kimiko, Maro Akaji. Pro: Cinema Placet, Arato Genjirō (Akiyama Michio, Son Kahō). Scr: Tanaka Yōzō. M: Umebayashi Shigeru, Kawachi Kaname. Ph: Fujisawa Junichi. Ed: Suzuki Akira. Pd: Ikeya Noriyoshi. O: Saisha Yasushi (asst. dir.). Japan, 13.4.1991.

Plot: Fantasia on the life of the amorous watercolorist and poet Yumeji Takehisa, centering around a visit to the mountains of Kanazawa. It begins with what seems to be a dream of Yumeji killed in a pistol duel by a strange man. In Kanazawa, he desires to paint or seduce (for he cannot tell the difference) an uncanny "widow" (Mariya) whom he sees on a lake. Her husband is apparently dead by a mad killer (Hasegawa) hiding in the mountains. But soon the husband Wakiya (Harada) turns up again, living the high life in the small village and drawing Yumeji into his revels. Yumeji is obsessed by with the widow, despite the danger of the lurking killer. The latter eventually hangs himself with Yumeji's help, while Wakiya departs by train—a strange behavior for a ghost. The widow finally offers herself to Yumeji, who demurs, and somehow his painting of her gets accomplished.

1993

Kekkon (結婚)/*Marriage*

Directors: Suzuki Seijun, Nagao Hiroshi, Onchi Hideo. Cast: Harada Yoshio, Harada Kiwako, Naitō Taketoshi, Matsubara Chieko, Bengaru, Jinnai Taketori, Natori Yūko, Musaka Naomasa, Nakai Kiichi, Satō Koichi, Hasegawa Hatsunori, Takeuchi Tōru, Kawakami Mieko, Washio Isako, Ishikawa Kimiko, Toni Pedecine. Pro: Seshīru/Shōchiku (Masaoka Dōitsu, Nakagawa Shigehiro, Nabeshima Tashio, Takeda Shigeru). Scr: Urasawa Yoshio. M: Inoue Takayuki. Ph: Fujisawa Junichi. Ed: Uraoka Keiichi. Pd: Ikeya Noriyoshi. O: Satō Yoshio (asst. dir.). Japan, 24.4.1993.

Plot: A triptych of three short films in which Suzuki directs the first segment. A vain actor (Jinnai) agrees to a marriage proposal in the hopes that the news will boost his popularity. But it turns out to be a sham as his intended (Harada Kiwako) is in a long-term affair with another actor which all parties want to conceal. The enraged groom wants to cancel the marriage but it is too late. However on the marriage day it is not the intended bride who shows up but, by some inexplicable cause, a loving high school sweetheart whom the actor had left behind.

2001

Pisutoru opera (ピストルオペラ)/*Pistol Opera*

Cast: Esumi Makiko, Yamaguchi Sayoko, Hira Mikijirō, Nagase Masatoshi, Kiki Kirin, Hanae Kan, Jan B. Woudstra, Sawada Kenji, Watanabe Kensaku, Kato Haruko, Aoki Tomio, Morishita Yoshiyuki, Tanaka Yōji. Pro: Shōchiku/Dentsu/JVC/TV Tokyo/Ogura Jimsyo Co. (Ogura Satoru, Katashima Ikki). Scr: Itō Kazunori, Guryū Hachizuke; Kimura Takeo and Suzuki Seijun (uncred.). M: Tezuma Masafumi, Uemura Shūta (musical directors). Ph: Maeda Yonezō. Ed: Suzuki Akira. Pd: Kimura Takeo. O: Higuchi Shinji (special effects), Ihara Shinji (asst. dir.), Nagamachi Kanako (costumes). Japan, 27.10.2001.

Plot: Stray Cat (Esumi) is The Guild's No. 3 assassin. She receives contracts from the veiled Guild agent Uekyo (Yamaguchi). A young girl (Hanae) seems to be present whenever she kills someone. Stray Cat lives a solitary, independent life in the country with an elderly woman (Kiki). Soon she is receiving contracts to kill the other, eccentric Guild assassins, including the unseen No. 1 Killer "Hundred Eyes." Stray Cat's competitiveness is recklessly encouraged by the aged, crippled Hanada Gorō (Hira), who survived his travails in 1967 but is a wreck of his former self. The infrared dot that signifies a sniper target starts appearing everywhere in Stray Cat's path. A courteous sharpshooter in black (Nagase) appears claiming to be No. 1. Stray Cat slays him in the forest, but the red dot does not disappear . . . Hanada claims that No. 1 is still alive and that he/she has a list of the real names of all the killers. Stray Cat and her sexually precocious follower seem to drift until she confronts the agent Uekyo as the *real* Hundred Eyes. Uekyo uses the young girl (and other street girls) as her "eyes"; they, mysteriously, even share her name. Uekyo grew bored and created a competition amongst the assassins, waiting to challenge the last survivor. In a monologue, Uekyo confesses that at first she was appalled by the Americanization of Japan evident in post-war films, but then had a vision in which all flags, Japanese, American, etc., were all "bloody, muddy, and shitty." In a location that seems like a time-warp or metamorphosing theatre full of mobile artistic and cultural artefacts, Uekyo is killed by Stray Cat. The latter is now No. 1, and so Hanada makes a pathetic attempt, in front of Mt. Fuji, to kill her. Stray Cat tells him piteously that he is not a "pro," and promptly shoots herself.

2005

Operetta tanuki goten (オペレッタ狸御殿)/*Princess Raccoon* aka *Raccoon Palace*

Cast: Zhang Ziyi, Odagiri Jō, Hira Mikijirō, Yakushimaru Hiroko, Saori Yuki, Takahashi Gentarō, Yamamoto Tarō, Papaya Suzuki, Ichikawa Miwako, Onoe Murasaki, Sasai Eisuke. Pro: Ogura Jimsyo Co./Dentsu/Eisei Gekijo/Geneon/Nippon Herald/Shōchiku (Ogura Satoru, Katashima Ikki), Suzuki Seijun (exec.). Scr: Urasawa Yoshio. M: Ōshima Michiru, Shirai Yoshiaki. Ph: Maeda Yonezō. Ed: Itō Nobuyuki. Pd: Ataka Norifumi. O: Itō Sachiko (costumes); Tsugi Isao (make-up design); Suenaga Ken (asst. dir.). Japan, 28.5.2005.

Plot: A musical revue version of a famous fairy tale. A vain king of ancient Yamato, Azuchi (Hira) loathes his son (Odagiri) for his beauty. Failing to have him assassinated, Azuchi banishes the prince instead. The prince strays into the sacred woods beneath Mt. Kiraisu, where he encounters a beautiful woman speaking a strange tongue (Mandarin). They share a romantic reverie in the woods. She is a princess (Zhang) of the raccoon (*tanuki*) palace, and their attraction is looked on with dismay by the court. The prince is imprisoned by the raccoons; the princess and her handmaidens save him, but even her loyal followers demand that the lovers be separated. She falls ill in despair, and the prince journeys up the mountain to find the "Frog of Paradise" to heal her. But the star-crossed lovers are destined to die for their passion.

Notes

Introduction

1. *Style to kill: Koroshi no rakuin bijuaru direkutori* (Tokyo: Puchigura paburisshingu, 2001), A17-A26; Stephen Teo, "Seijun Suzuki: Authority in Minority," *Senses of Cinema* 8 (July-August 2000), http://archive.sensesofcinema.com/contents/festivals/oo/8/miff/suzuki.html; Isoda Tsutomu and Todoroki Yukio, *Sei/jun/ei/ga* (Tokyo: Waizu shuppan, 2006), 312; Gerald Peary, ed., *Quentin Tarantino: Interviews* (University Press of Mississippi, 2013), 123-24; Logan Hill, "Even Tarantino Was Shocked," *The Telegraph* (12 February 2006); Suzuki Seijun obituary, https://www.japantimes.co.jp/news/2017/02/23/national/director-musicals-guns-b-movies-seijun-suzuki-dead-93/ (23 February 2017).

2. Suzuki interview by Tom Mes for the website Midnight Eye (11 October 2001), http://www.midnighteye.com/interviews/seijun-suzuki/

3. Harold Bloom, *A Map of Misreading*, 2nd ed. (London: Oxford University Press, 2003), xiv.

4. In David Bordwell, *Narration in the Fiction Film* (Madison: University of Wisconsin Press, 1985), 150.

5. Dudley Andrew, *Concepts in Film Theory* (London: Oxford University Press, 1984), 166.

6. Andrew, 167.

7. Although the above characterization of "difference" is formulated without reference to or reliance upon Ueno Kōshi's concept of *zure* ("deviation")—a concept which he brought to bear on his 1986 book *Seijun Suzuki zen eiga*—there is clearly some degree of affinity between them insofar as William Carroll's recent (and valuable) interpretation of Ueno is right to characterize *zure* as primarily a deviation from "expectations set up by social and genre conventions." My deployment of "difference" and the "differential," however, quite clearly betrays its allegiance to a different school of thought in that I view difference and negation as essential to the creation and interpretative construction of meaning (including the socio-political), whereas the tendency (as I discuss in chapter 6) of the "formalist" school of criticism with which Ueno is associated is to deny the semantic effect of a stylistic event, particularly as it relates to narrative meaning, or at the very least to bracket concerns about how such meaning may be generated by non-verbal content; William Carroll, *Suzuki Seijun and Postwar Japanese Cinema* (Columbia University Press, 2022), 48-52, 91-92.

8. "What is an Author?" (February 1969), translated by Josué V. Harari in Foucault, *Aesthetics, Method and Epistemology*, edited by James D. Faubion (London: Allen Lane, Penguin Press, 1998), 221-22. At this point in the evolution of our digital culture, as characterized by a seemingly endless proliferation of pragmatically anonymous texts, tweets, and posts, I do not share Foucault's 50-year-old estimation that there is a verifiable political or polemical value in replacing the author function with whatever blunter structure of signifying constraint—as Foucault himself predicts—is bound to come after.

9. Berys Gaut, "Film Authorship and Collaboration," in Richard Allen and Murray Smith, eds., *Film Theory and Philosophy* (Oxford: Clarendon Press, 1997), 158.

10. Yoshimoto Mitsuhiro's treatment of Kurosawa's films in his book *Kurosawa: Film Studies and Japanese Cinema* (Raleigh: Duke University Press, 2000), 55, 58-61, cannot, on my reading, quite overcome its acute self-consciousness of this and a number of other traditional objections to director study. Yoshimoto's lucid doubts remain substantially, if understandably, unresolved in and by the subsequent analyses.

11. I owe the concept of directorial endorsement largely to the late Victor Perkins, although Perkins's concept of the director is (in essence) more empirical and, metaphorically-speaking, more "conductorial" than mine, which is based in the reconstruction of a composite textual agency; cf. Perkins, "Moments of Choice," *Rouge* 9 (2006), http://www.rouge.com.au/9/index.html

12. Geoffrey Nowell-Smith, "Six Authors in Pursuit of *The Searchers*," in John Caughie, ed., *Theories of Authorship* (London: Routledge, 1981), 222.

13. William Carroll notes that major Japanese film critics of the 1930s, such as Kishi Matsuo and Murakami Tadahisa, endorsed and expounded upon the "authorism" (*sakka shugi*) of the director. Carroll, 44-45.

14. David Bordwell, "Visual Style and the Japanese Cinema," *Film History* 7:1 (Spring 1995): 22, 6-7.

15. David Bordwell, "A Cinema of Flourishes: Japanese Decorative Classicism of the Prewar Era," in Arthur Nolletti Jr. and David Desser, eds., *Reframing Japanese Cinema* (Bloomington: Indiana University Press, 1992), 331, 338.

16. Bordwell, *Narration in the Fiction Film*, 162.

17. Following on from a concept in French film theory introduced, more or less, by Étienne Souriau, my use of the term relies on what Thomas Elsaesser specifies as "single diegesis" in his "Discipline Through Diegesis," in Wanda Strauven, ed., *The Cinema of Attractions Reloaded* (Amsterdam University Press, 2006), 216.

18. Bordwell, *Narration in the Fiction Film*, 161-62.

19. Bordwell, 168.

20. Bordwell, 163-64.

21. Miriam Bratu Hansen, "The Mass Production of the Senses," in Christine Gledhill and Linda Williams, eds., *Reinventing Film Studies* (Oxford: Oxford University Press, 2000), 337-38.

22. Catherine Russell's *Japanese Classical Cinema Revisited* (New York: Continuum, 2011), 10-14, is a critique of Bordwell's evidence that clearly fails without counter-examples. On the use of examples, see Catherine Constable, *Thinking in Images: Film Theory, Feminist Philosophy and Marlene Dietrich* (London: British Film Institute, 2005), 21-22.

23. Bordwell's tendency (like that of the Japanese critic Hasumi Shigehiko) is to deny the semantic effect of any stylistic event, though this was not the case in his early essay "Mizoguchi and the Evolution of Film Language," in Stephen Heath and Patricia Mellencamp, eds., *Cinema and Language* (Frederick, MD: University Publications of America, 1983), 110-13. See also Donald Kirihara's corrective, "Reconstructing Japanese Film," in David Bordwell and Noël Carroll, eds., *Post-theory* (Madison: University of Wisconsin Press, 1996), 514-15.

24. Burch's presentation of the argument is somewhat haphazard, but valuable nonetheless: Noël Burch, *To the Distant Observer: Form and Meaning in the Japanese Cinema*, rev. ed. (University of California-Berkeley, 1979), 243-44, 275-78, 284-85, 287-88, 299. Richie in his *A Hundred Years of Japanese Film* (Kodansha, 2001), 116-19, speaks of a new realism or verisimilitude but does not specify its formal parameters; he also notes, 115, 134, a new "imitation" of Hollywood based on viewing of new American films. More revealing is his earlier condemnation of "one of the most conservative, artistically reactionary . . . and unprofessional film industries in the world," at exactly the time in question here, the mid-to-late 1950s: Joseph Anderson and Donald Richie, *The Japanese Film: Art and Industry*, rev. ed. (Princeton, 1982), 332, 345.

25. William Carroll points out that the leftist film critic Matsuda Masao expressed essentially the same idea in 1968, although his comments reached far further into the realms of hyperbole and speculation; Caroll, 24.

26. Andrew, 162.

27. Richie, *A Hundred Years of Japanese Film*, 201.

28. Jacques Rivette, "Time Overflowing" (September 1968), translated in *Cahiers du Cinéma 1960-1968*, edited by Jim Hillier (Cambridge: Harvard University Press, 1986), 321.

29. Satō Tadao, *Shinema '69* (no. 2), in *Currents in Japanese Cinema*, translated by Gregory Barrett (Tokyo: Kodansha, 1983), 224.

30. Gilles Deleuze, *Masochism: Coldness and Cruelty*, translated by Jean McNeil (New York: Zone Books, 1991), 27-29.

31. Deleuze, 32-33.

32. Foreword to Klaus Theweleit, *Male Fantasies, Vol. 1: Women, Floods, Bodies, History* (Minneapolis: University of Minnesota Press, 1987), xii.

33. Gaylyn Studlar remarks that "paradoxically, the structure of disavowal guarantees a continual, suspended acknowledgement of the very thing denied." Studlar, *In the Realm of Pleasure: Von Sternberg, Dietrich, and the Masochistic Aesthetic* (New York: Columbia University Press, 1991), 93.

34. It is strongly recommended that readers who are not familiar with Suzuki's

Chapter 1

1. Ueno Kōshi, *Suzuki Seijun zen eiga* (Tokyo: Rippu shobō, 1986), 359, among others. The Sumida river divides Sumida and Chūō wards.
2. Ueno, 359; "Biography," compiled by Hasumi Shigehiko in Suzuki Seijun, Hasumi Shigehiko, *Suzuki Seijun: the Desert Under the Cherry Blossoms* (Rotterdam: Film Festival Rotterdam, NFM/IAF et al., 1991), hereafter referred to in this chapter as "Hasumi (1991)," 80.
3. Mark Schilling, *No Borders, No Limits: Nikkatsu Action Cinema*, 2nd ed. (Godalming: FAB Press, 2008), 142. This description of his father's business is either fortuitous or too good to be true, considering that the first character making up the family name "Suzuki" means "bell."
4. Hasumi (1991), 80.
5. Schilling, 142.
6. Ueno, 360.
7. Suzuki in Mark Schilling, *The Yakuza Movie Book* (Berkeley: Stone Bridge Press, 2003), 103.
8. Translated in Miriam Silverberg, *Erotic Grotesque Nonsense: The Mass Culture of Japanese Modern Times* (Berkeley: University of California Press, 2009), 25-29.
9. Ueno, 360.
10. Silverberg, 28-29.
11. Ueno, 360.
12. Hasumi (1991), 80.
13. The more detailed source, Ueno, 360, says eight hours; but Schilling, 142, seemingly as a result of his interview with Suzuki, says "several days." Suzuki was understandably reticent about this period of service, for example omitting it from his memoir of the war translated in Hasumi (1991), 29.
14. Suzuki, "My Work," in Hasumi (1991), 29.
15. Suzuki, "My Work," 29.
16. Suzuki, *Kenka erejii*, 2nd ed. (Tokyo: Nihon tosho sentā, 2003), 26-35.
17. Suzuki in Hasumi (1991), 30.
18. Isoda Tsutomu and Todoroki Yukio, eds., *Sei/jun/ei/ga* (Tokyo: Waizu shuppan, 2006), 402.
19. Isoda and Todoroki, 402.
20. Isoda and Todoroki, 402-3.
21. Suzuki in Hasumi, 31.
22. Suzuki in Hasumi, 31.
23. Hasumi (1991), 80.

24. *"Isetsu: Shōchiku gakkō"* ("Opinions: The Shochiku School") in Motomura Shūji, ed., *Suzuki Seijun sōtokushū* (Tokyo: Kawade shobō shinsha, 2001), 83.

25. Chris Desjardins, *Outlaw Masters of Japanese Film* (London: I.B. Taurus, 2005), 145.

26. Isoda and Todoroki, 402-3.

27. Isoda and Todoroki, 404.

28. Ueno, 112-13.

29. Ueno, 112.

30. A similar but certainly smaller development took place at Tōei, which remained the major producer of *jidai-geki* and *chanbara* for another decade.

31. Isoda and Todoroki, 404.

32. These two films, Furukawa Takumi's *Taiyō no kisetsu/Season of the Sun* and Nakahira Kō's *Kurutta kajitsu/Crazed Fruit*, begat a national scandal and debate over permissiveness in the cinema: Michael Raine, "Yūjiro: Youth, Celebrity, and the Male Body," in Dennis Washburn and Carole Cavanaugh, eds., *Word and Image in Japanese Cinema* (Cambridge University Press, 2000), 204-5, 211.

33. Schilling, 98.

34. Suzuki in Hasumi (1991), 33-34.

35. Suzuki, 99.

36. Schilling, *No Borders, No Limits* (2008), 14.

37. Paul Kerr, "Out of What Past? Notes on the B *film noir*," in Alain Silver and James Ursini, eds., *Film Noir Reader* (New York: Limelight Editions, 1996), 108-25.

38. Schilling, 99.

39. Suzuki in Hasumi, (1991), 38; Interview with Brian Puterman and Robert Graves, *Asian Cult Cinema* v. 21 (1998): 45.

40. Suzuki quoted in Ian Buruma, "The Eccentric Imagination of a Genre Filmmaker," in Simon Field and Tony Rayns, eds., *Branded to Thrill: The Delirious Cinema of Suzuki Seijun* (London: Institute of Contemporary Arts, 1994), 20.

41. *Asian Cult Cinema* v. 21, (1998), 56.

42. *Asian Cult Cinema* v. 21, (1998), 42.

43. Suzuki in Desjardins, 146; *Asian Cult Cinema* v. 21, 46.

44. In a monograph published a matter of weeks before this present volume, William Carroll also recognizes the analogy at some length: Carroll, *Suzuki Seijun and Postwar Japanese Cinema* (New York: Columbia University Press, 2022), 39-40, 82.

45. Fukasawa Tetsuya, review of *Hachi jikan no kyōfu*, *Kinema junpō* no. 172 (Early April 1957): 109. The reviewer (once again rather randomly) compared the actors in the picture, unfavorably, to Rod Steiger!

46. Suzuki, "My Work," 34.

47. Kosuge Haruo, *Kinema junpō* (Late September, 1958): 76.

48. William Carroll, in a very recent monograph, finds much significance in the fact that this film and its immediate successor were in fact the "A-features" on a double bill, with the B-features typically running less than an hour in length.

However, since these are the only two such instances from the 1950s, and since, as Carroll recognizes, the first-run status of Suzuki's longer pictures from 1960-1962 is ambiguous at best, I do not regard them as significant evidence of what Carroll invokes as the possibility that Suzuki enjoyed a significantly higher status at Nikkatsu than he claimed to have done. Granting the well-advised caution about autobiographical myth-making, there is little evidentiary basis for dismissing or even casting into doubt Suzuki's frequent and bald testimonies of criticism from the studio and consequent career anxieties; Carroll, 64, 68-70.

49. Masumura was a frequent contributor: for example, the *Kinema junpō*, no. 261 (Late June 1960): 50-55, roundtable on "Cine-realism"; *Kinema junpō* no. 145 (May 1956): 48-50: *Kinema junpō* no. 415 (May 1966): 63; *Kinema junpō* no. 428 (Dec. 1966), 30-35. The Late July 1964 issue (no. 370) celebrates Masumura's *Manji* (Daiei, 1964) on the very same page (80-81) as a condescending, diatribe against Suzuki's *Nikutai no mon* (1964) by Oguri Masami. As for Imamura, the magazine visited him on set for photographs and a feature article in *Kinema junpō* no. 357 (early Feb. 1964): 13-25.

50. Okada Seizō, *Kinema junpō* no. 212 (Early Sept. 1958): 77.

51. Isoda and Todoroki, 112; Suzuki in *Asian Cult Cinema*, v. 21, 58.

52. Thomas Weisser, "The Films of Seijun Suzuki," *Asian Cult Cinema* v. 21 (4th Quarter 1998): 43, 47, 49. Riddled with careless factual and linguistic errors, this annotated filmography contains invaluable anecdotes based on unpublished exchanges with the director.

53. Interview with Ueno in Hasumi (1991), 71.

54. For *Kemono no nemuri* (1960), *Kinema junpō* no. 258 (Early May 1960): 84.

55. Weisser, 51. Weisser did not, unfortunately, reveal his source.

56. Suzuki in *Asian Cult Cinema* v. 21, 44.

57. From the documentary *Inside Doctor No*, originally produced for the MGM DVD release (2000).

58. Some formative films include Hasebe's *Nora neko rokku/Stray Cat Rock* series, featuring superstar Kaji Meiko, especially *Sekkusu hantā/Sex Hunter* (1970), and Sone's *Seidan botan-dōrō/Hellish Love* (1972).

59. Review by Nakahara Yumihiko, *Eiga hyōron* (July 1963), 34-35.

60. Nakahara, 36.

61. Not all of the magazine's articles were laudatory; Kazuki Ryōsuke, "*Suzuki Seijun yo, ongaku ni motto aijō wo . . .*" ("Suzuki Seijun, Love Music a Little More . . ."), *Eiga hyōron* (Nov. 1964), accuses the director's lack of regard for compositional harmony: 85-86. Carroll notes that Kazuki was revealed, much later, to have been a pen name of the young avant-garde filmmaker Obayashi Nobuhiko; Carroll, 17.

62. Hasumi "A World Without Seasons" in Hasumi (1991), 9.

63. Kajiwara, *Eiga hyōron* (July 1964), reprinted in Motomura, ed., *Suzuki Seijun sōtokushū*, 120-22.

64. Kajiwara, 122. It is telling that, as William Carroll points out, the article to

start this trend in Suzuki's favor was not in fact by a staff critic but was chosen from amongst the reader submissions; Carroll, 17.

65. *Kinema junpō* no. 370 (Late July 1964): 80-81, *Kinema junpō* no. 388 (Early April 1965): 87; Kazuki in *Eiga hyōron* (Nov. 1964): 86; Sano Mitsuo, "*Koroshiya to shunpu no aida no kyokōsei* (Fictionality Amidst Killers and Whores)," *Eiga geijutsu* (May 1965): 49-50.

66. Kazuki, 86.

67. Shirai Yoshio and Iijima Tetsuo, "*Nihon eiga no ransei 'itanji'*" (The *Enfants Terribles* of Japanese Cinema's Troubled Times), *Kinema junpō* no. 440 (June 1967): 41-46; Iijima, "*Katō Tai to Suzuki Seijun: insaido de wa hanasakanu ninin no Taishō senchūha*" (Katō Tai and Suzuki Seijun: On the Inside, Two Men of the Taishō War Generation Who Did not Bloom), *Eiga geijutsu* (March 1967): 36-38; interview with Suzuki and his *kumi* by Satō Tadao in *Eiga hyōron* (Nov. 1966): 19-36.

68. Ishigami Mitsutoshi, "*Tokyo nagaremono igo he,*" *Eiga hyōron* (August 1966), in Motomura, 131; Satō, *Nihon eigashi vol. 3* (Tokyo: Iwanami shoten, 1996), 37. In addition to Ishigami, Carroll mentions future director Adachi Masao and leftist critic Matsuda Masao as demonstrative Suzuki admirers; Carroll, 17.

69. Satō Tadao, *Currents in Japanese Cinema*, trans. Gregory Barrett (Tokyo: Kodansha, 1983), 227.

70. Suzuki in Isoda and Todoroki, 274, 277; Shindō in Motomura, 23.

71. Desjardins, 148.

72. Isoda and Todoroki, 74-80.

73. Isoyama Hiroshi, *Kinema junpō* no. 415 (May 1966): 62.

74. Ogawa Yoshiyuki, *Kinema junpō* no. 430 (Jan. 1967): 121; *Kinema junpō* no. 428 (Dec. 1966): 107-26.

75. "*Wakaki hi no Seijun no shōzō*" (Portrait of Seijun's Youth), *Eiga hyōron* (Feb. 1967), reprinted in Motomura, 131.

76. Ueno Kōshi, "Suzuki Battles Nikkatsu," in Alastair Phillips, ed., *The Films of Seijun Suzuki* (Edinburgh Festival Program, 1988), 40.

77. For example, Kawarabata Yasushi, "*Suzuki Seijun mondai repōto: wakai kōshō he ba wo utsusu,*" *Eiga hyōron* 28:6 (1971): 60-62.

78. Translated in Daisuke Miyao, "Dark Visions of Japanese Film Noir: Suzuki Seijun's *Branded To Kill,*" in Alastair Phillips and Julian Stringer, eds., *Japanese Cinema: Texts and Contexts* (Abingdon, Oxon: Routledge, 2007), 194-95.

79. In Miyao, 194, and Lisa Spalding in Phillips., ed., *The Films of Seijun Suzuki*, 40.

80. The "Joint Struggle Committee" Statement of July 13th in Ueno, 222-23. The final settlement with Nikkatsu included a donation of *Koroshi no rakuin* and *Kenka erejii* to the National Film Centre in Tokyo (227), reflecting concerns that a vindictive Nikkatsu might destroy or "bury" the prints of Suzuki's films.

81. Ueno in Phillips, 40.

82. Ueno in Phillips, 40.

83. Ueno, 221-22.

84. *Eiga hyōron* (August 1968) featured three articles comparing the Suzuki Affair with the Langlois Affair in Paris, 59-92.

85. Interview with Hubert Niogret, *Positif* (June 1990): 26

86. For example, Kanai Toshio, *"Tokubetsu repo: Shine-kurabu to Suzuki Seijun jōei mondai"* (Special Report on Problems Screening Suzuki Seijun's Works), *Kinema junpō* no. 469 (June 1968): 92-94; Kawarabata Yasushi, "Suzuki Seijun jiken repōto: sakka ni osareta Koroshi no rakuin" (Report on the Suzuki Seijun Affair: *Branded to Kill* Branded on the Author), *Eiga hyōron* 25:7 (1968): 18-21.

87. Ueno in Phillips, 40.

88. Ueno in Phillips, 40. The studios were gradually sold off throughout the dispute, and in 1971 Nikkatsu removed Hori and announced that they would exclusively produce soft-core pornography, or *roman poruno*.

89. For example, Sone Yoshitada, *"Suzuki Seijun-ron: utae, odore"* (The Theory of Suzuki: Dance, Sing), *Eiga geijutsu* no. 255 (Nov. 1968): 52-54; Roland Lethem, "Suzuki Seijun to *Nikutai no mon*," *Eiga hyōron* (Jan. 1969): 42-47; Ueno Kōshi, "Rojin ga rojin de aru tame ni ha: shinario⌈Iken⌋he no Suzuki Seijun no michinori" (Lu Xun for his own sake: Suzuki Seijun's road to the screenplay *"Iken"*), *Eiga hihyō* (Nov. 1970): 63-75.

90. Hatano Tetsurō, *"Haigo no nai sekai"* (A World Without a Backdrop), *Bijutsu techō*, no. 398 (Sept. 1975): 235-47; Tayama Rikiya, *"Bi no seiri*: Suzuki Seijun," *Kokubungaku* v. 22 (June 25, 1977): 155-58; "Suzuki Seijun san: damashiai ni ikiru eiga kantoku" (Suzuki-san: A Film Director Who Lives for Trickery), *Asahi Journal* 23 (1981): 92-97.

91. *Kinema junpō* no. 627 (March 1974) to no. 650 (Late February 1975).

92. Satō Tadao, *Nihon eiga shisōshi* (Tokyo: Sanichi shobō, 1970).

93. This has been available—and highly influential—in English translation in Satō, *Currents in Japanese Cinema*, 221-29.

94. Translated in Satō, *Currents in Japanese Cinema*, 225.

95. Satō, *Currents in Japanese Cinema*, 225.

96. Hatano, 235-36.

97. For example, Ueno, *Suzuki Seijun zen eiga*, 230-42.

98. Donald Richie, *A Hundred Years of Japanese Film* (Tokyo: Kodansha, 2001), 181.

99. Interview included on the 2006 Kino DVD of *Zigeunerweisen*.

100. *Eiga geijutsu* no. 27 (April 1977): 31-46; no. 29 (June 1977): 31-47; no. 31 (August 1977): 39-117.

101. For example, *Ātto shiata* no. 144 (January 1981): 8-30, 38-60; Akiyama Kiyoshi, *Nihon eiga kenkyū* 4 (May 1981): 4-6.

102. In what can only be described as a *haute culture* takedown, the fiction writer Kanai Mieko, no film scholar, accused Suzuki of a "dogmatism that operates as if only the appetite for aesthetic expression existed," which, she claimed, could be culpably associated with fascism: *Bungei* v. 20 (September 1981), 186-89.

103. Nevertheless, a special issue of *Yuriika* magazine anticipated *Yumeji*: *Yuriika* 23:4 (1991).

104. Stephen Teo, "Suzuki Seijun: Authority in Minority," *Senses of Cinema* 8 (July-August 2000); Akahori Masako and Tanabe Kaori, *Style to Kill: Koroshi no rakuin bijuaru direkutori* (Tokyo: Puchigura Publishing, 2001), A17-A27; Chuck Stephens, "Kiyoshi Kurosawa Begins at the End," *New York Times* (24 July 2001).

105. Schilling, *Yakuza Movie Book*, 95-96; Stephen Teo, "Authority in Minority."

106. "Bullet Ballet," *Chicago Reader* (22 August 2003), http://www.jonathanrosenbaum.net/2013/10/bullet-ballet/

107. Watanabe Takenobu's *Nikkatsu akushon no kareina sekai, vol. 2 1963-1967* (Tokyo: Miraisha, 1981-82) offers remarkably close readings of a few films, though the focus is on defining the Nikkatsu "house style."

108. Ueno, *Suzuki Seijun zen eiga*, featuring a superbly researched bibliography. A second book, edited by Isoda and Todoroki in 2006, invaluable for its production information, simply features a long interview with a famously reticent director.

109. Carroll, 94.

110. Carroll, 31

111. Carroll, 27, 30.

112. Carroll, 107-14, 40, 126, 32, 36.

113. Carroll, for example, accepts the periodization of Nikkatsu Action Cinema that was set out by Watanabe Takenobu; 72.

114. In Yamane Sadao, *Eiga ga hadaka ni naru toki* (Tokyo: Seidōsha, 1988), 35.

Chapter 2

1. Review of *Rajo to kenjū*, *Asahi Shinbun* (9 Dec. 1957); Review of *Aoi Chibusa*, *Asahi shinbun* (8 Sept. 1958).

2. The marketing of the *nuberu bagu* remains astonishingly underdeveloped in Film Studies: see Turim's brief comments in *The Films of Ōshima Nagisa: Images of a Japanese Iconoclast* (Berkeley: University of California Press, 1998), 12-14, 34-35.

3. Schilling, *No Borders, No Limits*, 135.

4. Suzuki, "Forgetting Foreign Names," in Suzuki and Hasumi, *The Desert Under the Cherry Blossoms*, 75.

5. Satō, *Currents in Japanese Cinema*, 226.

6. Ueno Kōshi, ed., *Seijun Suzuki zen eiga*, 120.

7. Interview with Tony Rayns (28 June 2006), from the 2007 Yume Pictures DVD release of *Tokyo Drifter*.

8. Satō Shigeomi, review of *Ankokugai no taiketsu*, *Eiga geijutsu* 8:3 (1960): 73; Fukasawa, *Kinema junpō* no. 347 (June 1963): 86.

9. Nakahara, review of *Yajū no seishun*, 36.

10. For example, *Kinema junpō*'s review (late Oct. 1958) of Noguchi's *Jigoku no satsutaba/Bankroll from Hell* (1958); Fukasawa's review of Suzuki's *Hachi jikan no kyōfu* (*Kinema junpō* no. 172, Early April 1957): 109. The *katakana* (borrowed) term *gangu* seems to have signified more the Americanized, movie-fantasy crime syndi-

cates that appeared in Nikkatsu's films of the 1950s than the native *yakuza* milieu which appeared in later genre films.

11. James Naremore, *More Than Night: Film Noir in its Contexts* (Berkeley: University of California Press, 1998), 46.

12. For example, James M. Cain's *The Postman Always Rings Twice* (1934) and *Double Indemnity* (1936) have little to do with private detectives, yet are widely considered as examples of "hard-boiled": Naremore, 52.

13. Gene D. Phillips, *Out of the Shadows* (Lanham, MD: Scarecrow Press, 2012), 12-13.

14. See Komatsu Hiroshi, "Representations of the Dark World in Japanese Silent Films," in Roberto Cueto, ed., *Japón en negro* (Festival Internacional de cine de Donostia-San Sebastian, S.A., 2008), 279.

15. This included the British writers James Hadley Chase and Graham Greene, who did not focus on private eyes.

16. Japan's most popular mystery writer, Matsumoto Seichō, wrote in a more Japanese idiom and with echoes of Simenon more than American writers. The crime films of Nomura Yoshitarō at Shōchiku were almost exclusively Matsumoto adaptations, which further confuses the task of classifying the crime films of the 1950s.

17. Other influences on Kurosawa's crime films included Simenon, German thrillers such as *M* (Fritz Lang, 1931) and the new urban realism of Rossellini's *Roma Città Aperta* (1945).

18. For example, Huston's *The Maltese Falcon* (1941, released in Japan in 1951); Wilder's *Double Indemnity* (1944, released in 1953), Preminger's *Laura* (1944, released in Japan in 1947): Hirano Kyoko, "Japanese Crime Films in the 1940s and 1950s," in Cueto, ed., *Japón en negro*, 291. These films were all key texts of Borde and Chaumeton's seminal 1955 work *Panorama du films noir Americain/A Panorama of American Film Noir,* translated by Paul Hammond (San Francisco: City Lights Books, 2002).

19. Schilling, 11.

20. Suzuki mentions his reading of Hammett in Isoda and Todoroki, 168; he refers to his knowledge of John Huston in Chris Desjardins, *Outlaw Masters of Japanese Film*, 145.

21. Tsuda Yukio in *Kinema junpō* no. 195 (late Jan. 1958): 70; see also see an unattributed review in *Asahi shinbun* (Dec. 9, 1957).

22. The choreography of this second shot also resembles the visual introduction of Gilda (Hayworth) in Charles Vidor's 1946 film of that name for Columbia Pictures.

23. Suzuki later claimed, "I never use shot-reverse shot" in two-person dialogue scenes: "Forgetting Foreign Names," translated in Suzuki and Hasumi, 73.

24. Kurahara Koreyoshi also created a diegetically problematic flashback in his *Ore wa matteiru ze* of the same year, albeit in a more conventional narrative context of a hero imagining the circumstances of his brother's death.

25. Janey Place, "Women in Film Noir," in E. Ann Kaplan, ed., *Women in Film Noir*, rev. ed. (London: BFI, 2008), p. 48.

26. Hasumi, "A World Without Seasons," in Suzuki and Hasumi, *The Desert Under the Cherry Blossoms*, 14.

27. Eric Crosby, "Widescreen Composition and Transnational Influence: Early Anamorphic Filmmaking in Japan," in Steve Neale and Sheldon Hall, eds., *Widescreen Worldwide* (Bloomington: Indiana University Press, 2010), 183-84.

28. Crosby, 184.

29. Crosby, 184-85.

30. Crosby, 185. Italics mine.

31. The surrealist films of Buñuel and Dali also make heavy use of carnal simulacra. Nagatsuka's close-up on a putrefied cat may be an homage to the rotting ass of *Un Chien Andalou*.

32. Publicity stills exist, possibly unused, for Suzuki's *Raburetaa* (1959) featuring the heroine baring her breasts during a love scene (see Suzuki and Hasumi, 42). No such nudity or love scene exists in the theatrical release of this (suspiciously short) film: it may have been removed.

33. See note 44 below.

34. In Deleuze, 118.

35. "Forgetting Foreign Names," in Suzuki and Hasumi, 70.

36. Deleuze, 120.

37. On the connection between the cinematic female subject, her preoccupied vision of indeterminate post-war spaces, and post-war national identity crises in Europe, see Mark Betz, *Beyond the Subtitle: Remapping European Art Cinema* (Minneapolis: University of Minnesota Press, 2009), 93-95, 97-99, 119-21, 131-35, 140-41, 144-46, 155-57, 160-64.

38. On color usage in pre-modern painting and in *ukiyo-e*, see Satō, "Japanese Cinema and the Traditional Arts," in Linda Erlich and David Desser, eds., *Cinematic Landscapes* (Austin: University of Texas, 1994), 299-321, 165, 171-75, and Utagawa Hiroshige, *The Moon Reflected* (London: IKON/British Museum, 2008), 22-23, 27. For the cinematic legacy, see Desser, "Gate of Flesh(tones): Color in the Japanese Cinema," in Erlich and Desser, eds., *Cinematic Landscapes: Observations on the Visual Arts of China and Japan* (Austin, University of Texas, 1994), 316-17 and Steven Peacock, *Colour* (Manchester, 2010), 30-33.

39. Translated in Weisser, *Asian Cult Cinema* v. 21, 51.

40. Carroll, 107-9, quite independently noticed what the film scholar Paul Coates defines as "the complete separation of color and object." Carroll relies on Coates and Richard Misek for his discussion of this phenomena, whereas I rely on the tradition and historical context underpinning Deleuze's treatment of "colourism."

41. Kandinsky, "Concerning the Spiritual in Art," quoted in Peacock, 16.

42. Ford's *Drums Along the Mohawk* (Fox, 1939) climaxes with an abstract iconography of American democracy, that is, people of various classes set against non-diegetic backdrops of the colors of the American flag.

43. See Yoshimoto's reading of *Seishun zankoku monogatari*, "Questions of the New: Ōshima Nagisa *Cruel Story of Youth*," in Phillips and Stringer, eds., *Japanese Cinema: Texts and Contexts*, 168-80. Dennis Washburn's "The Arrest of Time: The Mythic Transgressions of *Vengeance is Mine*" is relevant to early Kurahara as well as Imamura: in Dennis Washburn and Carole Cavanaugh, eds., *Word and Image in Japanese Cinema* (Cambridge: Cambridge University Press, 2000), 319, 321, 324-26, 336-39.

44. In 1960, the proposed revision and renewal of the U.S. Japan Security Treaty of 1952, a major determinant of Japan's political and economic positioning within the Cold War system, was opposed by massive citizen opposition and protest carried out by a broad coalition of social groups, for example students, women's groups, and intellectuals. There were also many attempts by leftist students to radicalize the broadly democratic, pro-constitutional nature of the coalition. In May 1960, the revision of the treaty passed the Diet, but the outcome of this and many other mass protest movements of the time was the fall of Prime Minister Kishi Nobusuke's administration. See Koschmann, "Intellectuals and Politics," in Andrew Gordon, ed., *Postwar Japan as History* (Berkeley: University of California Press, 1993), 406-9.

45. William Carroll also noted a "media hyperconsciousness" in the film that linked it to the *nuberu bagu*, although Carroll's immediate focus is on the use of found footage and films-within-films rather than on the mass media's commercial imperatives and economic imperialism; Carroll, 36.

46. Hasumi, "A World Without Seasons," 16.

47. Hasumi, 17-18.

48. In Ueno, 71.

49. For example, Tayama Rikiya, "*Bi no seiri*: Suzuki Seijun," *Kokubungaku* 22:8 (June 1977): 155-58; Ryōgoku, "Suzuki Seijun *ni tsuite*," *Eiga hyōron* (May 1966), in Motomura, 127-29.

50. Recall, e.g. the director's meditation on the period as quoted in chapter 1.

51. Bordwell, *Narration in the Fiction Film*, 317, 320.

52. The final close-ups on the heroine of *Hishū monogatari/A Tale of Sorrow* (1977) are directly referential to those of Joan of Arc (Mme. Falconetti) in Dreyer's *Le Passion de Jeanne D'Arc* (1928).

Chapter 3

1. See Kagami Saburō, ed., *Hādoboirudo no tanteitachi* (Tokyo: Pashifika, 1979).

2. In Isoda and Todoroki, *Sei/jun/ei/ga*, 168.

3. Ōyabu (1935-1996) was born in colonial Seoul and returned to Japan to suffer its post-war depredations. A reader of American fiction, Ōyabu met instant success publishing his *Yajū no shisu beshi* in a Waseda University magazine.

4. Schilling, *No Borders, No Limits*, 17-18.

5. 2017 interview for the Arrow Films box set, "Seijun Suzuki: The Early Years, Volume 2."

6. *Kutabare akutō-domo*: *Tantei jimusho 2-3* was successful enough commercially to be followed by a now-forgotten sequel with the same leading actors (Shishido, Hatsui, and Kaneko Nobuo), directed by another former Noguchi A.D., the forgotten Yanase Nozomu.

7. Furukawa Takumi's *Kenjū zankoku monogatari*/Cruel Gun Story (1964), also from an Ōyabu novel, notably took the path of trying to recreate the older, hard-boiled stylistic milieu.

8. Watanabe, *Nikkatsu akushon no kareina sekai*, vol. 2, 115-16.

9. According to Nakahara, *Eiga hyōron* (July 1963): 34.

10. Nakahara, 35.

11. Interview in Chris Desjardins, *Outlaw Masters of Japanese Film* (I.B. Taurus, 2005), 145.

12. For example, Borde and Chaumeton, *A Panorama of American Film Noir*, 92-93, 34-35.

13. Cueto, "Shades of Black," *Japón en negro*, 267-71.

14. Naremore, *More Than Night*, 38.

15. Naremore, 36.

16. J.P. Telotte, *Voices in the Dark: The Narrative Patterns of* Film Noir (University of Illinois, 1989), 203.

17. Marilyn Ivy, "Formations of Mass Culture," in Andrew Gordon, ed., *Postwar Japan as History* (Berkeley: University of California Press, 1993), 250.

18. These are, of course, legally unsubstantiated allegations, but for the testimony of insiders such as Fukasaku, especially as regards the criminal connections of producer Shundō Kōji, see Federico Varese, "The Secret History of Japanese Cinema: Yakuza Movies," *Global Crime* 7:1 (February 2006): 117.

19. Isoda and Todoroki, 165

20. In Laura Mulvey's Lacanian view, this form of identification, the lynchpin of mainstream cinema's ideological operations, served to construct a male protagonist as a pleasurable ego ideal and hence justify his (largely reactionary) behaviour towards women. Mulvey, "Visual Pleasure and Narrative Cinema," in *Visual and Other Pleasures* (London: Macmillan, 1989), 16-21, 25-26.

21. For Smith, sympathetic engagement with a character requires *recognition*, *alignment*, and *allegiance* to one character's POV over another's: *Engaging Characters: Fiction, Emotion, and the Cinema* (Oxford: Clarendon Press, 1995), 81-86.

22. See Paul Schrader, "The Yakuza Film: A Primer," in Alain Silver and James Ursini, eds., *The Gangster Film Reader* (New York: Limelight, 2007), 78; and Isolde Standish, *A New History of Japanese Cinema* (New York: Continuum, 2005), 294-300.

23. John W. Dower, "Peace and Democracy in Two Systems," in Gordon, ed., *Postwar Japan as History*, 18.

24. Isoda and Todoroki, 167.

25. See Standish on the satirical motif of male impotence: Isolde Standish, *Politics, Porn and Protest* (London: Continuum, 2011), 95-113.

26. In my view, Burch's strong critique of Wakamatsu remains relevant, in *To the Distant Observer: Form and Meaning in the Japanese Cinema*, rev. ed. (Berkeley: University of California Press, 1979), 351-55.

27. See Brian Moeran, "The Beauty of Violence: *Jidai-geki, yakuza*, and *eroduction* Films in Japan," in David Riches, ed., *The Anthropology of Violence* (Oxford: Blackwell, 1986), 103-18.

28. Chandler, *The Big Sleep* (New York: Vintage, 1988 [1939]), 14.

29. In Isoda and Todoroki, 170.

30. Suzuki, *Kenka ereji*, 2nd ed. (Tokyo: Nihon Tosho Sentā, 2003), 129.

31. Cf. Moeran, 104, 111-12.

32. Hubert Niogret, "Entretien avec Seijun Suzuki," *Positif* n. 352 (June 1990): 27-28.

33. See Telotte, "A Fate Worse Than Death: Racism, Transgression, and Westerns," *Journal of Popular Film and Television* 26:3 (January 1998): 120-27, on the significance of "borders."

34. One memorable scene involving Shishido's fingernail was awkwardly affected by censorship, while, ironically, the gory, excised footage found its way into the trailer. Suzuki's dehumanizing original cut of the final sequence was also censored, famously including a close-up of Mrs. Takeshita "slashed like a Venetian blind": Isoda and Todoroki, 165, 168.

35. This applied not only to policies relating to reproductive sexuality but also to issues such as welfare, education, and employment: Kathleen Uno, "The Death of 'Good Wife, Wise Mother'?" in Gordon, ed., *Postwar Japan as History*, 295.

36. Mizuno's actions towards Mrs. Takeshita are highly reminiscent of Chandler's late novel, *The Little Sister* (1949).

37. Ivy, "Formations of Mass Culture," in Gordon, 249.

38. Naremore, 43.

39. "Women in Film Noir," in Kaplan, ed., *Women in Film Noir*, 47

40. "Woman's Place: The Absent Family of Film Noir," in Kaplan, 42.

41. Uno, 210.

42. On this aesthetic of the female body "dissected" by partial views, e.g., Vadim's *Et Dieu . . . Créa la Femme* (1956), see Susan Hayward, *French National Cinema* (London: Routledge, 1993), 180-91.

43. William Carroll, in a study that was released shortly before this present volume, relates the two-dimensionality of the mirror/screen to the rejection of a "narrative" hierarchy of visual events in the shot. Carroll, however, does not approach the sequence from the perspective of spectatorship and figuration, but rather in reference to perspective, Hasumi's formalism (see the footnote below), and to 21st century studies in the "flatness" of digital screen culture; Carroll, 56-57.

44. In Hasumi's exegesis, "because of the rectangular screen's limitations, Suzuki is a rigid realist. . . . The pure action shown on the surface is the cinema's most

concrete mode of existence. And when it reached real concreteness, the film become abstract and the medium has to believe in its own limitations. Suzuki is, perhaps with Godard, one of the few directors who are not afraid to be concrete": Hasumi, "A World Without Seasons," 18, 23.

45. Robert Stam, *Reflexivity in Film and Literature* (New York: Columbia University Press, 1992), 13-15. Norman Bryson writes, "it is clear the term 'realism' cannot draw its validity from any absolute conception of 'the real', because that conception cannot account for the changing historical character of the real . . . which involves complex formations of representations and codes . . .": Bryson, *Word and Image* (Cambridge University Press, 1981), 1-10.

46. Metz, *Impersonal Enunciation, or, The Place of Film*, trans. Cormac Deane (New York: Columbia, 1987), 10-11, 22.

47. In Isoda and Todoroki, 170. Emphasis mine.

48. Interview in Schilling, *The Yakuza Movie Book*, 99.

49. In Schilling, 102.

50. See Tom Gunning on Lang's use of cinematic allegory in his *Films of Fritz Lang: Allegories of Vision and Modernity* (London: British Film Institute, 2001), 26-30.

51. Gunning, 55

52. For, M.H. Abrams, this "relatively determinate reference" of an allegorical correlation makes it unlike the "further range of suggested but unspecified reference" of the symbolic: Abrams, *A Glossary of Literary Terms*, 4th edition (Boston: Heinle & Heinle, 1999), 311.

53. Metz, "Current Problems in Film Theory," in Bill Nichols, ed., *Movies and Methods* (Berkeley: University of California Press, 1976), 571.

54. Trevor Whittock, *Metaphor and Film* (Cambridge: Cambridge University Press, 1990), 12-16, 30-32.

55. Laurot, "From Logos to Lens," in Nichols, 578-82.

56. Noël Carroll, *Interpreting the Moving Image* (Cambridge: Cambridge University Press, 1998), 212-23.

57. In Whittock, 10.

58. In Stam, xiv.

59. Stam, xiv.

60. Whittock, 42.

61. Gilles Deleuze, *Cinema 1: The Movement-Image*, translated by Hugh Tomlinson and Barbara Haberjam (Minneapolis: University of Minnesota Press, 1983), 199-204.

Chapter 4

1. In Rayns, ed., "Suzuki on Suzuki," in Field and Rayns, eds., *Branded to Thrill*, 26. Sawashima's *Matabi san-nin yakuza* was made for Tōei in 1965.

2. Joaqúin da Silva, "Fukasaku and Scorsese," in Silver and Ursini, eds., *Gangster Film Reader*, 344.

3. Iijima Tetsuo, *Eiga geijutsu* (March 1967), 36-38; Shirai and Iijima, *Kinema junpō* no. 440 (June 1967): 41-46.

4. Keiko Iwai McDonald, "The Yakuza Film: An Introduction," in Nolletti and Desser, eds., *Reframing Japanese Cinema*, 185-93; Isolde Standish, *Myth and Masculinity in the Japanese Cinema* (Richmond, Surrey: Curzon, 2000), 158-81.

5. Schrader, 78.

6. McDonald, 174-79.

7. David E. Kaplan and Alec Dubro, *The Yakuza: Japan's Criminal Underworld*, second edition (Berkeley: University of California Press, 2003), 151.

8. Standish, 160-62, 170, 172-75.

9. Certain comic directors such as Yamanaka Sadao were noted for using such "antiheroes" for provocative social criticism: Satō, 222-23; Richie, *A Hundred Years of Japanese Film*, 66-73.

10. Suzuki, "The Days of *Kantō mushuku*," in Suzuki and Hasumi, *The Desert Under the Cherry Blossoms*, 39.

11. Satō, 52-53; cf. Standish, *A New History of Japanese Cinema* (New York: Continuum: 2005), 309.

12. Standish, *Myth and Masculinity*, 167-69; also *A New History of Japanese Cinema*, 256-59.

13. Standish, *Myth and Masculinity*, 316.

14. Yamaguchi, "*Wakakihi no Seijun no shōzō*," in Motomura, ed., *Suzuki Seijun sōtokushū*, 131.

15. In Schilling, *The Yakuza Movie Book*, 98.

16. Rayns, in Field and Rayns, eds., *Branded to Thrill*, 6.

17. In youth, Hirabayashi (1905-1972) was a member of the Taishō proletarian literary movement and was arrested for sedition, along with hundreds of other cultural figures, in 1923. During and after the war she received several literary prizes.

18. "Suzuki on Suzuki," in Field and Rayns, 25-26.

19. Satō, *Currents in Japanese Cinema*, 227.

20. Suzuki, *Kenka erejii*, 2nd ed. (Tokyo: Nihon tosho senta, 2003), 128-29.

21. Jacoby, *A Critical Handbook of Japanese Film Directors* (Berkeley: Stonebridge Press, 2008), 289.

22. Suzuki, "The Days of *Kantō mushuku*," in Suzuki and Hasumi, 39.

23. Harold Bloom, *Shakespeare: The Invention of the Human* (New York: Harcourt, 1998), 340; the transposition of genders is, of course, mine.

24. Bloom, 336, 361-62.

25. In Field and Rayns, 35.

26. Hasumi, "A World without Seasons," in Suzuki and Hasumi, 7-11.

27. Jordan Sand shows that the 1920s saw the beginning of a defence of "nativist" elements of domestic architecture within a larger disavowal of capitalism. Sand

regrettably does not address the changing symbolic connotations of "traditional" interiors throughout the century as much as their opposite, the provocative Westernized "culture house": *House and Home in Modern Japan: Architecture, Domestic Space, and Bourgeois Culture, 1880-1930* (Cambridge: Harvard University Press, 2005), 100-102; 338-44; 363; 370-78.

28. See Standish's preliminary observations on bodily endurance and stillness: *Myth and Masculinity*, 174, 176, 178-79.

29. Many film series of the 1930s, such as the *Rikōran* films of Shirley Yamaguchi, were devoted to such pastoral propaganda; Standish, *A New History of Japanese Cinema*, 124-27.

30. In Alastair Phillips, ed., *The Films of Suzuki Seijun* (Edinburgh Festival Programme, 1988), 41.

31. A famous symbol of Meiji modernization, also known as the *jūnikai* (twelve floors), this leisure complex was built by Scottish engineer W.K. Burton in 1890 but effectively destroyed in the Great Kantō Earthquake of 1923.

32. Originally a protective garrison for the leased territory along the South Manchurian Railway after the Russo-Japanese War, the Kwantung army became so influential as an agent of imperial expansion in Northern China—and Ultra-Nationalist political thought at home—that they single-handedly engineered the Manchurian Incident of 1931, an invasion based on the false accusation of Chinese dissidents for attempting to blow up the rail line. They then forced the Imperial Command into establishing the colonial Manchukuo state which they administered: Marius Jansen, *The Making of Modern Japan* (Cambridge: Belknap Press, 2000), 578-89.

33. Some examples of the genre, which focused overwhelmingly on the heroism of fighter pilots in different phases of the war, include *Hawaii Middowei daikaikûsen: Taiheiyô no arashi*/I Bombed Pearl Harbour (Tōei, 1960) and *Kurenai no umi*/Blood on the Sea (Tōhō, 1961).

34. Standish, *Myth and Masculinity*, 108.

35. Ryōgoku, "*Onna jōi no shisō: Suzuki Seijun ni tsuite,*" *Eiga hyōron* (May 1966) in Motomura, 129.

36. Kurahara had depicted a similar quest of social escape in *Nikui an-chikushō/I Hate but Love* (Nikkatsu 1962), though it is dramatized in such blatantly gendered, misogynistic terms that the self-righteous hero strikes his girlfriend, who cannot comprehend his desire for freedom, no less than six times during the film.

37. Standish, *A New History of Japanese Cinema*, 309, 316-17; *Myth and Masculinity*, 51, 82, 92, 169, 173-74, 179-80.

38. McDonald mentions a prewar precedent for both the "romantic" and the "truly" outcast hero in Tsuji Yorihoro's *Kaketoji Tokijirō* (1929), 172.

39. Standish, *A New History of Japanese Cinema*, 295.

40. Ryōgoku, 129-30.

41. Standish, *Myth and Masculinity*, 160-62, 165.

Chapter 5

1. Ueno Kōshi, ed., *Suzuki Seijun zen eiga* (Tokyo: Rippu shobō, 1986), 70, and Isoda/Todoroki, *Sei/jun/ei/ga* (Tokyo: Waizu shuppan, 2006), 208.

2. The instant success, in March 1947, of Tamura's short story *Nikutai no mon* sparked this much-publicized literary cycle. See Yoshikuni Igarashi, *Bodies of Memory: Narratives of War in Postwar Japanese Culture, 1945-1970* (Princeton University Press, 2000), 55-61; J. Victor Koschmann, *Revolution and Subjectivity in Postwar Japan* (University of Chicago Press, 1996), 57-60.

3. Isoda/Todoroki, 208; and Suzuki in Chris Desjardins, *Outlaw Masters of Japanese Film* (New York: I.B. Taurus, 2005), 147. Both Kitahara Mie and the minor star Shiraki Mari had long departed these ranks.

4. See Igarashi on prostitution and the female body as allegory in post-war popular culture, 57-58, 108-14.

5. Suzuki's films were frequently attached to those of Imamura as B-pictures and Suzuki has frequently stated that he shot his own films with anxious regard for the A-pictures that they would precede: for example, a 1972 lecture in Suzuki and Hasumi, 38.

6. See John Dower, *Embracing Defeat* (London: Allen Lane, 1999), 89-104, 107-10.

7. Nikkatsu released the film under the "adults only" certificate that had plagued the production of *Yajū no seishun*.

8. Isoda and Todoroki, 210; general overviews of the *roman poruno*, including Jasper Sharp's *Behind the Pink Curtain* (Godalming: FAB Press, 2008) and Satō's *Nihon eigashi, Volume 3* (Tokyo: Iwanami shoten, 1996), 160-66, have ignored the rather obvious influence of Suzuki's film. Earlier French critics tacitly recognized the connection: Jean-Paul Le Pape, "Le Cinema Pink: Un Certain Miroir," *Le Cinema Aujourd'hui* no. 15 (Hiver 1979-80), 51-54; Max Tessier, "L'exutoire du Roman Poruno," from the same volume, 56-63.

9. These include a 1977 remake by Nikkatsu under the generic banner of *roman poruno*, directed by Nishimura Shōgorō, Suzuki's former Assistant Director, and a 1988 version for Tōei by the well known *yakuza* film director Gosha Hideo.

10. Isoda and Todoroki, 210-11.

11. This was to prevent the revelation of pubic hair onscreen in accordance with Eirin's self-censorship standards; the *maebari* became standard practice for Nikkatsu's erotic films. This development, which Suzuki takes credit for and seems to predate the use of a similar device in Hollywood, had a tremendous impact on the aesthetics and representation of sexuality in Japanese, if not international, cinema. Isoda and Todoroki, 210.

12. Makino's film was independently produced; Taniguchi's film, for Tōhō, was under the title *Escape at Dawn/Akatsuki no dassō*.

13. Koschmann, 51-57, explores the relation of negativity and irony to early post-war "humanist" literature, but the realist practice of studio cinema during the

Occupation was predominantly reconstructionist in tone. Even in Kurosawa's *Nora inu*, studio realism tended to come down in favor of the restoration of law and order.

14. On the cinematic representation of post-war discourses of "victim consciousness" (*higaisha ishiki*), see Standish's *Myth and Masculinity*, 146-58 and *Politics, Porn, and Protest*, 52-57. Yoshimoto argues, persuasively, that the rejection of victim consciousness defined Ōshima's early films such as *Shiiku/The Catch* (Sōzōsha, 1963): Yoshimoto, "Questions of the New: Ōshima Nagisa *Cruel Story of Youth*," in Alastair Phillips and Julian Stringer, eds., *Japanese Cinema: Texts and Contexts* (Abingdon, Oxon: Routledge, 2007), 176-80, and likewise the early *nuberu bagu*: see Standish *Politics, Porn and Protest*, 27-30.

15. Standish, *Myth and Masculinity*, 69-72, 86, 95, 117, 151, 154.

16. Gluck, "The Past in the Present," in Gordon, ed., *Postwar Japan as History*, 82.

17. Gluck, 83.

18. Igarashi, 13.

19. While the Japanese Right (including unreconstructed militarists) forged cooperative ties with American authorities during and after the Occupation (1945-1952), in order to combat socialism, suppress trade unionism, and reinvigorate Corporate Japan as a link in the economic world system (as a military supplier during the Korean War), the Left therefore reacted to the Occupation's Red Purge of 1950 with bitter Anti-Americanism, a sense of betrayal by the "agents" of a democracy that the Left had been, in theory, prepared to extol as Japan's bright future. Dower, 4-5, 9-10, 13-16, 18-27; Koschmann, 44-48.

20. Igarashi, 55-57, 60-61.

21. Igarashi, 59-60.

22. Igarashi, 106-13.

23. Ōshima, in David Desser, *Eros Plus Massacre* (Bloomington: Indiana University Press, 1988), 52.

24. The post-war theorist Maruyama Masao criticized Tamura's *Nikutai bungaku* as a shallow and limiting "realism" (i.e., naturalism), which lacked thoroughly modern political subjectivity: Igarashi, 61-63.

25. Interview with Mori Jun (2005), from the Criterion DVD release of *Story of a Prostitute*.

26. This refers to the legendary pre-historic kingdom of *yamato* under the mythical Emperor Jimmu. A way of separating "native" Japanese from Chinese culture in the middle ages, *Yamato damashii* evolved into a transcendental guarantee of national exceptionalism through martial valor and (eventually) a quasi-official battle cry of Japanese troops during the war period 1932-1945.

27. Eiko Maruko Siniawer, *Ruffians, Yakuza, Nationalists* (Ithaca: Cornell University Press, 2008), 139-61; David E. Kaplan and Alec Dubro, *The Yakuza*, rev. ed. (Berkeley: University of California Press, 2003), 32-42, 46-66.

28. From a documentary on the making of *Kenkei tai soshiki boryoku* (1975), recently made available on the 2017 Arrow blu-ray of the film.

29. Silverberg discusses the domestic and imperial emphasis of even a comparatively modern, Westernized magazine such as *Shufu no tomo* (*Housewife's Friend*), 143-53.

30. While the heroine of Tamura's story is explicitly Chinese, the ethnic identity of Harumi, who first appears in Shanghai with a Japanese lover, is never explicitly revealed in Suzuki's version. I do not know the motivation for this decision, but the Japanese cultural attachments of the couple suit its satirical focus.

31. William W. Kelly, "Finding a Place in Metropolitan Japan," in Gordon, 194. This was accompanied by a vast advertising regime aimed at housewives.

32. Interview conducted for the 2005 Criterion collection DVD.

33. Iida Kokomi, *Kinema junpō* no. 388 (Early April 1965): 87.

34. Review by Ogura Masami, *Kinema junpō* no. 370 (Late July 1964): 80-81.

35. *Eiga hyōron* (Nov. 1964): 86.

36. Satō, *Currents in Japanese Cinema*, 225.

37. Standish, *A New History of Japanese Cinema* (New York: Continuum, 2005), 259.

38. Standish, 259.

39. Ogawa Yoshiyuki, *Kinema junpō* no. 370 (Late July 1964): 80.

40. The very iconography of "hanging" in erotic narrative specifies a masochistic scenario, as Deleuze shows in relation to von Sacher-Masoch's fiction: "the masochistic rites of torture and suffering imply actual physical suspension (the hero is hung up, crucified, or suspended)." Deleuze, *Masochism: Coldness and Cruelty*, 33.

41. Deleuze, 14, 32, 37-46.

42. Catherine Constable, in her book *Thinking in Images* (London: British Film Institute, 2005), 57-58, 63, effectively criticized the account of masochism in Studlar's *In the Realm of Pleasure: Von Sternberg, Dietrich, and the Masochistic Aesthetic* (New York: Columbia University Press, 1993), insofar as it relates to early female psychological development. I bracket these concerns here and concentrate on Studlar's account of male masochism as it relates the masochistic contours of a male filmmaking practice.

43. Deleuze, 13-16, 34-35.

44. Studlar, *In the Realm of Pleasure*, 14-15.

45. Theodor Reik, *Masochism and Modern Man*, quoted in Studlar, 16.

46. Deleuze, 60.

47. Brian Moeran, 105. Needless to say, the notion of the sadistic male seeking out a "masochistic" (hence willing) victim is incoherent on the level of clinical symptomology.

48. Kinder, *Blood Cinema; The Reconstruction of National Identity in Spain* (Berkeley: University of California Press, 1993), 149-50.

49. Kinder, 148-50, 197-98, 210-21, 250. Kinder's Phallic Mother as an overbearing stand-in for the patriarch is notably antithetical to Deleuze's configuration of a tripartite maternal archetype dominated by the "Oral Mother" who rebellious-

ly supplants both the Oedipal mother *and* the father. Deleuze is explicitly hostile to "a disguised father image in the masochistic ideal . . . detecting the presence of the father behind the women torturer.": Deleuze, 55.

50. This is a rather common *topos* of Hollywood *film noir* and its descendants: see William B. Covey, "*Pères Fatales*: Character and Style in Postmodern Neo-Noir," *Quarterly Review of Film and Video* 28:1 (2010): 41-52.

51. See Standish, *Myth and Masculinity*, 40-45.

52. Deleuze, "Bartleby, or the Formula," in *Essays Clinical and Critical* (London: Athlone Press, 1993), 71-73.

53. David Rodowick argues that at least the male masochist can "formulate subjectivities that resist patriarchal authority and phallic sexuality" even if through negativity and self-castration: Rodowick, *The Difficulty of Difference* (New York: Routledge, 1991), 84-88. Studlar argues for masochism as representational mode or dynamic that enables female resistance to prevailing patriarchal forms: 7-8, 50-52, 73, 77, 82.

54. Satō, 225.

55. Deleuze, 22, 31-33, emphasizes a related, general masochistic disavowal of gender difference.

56. Translated by Igarashi in his *Bodies of Memory*, 59.

57. "Gaylyn Studlar responds to Miriam Hansen . . . ," *Cinema Journal* v. 26 (Summer 1987): 53.

58. Hasumi, "A World Without Seasons," in Hasumi and Suzuki, 21.

59. Hasumi, "A World Without Seasons," in Hasumi and Suzuki, 21.

60. Studlar, 52.

61. It should be noted that in Japan, von Sternberg was perhaps the most revered of Hollywood directors: Richie and Anderson, *The Japanese Film: Art and Industry*, rev. ed. (Princeton University Press, 1982), 247; Satō, *Currents in Japanese Cinema*, 32.

62. Deleuze recognizes that "dialectic implies transposition and displacements of this kind, resulting in a scene being enacted simultaneously . . . with reversals and reduplications in the allocation of roles and discourse": Deleuze, 22.

63. Kinder, 136-37.

64. Kinder, 149-50.

65. Kinder, 146. Deleuze might interpret the (specifically Catholic) imageries that Kinder identifies as an aspect of the "masochism specific to the sadist and equally a sadism specific to the masochist" that are both fundamentally distinct from the independent cultural regimes of sadism and masochism properly so-called. Deleuze, 67, 144.

66. Studlar, 18.

67. Deleuze, 59.

68. Studlar, 19.

69. Studlar, 20-21.

70. Studlar, 21.

71. Deleuze, 26. See also Studlar, 20, 70.
72. Studlar, 27.
73. Studlar, 61.
74. Studlar, 24.
75. Studlar, 116.
76. Studlar, 116.
77. Studlar, 136.
78. Studlar, 131.
79. In Motomura Shūji, ed., *Suzuki Seijun sōtokushū*, 121.
80. Ōshima's statements during this period on the use of gender in political allegory betray a comparative lack of clarity: for example, in *Cinema, Censorship, and the State*, 109. Like Wakamatsu's films, *Hakuchū no tōrima/Violence at Noon* speculates about rape as a dissentient political gesture: Satō argued that such films "became an attempt to liberate the self from the deformity [of psychological repression] through sudden violent acts," aimed, of course, at women: *Currents in Japanese Cinema*, 230. The films are thus perennially problematic for feminist theory: cf. Maureen Turim, *The Films of Oshima Nagisa: Images of a Japanese Iconoclast* (Berkeley: University of California Press, 1998), 246-68.

Chapter 6

1. Yamaguchi, *Eiga hyōron* (Feb. 1967), in Motomura, ed., *Suzuki Seijun: sōtokushū*, 131-32.
2. Isoyama Hiroshi, Review of *Tokyo nagaremono*, *Kinema junpō* no. 415 (May 1966): 62. See also Ishigami Mitsutoshi, "*Tokyo nagaremono igo he*" (After *Tokyo Drifter*), *Eiga hyōron* (August 1966), in Motomura, 130-31.
3. *Kinema junpō* no. 428 (Dec. 1966), 107-26.
4. Isoda and Todoroki, eds., *Sei/jun/ei/ga*, 274. Nikkatsu devotees may notice that the same tune had appeared under the title "*Kanto nagaremono*" in *Kutabare gurentai* (1960), also adapted for a male singer but in a slightly different arrangement.
5. The photograph below is a publicity still for the film *Daisōgen no wataridori/Plains Wanderer*, reproduced in Schilling's *No Borders, No Limits*, 48. The Nikkatsu still is unattributed.
6. Desser, *Eros Plus Massacre*, 68-69; Watanabe, *Nikkatsu akushon no kareina sekai 1954-1962*, 110-23.
7. *Mukokuseki* is notoriously ill-defined, both critically and in popular usage, taking on different meanings with each decade. Recently it has described the not-quite-racially defined appearance of popular anime characters. In the 1960s, one could argue that Honda Ishirō's globalist, futurist, multi-racial fantasies (e.g., *Kaijū daisensō*, 1965) were more *mukokuseki* than anything Nikkatsu ever made. While I do not dismiss the term in this study, neither do I rely on it.

8. Isoda and Todoroki, 275.

9. This sequence functions, in part, as an homage to Ford's *Stagecoach* (1939) in which John Wayne, in a rifle stand-off with the villains, walks boldly towards them and drops to the ground before firing. Since Wayne's purpose is clearly to be the first one to fire, it only underscores the arbitrariness of Suzuki's version.

10. Hasumi, "A World Without Seasons," 14. The textual evidence Hasumi provides for these general claims is from the earlier *yakuza* sequence.

11. Hasumi, 13, 22.

12. Hasumi, 5-9.

13. Satō, *Currents in Japanese Cinema*, 227.

14. Translated in Phillips, ed., *The Films of Seijun Suzuki*.

15. Hasumi, 14.

16. Hasumi, 18.

17. Deleuze, *Cinema 1*, 141-42.

18. Hasumi, 21-22.

19. This is quite clearly the case, for instance, in surrealist films such as Rene Clair's *Entr'acte* (1924), which were certainly revived and discussed by the critics of *Kinema junpō* in the late 1950s and 1960s.

20. Hasumi, 20-22.

21. Iser, "The Pattern of Negativity in Beckett's Prose," in Harold Bloom, ed., *Samuel Beckett: Modern Critical Views* (Englewood Cliffs, NJ: Chelsea House, 1985), 126-28 [italics mine].

22. Hasumi, 17-18, 21-22. William Carroll, in a recent publication, usefully emphasizes, throughout Suzuki's career, the denial or the compromise of the cinematic illusion of depth in favor of flatness, but, following Hasumi, does not pursue the motif in relation to narrative and social allegory; Carroll, 92, 56-57.

23. Hasumi, 20, writes that Suzuki "gradually evolved" toward an idiosyncratic "kind of avant-garde."

24. Stam, *Reflexivity in Film and Literature*, xiv, 2, 7, 128-30, 138-40, 142-44, 151-52. Stam, it must be said, does not *systematically* address processes of cinematic narration.

25. Studlar, *In the Realm of Pleasure*, 87.

26. In Studlar, 90.

27. Studlar, 92.

28. *Oxford English Dictionary* [Online].

29. The director commented, "certainly it was a new city," in Isoda and Todoroki, 276.

30. Problems with waste disposal and water supply became national scandals; the authorities pushed the lower classes and the homeless from the metropole; domestic space became smaller and smaller while public crowding became endemic; Edward Seidensticker, *Tokyo Rising* (New York: Alfred A. Knopf, 1990), 227, 233-35, 259; Roman A. Cybriwsky, *Tokyo: The Shogun's City at the Twenty-First Century*, rev. ed. (Chichester: John Wiley & Sons, 1998), 93-97.

31. Cybriwsky, 125-26.
32. Standish, *Myth and Masculinity*, 184.
33. Cohan, 203.
34. Satō, "Kaneto Shindo," in John Wakeman, ed., *World Film Directors, Volume 2* (New York: H. W. Wilson, 1988).
35. Eiko Maruko Siniawer, *Ruffians, Yakuza, Nationalists* (Ithaca: Cornell University Press, 2008), 176.
36. My sense of Suzuki's considerable, but scattered and unsystematic knowledgeability and *penchant* for semantic gamesmanship suggest that he would have been conscious of the use of roman initials. The extent to which Japanese print and media culture in the 1960s fostered this consciousness may be noted by the use of "BBS" for the NGO organisation *Biggu Burazāsu ando Shisutāsu* (Big Brothers and Sisters) in *Fumihazushita haru* (1958) and Kosuge Haruo's review for *Kinema junpō* no. 213 (Early Sept. 1958): 76.
37. Gay supporting characters are relatively common in Nikkatsu's light *akushon* pictures (e.g., *Kutabare gurentai*), but these, as in the British cinema of the time, are "fey" and comic characters, likeable but weak, unthreatening, and unheroic.
38. Isoda and Todoroki, 275; Suzuki, *Kenka erejii* (2nd ed., 2003), 127.
39. Cohan, 83-84.
40. Barber, *Projected Cities* (London: Reaktion, 2006), 130.
41. Cohan, 19.
42. See Satō, n. 34 above; Itami Jūzō, a contemporary of the *nuberu bagu*, opined in retrospect that "the major problem with the young generation, as I see it, is that the role of the father has become extremely weak. Because Japanese men fought the war and lost it, their value as role models has really declined. So now we have a generation of young people who . . . have no underlying principles for controlling their desires. . . . Japan has become a country in which only the pleasure principle matters"; in Schilling, *Contemporary Japanese Film* (New York: Weatherhill, 1999), 79-80. In the United States, *Life Magazine* observed the habits of "the new American domesticated male"; *Look Magazine*'s 1958 cover story, "The Decline of the American Male," fretted that "men let themselves be dominated . . . they conform to the values of the crowd much too readily," in Cohan, xix, 4-6, 54-55.
43. Cohan, 9.
44. Shindō on *Kenka erejii* (1967), in Motomura, 23.
45. In Keiko I. McDonald, "Defeat Revisited," in *Reading a Japanese Film* (Honolulu: University of Hawai'i Press, 2005), 152.
46. Emiko Ohnuki-Tierney, *Kamikaze, Cherry Blossoms, Nationalisms: The Militarization of Aesthetics in Japanese History* (University of Chicago Press, 2000), 112.
47. Translated in Ohnuki-Tierney, 72.
48. Ohnuki-Tierney, 82, 131.
49. On the so-called "Nikudan incident," in which military commanders sent

three soldiers to their death in Shanghai simply to make media heroes out of them, see Ohnuki-Tierney, 113; Battleship Yamato, the Pacific War's largest and costliest battleship, was sent into combat in wilful disregard of its strategic uselessness: see Yoshida Mitsuru's memoir, *Requiem for Battleship Yamato* (Naval Institute Books, 1999).

50. See Dower, *Embracing Defeat* (London: Allen Lane, 1999), 34.

51. Richie, *A Hundred Years of Japanese Film*, 180.

52. Yoshikawa's serialized 1935 novel *Musashi*, the most popular retelling of Miyamoto Musashi's biographical legend, emphasizes the hero's renunciation of love for the sake of his martial training.

53. Standish, 45.

54. Standish, 37, 82, 89.

55. Tanabe was the author most extensively read by the *kamikaze* pilots and doubtless other servicemen as well, and, according to Ohnuki-Tierney, 5, "delivered the now infamous speech on May 19, 1943 . . . advocating the intellectual's involvement in society as a means to change society. For the students, his message was to go to war." Dr. Nitobe's influential revision of the myth of the samurai "code" imported concepts of European chivalry into the mix: see G. Cameron Hurst's "Death, Honour and Loyalty: The Bushidō Ideal," *Philosophy East and West* 40:4 (Oct. 1990): 511-14, 516.

56. Rayns, essay for the 2005 Criterion collection DVD.

57. Ian Buruma, *A Japanese Mirror: Heroes and Villains of Japanese Culture* (London: Penguin, 1984), 146; cf. Standish, 123.

58. Ohnuki-Tierney, 109.

59. Among the many popular film versions of this story both during and after the war, Inagaki Hiroshi's *Miyamoto Musashi* trilogy from 1940-42, for Tōhō, was arguably the most influential.

60. Silverberg, *Erotic Grotesque Nonsense*, 145-48; Uno, "The Death of 'Good Wife, Wise Mother'?", 296-98; Ohnuki-Tierney, 78.

61. There was a prevailing naïve hope throughout late 1941 that a war with United States would be short and light on resources. See Marius Jansen, *The Making of Modern Japan* (Cambridge, MA: Belknap, 2000), 636-39.

62. Ohnuki-Tierney, 5.

63. The Meiji oligarchy's Imperial Rescript to Soldiers (*gunjin chokuyu*) "linked mountain worship to imperial duty" in proclaiming that the "obligation [to the emperor] is heavier than the mountain but death is lighter than a feather"; in Ohnuki-Tierney, 62.

64. Water imagery was so associated with military culture that a post-war academic volume of writings left behind by student soldiers was entitled *Listen to the Voices of the Sea Gods*; Ohnuki-Tierney, 188.

65. Ohnuki-Tierney, 38.

Chapter 7

1. Suzuki in Satō Tadao, *Currents in Japanese Cinema* (Tokyo: Kodansha, 1983), 224.

2. Translated in Daisuke Miyao, "Dark Visions of Japanese Film Noir," in Alastair Phillips and Julian Stringer, eds., *Japanese Cinema: Texts and Contexts* (Abingdon, Oxon: Routledge, 2007), 193.

3. Standish, *Politics, Porn and Protest*, 6.

4. Suzuki, in Mark Schilling, *The Yakuza Movie Book*, 102; Naremore, *More Than Night*, 17-25, 28.

5. Miyao, "Dark Visions of Japanese Film Noir," 200.

6. See Tanemura Suehiro, "Ruizu bunyueru ron," *Eiga geijutsu* (May 1966): 20-22; Ōshima among others is known to have corresponded about the film: Ōshima, *Cinema, Censorship and the State*, 112.

7. Cf. Miryam Sas, *Fault Lines: Cultural Memory and Japanese Surrealism* (Stanford University Press, c1999), 159-77. The surrealist poet and art critic Takiguchi Shūzō evaded the notorious persecution or "conversion" of Japanese avant-garde artists in the 1930s, in order to become a prominent post-war intellectual and father figure to the 1950s Tokyo avant-garde.

8. Sas, *Fault Lines*, 159, 166.

9. Sas, *Experimental Arts in Post-war Japan* (Cambridge: Harvard East Asian Monographs, 2011), 39-42.

10. Suzuki displayed a calculating consciousness of the era in Schilling, 102.

11. In Miryam Sas, *Fault Lines: Cultural Memory and Japanese Surrealism*, 30.

12. Sas, 68.

13. John Clark, *Surrealism in Japan* (Clayton, Victoria: Monash Asia Institute, 1997), 30.

14. Translated in Clark, 20. Kanbara was not a surrealist but an influential futurist within the 1920s avant-garde.

15. For example, Warshow's famous essay, reprinted in Ursini and Silver's *Gangster Film Reader*, 11-18. There is a certain iconic resemblance between Shishido's character and the dark, bestial Tony Comante of Hawks's *Scarface* (Universal, 1932).

16. Ohnuki-Tierney, 131.

17. Satō, *Currents of Japanese Cinema*, 53.

18. By 1967, robots were already a national obsession of mass media youth culture; for example, Tezuka Osamu's benign *Astroboy* manga and television series and Tsuburuya Eiji's rather violent *Urutora Q* (1965).

19. Klaus Theweleit, *Male Fantasies, Vol. 1: Women, Floods, Bodies, History* (Minneapolis: University of Minnesota Press, 1987), 242.

20. Watanabe Takenobu, *Nikkatsu akushon no kareina sekai*, vol. 2, 133-37.

21. Watanabe, 134-35.

22. Watanabe, 133, 135.

23. Standish, *Myth and Masculinity*, 160-62, 165.

24. Number One's uncanny ability to disappear and reappear recalls the earliest Japanese crime films, remakes of the then scandalous French film *Zigomar* (1911), about a disappearing/reappearing criminal. See Aaron Gerow, *Visions of Japanese Modernity: Articulations of Cinema, Nation, and Spectatorship, 1895-1925* (Berkeley: University of California Press, 2010), 50-65.

25. Melville, quoting Mark Cousins, in "Confessions of a Stray Cat: *Pistol Opera*," *Senses of Cinema* 50 (2009), http://www.sensesofcinema.com/2009/cteq/pistol-opera

26. Bordwell, *Narration in the Fiction Film*, 163-64.

27. I am uncertain that this remarkable gesture can be satisfactorily explained—or defanged, as it were—by William Carroll's use of the term "subjective register." The butterflies, of course, in some sense relate Hanada's memory and traumatized imagination (see chapter 8); but this does not explain the *physical* reactions of Hanada's head, eyes, and face to the non-diegetic butterflies. It seems to me a further level or "register" needs to be accounted for beyond the mere visual corollary of a character's internal space of mood and thought. Carroll also uses an example from *Tokyo nagaremono* of the non-diegetic red line on the train tracks that Tetsu strives to reach (see fig. 6.11). But granting Tetsu's subjective concentration on that area, surely the "redness" of the track may be defined as an ("objective" or "third-person") figure for Tetsu's interest; Carroll, 134-35.

28. I cannot agree with Carroll's generalization, at least as it is stated, that "Seijunesque editing cannot be defined as being continuous or discontinuous" on the basis that Suzuki (like virtually any narrative filmmaker) uses classical continuity as a baseline. Although Carroll's ultimate purpose is quite properly to locate the Suzuki signature in a tension between formal oppositions, the generalization treats obedience to and violation of a well-established system of conventions as proportionate to one another. But the intentional disruption of a system is more remarkable, questionable, provocative, and rarer than simple adherence. The latter is more or less self-effacing; the former demands thought and recognition from the viewer. Thus the pertinent question is whether Suzuki's films are *more* discontinuous than other relevant films, and if so, how and why? Carroll refers to "jarring cuts" in Suzuki as a matter of "setting up expectations and upending them," particularly emphasizing the "initial elision through editing of motivating information that is only revealed in retrospect." These techniques are highly significant (as in, e.g., Harumi's "breakdown" in *Shunpuden*), but so are unmotivated cutaways, jump cuts, repetitions, and spatio-temporal impossibilities (some of which I discuss below) that cannot be said to be related to specific viewer expectations. They relate only in the most general sense to the cinemagoer's expectation of "clarity" as based on a lifetime of absorption in classical conventions; Carroll, 15, 123, 130.

29. Gilles Deleuze, *Cinema 2: The Time-Image*, translated by Hugh Tomlinson and Roberta Galeta (London: Athlone Press, 1989), xi.

30. Deleuze, xi.

31. Deleuze, 127.
32. Deleuze, *Cinema 2*, 102-3.
33. Deleuze, *Cinema 2*, 102-3.
34. Deleuze, 103.
35. Deleuze, 274.
36. Imamura's films of the period develop other, interesting avenues of formal reflexivity, but not of the type that Suzuki developed here, which better resembles British "New Wave" films such as *Performance* (1968/1970).
37. Deleuze, 129.
38. Deleuze, 130. Emphasis mine.
39. Deleuze, 129, 133.
40. Deleuze, 133.
41. Hasumi, "A World Without Seasons," in Suzuki and Hasumi, 21.
42. Deleuze, *Cinema 1*, 214.
43. Deleuze, *Cinema 2*, 137.
44. Deleuze, *Cinema 2*, 138.
45. Deleuze, 142.
46. Gray, *Straw Dogs* (London: Continuum), 79-80.
47. *Eiga geijutsu* no. 255 (November 1968): 52.
48. Deleuze, *Cinema 1*, 127-29.
49. *Kinema junpo* no. 440 (June 1967): 465.
50. In Ōgai's sublime historical tale *Abe ichizoku*, the suicide or *junshi* of a loyal clan retainer elicits inconceivable reactions in the community quite opposite to the ones he intended.
51. Early Shōwa commentators considered the *chanbara* films of Bando Tsumasaburō, as written by scenarist Suzukita Rokuhei, to be "nihilistic": Richie, *A Hundred Years of Japanese Film*, 65. Indeed, the inter-titles of *Orochi* (Futagawa, 1925) posit that "there is no justice, society judges based on appearance, the world is full of lies."
52. Aaron Gerow, *Kitano Takeshi* (London: British Film Institute, 2007), 185.
53. Koschmann treats in similar regard the post-war philosopher Takukawa Sumio, who decried the influence (or misreading) in Japan of the so-called "nihilism" of European philosophy from Kierkegaard to Sartre: Koschmann, 136-40.
54. Isoda and Todoroki, 386.
55. For example, *Noraneko Rokku Sekkusu Hantā/Stray Cat Rock: Sex Hunter* (Nikkatsu, 1971).
56. I take as axiomatic Northrop Frye's definition of myths as narratives that are central to, rather than peripheral to, the dominant culture of any community: Frye, *The Secular Scripture* (Cambridge, MA: Harvard University Press, 1978).
57. Gerow, 184.
58. Alan Wolfe, "Suicide and the Japanese Postmodern," in Masao Miyoshi and Harry D. Harootunian, eds., *Postmodernism and Japan* (Durham: Duke, 1989), 220. I view *Pisutoru opera*'s invocation of Mishima as parodical rather than what Wolfe invokes as a self-aware Jamesian pastiche of itself: 222-24.

59. Wolfe, 216. *Pisutoru opera* is the only Suzuki film that I would describe with any confidence as "post-modern."

60. Kurita Isamu, in an *Eiga geijutsu* (Feb. 1966) article on Yoshida, wrote that "the sexual act is the only one that exists as a moment"; translated in Standish, *Politics, Porn and Protest*, 56. See also Ogawa Tōru in *Eiga geijutsu* (Sept. 1964), on Imamura, in Standish, 79-88.

61. This includes an inebriated interview in *Asian Cult Cinema* v. 21 (1988) reprinted at http://seijunsuzuki.blogspot.com/p/films-of-seijun-suzuki-complete_29.html

62. Translated by Barrett in Satō, *Currents in Japanese Cinema*, 228.

Chapter 8

1. Interview included on the 2006 Kino DVD of *Zigeunerweisen*.

2. Isoda and Todoroki, *Sei/jun/ei/ga*, 350-51.

3. Accounts differ of how Arato and Suzuki initiated their collaboration, but certainly a major catalyst was Arato's appearance as an actor in an avant-garde "roman poruno" film planned by Tanaka and written by Yamatoya; Isoda and Todoroki, 350.

4. Also known as Kara Jūrō's "*Jokyō gekijō*" or "Situation Theatre," which Arato had been a member of, then fired from, before he created his own troupe, the Tenshogikan, in 1972: Benito Ortolani, *The Japanese Theatre: from Shamanistic Ritual to Contemporary Pluralism*, rev. ed. (Princeton: Princeton University Press, 1995), 260.

5. Bourdieu, *The Field Of Cultural Production* (Cambridge: Polity, 2004), 188. See also Roland Domenig, "The Anticipation of Freedom: Art Theatre Guild and Japanese Independent Cinema," Midnight Eye (28 June 2004), http://www.midnighteye.com/features/the-anticipation-of-freedom-art-theatre-guild-and-japanese-independent-cinema/

6. Kyōka (1873-1939) was the principal literary figure of Japanese romanticism in the Meiji era. His 1906 short story, *Shunchū*, and the sequel he wrote immediately afterwards, form the literary basis of *Kagerō-za*. They concern the suicide of a mysterious wife but also feature the protagonist encountering a supernatural theatre performance in the mountains of Kanazawa. Uchida Hyakken (1889-1971) was a short story writer, diarist, and teacher of German. Partially due to the Great Kantō Earthquake, Uchida's Taishō stories of the uncanny were obscure until his reputation for *zuihitsu* (diaries and observational writings) burgeoned in the 1930s. *Zigeunerweisen* is based loosely on Uchida's belated "gothic" novella *Sarasate no ban/The Sarasate Record* (1952) and an earlier story, "Yamakata bōshi" or "The Bowler Hat" (1934). See Rachel DiNitto, *Uchida Hyakken: A Critique of Modernity and Militarism in Prewar Japan* (Cambridge: Harvard University Asia Center, 2008).

7. There was a pronounced effort amongst the intellectual elite of Late Meiji and early Taishō to revitalize kabuki, which was felt to have declined in the early Meiji period due to, amongst other things, state intervention: Ortolani, 183.

8. In Isoda and Todoroki, 349.

9. Richard N. Tucker in Colette Balmain, *Introduction to Japanese Horror Film* (Edinburgh University Press, 2008), 53.

10. Colette Balmain, *Introduction to Japanese Horror Film*, x.

11. Richard J. Hand, "Aesthetics of Cruelty: Traditional Japanese Theatre and the Horror Film," in Jay McRoy, ed., *Japanese Horror Cinema* (Honolulu: University of Hawaii, 2005), 19.

12. Suzuki in Isoda and Todoroki, 352.

13. Quoted in Fujita Masao's review of *Zigeunerweisen*, *Kinema junpō* no. 786 (Late May, 1980): 152.

14. I am uncertain of William Carroll's belief, stemming from Todorov, that the mere presence of potentially supernatural elements in a narrative film necessarily "throws the laws of the film's diegesis into question" to a much greater degree than, say, a cinematic murder mystery. It is after all evident that many narrative genres include fantastic elements that film viewers expect and incorporate as diegetic features even when the characters regard them as supernatural. As I essay it here, the connection between the supernatural and cinematic form is best described as allegorical; Carroll, 143-47.

15. Of many post-war versions of the *Yotsuya kaidan* story (e.g., Kinoshita's 1949 version for Shōchiku), this was a modernized version which emphasized psychological guilt over the supernatural. Keiko I. McDonald, *Japanese Classical Theatre in Films* (London: Associated University Presses, 1994), 49.

16. This motif also occurs in Teshigahara's *Tanin no kao/Face of Another* (Tōhō, 1966).

17. Harry D. Harootunian, *Overcome by Modernity: History, Culture, and Community in Interwar Japan* (Princeton: Princeton University Press, 2000), xvii.

18. "Cinema, Film Directors, and Oshima," in Suzuki and Hasumi, *The Desert Under the Cherry Blossoms*, 48.

19. Toyoda's films include *Yotsuya kaidan* (Tōhō, 1965) and *Jigokuhen/Portrait of Hell* (1969).

20. The fox is central to folklore and extant medieval prose collections such as the *Konjaku monogatari*. Beautiful women who seduce men often turn out to be foxes in disguise.

21. DiNitto, "Translating Prewar Culture into Film: The Double Vision of Suzuki Seijun's *Zigeunerweisen*," *Journal of Japanese Studies* 30 (Winter 2004): 54.

22. McDonald, 92.

23. Tzvetan Todorov, *The Fantastic: A Structural Approach to Genre* (Ithaca: Cornell University Press, 1975), 26-41.

24. Charles Shirō Inouye, "Afterward" to Izumi Kyōka, *Japanese Gothic Tales*, trans. Inouye (Honolulu: University of Hawai'i Press, 1996), 162-66.

25. Balmain, 50-70.
26. John Orr, *Cinema and Modernity* (Cambridge: Polity, 1993), 37.
27. Kyōka and his critics alike recognized Hugo as the literary antecedent to his creation of a "Japanese gothic": Inouye "Afterward" to *Japanese Gothic Tales*, 161-62. Mishima compared Kyōka's use of the doppelganger motif to that of E. T. A. Hoffmann: Inouye, "Introduction" to *Japanese Gothic Tales*, 7. Uchida produced scholarly translations of the German romantics.
28. The relationship between Uchida and Akutagawa is fictionalized in Uchida's short story "Yamakata bōshi," or "The Bowler Hat." DiNitto, *Uchida Hyakken*, 9, 16, 26, 200, 206.
29. Orr, 40.
30. DiNitto, "Translating Prewar Culture into Film," 41.
31. Orr, 39.
32. Orr, 39.
33. Charles Shirō Inouye, *Evanescence and Form* (New York: Palgrave Macmillan, 2008), 122-27.
34. Orr, 44.
35. Cf. Standish, *Politics, Porn and Protest*, 120-44, for the self-acknowledged conundrums of *nuberu bagu* documentary practice (Imamura, Hara, Ōshima).
36. This recalls the use of tape recorders by Number One in *Koroshi no rakuin*.
37. Harootunian, xvii.
38. DiNitto, 48, 41.
39. Suzuki (from the magazine *Shinema '69*) in Satō, *Currents of Japanese Cinema*, 228.
40. McDonald defines "erotetic," following Noël Carroll, thusly: "the audience is expected to frame narrative questions about the fictional world of the film, especially cause/effect chains . . .": McDonald, 13.
41. For Gilles Deleuze, the experience of time logically obliges us to accept that the past "is not necessarily true," therefore enabling a multiplicity of "virtual" or "not necessarily true" versions of it. *Cinema 2*, 130.
42. Lecture at the Bethnal Green Working Men's Club, London, 28 July 2011.
43. See Suzuki in Suzuki and Hasumi, *The Desert Under the Cherry Blossom*, 60.
44. These scatological gestures recall Sakaguchi Ango's highly influential postwar concept of decadence (*daraku*), a kind of resistance to power (or opting out of power) through self-annihilating acts of degradation: Sas, 5-7.
45. Suzuki had originated the motif of children performing traditional theatre in the festival sequence of *Kutabare gurentai* (1960).
46. Silverberg, *Erotic Grotesque Nonsense*, 28-35, 237-48.
47. Ortolani, 260-61.
48. The *aragoto* or "rough" style of kabuki performance is characterized by exaggerated gesture and was pioneered by Edo actor Ichikawa Danjūrō I (1660-1704) as a contrast to the *wagoto* or "soft" style of performance used by Osaka and Kyoto performers.

49. Burch, *To the Distant Observer*, 81, 84-85, 108-9; Kirihara's "Kabuki, Cinema, and Mizoguchi Kenji" offers a more thorough treatment of theatrical mise-en-scène on film, but only in reference to Mizoguchi: in Heath and Mellencamp, 97-106.

50. Sas, *Experimental Arts in Post-war Japan*, xiv, 3.

51. Goodman, *Japanese Drama and Culture in the 1960s: The Return of the Gods* (Armonk, NY: M. E. Sharpe, 1988), 12-19.

52. Goodman in Ortolani, 259.

53. Ortolani, 181.

54. Inouye, "Afterward" to Izumi Kyōka, *Japanese Gothic Tales*, 166.

55. This included advocacy of women's rights, an anti-marriage and anti-war stance: Inouye, "Afterward," 166.

56. On the prehistoric political centrality of *matsuri*, see Joseph M. Kitagawa, "Preface" to Donald L. Philippi, trans., *Norito, A Translation of Ancient Japanese Ritual Prayers* (Princeton: Princeton University Press, 1990), xxii.

57. Hori Ichirō, "Shamanism in Japan," *Japanese Journal of Religious Studies* 2:4 (Dec. 1975): 235-36.

58. In Samuel L. Leiter and James Brandon, eds., *Japanese Theater in the World* (New York: Japan Society, 1997), 17.

59. Oine was originally German: strangers, especially foreigners, were often treated as *kami* (deities) in archaic Japanese folk tradition: Yoshida Teigo, "The Stranger as God," *Ethnology* 20:2 (April 1981): 87-99.

60. On this major motif of female bodily transformation, Susan Napier has argued that *hentai* (erotic) anime of the 1990s emphasizes the "female body in a frenzy of metamorphosis" that is not simply a portrait of "submission and abjection" but an "intricate series of contesting hierarchical relations" that "suggests new kinds of power": Napier, "The Frenzy of Metamorphosis: The Body in Japanese Pornographic Animation," in Dennis Washburn and Carole Cavanaugh, eds., *Word and Image in Japanese Cinema* (Cambridge: Cambridge University Press, 2000), 361.

61. Ronald Bogue, *Deleuze on Cinema* (New York: Routledge, 2003), 117-24.

62. Deleuze, *Cinema 2*, 44, 47.

63. Deleuze, 54-55. See, further, Yacavone, *Language and Semiotic Studies* 3:1, 79-124.

64. Orr, 7, 9.

65. Itō Kazunori, esteemed writer of such anime as *Ghost in the Shell* (1995-), *Patlabor* (1989-) and *Urusei yatsura* (1983-1991), discusses the influence of *Koroshi no rakuin* in Akahori Masako and Tanabe Kaori, eds., *Style to Kill: Koroshi no rakuin bijuaru direkutori* (Tokyo: Puchigura paburisshingu, 2001), A30-A34.

Bibliography

Abrams, M.H., *A Glossary of Literary Terms*, 4th ed. (Boston: Heinle & Heinle, 1999).
Akahori Masako and Tanabe Kaori, eds., *Style to kill: Koroshi no rakuin bijuaru direkutori* (Style to Kill: *Koroshi no rakuin* Visual Directory) (Tokyo: Puchigura paburisshingu, 2001).
Akiyama Kiyoshi, *Kaiki "Tsigoineruwaizen"* (The Bizarre *Zigeunerweisen*). *Nihon eiga kenkyū* 4 (May 1981): 4-6.
Anonymous, Review of *Rajo to kenjū*. *Asahi shinbun* (Dec. 9, 1957).
Anonymous, Review of *Aoi chibusa*. *Asahi shinbun* (Sept. 8, 1958).
Anderson, Joseph L., and Donald Richie, *The Japanese Film: Art and Industry*, rev. ed. (Princeton University Press, 1982).
Andrew, Dudley, *Concepts in Film Theory* (Oxford: Oxford University Press, 1984).
Asada Akira, "Infantile Capitalism." In H. D. Harootunian and Masao Miyoshi, eds., *Postmodernism and Japan* (Durham: Duke University Press, 1989), 273-79.
Balmain, Colette, *Introduction to Japanese Horror Film* (Edinburgh University Press, 2008).
Barber, Stephen, *Projected Cities* (London: Reaktion, 2002).
Betz, Mark, *Beyond the Subtitle: Remapping European Art Cinema* (Minneapolis: University of Minnesota Press, 2009).
Bloom, Harold, *A Map of Misreading*, 2nd ed. (Oxford: Oxford University Press, 2003).
Bloom, Harold, *Shakespeare: The Invention of the Human* (New York: Harcourt Brace, 1998).
Bogue, Ronald, *Deleuze on Cinema* (New York: Routledge, 2003).
Borde, Raymond, and Étienne Chaumedon, *A Panorama of American Film Noir*. Translated by Paul Hammond (San Francisco: City Lights Books, 2002).
Bordwell, David, "A Cinema of Flourishes: Japanese Decorative Classicism of the Prewar Era." In David Desser and Arthur Nolletti, eds., *Reframing Japanese Cinema* (Bloomington: Indiana University Press, 1992), 327-45.
Bordwell, David, "Mizoguchi and the Evolution of Film Language." In Stephen Heath and Patricia Mellencamp, eds., *Cinema and Language* (Frederick, MD: University Publications of America, 1983), 107-16.
Bordwell, David, *Narration in the Fiction Film* (Madison: University of Wisconsin Press, 1985).

Bordwell, David, "Visual Style and the Japanese Cinema." *Film History* 7:1 (Spring 1995): 5-31.
Bourdieu, Pierre, *The Field of Cultural Production* (Cambridge: Polity, 2004 [1985]).
Burch, Noël, *Theory of Film Practice* (Princeton: Princeton University Press, 1981).
Burch, Noël, *To the Distant Observer: Form and Meaning in the Japanese Cinema*, Rev. ed. (Berkeley: University of California Press , 1979).
Buruma, Ian, *A Japanese Mirror: Heroes and Villains of Japanese Culture* (London: Penguin, 1984).
Carroll, Noël, *Interpreting the Moving Image* (Cambridge: Cambridge University Press, 1998).
Carroll, William, *Suzuki Seijun and Postwar Japanese Cinema* (Columbia University Press, 2022).
Cavanaugh, Carole, "Eroticism in Two Dimensions: Shinoda Masahiro's *Double Suicide*." In Alastair Phillips and Julian Stringer, eds., *Japanese Cinema: Texts and Contexts* (Abingdon: Routledge, 2007), 205-17.
Clark, John, *Surrealism in Japan* (Clayton, Victoria: Monash Asia Institute, 1997).
Cohan, Stephen, *Masked Men* (Bloomington: Indiana University Press, 1997).
Comolli, Jean-Louis, and Jean Narboni, "Cinema/Ideology/Criticism." In Bill Nichols, ed., *Movies and Methods*, Volume I (Berkeley: University of California Press, 1976), 22-30.
Constable, Catherine, *Thinking in Images: Film Theory, Feminist Philosophy and Marlene Dietrich* (London: British Film Institute, 2005).
Covey, William B., "Pères Fatales: Character and Style in Postmodern Neo-Noir." *Quarterly Review of Film and Video* 28:1 (2010): 41-52.
Crosby, Eric, "Widescreen Composition and Transnational Influence: Early Anamorphic Filmmaking in Japan." In Steve Neale and Sheldon Hall, eds., *Widescreen Worldwide* (Bloomington: Indiana University Press, 2010), 173-99.
Cueto, Roberto, ed., *Japón en negro* (Festival Internacional de Cine de Donostia-San Sebastián, S.A., 2008).
Cybriwsky, Roman A., *Tokyo: The Shogun's City at the Twenty-First Century*, revised edition (Chichester: John Wiley & Sons, 1998).
Da Silva, Joaquín, "Fukusaku and Scorsese: Yakuza and Gangsters." In Alain Silver and James Ursini, eds., *Gangster Film Reader* (Pompton Plains, NJ: Limelight Books, 2007), 343-57.
De Bary, Brett, "Not Another Double Suicide: Gender, National Identity, and Repetition in Shinoda Masahiro's *Shinjuten no Amijima*." *Iris* 16 (Spring 1993): 57-86.
Deleuze, Gilles, *Cinema 1: The Movement-Image*. Translated by Hugh Tomlinson and Barbara Haberjam (Minneapolis: University of Minnesota Press, 1983).
Deleuze, Gilles, *Cinema 2: The Time-Image*. Translated by Hugh Tomlinson and Robert Galeta (London: Athlone Press, 1989).
Deleuze, Gilles, *Masochism: Coldness and Cruelty*. Translated by Jean McNeil (New York: Zone Books, 1991).

Deleuze, Gilles, "Bartleby, or the Formula." In *Essays Clinical and Critical* (London: Athlone Press, 1993), 68-91.

Desjardins, Chris, *Outlaw Masters of Japanese Film* (New York: I. B. Taurus, 2005).

Desser, David, *Eros Plus Massacre: An Introduction to the Japanese New)Wave Cinema* (Bloomington: Indiana University Press, 1988).

Desser, David, "Gate of Flesh(tones): Color in the Japanese Cinema." In Linda C. Erlich and David Desser, eds., *Cinematic Landscapes: Observations on the Visual Arts of China and Japan* (Austin: University of Texas, 1994), 299-321.

DiNitto, Rachel, "Translating Prewar Culture into Film: The Double Vision of Suzuki Seijun's *Zigeunerweisen*." *Journal of Japanese Studies* 30 (Winter 2004): 35-63.

DiNitto, Rachel, *Uchida Hyakken: A Critique of Modernity and Militarism in Prewar Japan* (Cambridge: Harvard University Asia Center, Harvard University Press, 2008).

Domenig, Roland, "The Anticipation of Freedom: Art Theatre Guild and Japanese Independent Cinema," Midnight Eye (28 June 2004), http://www.midnighteye.com/features/the-anticipation-of-freedom-art-theatre-guild-and-japanese-independent-cinema/

Dower, John, *Embracing Defeat* (London: Allen Lane, 1999).

Dower, John W., "Peace and Democracy in Two Systems: External Policy and Internal Conflict." In Andrew Gordon, ed., *Postwar Japan as History* (Berkeley: University of California Press, 1993), 3-33.

Dyer, Richard, "Resistance through Charisma: Rita Hayworth and *Gilda.*" In E. Ann Kaplan, ed., *Women in Film Noir*, rev. ed. (London: British Film Institute, 2008), 115-23.

Elsaesser, Thomas, "Discipline Through Diegesis." In Wanda Strauven, ed. *The Cinema of Attractions Reloaded* (Amsterdam University Press, 2006), 205-26.

Field, Simon, and Tony Rayns, eds., *Branded to Thrill: The Delirious Cinema of Suzuki Seijun* (London: Institute of Contemporary Arts, 1994).

Foucault, Michel, "Sade, Sergeant of Sex." In *Aesthetics, Method and Epistemology*, translated by Josué V. Harari and edited by James D. Faubion (London: Allen Lane, Penguin Press, 1998), 223-28.

Foucault, Michel, "What is an Author?" (February 1969). In *Aesthetics, Method and Epistemology*, translated by Josué V. Harari and edited by James D. Faubion (London: Allen Lane, Penguin Press, 1998), 205-22.

Fujita Masao, Review of *Zigeunerweisen*. *Kinema junpō* no. 786 (Late May, 1980): 152.

Fukasawa Tetsuya, "Review of *Hachi jikan no kyōfu*." *Kinema junpō* no. 172 (Early April 1957): 109.

Fukasawa Tetsuya, "Review of *Yajū no seishun*." *Kinema junpō* no. 347 (June 1963): 86.

Gaut, Berys, "Film Authorship and Collaboration." In Richard Allen and Murray D. Smith, eds., *Film Theory and Philosophy* (Oxford: Clarendon Press, 1997), 147-72.

Gerow, Aaron, *Kitano Takeshi* (London: British Film Institute, 2007).
Gerow, Aaron, *Visions of Japanese Modernity: Articulations of Cinema, Nation, and Spectatorship, 1895-1925* (Berkeley: University of California Press, 2010).
Gluck, Carol, "The Past in the Present." In Andrew Gordon, ed., *Postwar Japan as History* (Berkeley: University of California Press, 1993), 64-98.
Goodman, David G., *Japanese Drama and Culture in the 1960s: The Return of the Gods* (Armonk, NY: M. E. Sharpe, 1988).
Gordon, Andrew, ed., *Postwar Japan as History* (Berkeley: University of California Press, 1993).
Gunning, Tom, *The Films of Fritz Lang: Allegories of Vision and Modernity* (London: British Film Institute, 2001).
Hand, Richard J., "Aesthetics of Cruelty: Traditional Japanese Theatre and the Horror Film." In Jay McRoy, ed., *Japanese Horror Cinema* (Honolulu: University of Hawaii Press, 2005), 18-28.
Hansen, Miriam Bratu, "The Mass Production of the Senses." In Christine Gledhill and Linda Williams, eds., *Reinventing Film Studies* (Oxford: Oxford University Press, 2000), 337-38.
Harootunian, Harry, "Ghostly Comparisons." In Thomas LaMarre and Kang Nae-hui, eds., *Impacts of Modernities* (Hong Kong University Press, 2004), 39-52.
Harootunian, Harry D., *Overcome by Modernity: History, Culture, and Community in Interwar Japan* (Princeton: Princeton University Press, 2000).
Harvey, Sylvia, *May '68 and Film Culture* (London: British Film Institute, 1980).
Harvey, Sylvia, "Woman's Place: The Absent Family of Film Noir." In E. Ann Kaplan, ed., *Women in Film Noir*, rev. ed., (London: British Film Institute, 2008), 35-47.
Hasumi Shigehiko. "Biography of Seijun Suzuki". In Seijun Suzuki and Shigehiko Hasumi, *Suzuki Seijun: de woestijn onder de kersebloesem/Suzuki Seijun: the Desert Under the Cherry Blossoms* (Rotterdam: Film Festival Rotterdam, NFM/IAF, VPRO, Uitgeverij Uniepers Abcoude, 1991), 80-82.
Hasumi Shigehiko, "A World Without Seasons." In Seijun Suzuki and Shigehiko Hasumi, *Suzuki Seijun: de woestijn onder de kersebloesem/Suzuki Seijun: the Desert Under the Cherry Blossoms* (Rotterdam: Film Festival Rotterdam, NFM/IAF, VPRO, Uitgeverij Uniepers Abcoude, 1991), 7-26.
Hasumi Shigehiko, "*Miburi wo kaita temaneki*" (Beckoning Without a Gesture). *Eiga geijutsu* 31 (August 1977): 110-12.
Hasumi Shigehiko, "*Suzuki Seijun mata wa kisetsu no fuzai*." *Yuriika* 23:4 (1991): 38-57.
Hasumi Shigehiko, "*Yūrei wa kawaita oto wo hibikaseru*" ("The Ghost Makes the Noises Reverberate"). *Eiga geijutsu* (April-June 1980): 32-33.
Hatano Tetsurō, "*Haigo no nai sekai: Suzuki Seijun to sono shinwa*" (A World Without a Backdrop: Suzuki and that Myth). *Bijutsu techō* no. 398 (Sept. 1975): 235-47.
Hayward, Susan, *French National Cinema* (London: Routledge, 1993).
Hill, Logan, "Even Tarantino Was Shocked." *The Telegraph* (12 February 2006).
Hirano Kyoko, "Japanese Crime Films in the 1940s and 1950s." In Roberto Cueto,

ed., *Japón en negro* (Festival Internacional de Cine de Donostia-San Sebastián, S.A., 2008), 283-97.
Hori Ichirō, "Shamanism in Japan." *Japanese Journal of Religious Studies* 2:4 (Dec. 1975): 231-87.
Hurst, G. Cameron, III, "Death, Honour and Loyalty: The Bushidō Ideal." *Philosophy East and West* 40:4 (Oct. 1990): 511-27.
Igarashi, Yoshikuni, *Bodies of Memory: Narratives of War in Postwar Japanese Culture, 1945-1970* (Princeton: Princeton University Press, 2000).
Iida Kokomi, Review of *Shunpuden. Kinema junpō* no. 388 (Early April 1965): 87.
Iijima Tesuo, "Katō Tai to Suzuki Seijun: *insaido de wa hanasakanu ninin no* Taishō *senchūha*" (Katō Tai and Suzuki Seijun: On the Inside, Two Men of the Taishō War Generation Who Did Not Bloom). *Eiga geijutsu* (March 1967): 36-38.
Inouye, Charles Shirō, "Afterward" to Izumi Kyōka, *Japanese Gothic Tales* (Honolulu: University of Hawai'i Press, 1996), 159-202.
Inouye, Charles Shirō, *Evanescence and Form* (New York: Palgrave Macmillan, 2008).
Inuhiko Yomota, *Ajia no naka no Nihon eiga* (Tokyo: Iwanami shōten, 2001).
Ishigami Mitsutoshi, "Tokyo nagaremono igo he" (After *Tokyo Drifter*), *Eiga hyōron* (August 1966). In Motomura Shūji, ed., *Suzuki Seijun sōtokushū* (Tokyo: Kawade shobō shinsha, 2001), 130-31.
Iser, Wolfgang, "The Pattern of Negativity in Beckett's Prose." In Harold Bloom, ed., *Samuel Beckett: Modern Critical Views* (Englewood Cliffs, NJ: Chelsea House, 1985), 125-37.
Isoda Tsutomu and Todoroki Yukio, *Sei/jun/ei/ga* (Tokyo: Waizu shuppan, 2006).
Isoda Tsutomu, *Seijun sutairu: Seijun style* (Tokyo: Waizu shuppan, 2001).
Isoyama Hiroshi, Review of *Tokyo nagaremono. Kinema junpō* no. 415 (Late May 1966): 62.
Ivy, Marilyn, "Formations of Mass Culture." In Andrew Gordon, ed., *Postwar Japan as History* (Berkeley: University of California Press, 1993), 239-57.
Izumi Kyōka, *In Light of Shadows: More Japanese Gothic Tales*. Translated by Charles Shirō Inouye (Honolulu: University of Hawai'i Press, 2005).
Izumi Kyōka, *Japanese Gothic Tales*. Translated by Charles Shirō Inouye (Honolulu: University of Hawai'i Press, 1996).
Izumiya Shigeru, "Tsigoineruwaizen." *Kinema junpō* (Late June 1980): 138.
Jacoby, Alexander, *A Critical Handbook of Japanese Film Directors* (Berkeley: Stonebridge Press, 2008).
Jansen, Marius, *The Making of Modern Japan* (Cambridge: Belknap Press, 2000).
Kagami Saburō, ed., *Hādoboirudo no tanteitachi* (Tokyo: Pashifika, 1979).
Kajiwara Ryūji, "Suzuki Seijun no bi (The Beauty of Suzuki Seijun)." *Eiga hyōron* (July 1964), reprinted in Motomura Shūji, ed., *Suzuki Seijun sōtokushū* (Tokyo: Kawade shobō shinsha, 2001), 120-22.
Kanai Mieko, "*Eiga jihyō*" (Film Comment). *Bungei* v. 20 (September 1981): 186-89.
Kanai Toshio, "*Tokubetsu repo: Shine-kurabu to Suzuki Seijun jōei mondai*" (Special Report on CinéClub Problems Screening Suzuki Seijun's Works). *Kinema junpō* no. 469 (June 1968): 92-94.

Kaplan, David E., and Alec Dubro, *The Yakuza: Japan's Criminal Underworld*, 2nd edition (Berkeley: University of California Press, 2003).

Kaplan, E. Ann, ed., *Women in Film Noir*, rev. ed. (London: British Film Institute, 2008).

Kawarabata Yasushi, "*Sakuhin kenkyū 'Tsigoineruwaizen' oni to obake ni itaburare*" (Studying the film *Zigeunerweisen*: Torment Demons and Ghosts). *Ātto shiata* (Art Theatre) 144 (January 1981): 8-12.

Kawarabata Yasushi, "Suzuki Seijun jiken repōto: sakka ni osareta *Koroshi no rakuin*" (Report on the Suzuki Seijun Affair: *Branded to Kill* Branded on the Author). *Eiga hyōron* (July 1968): 18-21.

Kawarabata Yasushi, "Suzuki Seijun jiken repōto 2: Oretachi no chi ga yurusanai" (Report on the Suzuki Seijun Affair: Our Blood Will Not Forgive). *Eiga hyōron* (August 1968): 63-67.

Kawarabata Yasushi, "*Suzuki Seijun mondai repōto: wakai kōshō he ba wo utsusu*" (Report on the Suzuki Problem: Approaching Preliminary Negotiations). *Eiga hyōron* (June 1971): 60-62.

Kazuki Ryōsuke, "*Suzuki Seijun yo, ongaku ni motto aijō wo . . .*" ("Suzuki Seijun, Love Music a Little More . . ."). *Eiga hyōron* (Nov. 1964): 85-86.

Kelly, William W., "Finding a Place in Metropolitan Japan: Ideologies, Institutions, and Everyday Life," in Andrew Gordon, ed., *Postwar Japan as History* (Berkeley: University of California Press, 1993), 189-238.

Kerr, Paul, "Out of What Past? Notes on the B *film noir*." In Alain Silver and James Ursini, eds., *Film Noir Reader* (New York: Limelight Editions, 2004), 107-27.

Kimura Takeo, "*Kotoshi koso Suzuki Seijun ni eiga wo totte morau tame ni*" (To Shoot a Film for Suzuki Seijun This Year!). *Kinema junpō* no. 627 (March 1974): 96-101.

Kinder, Marcia, *Blood Cinema: The Reconstruction of National Identity in Spain* (Berkeley: University of California Press, 1993).

Kirihara, Donald, "Kabuki, Cinema, and Kenji Mizoguchi." In Stephen Heath and Patricia Mellencamp, eds., *Cinema and Language* (Frederick, MD: University Publications of America, 1983), 97-106.

Kirihara, Donald, "Reconstructing Japanese Film Studies." In David Bordwell and Noël Carroll, eds., *Post-Theory* (Madison: University of Wisconsin Press, 1996), 501-19.

Kitagawa, Joseph M., "Preface" to *Norito, A Translation of Ancient Japanese Ritual Prayers*. Translated by Donald L. Philippi (Princeton: Princeton University Press, 1990), vii-xxxvi.

Komatsu, Hiroshi, "Representations of the Dark World in Japanese Silent Films." In Roberto Cueto, ed., *Japón en negro* (Festival Internacional de Cine de Donostia-San Sebastian, S.A., 2008), 271-83.

Koschmann, J. Victor, "Intellectuals and Politics." In Andrew Gordon, ed., *Postwar Japan as History* (Berkeley: University of California Press, 1993), 395-424.

Koschmann, J. Victor, *Revolution and Subjectivity in Postwar Japan* (Chicago: University of Chicago Press, 1996).

Kosuge Haruo, Review of *Fumihazushita haru*. *Kinema junpō* no. 213 (Late Sept. 1958): 76.
Kosuge Haruo, Review of *Kemono no nemuri*. *Kinema junpō* no. 258 (Early May 1960): 84.
Krutnik, Frank, *In a Lonely Street: film noir, genre, masculinity* (London: Routledge, 1991).
Leiter, Samuel L., and James Brandon, eds., *Japanese Theater in the World* (New York: Japan Society, 1997).
Le Pape, Jean-Paul, "Le Cinema Pink: Un Certain Miroir."' *Le Cinema Aujourd'hui* no. 15 (Hiver 1979-80): 51-54.
Lethem, Roland, "Suzuki Seijun to *Nikutai no mon.*" *Eiga hyōron* (Jan. 1969): 42-47.
McDonald, Keiko I., *Japanese Classical Theater in Films* (London: Associated University Presses, 1994).
McDonald, Keiko I., *Reading a Japanese Film* (Honolulu: University of Hawai'i Press, 2005).
McDonald, Keiko Iwai, "The Yakuza Film: An Introduction." In Arthur Nolletti Jr. and David Desser, eds., *Reframing Japanese Cinema* (Bloomington: University of Indiana Press, 1992), 165-92.
Masumura Yasuzō and Ogi Masahiro, "*Zankoku byōsha to sakka no shiten*" (Cruel Representations and the Author's Point of View). *Kinema junpō* no. 428 (December 1966): 30-35.
Masumura Yasuzō et al., "*Shine rearizumu*" (Cine-Realism). *Kinema junpō* no. 261 (Late June 1960): 50-55.
Matsuda Masao, Review of *Hishū monogatari*. *Kinema junpo* no. 710 (Late June 1977): 154-55.
Melville, David, "Confessions of a Stray Cat: *Pistol Opera.*" *Senses of Cinema* 50 (2009), http://www.sensesofcinema.com/2009/cteq/pistol-opera (accessed September 11, 2010).
Mes, Tom, "Suzuki Seijun." *Midnight Eye* (October 2011). http://www.midnighteye.com/interviews/seijun-suzuki/
Miyao, Daisuke, "Dark Visions of Japanese Film Noir: Suzuki Seijun's *Branded To Kill.*" In Alastair Phillips and Julian Stringer, eds., *Japanese Cinema: Texts and Contexts* (Abingdon, Oxon: Routledge, 2007), 193-204.
Moeran, Brian, "The Beauty of Violence: *Jidai-geki, yakuza,* and *ero-duction* Films in Japan." In David Riches, ed., *The Anthropology of Violence* (Oxford: Blackwell, 1986), 103-18.
Motomura Shūji, ed., *Suzuki Seijun: sōtokushū* (Tokyo: Kawade shobō shinsha, 2001).
Motomura Toshihiro, "The Poisonous Women of the Meiji, Taishō, and Shōwa: Do Not Touch Me, I am Dangerous." In Roberto Cueto, ed., *Japón en negro* (Festival Internacional de Cine de Donostia-San Sebastián, S.A., 2008), 402-14.
Mulvey, Laura, "Visual Pleasure and Narrative Cinema." In *Visual and Other Pleasures* (London: Macmillan, 1989), 14-28.

Nakahara Yumihiko, Review of *Yajū no seishun*. *Eiga hyōron* (July 1963): 34-36.
Napier, Susan J., "The Frenzy of Metamorphosis: The Body in Japanese Pornographic Animation." In Dennis Washburn and Carole Cavanaugh, eds., *Word and Image in Japanese Cinema* (Cambridge: Cambridge University Press, 2000), 342-64.
Naremore, James, *More Than Night: Film Noir in its Contexts* (Berkeley: University of California Press, 1998).
Nichols, Bill, ed., *Movies and Methods*, Volume I (Berkeley: University of California Press, 1976).
Niogret, Hubert, "Entrètien avec Seijun Suzuki." *Positif* n. 352 (June 1990): 26-28.
Nishikawa Katsumi, Inoue Kazuo, Takahashi Osamu, Shinoda Masahiro, "Isetsu: Shōchiku gakkō: Seijun wa doko kara yatta kita no ka" (Opinions: the Shōchiku School: Where did Suzuki Start?). In Motomura Shūji, ed., *Suzuki Seijun sōtokushū* (Tokyo: Kawade shobō shinsha, 2001), 82-94.
Nowell-Smith, Geoffrey, "Six Authors in Pursuit of *The Searchers*." In John Caughie, ed., *Theories of Authorship* (London: Routledge, 1981), 221-23.
Nozawa Kazuma, ed., *Nikkatsu 1954-1971: eizō wo sōzō suru samurai-tachi* (Tokyo: Waizu shuppan, 2000).
Ogawa Yoshiyuki, Review of *Kenka erejii*. *Kinema junpō* 430 (Jan. 1967): 121.
Ogawa Yoshiyuki, Review of *Nikutai no mon*. *Kinema junpō* no. 370 (Late July 1964): 80-81.
Ohnuki-Tierney, Emiko, *Kamikaze, Cherry Blossoms, Nationalisms: The Militarization of Aesthetics in Japanese History* (Chicago: University of Chicago Press, 2000).
Okada Seizō, Review of *Ankokugai no bijo*. *Kinema junpō* no. 212 (Early Sept. 1958): 77.
Orr, John, *Cinema and Modernity* (Cambridge: Polity, 1993).
Ortolani, Benito, *The Japanese Theatre: from Shamanistic Ritual to Contemporary Pluralism*, rev. ed. (Princeton: Princeton University Press, 1995).
Ōshima, Nagisa, *Cinema, Censorship, and the State*. Edited by Maureen Turim (Cambridge: MIT Press, 1992).
Ōyabu Haruhiko, *Yajū shisu beshi* (Tokyo: Dainihon yūbenkai kōdansha, 1958).
Peacock, Steven, *Colour* (Manchester: University of Manchester Press, 2010).
Perkins, V.F. *Film as Art* (London: Da Capo Press, 1993).
Perkins, Victor, "Moments of Choice." *Rouge* [online journal] 9 (2006), http://www.rouge.com.au/9/index.html
Phillips, Alastair, ed., *The Films of Seijun Suzuki* (Edinburgh Festival Programme, 1988).
Phillips, Alastair, *Rififi* (London: I.B. Taurus, 2009).
Phillips, Alastair, and Julian Stringer, eds., *Japanese Cinema: Texts and Contexts* (Abingdon, Oxon: Routledge, 2007).
Phillips, Gene D., *Out of the Shadows* (Lanham, MD: Scarecrow Press, 2012).
Place, Janey, "Women in Film Noir." In E. Ann Kaplan, ed., *Women in Film Noir*, rev. ed. (London: British Film Institute, 2008), 47-69.

Raine, Michael, "Yūjirō: Youth, Celebrity, and the Male Body." In Dennis Washburn and Carole Cavanaugh, eds., *Word and Image in Japanese Cinema* (Cambridge: Cambridge University Press, 2000), 202-25.

Rayns, Tony, "The *Kyoka* Factor." In Simon Field and Tony Rayns, eds., *Branded to Thrill: The Delirious Cinema of Suzuki Seijun* (London: Institute of Contemporary Arts, 1994), 7-10.

Richie, Donald, *A Hundred Years of Japanese Film* (Tokyo: Kodansha, 2001).

Ridgely, Steven C., *Japanese Counterculture: The Antiestablishment Art of Terayama Shūji* (Minneapolis: University of Minnesota Press, 2010).

Rivette, Jacques, "Time Overflowing." In Jim Hillier, ed., *Cahiers du Cinéma 1960-1968* (Cambridge: Harvard University Press, 1986), 321.

Rodowick, D. N., *The Crisis of Political Modernism: Criticism and Ideology in Contemporary Film Theory* (Urbana: University of Illinois Press, 1988).

Rodowick, D. N., *The Difficulty of Difference* (New York: Routledge, 1991).

Rosenbaum, Jonathan, "Bullet Ballet." *Chicago Reader* (22 August 2003), http://www.jonathanrosenbaum.net/2013/10/bullet-ballet/

Russell, Catherine, *Classical Japanese Cinema Revisited* (New York: Continuum, 2011).

Ryōgoku Midori, "*Onna jōi no shisō: Suzuki Seijun ni tsuite*" (Thoughts of a Superior Woman: On Suzuki Seijun)," *Eiga hyōron* (May 1966), in Motomura Shūji ed., *Suzuki Seijun sōtokushū* (Tokyo: Kawade shobō shinsha, 2001), 128-30.

Sand, Jordan, *House and Home in Modern Japan: Architecture, Domestic Space, and Bourgeois Culture, 1880-1930* (Cambridge, MA: Harvard University Press, 2005).

Sano Mitsuo, "*Koroshiya to shunpu no aida no kyokōsei*" (Fictionality Amidst Killers and Whores). *Eiga geijutsu* (May 1965): 48-50.

Sas, Miryam, *Experimental Arts in Post-war Japan* (Cambridge: Harvard East Asian Monographs, 2011).

Sas, Miryam, *Fault Lines: Cultural Memory and Japanese Surrealism* (Stanford: Stanford University Press, c1999).

Satō Katsuji, Review of *Minato no kampai: shōri wo waga te ni. Kinema junpō* no. 145 (May 1956): 94-95.

Satō Shigeomi, Review of *Ankokugai no taiketsu. Eiga geijutsu* v. 8:3 (1960): 73.

Satō Tadao, *Currents in Japanese Cinema*. Translated by Gregory Barrett (Tokyo: Kodansha, 1983).

Satō Tadao, "Kaneto Shindo." In John Wakeman, ed., *World Film Directors, Volume 2* (New York: H. W. Wilson, 1988).

Satō Tadao, "Japanese Cinema and the Traditional Arts." In Linda C. Erlich and David Desser, eds. *Cinematic Landscapes: Observations on the Visual Arts of China and Japan* (Austin: University of Texas, 1994), 165-86.

Satō Tadao, *Nihon eigashi 1960-1990*, vol. 3 (Tokyo: Iwanami shoten, 1996).

Satō Tadao, *Nihon eiga shisōshi* (Tokyo: Sanichi shobō, 1970).

Satō Tadao, "*Suzuki Seijun-ron*." *Ātto shiata* (Art Theatre) no. 144 (January 1981): 18-22.

Schilling, Mark, *No Borders, No Limits: Nikkatsu Action Cinema*, 2nd ed. (Godalming: FAB Press, 2008).

Schilling, Mark, *The Yakuza Movie Book* (Berkeley: Stone Bridge Press, 2003).

Schrader, Paul, "The Yakuza Film: A Primer." In Alain Silver and James Ursini, eds., *The Gangster Film Reader* (Pompton Plains, NJ: Limelight, 2007), 65-83.

Seidensticker, Edward, *Tokyo Rising* (New York: Alfred A. Knopf, 1990).

Sharp, Jasper, *Behind the Pink Curtain* (Godalming: FAB Press, 2008).

Shirai Yoshio and Iijima Tetsuo, "Nihon eiga no ransei 'itanji'" (The *Enfants Terribles* of Japanese Cinema's Troubled Times). *Kinema junpō* no. 440 (June 1967): 41-46.

Silverberg, Miriam Rom, *Erotic Grotesque Nonsense: The Mass Culture of Japanese Modern Times* (Berkeley: University of California Press, 2009).

Siniawer, Eiko Maruko, *Ruffians, Yakuza, Nationalists* (Ithaca: Cornell University Press, 2008).

Sone Yoshitada, "Suzuki Seijun-ron: utae, odore" (The Theory of Suzuki: Dance, Sing). *Eiga geijutsu* no. 255 (Nov. 1968): 52-54.

Spalding, Lisa, "Period Films in the Pre-War Era." In Arthur Nolletti Jr. and David Desser, eds., *Reframing Japanese Cinema* (Bloomington: Indiana University Press, 1992), 131-45.

Stam, Robert, *Reflexivity in Film and Literature* (New York: Columbia University Press, 1992).

Standish, Isolde, *A New History of Japanese Cinema* (New York: Continuum, 2005).

Standish, Isolde, *Myth and Masculinity in the Japanese Cinema* (Richmond, Surrey: Curzon, 2000).

Standish, Isolde, *Politics, Porn and Protest* (London: Continuum, 2011).

Stephens, Chuck, "Kiyoshi Kurosawa Begins at the End," *New York Times* (24 July 2001).

Studlar, Gaylyn, *In the Realm of Pleasure: Von Sternberg, Dietrich, and the Masochistic Aesthetic* (New York: Columbia University Press, 1993).

Suzuki Seijun, "Cinema, Film Directors, and Ōshima." In Seijun Suzuki and Shigehiko Hasumi, *Suzuki Seijun: de woestijn onder de kersebloesem/Suzuki Seijun: the Desert Under the Cherry Blossoms* (Rotterdam: Film Festival Rotterdam, NFM/IAF, VPRO, Uitgeverij Uniepers Abcoude, 1991), 41-51.

Suzuki Seijun, "The Days of *Kantō mushuku*." In Seijun Suzuki and Shigehiko Hasumi, *Suzuki Seijun: de woestijn onder de kersebloesem/Suzuki Seijun: the Desert Under the Cherry Blossoms* (Rotterdam: Film Festival Rotterdam, NFM/IAF, VPRO, Uitgeverij Uniepers Abcoude, 1991), 33-41.

Suzuki Seijun, "Forgetting Foreign Names (Interview by Ueno Kōshi)." In Suzuki Seijun, Hasumi Shigehiko, *Suzuki Seijun: de woestijn onder de kersebloesem/Suzuki Seijun: The Desert Under the Cherry Blossoms* (Rotterdam: Film Festival Rotterdam, NFM/IAF, VPRO, Uitgeverij Uniepers Abcoude, 1991), 67-79.

Suzuki Seijun, *Hanajigoku* (Tokyo, Hokutō shobō, 1972).

Suzuki Seijun, "Interview," *Asian Cult Cinema* 21 (4th Quarter 1998): 42-58.

Suzuki Seijun, *Kenka erejii*, 2nd ed. (Tokyo: Nihon tosho sentā, 2003).

Suzuki Seijun, *Koshū* (Tokyo: Hokuto shobō, 1980).
Suzuki Seijun, "Midnight Eye Interview—Seijun Suzuki." 11 Oct. 2001. Accessed 8 Nov 2010. http://midnighteye.com/interviews/seijun_suzuki.shtml
Suzuki Seijun, Kimura Takeo, Ishigami Mitsutoshi, Satō Tadao, "*Jumon ni miirarete*" (Charmed by a Spell). *Eiga hyōron* (Nov. 1966): 19-36.
Tanemura Suehiro, "Ruizu bunyueru ron." *Eiga geijutsu* (May 1966): 20-22.
Tanemura Suehiro, "Suzuki Seijun-ron: aru chūsei shugiya Meeubisu wa" (The Moebius Strip of a Medieval Anarchist). *Eiga hyōron* (August 1968): 59-63.
Tayama Rikiya, "Bi no seiri: Suzuki Seijun (Suzuki Seijun: The Physiology of Beauty)." *Kokubungaku* 22:8 (June 1977): 155-58.
Telotte, J. P., "A Fate Worse Than Death: Racism, Transgression, and Westerns." *Journal of Popular Film and Television* 26, no. 3 (January 1998): 120-27.
Telotte, J. P., *Voices in the Dark: The Narrative Patterns of Film Noir* (University of Illinois, 1989).
Teo, Stephen, "Seijun Suzuki: Authority in Minority." *Senses of Cinema* 8 (July-August 2000), http://archive.sensesofcinema.com/contents/festivals/00/8/miff/suzuki.html
Tessier, Max, "'L'exutoire du Roman Poruno," *Le Cinema Aujourd'hui* no. 15 (Hiver 1979-80): 56-63.
Tessier, Max, *Images du cinema japonais* (Paris: Lherminier, 1981).
Theweleit, Klaus, *Male Fantasies, Volume 1: Women, Floods, Bodies, History* (Minneapolis: University of Minnesota Press, 1987).
Todorov, Tzvetan, *The Fantastic: A Structural Approach to Genre* (Ithaca: Cornell University Press, 1975).
Tsuda Yukio, Review of *Rajo to kenjū*. *Kinema junpō* no. 195 (Late Jan. 1958): 70.
Turim, Maureen, *The Films of Oshima Nagisa: Images of a Japanese Iconoclast* (Berkeley: University of California Press, 1998).
Uchida, Hyakken. *Realm of the Dead*. Translated by Rachel DiNitto (New York: Dalkey Archive Press, 2006 [1924]).
Ueno Kōshi, *Nikutai no jidai* (Tokyo: Gendai shokan), 1989.
Ueno Kōshi, "Suzuki Battles Nikkatsu." In Alastair Phillips, ed., *The Films of Seijun Suzuki* (Edinburgh Festival Program, 1988), 40.
Ueno Kōshi, ed., *Suzuki Seijun zen eiga* (Tokyo: Rippu shobō, 1986).
Uno, Kathleen S., "The Death of 'Good Wife, Wise Mother'?" In Andrew Gordon, ed. *Postwar Japan as History* (Berkeley: University of California Press, 1993), 293-324.
Utagawa Hiroshige, *The Moon Reflected* (London: IKON/British Museum, 2008).
Varese, Federico, "The Secret History of Japanese Cinema: Yakuza Movies." *Global Crime* 7:1 (February 2006): 105-24.
Vick, Tom, *Time and Space Are Nonsense* (Washington, DC: Smithsonian Institution/Freer Gallery of Art, 2015).
Warshow, Robert, "The Gangster as Tragic Hero." In James Ursini and Alain Silver, eds., *The Gangster Film Reader* (Pompton Plains, NJ: Limelight, 2007), 11-18.

Washburn, Dennis, "The Arrest of Time: The Mythic Transgressions of *Vengeance is Mine.*" In Dennis Washburn and Carole Cavanaugh, eds., *Word and Image in Japanese Cinema* (Cambridge: Cambridge University Press, 2000), 318-41.

Watanabe Takenobu, *Nikkatsu akushon no kareina sekai 1954-1962* (Tokyo: Miraisha, 1981).

Watanabe Takenobu, *Nikkatsu akushon no kareina sekai, vol. 2 1963-1967* (Tokyo: Miraisha, 1981-82).

Weisser, Thomas, "The Films of Seijun Suzuki: A Complete Filmography with Additional Commentary." *Asian Cult Cinema* 21 (4th Quarter 1998): 43-59.

Whittock, Trevor, *Metaphor and Film* (Cambridge: Cambridge University Press, 1990).

Wolfe, Alan, "Suicide and the Japanese Postmodern." In Masao Miyoshi and Harry D. Harootunian, eds., *Postmodernism and Japan* (Durham: Duke University Press, 1989).

Wollen, Peter, *Signs and Meaning in the Cinema*, expanded edition (London: British Film Institute, 1997).

Yacavone, Peter, "Melville's *Pierre*: Metaphor as Smokescreen and Enthusiasm." *Language and Semiotics Studies* vol. 3:1 (Spring 2017): 80-113.

Yamaguchi Tetsu, "*Wakaki hi no Seijun no shōzō* (Portrait of Seijun's Youth)." *Eiga hyōron* (February 1967), in Motomura Shūji, ed., *Suzuki Seijun: sōtokushū* (Tokyo: Kawade shobō shinsha, 2001), 131-32.

Yamane Sadao, *Eiga ga hadaka ni naru toki* (Tokyo: Seidōsha, 1988).

Yoshida Mitsuru, *Requiem for Battleship Yamato* (Washington, DC: Naval Institute Books, 1999).

Yoshida Teigo, "The Stranger as God." *Ethnology* 20:2 (April 1981): 87-99.

Yoshimoto, Mitsuhiro, *Kurosawa: Film Studies and Japanese Cinema* (Richmond: Duke University Press, 2000).

Yoshimoto, Mitsuhiro, "Questions of the New: Ōshima Nagisa *Cruel Story of Youth.*" In Alastair Phillips and Julian Stringer, eds., *Japanese Cinema: Texts and Contexts* (Abingdon, Oxon: Routledge, 2007), 168-80.

Filmography

***Abashiri bangaichi**/Abashiri Prison*. Dir. Ishii Teruo. Prod. Tōei. Japan, 1965. Main cast: Takakura Ken, Arashi Kanjūrō, Abe Tōru, Kunie Tanaka.

***À bout de souffle**/Breathless*. Dir. Jean-Luc Godard. Prod. Productions Georges de Beauregard. France, 1960. Main cast: Jean-Paul Belmondo, Jean Seberg.

***L'âge d'Or**/The Golden Age*. Dir. Salvador Dali and Luis Buñuel. Prod. Charles de Noailles. France, 1930. Main cast: Gaston Modot, Lydia Lys.

***Ai no korida**/In the Realm of the Senses*. Dir. Ōshima Nagisa. Prod. Argos Films/Ōshima Production. France, 1976. Main cast: Fujita Tatsuya, Matsuda Eiko.

***Akai hankachi**/Red Handkerchief*. Dir. Masuda Toshio. Prod. Nikkatsu. Japan, 1964. Main cast: Ishihara Yūjirō, Asaoka Ruriko, Nitani Hideaki, Kawachi Tamio, Kaneko Nobuo.

***Akatsuki no dassō**/Escape at Dawn* aka *Desertion at Dawn*. Dir. Senkichi Taniguchi. Prod. Tōhō. Japan, 1950. Main cast: Ikebe Ryō, Yamaguchi Yoshiko (aka Shirley Yamaguchi), Ozawa Eitarō.

***Ankokugai**/Underworld*. Dir. Yamamoto Kajirō. Prod. Tōhō. Japan, 1956. Main cast: Tsuruta Kōji, Shimura Takashi, Aoyama Kyōko, Miyaguchi Seiji.

***Ankokugai no taiketsu**/The Last Gunfight*. Dir. Okamoto Kihachi. Prod. Tōhō. Japan, 1959. Main cast: Mifune Toshirō, Tsuruta Kōji, Satō Makoto, Hirata Akihiko.

***Aoi sanmyaku**/Blue Mountains*. Dir. Imai Tadashi. Prod. Shōchiku. Japan, 1949. Main cast: Hara Setsuko, Ikebe Ryō, Kogure Michiyo.

Belle de Jour. Dir. Luis Buñuel. Prod. Hakim/Paris Film. France, 1966. Main cast: Catherine Deneuve, Jean Sorel, Michel Piccoli, Geneviève Page.

***Buta to gunkan**/Pigs and Battleships*. Dir. Imamura Shohei. Prod. Nikkatsu. Japan, 1961. Main cast: Nagato Hiroyuki, Yoshimura Jitsuko, Tanba Tetsurō.

***Das Cabinet des Caligari**/The Cabinet of Dr. Caligari*. Dir. Robert Wiene. Prod. Decla-Bioscop AG. Germany, 1919. Main cast: Werner Krauss, Conrad Veidt, Friedrich Feher, Lil Dagover.

***Chitei no uta**/Song of the Underworld*. Dir. Noguchi Hiroshi. Prod. Nikkatsu. Asst. Dir. Suzuki Seitarō. Japan, 1956. Main cast: Nawa Hiroshi, Ishihara Yūjirō, Sugai Ichirō, Takashina Kaku.

***Chūji no tabi nikki**/Chūji's Travel Diary*. Dir. Itō Daisuke. Prod. Nikkatsu. Japan, 1927. Main cast: Ōkochi Denjirō, Nakamura Hideo, Nakamura Kichiji, Kinoshita Chiyoko.

***Der Congress Tanzt**/Congress Dances*. Dir. Erik Charell. Prod. UFA. Germany, 1931. Main cast: Conrad Veidt, Willi Fritsch, Lil Dagover, Lilian Harvey.

Cotton Comes to Harlem. Dir. Ossie Davis. Prod. Formosa/United Artists. USA, 1970. Main cast: Raymond St. Jacques, Godfrey Cambridge, Calvin Lockhart, Redd Foxx.

Destry Rides Again. Dir. George Marshall. Prod. Universal. USA, 1938. Main cast: Marlene Dietrich, James Stewart, Brian Donlevy, Charles Winninger.

Dr. No. Dir. Terence Young. Prod. Eon/Batjac/United Artists. UK, 1962. Main cast: Sean Connery, Ursula Andress, Joseph Wiseman, Jack Lord.

Drums Along the Mohawk. Dir. John Ford. Prod. Twentieth Century Fox. USA, 1939. Main cast: Henry Fonda, Claudette Colbert, Edna May Oliver, Chief John Big Tree.

***Edojō saigo no hi**/Last Days of Edo Castle*. Dir. Inagaki Hiroshi. Prod. Tōhō. Japan, 1941. Main cast: Hara Kensaku, Kagawa Ryōsuke, Shimura Takashi.

***Ero shogun to nijūichi nin no aishō**/Lustful Shogun and his 91 Concubines*. Dir. Suzuki Norifumi. Prod. Tōei. Japan, 1972. Main cast: Hayashi Shinichirō, Watanabe Yayoi, Ike Reiko, Abe Tōru.

***Le fantôme de la liberté**/Phantom of Liberty*. Dir. Luis Buñuel. Prod. EIA/Greenwich. France, 1974. Main cast: Michel Lonsdale, Monica Vitti, Adolfo Celi, Julein Bertheu.

***Getsuyōbi no Yuka**/Monday Girl* aka *Only on Mondays*. Dir. Nakahira Kō. Prod. Nikkatsu. Japan, 1964. Main cast: Kaga Mariko, Nakao Akira, Hino Michio.

Gilda. Dir. Charles Vidor. Prod. Columbia. USA, 1946. Main cast: Rita Hayworth, Glenn Ford, George Macready.

***Gitā o motta wataridori**/Rambling Guitarist*. Dir. Buichi Saitō. Prod. Nikkatsu. Japan, 1959. Main cast; Kobayashi Akira, Shishido Jō, Kaneko Nobuo.

***Jigoku**/Inferno* aka *The Sinners from Hell*. Dir. Nakagawa Nobuo. Prod. Shintōhō. Japan, 1960. Main cast: Amachi Shigeru, Mitsuya Utako, Numata Yoichi, Nakamura Torahiko.

***Jigoku no satsutaba**/Bankroll from Hell*. Dir. Noguchi Hiroshi. Prod. Nikkatsu. Japan, 1958. Main cast: Mizushima Michitarō, Sugai Ichirō, Hirōka Mieko.

***Jōi-uchi: hairyō tsuma shimatsu**/Rebellion*. Dir. Kobayashi Masaki. Prod. Tōhō. Japan, 1965. Main cast: Mifune Toshirō, Nakadai Tatsuya, Mishima Masao, Tsukasa Yoko.

***Karadatachi no hana**/Orange Flower*. Dir. Saeki Kiyoshi. Prod. Nikkatsu. 2nd Asst. Dir. Suzuki Seitarō. Japan, 1954. Main cast: Amimaya Setsuko, Chō Hirsohi, Itō Yūnosuke.

***Kawaita hana**/Pale Flower*. Dir. Shinoda Masahiro. Prod. Shōchiku. Japan, 1963/4. Main cast: Ikebe Ryō, Kaga Mariko, Miyaguchi Seiji, Tōno Eijirō.

***Kenjū buraichō: Nukiuchi no Ryūji**/Ryūji the Gunslinger*. Dir. Noguchi Hiroshi. Prod. Nikkatsu. Japan, 1960. Main cast: Akagi Keihachirō, Shishido Jō, Asaoka Ruriko, Sugai Ichirō.

***Kenjū zankoku monogatari**/Cruel Gun Story*. Dir. Furukawa Takumi. Prod. Nikkatsu. Japan, 1964. Main cast: Shishido Jō, Matsubaira Chieko, Kawachi Tamio.

Kiss Me Deadly. Dir. Robart Aldrich. Prod. Parklane Pictures. USA, 1955. Main cast: Ralph Meeker, Albert Dekker, Paul Stewart, Cloris Leachman.

Kōkaku Kidōtai/Ghost in the Shell. Dir. Oshii Mamoru. Prod. Bandai visual/Kōdansha, Production I.G. Japan, 1995. Main cast: Tanaka Atsuko, Ōtsuka Akio, Ōki Tamio, Iemasa Kayumi.

Koruto wa ore no pasupōto/A Colt Is My Passport. Dir. Nomura Takashi. Prod. Nikkatsu. Japan, 1967. Main cast: Shishido Jō, Jerry Fujio, Kobayashi Chitose, Esumi Eimei.

Koshiben ganbare/Flunky, Work Hard! Dir. Naruse Mikio. Prod. Shōchiku. Japan, 1930. Main cast: Yamaguchi Isamu, Naniwa Tomoko, Akiyama Shizue, Katō Seiichi.

Kunisada Chūji. Dir. Takizawa Eisuke. Prod. Nikkatsu. Asst. Dir. Suzuki Seitarō. Japan, 1954. Main cast: Tatsumi Ryotarō, Tsushima Keiko.

Kuroi shio/Black Tide. Dir. Yamamura Sō. Prod. Nikkatsu. Asst. Dir. Suzuki Seitarō. Japan, 1954. Main cast: Yamamura Sō, Tōno Eijirō, Abe Tōru.

Kurutta kajitsu/Crazed Fruit. Dir. Nakahira Kō. Prod. Nikkatsu. Japan, 1956. Main cast: Ishihara Yūjirō, Kitahara Mie, Tsugawa Masahiko, Ishihara Shintarō.

Kyōjin to gangu/Giants and Toys. Dir. Masumura Yasuzō. Prod. Daiei. Japan, 1958. Main cast: Kawaguchi Hiroshi, Nozoe Hitomi, Takamatsu Hideo, Itō Yūnosuke.

Kyonetsu no kisetsu/Season of the Sun aka *Season of Heat* aka *The Warped Ones*. Dir. Kurahara Koreyoshi. Prod. Nikkatsu. Japan, 1960. Main cast: Kawachi Tamio, Matsumoto Noriko, Nagato Hiroyuki, Gō Eiji.

The Long Goodbye. Dir. Robert Altman. Prod. E-K Corporation/Lion's Gate Films. USA, 1973. Main cast: Elliott Gould, Nina van Pallandt, Sterling Hayden, Mark Rydell.

The Maltese Falcon. Dir. John Huston. Prod. Warner Brothers. USA, 1941. Main cast: Humphrey Bogart, Mary Astor, Peter Lorre, Sydney Greenstreet.

Metropolis. Dir. Fritz Lang. Prod. UFA. Germany, 1927. Main cast: Brigitte Helm, Gustav Frölich, Rudolf Klein-Rogge, Alfred Abel.

Nagaremono (film series). Dir. Yamazaki Tokujirō. Prod. Nikkatsu. Japan, 1960-61. Main cast: Kobayashi Akira, Shishido Jō, Asaoka Ruriko.

Naniwa erejii/Naniwa Elegy aka *Osaka Elegy*. Dir. Mizoguchi Kenji. Prod. Shōchiku. Japan, 1936. Main cast: Yamada Isuzu, Umemura Yōko, Asaka Shinhachirō, Shiganoya Benkei.

Narayama bushikō/Ballad of Narayama. Dir. Kinoshita Keisuke. Prod. Shōchiku. Japan, 1958. Main cast: Tanaka Kinuyo, Takahashi Teiji, Miyaguchi Seiji, Itō Yūnosuke.

Narayama bushikō/Ballad of Narayama. Dir. Imamura Shōhei. Prod. Tōei. Japan, 1983. Main cast: Ogata Ken, Sakamoto Sumiko, Aki Takejō, Takada Junko.

Night and the City. Dir. Jules Dassin. Prod. 20th Century Fox. UK, 1950. Main cast: Richard Widmark, Gene Tierney, Googie Withers, Francis L. Sullivan.

Nihon no yoru to kiri/Night and Fog in Japan. Dir. Ōshima Nagisa. Prod. Shōchiku. Japan, 1960. Main cast: Kuwano Miyuki, Watanabe Fumio, Tsugawa Masahiko.

***Nikui an-chikushō**/I Hate but Love*. Dir. Kurahara Koreyoshi. Prod. Nikkatsu. Japan, 1962. Main cast: Ishihara Yūjirō, Asaoka Ruriko, Nagato Hiroyuki, Kawachi Tamio.

***Nikutai no mon**/Gate of Flesh*. Dir. Makino Masahiro. Prod. Yoshimoto Production. Japan, 1948. Main cast: Aizome Yumiko, Haruna Kaoru, Kyokawa Sōji, Mizushima Michitarō.

***Nikutai no mon**/Gate of Flesh*. Dir. Nishimura Shōgorō. Prod. Nikkatsu. Japan, 1977. Main cast: Kayama Reiko, Yamaguchi Miyako, Watanabe Tokuko, Miyashita Junko.

***Nippon konchūki**/Insect Woman*. Dir. Imamura Shōhei. Prod. Nikkatsu. Japan, 1963. Main cast: Hidari Sachiko, Aizawa Keiko, Kawazu Seizaburō, Harukawa Masumi.

***Nora inu**/Stray Dog*. Dir. Kurosawa Akira. Prod. Tōhō. Japan, 1949. Main cast: Mifune Toshirō, Shimura Takashi, Miyoshi Eiko, Awaji Keiko.

***Nora neko rokku: Sekkusu hantā**/Stray Cat Rock: Sex Hunter*. Dir. Hasebe Yasuhara. Prod. Nikkatsu. Japan, 1970. Main cast: Kaji Meiko, Fuji Tatsuya, Okazaki Jirō.

North by Northwest. Dir. Alfred Hitchcock. Prod. M-G-M. USA, 1959. Main cast: Cary Grant, Eva Marie Saint, James Mason, Jessie Royce Landis.

***Okasareta hakui**/Violated Angels*. Dir. Wakamatsu Kōji. Prod. Wakamatsu Pro. Japan, 1967. Main cast: Kara Jūrō, Koyanagi Keiko, Natsu Junko.

Onibaba. Dir. Shindo Kaneto. Prod. Tōhō. Japan, 1964. Main cast: Otawa Nobuko, Yoshimura Jitsuko, Satō Kei, Uno Jukichi.

***Ore no kenjū wa subayai**/My Pistol Is Quick*. Dir. Noguchi Hiroshi. Prod. Nikkatsu. Japan, 1954. Asst. Dir. Suzuki Seitarō. Main cast: Kawazu Seizaburō, Sumiko Hidaka, Nawa Hiroshi.

***Ore wa matteiru ze**/I am Waiting*. Dir. Kurahara Koreyoshi. Prod. Nikkatsu. Japan, 1957. Main cast: Ishihara Yūjirō, Kitihara Mie, Nitani Hideaki, Kosugi Isamu.

***Otoko no monshō**/Gambler's Code*. Dir. Matsuo Akinori. Prod. Nikkatsu. Japan, 1966. Main cast: Takahashi Hideki, Izumi Masako, Kondō Hiroshi, Kijima Ichirō.

***La Passion de Jeanne D'Arc**/The Passion of Joan of Arc*. Dir. Carl Theodor Dreyer. Prod. Société Générale des Films. France, 1928. Main cast: Renée Falconetti, Eugene Silvain, Maurice Schutz, Antonin Artaud.

Performance. Dir. Donald Cammell and Nicolas Roeg. Prod. Warner Brothers. UK, 1968/70. Main cast: James Fox, Mick Jagger, Anita Pallenberg, Michèle Breton.

The President's Analyst. Dir. Theodore J. Flicker. Prof. Paramount. USA, 1967. Main cast: James Coburn, Severn Darden, Godfrey Cambridge, William Daniels.

***Le Procès**/The Trial*. Dir. Orson Welles. Prod. Paris/Europa Productions/Hisa Film/Finanziaria Cinematografica Italiana (FICIT). France, Germany, Italy, 1962. Main cast: Anthony Perkins, Jeanne Moreau, Romy Schneider, Orson Welles.

***Rakujitsu no kettō**/Duel at Sunset*. Dir. Noguchi Hiroshi. Prod. Nikkatsu. Written by Suzuki Seitarō and Ida Motomu. Asst. Dir. Suzuki Seitarō. Japan, 1955. Main cast: Bando Kōtarō, Akechi Jūzaburō.

Rear Window. Dir. Alfred Hitchcock. Prod. Universal. USA, 1954. Main cast: James Stewart, Grace Kelly, Thelma Ritter, Raymond Burr.

Red River. Dir. Howard Hawks. Prod. United Artists. USA, 1946/8. Main cast: John Wayne, Montgomery Clift, Walter Brennan, Joanne Dru.
Sabita naifu/*Rusty Knife*. Dir. Masuda Toshio. Prod. Nikkatsu. Japan, 1958. Main cast: Ishihara Yūjirō, Kitahara Mie, Kobayashi Akira, Shiraki Mari.
Scarface. Dir. Howard Hawks. Prod. Universal. USA, 1932. Main cast: Paul Muni, Ann Dvorak, George Raft, Boris Karloff.
The Searchers. Dir. John Ford. Prod. Warner Bros. USA, 1956. Main cast: John Wayne, Jeffrey Hunter, Natalie Wood, Ward Bond.
Seishun zankoku monogatari/*Cruel Story of Youth* aka *Naked Youth*. Dir. Ōshima Nagisa. Prod. Shōchiku. Japan, 1960. Main cast: Kuwano Miyuki, Kawazu Yūsuke, Kuga Yoshiko, Watanabe Fumio.
Shiiku/*The Catch*. Dir. Ōshima Nagisa. Prod. Sōzōsha. Japan, 1961. Main cast: Mikuni Rentarō, Hugh Hurd.
Shushin imada kiezu/*Red Lips Still Not Gone*. Dir. Shibuya Minoru. Prod. Shōchiku, 1949. 3rd Asst. Dir. Suzuki Seitarō. Main cast: Takasugi Sanae, Saburi Shin, Sada Keiji, Kuga Yoshiko.
Stagecoach. Dir. John Ford. Prod. Walter Wanger. USA, 1939. Main cast: John Wayne, Claire Trevor, Thomas Mitchell, John Carradine.
Taiyō no hakaba/*The Sun's Burial*. Dir. Ōshima Nagisa. Prod. Shōchiku. Japan, 1960. Main cast: Honō Kayoko, Tsugawa Masahiko, Sasaki Isao, Fujiwara Kamitari.
Taiyō no kisetsu/*Season of the Sun*. Dir. Furukawa Takumi. Prod. Nikkatsu. Japan, 1956. Main cast: Nagato Hiroyuki, Minamida Yōko, Tsugawa Masahiko, Ishihara Yūjirō.
Tanin no kao/*Face of Another*. Dir. Teshigahara Hiroshi. Prod. Teshigahara Production. Japan, 1966. Main cast: Nakadai Tatsuya, Kyō Machiko, Hira Mikijirō, Kishida Kyōko.
Tanuki goten/*Raccoon Palace*. Dir. Kimura Keigo. Prod. Shinko Kinema Oizuni Ltd. Japan, 1939. Main cast: Azuma Ryōnosuke, Bando Tarō.
Taxi Driver. Dir. Martin Scorsese. Prod. Italo/Judeo Films/Bill-Phillips/Columbia Pictures. USA, 1976. Main cast: Robert De Niro, Jodie Foster, Harvey Keitel, Cybill Shepherd.
Tobenai chinmoku/*Silence Has No Wings*. Dir. Kazuki Kuroi. Prod. ATG. Japan, 1964/6. Main cast: Kaga Mariko.
Tōkaidō yotsuya kaidan/*Yotsuya Ghost Story of Tokaidō*. Dir. Nakagawa Nobuo. Prod: Daiei. Japan, 1959. Main cast: Amachi Shigeru, Kitazawa Noriko.
Un Chien Andalou/*An Andalusian Dog*. Dir. Dali and Buñuel. Prod. Charles de Noailles. France, 1929. Main cast: Pierre Batcheff, Simone Mareuil.
Underworld. Dir. Josef von Sternberg. Prod. Paramount. USA, 1927. Main cast: George Bancroft, Clive Brook, Evelyn Brent.
Wataridori (film series). Dir. Saitō Buichi, Ushihara Yoichi, et al. Prod. Nikkatsu. Japan, 1959-62. Main cast: Kobayashi Akira, Asaoka Ruriko, Shishido Jō.
Yari no Gonza/*Gonza the Spearman*. Dir. Shinoda Masahiro. Prod. Shōchiku. Japan, 1986. Main cast: Iwashita Shima, Go Hiromi, Kawarazaki Chōichiro, Ōtaki Hideki.

***Yoidore tenshi**/Drunken Angel*. Dir. Kurosawa Akira. Prod. Tōhō. Japan, 1948. Main cast: Shimura Takashi, Mifune Toshirō, Kogure Michiyo, Kuga Yoshiko.

***Yotsuya kaidan**/Ghost Story of Yotsuya*. Dir. Kinoshita Keisuke. Prod. Shōchiku. Japan, 1949. Main cast: Tanaka Kinuyo, Uehara Ken, Sugimura Haruko, Sada Keji.

Zigomar. Dir. Victorin-Hippolyte Jasset. Prod. Société Française des Films Éclair. France, 1911. Main cast: Charles Krauss, Alexandre Arquillière.

Index

180 Degree Rule, 128, 130, 131. *See also* "axis (of action)"

Akuma no machi/Demon Town, 46, 320
Akutarō/The Bastard, vii, ix, 19, 30, 42, 67, 68, 70, 142, 163, 331
Akutarō-den: warui hoshi no shita de mo/ Stories of Bastards: Born Under a Bad Star, vii, 42, 70, 71, 163, 256, 312, 335
Ankokugai no bijo/Underworld Beauty, vii, ix, 28, 42, 44, 51, 52-54, 55, 321-22
Ankoku no ryoken/Passport to Darkness, 55, 57, 153, 180, 324
Aoi chibusa/Blue Breasts, 26, 61, 69, 322
Arato Genjirō, 37, 38, 265, 296, 341, 342, 344, 375nn3-4
auteur, auteurism, 2, 4, 10, 28, 36, 38, 40, 41, 42, 46, 88, 109, 157, 262, 266, 313
author (cinematic), authorial 4, 5, 32, 52, 105, 114, 166, 266, 286
"author function," 4, 348n8
avant-garde, xii, 18, 31, 34, 58, 144, 161, 191, 192, 225, 227, 265, 291, 293, 369n23, 372n7, 372n14
avant-garde theatre (Japanese), 37, 38, 101, 267, 296, 298, 299, 375n4
axis (of action), 7, 8, 123, 131, 132. *See also* 180 Degree Rule

Bordwell, David, 7-9, 70, 244, 349n22, 349n23, 384
Buñuel, Luis, 7, 16, 226, 246, 250-51, 258, 262, 357n31
Burch, Noël, 7, 9, 297, 349n24, 360n26

Carroll, William, v, 39-40, 347n7, 348n13, 349n25, 351-52n48, 353n68, 355n13, 357n40, 358n45, 360n43, 369n22, 373n27, 373n28, 376n14
Chandler, Raymond, 45, 77, 89, 360n36
classical cinema, 4, 6, 7-9, 12, 23, 27, 33, 35, 43, 47, 50, 52, 61, 100, 105, 106, 109, 115, 123, 132, 192, 222, 225, 229, 242, 248, 250, 253, 254, 255, 257, 290, 305, 316, 349n22
classical Hollywood cinema, 6, 7-9, 35, 244
continuity (editing), 8, 130, 172, 186, 251, 373n28
forms, conventions, norms, 33, 47, 50, 61, 62-68, 78-90, 107, 121, 123, 160, 373n28
movie stars, 167, 209
narration, 8, 52, 253, 290
narrative, 7, 8, 9, 27, 35, 109, 119, 138, 192
studio realism, 146, 160
style, 7, 115, 244
classical theatre (*i.e.*, Japanese classical theatre), 18, 22, 60, 126, 268, 269, 289, 293, 295, 296, 299, 302, 304, 376n15, 377n45
color, ix, x, xiii, 6, 18, 29, 30, 31, 33, 40, 43, 57, 58, 59, 60, 62, 66, 69, 74, 76-77, 80, 81, 87, 96, 111, 135, 269, 299, 357n38, 357n40
non-diegetic color, 60-61, 88, 115, 117, 119, 143, 174, 193, 200, 202, 286, 357n42
continuity (editing), 7, 8, 9, 125, 128, 130, 131, 133, 160, 172, 191, 222, 229, 248, 250, 251, 253, 268, 280, 290, 292, 293, 300, 305, 316, 373n28
crystal, crystalline image (Deleuze), 305-6, 310, 312

Deleuze, Gilles, 7, 14, 15, 17, 60, 66, 107, 161, 162, 163, 165, 168, 169, 170, 171, 174, 192, 225, 229, 246, 248, 249-51, 252, 253-54, 255, 256, 257, 271, 305, 306, 310, 315, 357n40, 366n40, 366n49, 367n55, 367n62, 367n65, 377n41

/ 397 /

398 / Index

Diegesis, diegetic, 8, 40, 49, 50, 51, 56, 61, 68, 70, 96, 103, 104, 106, 166, 182, 184, 189, 191, 195, 198, 199, 222, 244, 251, 252, 268, 271, 272, 274, 284, 292, 300, 305, 306, 308, 348, 356, 376
   non-diegetic style, ix, xii, 6, 8, 33, 52, 58, 60, 61, 62, 88, 89, 107, 110, 115, 116, 117, 119, 120, 135, 143, 144, 149, 157, 158, 161, 171, 174, 175, 177, 179, 187, 188, 190, 193, 194, 198, 200, 217, 218, 227, 245, 261, 272, 286, 291, 310, 313, 316, 357, 373
directorial style, 23, 31, 50, 180
director study, 5, 248n10
discontinuity (in film editing), xi, xii, xiii, 18, 115, 130-31, 144, 145, 160, 161, 179, 185, 186-91, 192, 193, 196, 222, 225, 227, 246, 247, 248, 249, 250, 252, 253, 254, 255, 256, 259, 268, 280, 283, 300, 316, 373n28

Eiga geijutsu, 32, 37, 223, 257, 375n60
Eiga hyōron, 31, 32, 35, 44, 79, 113, 180, 352n61, 353n68, 359n9
eroticism, eroticization, 32, 43, 48, 50, 87, 93, 96, 97, 107, 157, 168, 170, 172, 173, 222, 258, 263, 264, 267
expressionism, 32, 56, 57, 70, 71, 81, 111, 119, 135, 143, 144, 174, 241, 251, 267

figuration, 2, 3, 16, 17, 18, 40, 62, 107, 172, 193, 244, 260, 289, 316, 360
film noir, ix, xii, 46, 51, 76, 77, 80-81, 82, 84, 85, 92, 93, 226, 229, 230, 351, 353, 356n18, 367n50
Ford, John, 12, 27, 90, 357, 369
Fujita Toshiya, 265, 270, 341
Fukasaku Kinji, 17, 38, 151, 206, 230, 359n18
Fumihazushita haru/The Spring That Never Came, 27-28, 322, 370n36

gendered violence, ix, 15, 17, 76, 85, 88-89, 90-94, 157, 158, 161, 166, 168, 169, 170, 175, 204, 221, 226, 237, 284, 303, 304, 305, 307, 313, 363n36, 368n80
Godard, Jean-Luc, 6, 41, 42, 43, 47, 60, 66, 67, 70, 71, 79, 98, 110, 184, 185, 199, 250, 252, 312, 361n44

Hachi jikan no kyōfu/Eight Hours of Terror, 27, 320, 351n44

hādo-boirudo, ix, 44-45, 46, 47, 53, 77, 79, 80, 224
Hammett, Dashiell, 45, 77, 356
Hana to dotō/The Flowers and the Angry Waves, vii, 108, 133-39, 193, 263, 332-33
Harada Yoshio, 37, 270, 290, 294, 340, 341, 342, 344
hard-boiled, 25, 31, 44, 45-46, 48, 51, 55, 70, 76, 77, 80, 83, 84, 89, 92, 180, 186, 254
Hasebe Yasuharu, 2, 30, 252, 259, 352n58
Hasumi Shigehiko, 24, 31, 36, 39, 40, 52, 67, 69, 102, 126, 167, 168, 191-93, 194, 196, 249, 254, 349n23, 360n43, 360n44, 369n10, 369n23
Hatsui Kotoe, 29, 78, 155
Hishū monogatari/A Tale of Sorrow, vii, xiii, 37, 60, 265, 266, 314, 315, 340, 358n52
Hitchcock, Alfred, 5, 14, 27, 47, 67, 107
Hori Kyūsaku, 11, 27, 30, 33, 34, 35, 61, 223, 242, 304, 354n88
Huston, John, 27, 80, 356n20

iconicity, iconic (discourse), xi, xii, 18, 33, 196-201, 210, 222, 229, 244, 252, 316
Igarashi, Yoshikuni 146, 147, 148, 364n4
Inouye, Charles Shirō, 285, 303
intention (textual or cinematic), intentionality, 3-4, 6, 12, 53, 60, 70, 89, 240, 288, 313, 316, 373
Irezumi ichidai/A Generation of Tattoos, vii, 108, 133, 134, 135, 138, 139, 140, 297, 336
Isoda Tsutomu and Todoroki Yukio, 101, 268, 355n108
Iwami Tsuruo, 23, 24

Jūsangō taihisen yori: sono gosōsha wo nerae/Take Aim at the Police Van, vii, 7, 157, 179, 199, 324

kabuki, 22, 59, 60, 126, 193, 212, 268, 285, 295, 297, 299, 303, 376n7, 377n48, 378n49
Kagenaki koe/Voice Without a Shadow, 42, 50, 54-57, 60, 81, 111, 251, 305, 323
Kagerō-za/Mirage Theatre, vii, 38, 69, 254, 265, 267, 287, 289, 290, 291-313, 316, 342, 375n6

Kaikyō, chi ni somete/Bloody Channel, vii, 29, 42, 57, 110, 328
Kajiwara Ryūji, 32, 173, 352n64
Kantō mushuku/Kantō Wanderer, vii, 31, 108, 109, 111, 113, 114-33, 191, 263, 267, 297, 331
Kawachi karumen/ Carmen from Kawachi, vii, 144, 165, 176-78, 315, 336
Kawachi Tamio, 29, 64, 81, 90, 150, 187
Kemono no nemuri/Sleep of the Beast, vii, 55, 72, 99, 100, 104, 198, 325
Kenjū buraichō: nukiuchi no Ryūji ix, 48
Kenjū zankoku monogatari/Cruel Gun Story, 186, 198, 359, 392
Kenka erejii/Elegy For Violence, vii, 12
Kimura Takeo, 5, 30, 32, 35, 37, 109, 136, 137, 138, 143, 174, 185, 193, 202, 205, 254
Kinder, Marcia, 164-65, 169, 366n49, 367n65
Kinema junpō, 27, 28, 30, 31, 32, 33, 35, 37, 42, 51, 79, 156, 181, 258, 351n45, 352n49
Kinoshita, Keisuke, films of, 23, 59, 263, 376n15
Kobayashi Akira, xi, 13, 27, 29, 31, 33, 77, 108, 109, 115, 118, 134, 181, 182, 206
Kobayashi Masaaki, 12-13
Koroshi no rakuin/Branded to Kill, vii, xii, 30, 33, 35, 37, 38, 56, 108, 119, 179, 196, 207, 221, 223-59, 260, 262-64, 266, 284, 297, 306, 314, 315, 339, 353n80, 377n36
Kurahara Koreyoshi, 26, 27, 30, 43, 63, 71, 180, 185, 356n24, 358n43, 363n36
Kuroi Kazuki, 192, 227
Kurosawa, Akira, x, 5, 14, 21, 32, 34, 41, 45, 56, 57, 80, 111, 119, 134, 145, 146, 156, 257, 258, 314, 316, 348n10, 356n17, 365n13
Kutabare gurentai /Go to Hell Youth Gang, vii, ix, 29, 42, 58-61, 104, 107, 255, 317, 326, 368n4, 377n45
Kyōka Izumi, 38, 135, 267, 277, 303

male gaze, 43, 51-52, 85, 86, 106, 132, 135, 281
Maltese Falcon, 80, 356, 393
masochism, xi, 36, 148, 156, 161-63, 166, 168-73, 174, 176, 177, 208, 260, 278, 316, 366n40, 366n42, 367n53, 367n65

Masuda Toshio, 9, 46, 57, 186, 255
Masumura Yasuzō, 6, 28, 183, 312, 352n49
Matsumoto Seichō, 46, 56, 57, 356n16
McDonald, Keiko I., 112, 274, 363n38, 377n40
metaphor, 2, 13, 60, 61, 70, 83, 89, 92, 94, 98, 99, 102-4, 105, 106, 107, 126, 128, 130, 150, 171, 185, 199, 218, 220, 227, 228, 229, 232, 233, 234, 242, 244, 257, 267, 268, 283, 286, 288, 290, 310
metonymy, 2, 64, 127, 178, 179, 207, 226, 266, 277
Midori Ryōgoku, 32, 140-41
Mikko o-rain/Undercover o-Line, 179, 184-85
Minato no kanpai: shōri wo wagate ni/ Harbor Toast: Victory is in Our Grasp, 25, 319
Mine Shigeyoshi, 5, 29, 128, 148, 174, 254
mise-en-scène, 4, 14, 72, 82, 84, 90, 98, 101, 106, 110, 143, 154, 155, 158, 161, 162, 168-70, 175, 237, 242, 254, 266, 276, 288, 292, 297, 306, 378n49
Mizoguchi, Kenji, 148, 153, 258, 378n49
Mulvey, Laura, 85, 359n20

Nagatsuka Kazue, 5, 28-29, 37, 49, 56, 66, 90, 135, 144, 184, 229, 244, 245, 357n31
Nakagawa Nobuo, xiii, 268-69, 270, 274, 277
Nakahira Kō, 23, 32, 78, 176, 180, 256, 351n32
negation/negativity, 3, 7, 13, 14, 39, 40, 63, 105, 132, 140, 147, 170, 179, 193, 225, 232, 237, 238, 239, 240, 244, 257, 264, 289, 293, 302, 347n7
Nikkatsu Studios, 1, 2, 7, 9, 10, 11, 15, 23, 24, 25, 26, 27, 28, 29, 30, 31, 32, 34, 35, 36, 37, 39, 40, 41, 42, 43, 44, 46, 48, 54, 57, 58, 59, 61, 63, 64, 67, 68, 69, 71, 77, 78, 79, 80, 84, 88, 98, 99, 101, 105, 111, 112, 114, 133, 142, 145, 156, 157, 170, 175, 176, 180, 181-85, 190, 191, 202, 206, 207, 210, 223, 226, 247, 254-55, 256, 265, 266, 278, 284, 290, 297, 352n48, 353n80, 354n88, 356n10, 364n7, 364n11, 368nn4-7, 370n37
akushon (genre), 33, 109, 186, 224, 230, 240, 242, 355n107, 355n113

Nikutai no mon/Gate of Flesh, vii, x, 32, 58, 119, 142, 143, 145, 146, 147-48, 150-52, 156, 157, 161, 163, 165-68, 169, 171, 174-75, 181, 237, 256, 314, 333, 352n49, 364n2

ninkyō eiga, 84, 86, 87, 109, 111-13, 114, 116, 117, 118, 126, 127, 140, 141, 186, 206, 213, 230, 233, 236, 241

Nippon konchūki/Insect Woman, 31, 32, 142, 253

Nitani Hideaki, 56, 207

Nogawa Yumiko, 32, 70, 78, 142, 147, 148, 167, 176, 254, 256

Noguchi Hiroshi, ix, 2, 9, 24-25, 26, 28, 29, 44, 46-47, 48, 57, 67, 77, 80, 87, 110, 114, 186, 355n10, 359n6

noh, 69, 268, 293, 296

Operetta tanuki gotten/Princess Raccoon, 38, 346

Ore ni kaketa yatsura/Those Who Bet on Me, 61, 329-30

Oretachi no chi ga yurusanai/Our Blood Will Not Forgive, 108, 109-11, 165, 256, 333-34

Ōshima Nagisa, 1, 2, 6, 11, 12, 15, 30, 34, 41, 42, 62, 63, 66, 98, 101, 107, 115, 148, 180, 225, 269, 312, 365n14, 368n80, 372n6, 377n35

Ōyabu Haruhiko, 45, 77, 78, 358n3, 359n7

Pacific War/Second World War. *See* Second World War

patriarchy, patriarchal, 7, 51, 54, 63, 84, 87, 91, 92, 93, 113, 119, 131, 132, 133, 134, 137, 141, 146, 147, 148, 150, 151, 153, 156, 158, 161, 164, 167, 170, 171, 176, 177, 178, 179, 196, 203, 206, 207, 213, 214, 215, 216, 221, 222, 231, 235, 237, 239, 254, 255, 262, 267, 277, 278, 280, 284, 285, 293, 295, 298, 303, 304, 305, 312, 314, 340, 366n49, 367n53

Performance, xii, 235, 236, 316, 374n36

pinku eiga (pink films), 15, 145, 163, 164, 170, 364n8

Pisutoru opera/Pistol Opera, vii, xiii, 38, 224, 254, 256, 257, 259-61, 262, 263, 264, 314, 345

post-war period, ix, 10, 11, 12, 14, 15, 16-17, 32, 45, 46, 54, 58, 60, 61, 63, 64, 65, 73, 77, 81, 83, 84, 87, 91, 92, 93, 111, 112, 114, 140, 142, 146, 147, 148, 150, 151, 156, 164, 167, 205, 206, 207, 223, 225, 260, 314, 358n44, 365n19, 374n53

post-war (Japanese) film, 9, 18, 23, 24, 33, 109, 115, 126, 140, 163, 171, 206, 210, 232, 250, 254, 268-69, 277, 305, 316, 364-65n13, 376n15

Raburetaa/Love Letter, 69, 323, 357n32

Rajo to kenjū/Nude Girl With a Gun, vii, ix, 44, 46, 47-52, 85, 247, 321

Rayns, Tony, 78, 126, 214

realism, 12, 15, 17, 43, 44, 61, 63, 66, 68, 70-71, 90, 98, 99, 100, 101, 133, 143, 146, 148, 160, 161, 170, 175, 180, 194, 254, 267, 296, 299, 300, 313, 349n24, 360n44, 361n45, 364-65n13, 365n24

reflexivity (self-reflexivity), 7, 10, 15, 17, 39, 43, 44, 49, 54, 58, 61, 62, 70, 77, 80, 84, 90, 94, 98, 99, 102, 103, 104-5, 106, 107, 110, 157, 181, 193, 196, 222, 229, 237, 243, 244, 254, 268, 274, 276, 280, 286, 287, 296, 306, 315, 374n36

Rupan sansei: Babiron no ōgon no densetsu/Lupin the Third: The Legend of the Gold of Babylon

sadism, xi, 14, 15, 54, 87, 88, 148, 157, 158, 161, 162, 164, 165, 167, 168-71, 175, 199, 203, 232, 235, 237, 262, 366n47, 367n65

Saitō Buichi, 9, 182

Sandanjū no otoko aka *shotto gan no otoko/Man With a Shotgun*, 184, 185

Satō Tadao, 35-36, 43, 113, 117, 133, 156, 158, 166, 191, 192, 206, 214, 236, 364n8, 368n80

The Searchers, 90-91

Second World War/Pacific War, 16, 32, 33, 40, 63, 64, 88, 92, 140, 142, 145, 146, 147, 148, 150, 151, 154, 156, 159, 163, 165, 206, 207, 210-15, 219, 220, 221, 232, 249, 257, 259, 363nn32-33, 365n26, 370n42, 371-72n49, 371n55, 371n61

seishun eiga (youth films), 25, 70

Shinoda Masahiro, 30, 34, 42, 98, 111, 211, 303

Shiraki Mari, ix, 44, 47, 49, 50-51, 54, 364n3

Shishido Jō, ix, 31, 44, 56, 75, 76, 77, 78, 79, 82, 84, 87, 100, 148, 167, 226, 230-31, 240, 254, 360n34, 372n15

Shōchiku, 10, 11, 23, 24, 25, 26, 37, 43, 60, 67, 69, 70, 111, 303, 356n16, 376n15

Shōchiku *nuberu bagu* ("New Wave"), 29, 42, 62

Shunpuden/Story of a Prostitute, vii, 32, 142, 144, 145, 146, 150, 152-55, 156, 158-61, 165, 172-73, 179, 278, 315, 373

Sone Yoshitada/Sone Chūsei, 30, 257, 352n58

spectacle, 36, 44, 47, 61, 63, 66, 69, 76, 85, 94-95, 97, 100, 101, 102, 144, 172, 179, 185, 192, 193, 200, 201, 222, 229, 280, 284
  erotic spectacle, x, 95, 96, 104, 107, 133, 157, 169, 175

spectatorship, 9, 94, 97, 106, 157, 169, 171, 172, 175, 192, 284, 285, 315, 360n43

Standish, Isolde, 112, 113, 140-41, 161, 206, 213, 360n25, 364n14

Studlar, Gaylyn, 161-63, 167, 168-69, 170, 171-72, 175, 197, 349n33, 366n42, 367n53

Subete ga kurutteru/Everything Goes Wrong, vii, ix, 30, 43, 44, 63-67, 70, 326

surrealism, xii, 38, 56, 61, 71, 223, 225-28, 229, 257, 259, 262, 267

Suzuki Akira, 5, 29, 37, 43, 115, 161, 247, 254

Suzuki Seijun
  early life, 10, 21-23, 133, 296
  career at Shōchiku, 10, 11, 23-24, 42, 67
  career at Nikkatsu, 1, 10-11, 24-34, 42-43, 44, 46, 54, 57, 61, 67, 71, 77, 99, 101, 110, 111, 114, 133, 142, 145, 186, 223, 242, 351-52n48, 353n80, 354n88, 364n11
  career as independent, 37-38, 224, 265-66, 287, 291
  film/cinematic practice, 1, 3, 4, 6, 7, 11, 13, 44, 57, 58, 69, 70, 76, 94, 98, 99, 102, 105, 107, 115, 149, 222, 248, 249, 266, 272, 287, 291, 293, 297, 313
  film viewing, 12, 22, 27, 43, 66, 69, 79-80, 90, 184, 226, 312
  philosophy and aesthetics, 3, 6, 10, 11, 13-16, 17, 18, 36, 54, 63, 81, 105-6, 107, 109, 138, 145-46, 149, 161, 169, 172, 173, 175, 193, 196, 225, 242, 255-56, 257-58, 261-64, 266, 285, 290-91, 294, 298, 299-300, 313, 314, 315, 354n102

"Suzuki Problem" (April 1968), 11, 33-35, 39, 354n84

war experience, 10, 22, 36, 164, 166, 211, 263, 350n13

Taishō period (1912-1926), 21-22, 37, 38, 61, 67, 69, 108, 134, 136, 137, 154, 226, 227, 267, 268, 269, 276, 277, 278, 279, 280, 288, 289, 290, 291, 294, 297, 303, 312, 362n17, 375n6, 376n7

Tanaka Yōzō, 30, 37, 227, 265, 375n3

Tantei jimusho 2-3: Kutabare akutō-domo/Detective Bureau 2-3: Go to Hell Bastards!, vii, 72, 77-79, 89, 95, 96, 99-100, 330, 359

Teshigahara Hiroshi, 192, 249, 376n16

theatricality, theatrical, x, xi, 6, 32, 59, 96, 101, 133, 135, 136, 137, 138, 144, 193, 195, 254, 296, 297, 300, 304, 316, 378n49

Tōei, 15, 32, 33, 46, 84, 87, 109, 111, 112-13, 114, 117, 141, 145, 171, 206, 230, 241, 254, 351n30, 363n33, 364n9

Tōge wo wataru wakai kaze/The Wind of Youth Crosses the Mountain Pass, vii, 16, 42, 68-69, 328

Tōhō, 7, 12, 22, 33, 46, 77, 111, 134, 278, 364n12, 371n59

Tōkō Kon, 30, 142

Tokyo kishitai/Tokyo Knights, 42, 61, 327

Tokyo nagaremono/Tokyo Drifter, vii, ix, xii, 14, 32, 33, 66, 83, 111, 157-58, 170, 179-81, 184, 185-210, 368n4, 373n27

Uchida Hyakken, 11, 37, 267, 278, 279, 280, 283, 375n6, 377nn27-28

Ueno Kōshi, 35, 36, 39, 347n7, 350n13, 355n108

Umi no junjō/Pure Emotions of the Sea, 28, 319-20

Von Sternberg, Josef, 7, 162, 168, 197, 367n61

Wada Kōji, 29, 57, 58, 61, 68, 78, 109, 151, 165, 177

Wakamatsu Kōji, 15, 31, 88, 101, 237, 287, 360n26, 368n80
Watari Tetsuya, xi, 14, 33, 181, 185, 186, 196, 200, 206, 207
Welles, Orson, 7, 49, 250, 253, 255, 256, 261, 305
Whittock, Trevor, 103, 104, 106, 197

Yajū no seishun/Youth of the Beast, vii, ix, 31, 40, 43, 72-107, 113, 116, 143, 165, 173, 175, 189, 191, 230, 330, 355, 360n44, 364n7

yakuza, xi, 15, 48, 54, 63, 68, 78, 82, 83, 84, 100, 111, 112, 114, 117, 118, 119, 126, 127, 132, 134, 135, 146, 150, 151, 152, 167, 196, 202, 204, 205, 206, 207, 258

yakuza eiga, 18, 25, 29, 31, 32, 39, 44, 86, 108, 109, 111, 113, 114, 126, 138, 141, 163, 198, 222, 224, 240, 277, 355-56n10, 359n18

Yamane Sadao, 36, 39, 69, 305

Yoshida Kijū, 2, 42, 101, 163, 225, 262, 287, 375n60

Yoshimoto Mitsuhiro, 5, 348n10, 358n43, 365n14

Yumeji, vii, xiii, 38, 259, 265, 289, 290, 315, 345

Zigeunerweisen, vii, xiii, 11, 19, 37, 38, 251, 260, 265-66, 268-87, 288, 289, 291, 296, 297, 306, 312, 341, 375n6